Initiating Psychoanalysis

Initiating Psychoanalysis presents an international collection of papers brought together by the Working Party on Initiating Psychoanalysis of the European Psychoanalytic Federation and addresses the specific clinical and technical issues involved in launching the processes that are at the core of psychoanalysis and psychoanalytic treatment.

Expert contributors provide introductions and commentaries on a selection of psychoanalytic papers, including one by Freud himself, which refer to beginning psychoanalytic treatment in a wide range of settings. Divided into four main sections, areas of discussion include:

- historical and conceptual developments in the field
- practical, technical and ethical considerations
- unconscious transference and countertransference dynamics of initial interviews
- internal factors that can help or hinder psychoanalysts in work to initiate psychoanalysis.

This book will be helpful to all psychoanalytical practitioners in thinking about their work in first interviews with prospective patients, as well as psychoanalysts and psychotherapists at all levels of experience, who will be able to use this book to enrich their own practice.

Bernard Reith is a Psychoanalyst in private practice in Geneva, Switzerland, and Chair of the Working Party on Initiating Psychoanalysis of the European Psychoanalytic Federation.

Sven Lagerlöf is a Psychoanalyst in private practice in Stockholm, a Training Analyst at the Swedish Psychoanalytical Society, and former Chairman of the Clinic of the Institute of the Swedish Psychoanalytical Society.

Penelope Crick is a Fellow of the Institute of Psychoanalysis, British Psychoanalytic Society, Clinical Director of the London Clinic of Psychoanalysis and is also in private practice in London.

Mette Møller is a Training Analyst at the Danish Society and is in private practice, and a former Chair of the Danish Society's Psychoanalytic Consultation Service.

Elisabeth Skale is a Psychoanalyst, a Training Analyst and the President of the Vienna Psychoanalytical Society, and a former Clinical Director of the Vienna Psychoanalytical Ambulatorium.

THE NEW LIBRARY OF PSYCHOANALYSIS

General Editor Alessandra Lemma

The New Library of Psychoanalysis was launched in 1987 in association with the Institute of Psycho-Analysis, London. It took over from the International Psychoanalytical Library, which published many of the early translations of the works of Freud and the writings of most of the leading British and Continental psychoanalysts.

The purpose of the New Library of Psychoanalysis is to facilitate a greater and more widespread appreciation of psychoanalysis and to provide a forum for increasing mutual understanding between psychoanalysts and those working in other disciplines such as the social sciences, medicine, philosophy, history, linguistics, literature and the arts. It aims to represent different trends both in British psychoanalysis and in psychoanalysis generally. The New Library of Psychoanalysis is well placed to make available to the English-speaking world psychoanalytic writings from other European countries and to increase the interchange of ideas between British and American psychoanalysts. Through the *Teaching Series*, the New Library of Psychoanalysis now also publishes books that provide comprehensive, yet accessible, overviews of selected subject areas aimed at those studying psychoanalysis and related fields such as the social sciences, philosophy, literature and the arts.

The Institute, together with the British Psychoanalytical Society, runs a low-fee psychoanalytic clinic, organizes lectures and scientific events concerned with psychoanalysis and publishes the *International Journal of Psychoanalysis*. It also runs a training course in psychoanalysis which leads to membership of the International Psychoanalytical Association – the body which preserves internationally agreed standards of training, of professional entry, and of professional ethics and practice for psychoanalysis as initiated and developed by Sigmund Freud. Distinguished members of the Institute have included Michael Balint, Wilfred Bion, Ronald Fairbairn, Anna Freud, Ernest Jones, Melanie Klein, John Rickman and Donald Winnicott.

Previous general editors have included David Tuckett, who played a very active role in the establishment of the New Library. He was followed as general editor by Elizabeth Bott Spillius, who was in turn followed by Susan Budd and then by Dana Birksted-Breen.

The current General Editor of the New Library of Psychoanalysis is Alessandra Lemma, but this book was initiated and edited by Dana Birksted-Breen, former General Editor.

ALSO IN THIS SERIES

Impasse and Interpretation Herbert Rosenfeld
Psychoanalysis and Discourse Patrick Mahony
The Suppressed Madness of Sane Men Marion Milner
The Riddle of Freud Estelle Roith
Thinking, Feeling, and Being Ignacio Matte-Blanco
The Theatre of the Dream Salomon Resnik
Melanie Klein Today: Volume 1, Mainly Theory Edited by Elizabeth Bott Spillius
Melanie Klein Today: Volume 2, Mainly Practice Edited by Elizabeth Bott Spillius
Psychic Equilibrium and Psychic Change: Selected Papers of Betty Joseph Edited by Michael Feldman and Elizabeth Bott Spillius
About Children and Children-No-Longer: Collected Papers 1942–80 Paula Heimann. Edited by Margret Tonnesmann
The Freud–Klein Controversies 1941–45 Edited by Pearl King and Riccardo Steiner
Dream, Phantasy and Art Hanna Segal
Psychic Experience and Problems of Technique Harold Stewart
Clinical Lectures on Klein and Bion Edited by Robin Anderson
From Fetus to Child Alessandra Piontelli
A Psychoanalytic Theory of Infantile Experience: Conceptual and Clinical Reflections E. Gaddini. Edited by Adam Limentani
The Dream Discourse Today Edited and introduced by Sara Flanders
The Gender Conundrum: Contemporary Psychoanalytic Perspectives on Femininity and Masculinity Edited and introduced by Dana Birksted-Breen
Psychic Retreats John Steiner
The Taming of Solitude: Separation Anxiety in Psychoanalysis Jean-Michel Quinodoz
Unconscious Logic: An Introduction to Matte-Blanco's Bi-logic and Its Uses Eric Rayner
Understanding Mental Objects Meir Perlow
Life, Sex and Death: Selected Writings of William Gillespie Edited and introduced by Michael Sinason
What Do Psychoanalysts Want? The Problem of Aims in Psychoanalytic Therapy Joseph Sandler and Anna Ursula Dreher
Michael Balint: Object Relations, Pure and Applied Harold Stewart
Hope: A Shield in the Economy of Borderline States Anna Potamianou
Psychoanalysis, Literature and War: Papers 1972–1995 Hanna Segal
Emotional Vertigo: Between Anxiety and Pleasure Danielle Quinodoz
Early Freud and Late Freud Ilse Grubrich-Simitis
A History of Child Psychoanalysis Claudine and Pierre Geissmann
Belief and Imagination: Explorations in Psychoanalysis Ronald Britton
A Mind of One's Own: A Kleinian View of Self and Object Robert A. Caper
Psychoanalytic Understanding of Violence and Suicide Edited by Rosine Jozef Perelberg

On Bearing Unbearable States of Mind Ruth Riesenberg-Malcolm. Edited by Priscilla Roth
Psychoanalysis on the Move: The Work of Joseph Sandler Edited by Peter Fonagy, Arnold M. Cooper and Robert S. Wallerstein
The Dead Mother: The Work of André Green Edited by Gregorio Kohon
The Fabric of Affect in the Psychoanalytic Discourse André Green
The Bi-Personal Field: Experiences of Child Analysis Antonino Ferro
The Dove that Returns, the Dove that Vanishes: Paradox and Creativity in Psychoanalysis Michael Parsons
Ordinary People, Extra-ordinary Protections: A Post-Kleinian Approach to the Treatment of Primitive Mental States Judith Mitrani
The Violence of Interpretation: From Pictogram to Statement Piera Aulagnier
The Importance of Fathers: A Psychoanalytic Re-Evaluation Judith Trowell and Alicia Etchegoyen
Dreams That Turn Over a Page: Paradoxical Dreams in Psychoanalysis Jean-Michel Quinodoz
The Couch and the Silver Screen: Psychoanalytic Reflections on European Cinema Edited and introduced by Andrea Sabbadini
In Pursuit of Psychic Change: The Betty Joseph Workshop Edited by Edith Hargreaves and Arturo Varchevker
The Quiet Revolution in American Psychoanalysis: Selected Papers of Arnold M. Cooper Arnold M. Cooper. Edited and introduced by Elizabeth L. Auchincloss
Seeds of Illness and Seeds of Recovery: The Genesis of Suffering and the Role of Psychoanalysis Antonino Ferro
The Work of Psychic Figurability: Mental States Without Representation César Botella and Sára Botella
Key Ideas for a Contemporary Psychoanalysis: Misrecognition and Recognition of the Unconscious André Green
The Telescoping of Generations: Listening to the Narcissistic Links Between Generations Haydée Faimberg
Glacial Times: A Journey Through the World of Madness Salomon Resnik
This Art of Psychoanalysis: Dreaming Undreamt Dreams and Interrupted Cries Thomas H. Ogden
Psychoanalysis as Therapy and Storytelling Antonino Ferro
Psychoanalysis and Religion in the 21st Century: Competitors or Collaborators? Edited by David M. Black
Recovery of the Lost Good Object Eric Brenman. Edited and introduced by Gigliola Fornari Spoto
The Many Voices of Psychoanalysis Roger Kennedy
Feeling the Words: Neuropsychoanalytic Understanding of Memory and the Unconscious Mauro Mancia
Projected Shadows: Psychoanalytic Reflections on the Representation of Loss in European Cinema Edited by Andrea Sabbadini
Encounters with Melanie Klein: Selected Papers of Elizabeth Spillius Elizabeth Spillius. Edited by Priscilla Roth and Richard Rusbridger

Constructions and the Analytic Field: History, Scenes and Destiny Domenico Chianese
Yesterday, Today and Tomorrow Hanna Segal. Edited by Nicola Abel-Hirsch
Psychoanalysis Comparable and Incomparable: The Evolution of a Method to Describe and Compare Psychoanalytic Approaches David Tuckett, Roberto Basile, Dana Birksted-Breen, Tomas Böhm, Paul Denis, Antonino Ferro, Helmut Hinz, Arne Jemstedt, Paola Mariotti and Johan Schubert
Time, Space and Phantasy Rosine Jozef Perelberg
Rediscovering Psychoanalysis: Thinking and Dreaming, Learning and Forgetting Thomas H. Ogden
Mind Works: Technique and Creativity in Psychoanalysis Antonino Ferro
Doubt, Conviction and the Analytic Process: Selected Papers of Michael Feldman Michael Feldman. Edited by Betty Joseph
Melanie Klein in Berlin: Her First Psychoanalysis of Children Claudia Frank. Edited by Elizabeth Spillius
The Psychotic Wavelength: A Psychoanalytic Perspective for Psychiatry Richard Lucas
Betweenity: A Discussion of the Concept of Borderline Judy Gammelgaard
The Intimate Room: Theory and Technique of the Analytic Field Giuseppe Civitarese
Bion Today Edited by Chris Mawson
Secret Passages: The Theory and Technique of Interpsychic Relations Stefano Bolognini
Intersubjective Processes and the Unconscious: An Integration of Freudian, Kleinian and Bionian Perspectives Lawrence J. Brown
Seeing and Being Seen: Emerging from a Psychic Retreat John Steiner
Avoiding Emotions, Living Emotions Antonino Ferro
Projective Identification: The Fate of a Concept Edited by Elizabeth Spillius and Edna O'Shaughnessy
Insight: Essays on Psychoanalytic Knowing Jorge L. Ahumada

TITLES IN THE NEW LIBRARY OF PSYCHOANALYSIS TEACHING SERIES

Reading Freud: A Chronological Exploration of Freud's Writings Jean-Michel Quinodoz
Listening to Hanna Segal: Her Contribution to Psychoanalysis Jean-Michel Quinodoz
Reading French Psychoanalysis Edited by Dana Birksted-Breen, Sara Flanders and Alain Gibeault
Reading Winnicott Edited by Lesley Caldwell and Angela Joyce
Initiating Psychoanalysis: Perspectives Edited by Bernard Reith, Sven Lagerlöf, Penelope Crick, Mette Møller and Elisabeth Skale

THE NEW LIBRARY OF PSYCHOANALYSIS:
TEACHING SERIES

5

General Editor: Dana Birksted-Breen

Initiating Psychoanalysis

Perspectives

Edited by Bernard Reith, Sven Lagerlöf,
Penelope Crick, Mette Møller, Elisabeth Skale

Routledge
Taylor & Francis Group
LONDON AND NEW YORK

First published 2012
by Routledge
27 Church Road, Hove, East Sussex BN3 2FA

Simultaneously published in the USA and Canada
by Routledge
711 Third Avenue, New York NY 10017

Routledge is an imprint of the Taylor & Francis Group, an Informa Business

British Library Cataloguing in Publication Data
A catalogue record for this book is available from the British Library

Library of Congress Cataloging in Publication Data
Initiating psychoanalysis : perspectives / edited by Bernard Reith ... [et al.].
p. cm.—(New library of psychoanalysis teaching series)
ISBN 978-0-415-55497-8 (hardback)—ISBN 978-0-415-55498-5 (pbk.)
1. Psychoanalysis—Methodology. I. Reith, Bernard, 1954-
BF175.I5524 2011
616.89'17—dc22

2011004384

ISBN: 978-0-415-55497-8 (hbk)
ISBN: 978-0-415-55498-5 (pbk)
ISBN: 978-0-203-80198-7 (ebk)

Typeset in Bembo by RefineCatch Limited, Bungay, Suffolk
Paperback cover design by Sandra Heath
Printed by TJ International Ltd, Padstow, Cornwall

CONTENTS

Part III
The analyst's struggle with the experience of a first meeting 167

Part IV
Daring or reluctance to start analysis? 273

FOREWORD

Anne-Marie Sandler

It is a great honour for me to have been asked to write a brief foreword to this excellent publication, compiled by a group of psychoanalysts from different European psychoanalytical societies. It is important to welcome the fact that this book is taking a thoroughly psychoanalytic clinical stance in thinking about the role, meaning and aim of first interviews, with the emphasis on the dynamics of a first meeting between two people. The authors leave behind the traditional idea of the need for a thorough assessment of the patient, done without consideration of the impact that this unique encounter must have on both members of the dyad. I am thinking, for example, of Freud's writing about 'accessibility' or 'inaccessibility' as a quality of the patient which he thought was a necessary precondition for acceptance for psychoanalytic treatment. The book turns things around by raising the question of who is 'accessible' or 'inaccessible' in a first meeting and suggesting that it could be the analyst as much as the patient.

This highlights the fact that a first interview or consultation is for the patient and the analyst an encounter which evokes intense feelings in both protagonists. It is becoming increasingly recognized that the ability of the psychoanalyst to monitor the intense emotional climate that this encounter creates in both patient and analyst is of the greatest importance. The analyst must observe and monitor both the transference phantasies in the patient and his or her countertransference reactions, which give important indications of what is happening in the here and now of the interview. With this emphasis in mind, the first interview becomes a real initiation into the mystery of the unconscious mind of both patient and analyst and is thus a psychoanalytic experience.

This thoughtful book reminded me how difficult it can be to listen fairly and objectively to our colleagues' clinical material, particularly so when it concerns a first interview. I believe that this partly comes from the unconscious intensity of this kind of first encounter and that as we listen to a colleague, we are profoundly identified with the process. The moment the presenter deals with the material in a way which is alien to us, we are liable to be thrown into a state of confusion, which is often very difficult to bear. We then need to distance ourselves from the presentation and tend to become alienated from what has been going on in the interview.

This phenomenon has been discussed in much more depth by Dana Birksted-Breen *et al.* (2008), but I raise it here to link it with the fact that this book is the product of a working party. I believe that discussing clinical material, trying to assess it and to elevate it to a new level by suggesting that a first interview is an initiation to psychoanalysis, demands a great deal of inner work. To question one's practice and to reorganize one's opinion can be threatening and demands at times the inner security that a successful working group can offer. The presence of colleagues with whom one has worked and whom one has learned to trust and respect is, I believe, not only a prerequisite for harmonious work but also for an enhanced sense of safety which allows in us greater openness and flexibility. I congratulate the editors of this book for offering us a thoughtful, searching and important publication.

Reference

Birksted-Breen, D., Ferro, A., Mariotti, P. (2008). Work in progress: Using the two step method. In: Tuckett, D., Basile, R., Birksted-Breen, D., Böhm, T., Denis, P., Ferro, A., Hinz, H., Jemstedt, A., Mariotti, P., Schubert, J. (Eds), *Psychoanalysis Comparable and Incomparable: The Evolution of a Method to Describe and Compare Psychoanalytic Approaches* (Chapter 7). Hove, UK: Routledge, New Library of Psychoanalysis.

ACKNOWLEDGEMENTS

This book emerged out of the work of the *European Psychoanalytic Federation's Working Party on Initiating Psychoanalysis*, which began in 2004 as part of the *Ten Year Scientific Initiative* launched in 2001 by David Tuckett, then EPF President. David also chaired the WPIP during its first year and his enthusiasm has been a major source of support and inspiration.

We are grateful to the next presidents, Evelyne Séchaud and Peter Wegner, and the Executive and Council of the EPF for its economic support of the preparation of this book, which has taken place alongside the investigative work and seminar activities which are the main tasks of the WPIP. We are also indebted to the Developing Psychoanalytic Practice and Training program (DPPT) of the IPA, which helped to fund the WPIP conjointly with the EPF until 2007.

Present members of the WPIP are Bernard Reith (chair), John Boots, Penelope Crick, Alain Gibeault, Ronny Jaffè, Sven Lagerlöf, Mette Møller, Elisabeth Skale, Rudi Vermote and Peter Wegner. Former members who have made important contributions to the development of the WPIP are Rainer Dahlbender, Rachael Davenhill, Christine Diercks, Kari Hauge, Janet King and Ursula Walter.

Elisabeth Skale was the first to suggest that we publish a collection of the papers that we were finding particularly relevant to our work on the dynamics of first interviews. This led to an intense process of reading and discussion engaging all members of the working party till we had reached a consensus about the contents of this book. Sven Lagerlöf (as chair), Penny Crick, Mette Møller, Bernard Reith and Elisabeth Skale were appointed as Editing Group. We thank John Boots, Alain Gibeault, Ronny Jaffè and Peter Wegner for discussing and writing commentaries on a number of the papers. For all of us it has been both stimulating and fascinating to meet and confront different psychoanalytic cultures within our special field of interest.

We are particularly grateful to Antonino Ferro and Rudi Vermote, who both were kind enough to write a chapter especially for this book.

A lot of work has been put into translations: from French, German and Italian – often in several stages – for the selection process and in preparing for publication. The editing group as well as professional translators have been engaged in this work. We are grateful to David Alcorn, Maria Carla Belluci, Sophie Leighton, Beatrice Pahlabod, Gail Painitz and Andrew Weller.

Penny Crick and Bernard Reith have undertaken a special responsibility for the general condition of the final English texts. Penny has done a huge job on the final editing and has all along managed our contact with the Publisher. Dana Birksted-Breen, as General Editor of the New Library of Psychoanalysis, has given us strong and encouraging support from the very start of this project.

We are very grateful to Trudy Turmer who with patience and forbearance has put a vast typographic variety of texts into a uniform and presentable manuscript.

We would like to thank the following for their kind permission to reproduce copyright material:

Chapter 1. *Katharina: Case studies from Studies on Hysteria* (1893) by Sigmund Freud. Sigmund Freud © Copyrights, The Institute of Psycho-Analysis and the Hogarth Press for permission to quote from 'The Interpretation of Dreams' from *The Standard Edition of the Complete Psychological Works of Sigmund Freud* translated and edited by James Strachey. Reprinted by permission of The Random House Group Ltd. From Collected Papers Volume 2 by Sigmund Freud. Reprinted by permission of Basic Books, a member of Perseus Books Group.

Chapter 2. *The psychoanalytic initial interview and its method: A postscript to Freud's case 'Katharina'* by Hermann Argelander. Copyright © Wolfgang Argelander, reproduced by permission. First published 1978 in *Psyche* 32: 1089–1098.

Chapter 4. *Well, then, anything new? What that 'first' interview can teach us* by Evelyne Kestemberg. Copyright © Evelyne Kestemberg, reproduced by permission. First published 1985 in Gaeten Morin (Ed.), *Psychiatrie-Psychoanalyse. Jalons our une fécondation réciproque* (pp.11–20). Montreal: Chenelière Éducation.

Chapter 5. *Personal attitudes to psychoanalytic consultation* by John Klauber. Copyright © Ruth Brook Klauber, reproduced by permission.

Chapter 6. *The development of a therapeutic space in a first contact with adolescents* by Catalina Bronstein and Sara Flanders. Copyright © 1998, Taylor & Francis, reproduced with permission. First published in *Journal of Child Psychotherapy* 24(1): 5–36.

Chapter 7. *The analytic encounter: A historical and process-oriented perspective* by Jean-Louis Baldacci and Christine Bouchard. First published 1998 in *French Review of Psychoanalysis* 62(1): 13–24, reproduced by permission of University Press of France.

Chapter 8. *The analytical encounter* by Jean-Luc Donnet and Michel de M'Uzan. First published 1998 in *French Review of Psychoanalysis* 62(1): 189–208, reproduced by permission of University Press of France.

Chapter 9. *The profession of ferryman: Considerations on the analyst's internal attitude in consultation and in referral* by Stefano Bolognini. First published 2006 in *International Journal of Psychoanalysis* 87: 25–42, reproduced with permission of the publisher, Wiley-Blackwell.

Chapter 10. *Comments on transference and countertransference in the initial analytic meeting* by Thomas H. Ogden. First published 1992 in *Psychoanalytic Inquiry* 12: 225–247, reproduced with permission of the publisher, Taylor & Francis Ltd http://www.informaworld.com

Chapter 11. *Observations on the subjective indication for psychoanalysis* by Josef Dantlgraber. Copyright © Josef Dantlgraber, reproduced by permission. First published 1982 in *Psyche* 36: 193–225.

Chapter 12. *The opening scene and the importance of the countertransference* by Peter Wegner. Copyright © Peter Wegner, reproduced by permission. First published 1992 in *Psyche* 46: 286–307.

Chapter 13. *The consultation in psychoanalysis and its 'location': Working on the frontier* by Agostino Racalbuto. Published 2010 in *French Review of Psychoanalysis* 74(2): 507–519, reproduced by permission of University Press of France.

Chapter 15. *A perspective on doing a consultation and making the recommendation of analysis to a prospective analysand* by Arnold Rothstein. First published in © The Psychoanalytic Quarterly, 1994, *The Psychoanalytic Quarterly* LXIII: 680–695. Reproduced with permission.

Chapter 16. *In what frame of mind should the first interview be approached?* by Christian David. First published 1998 in *French Review of Psychoanalysis* 62(1): 87–99, reproduced by permission of University Press of France.

Chapter 17. *The Psychoanalyst of the future: Wise enough to dare to be mad at times* by Danielle Quinodoz. First published 2001 in *International Journal of Psychoanalysis* 82: 235–248, reproduced by permission of the publisher, Wiley-Blackwell.

Chapter 18. *The analyst's reluctance to begin a new analysis* by Lena Ehrlich. First published 2004 in *Journal of the American Psychoanalytic Association* 52(4): 1075–1093, reproduced with permission of the publisher, Sage Publications.

The WPIP would like to acknowledge appreciation of time spent staying and working together in Austria at the Knappenhof Reichenau, the hotel run in the past by the family of 'Katharina', and our inspirational visits to the Ottohaus on the nearby Rax mountain range, a pleasant refuge and cafe for walkers, and the very place where Freud was asked, 'Are you a doctor, Sir?' as described in Chapter 1.

Finally, we want to thank our families, who have coped with our moments of preoccupation and unavailability while working on the book with generous support and understanding.

GENERAL INTRODUCTION

Mette Møller, Sven Lagerlöf and Bernard Reith

This book is about beginning psychoanalytic treatment and, more specifically, about launching the psychoanalytic process that is at its core. Although the accent is on full psychoanalysis, which is no doubt the most challenging form of treatment to get going, the reader will see that many of the papers in this collection – beginning with that by Freud himself – refer to psychoanalytic treatment in general, whether in high frequency psychoanalysis on the couch, in face-to-face psychotherapy or in an even wider range of settings.

What is specific to psychoanalytic work in all contexts, including that of first encounters, is how the analyst listens and responds to the patient and, perhaps even more importantly, how he/she *reflects* on his/her mode of listening and responding. However, although these ways of working, and the theory that informs them, were developed by psychoanalysts as they treated people in very varied settings, it is clear that the process of full analysis (i.e. high frequency analysis on the couch) has been a major source of inspiration all along. It remains the most effective and most rewarding form of treatment for many patients, often helping them more profoundly and durably than the psychotherapeutic methods that are derived from and inspired by it (Sandell *et al.*, 2000). To a large extent, the efficacy of full analysis is due to its ability to afford both patient and analyst with an insight of unparalleled depth and precision into the workings of the unconscious mind. Efficacy, depth of understanding, and the advancement of the discipline are closely intertwined.

For all these reasons, it is important that psychoanalysis survive both as a therapeutic and as a research discipline. Sustained accession of patients to psychoanalysis is essential, foremost for our patients, but also for the discipline itself: ongoing clinical practice is the obvious prerequisite to the continued scientific development of the method and its concepts.

Patients entering psychoanalysis today are no longer necessarily the less disturbed – if ever they have been. Analysts can help patients with severe disturbance and suffering. Often such patients turn to analysis only after other treatments have failed. How then can we disseminate information about psychoanalysis as a necessary and valuable alternative to the various short-term psychotherapeutic treatments – psychodynamic as well as cognitive or other forms – that are on offer today to people who are looking for help?

In particular, how can psychoanalysts work with the patients they meet for consultation, or indeed in any other aspect of their day-to-day work, in such a way as to give them a taste of the unique experience of psychoanalysis? Neither our patients nor our fellow professionals are likely to be quite convinced by mere rational expositions of the method and of clinical and empirical evidence that it is effective. For our colleagues, familiarity with successful clinical cases will be important. But for our potential patients, only the direct experience of a subjectively meaningful encounter with a psychoanalyst is likely to give them a sense that it is worth their while to enter full psychoanalytic treatment. This may happen during preliminary interviews with patients who have already thought that psychoanalysis could be an option, but it may also happen during interviews with people who are looking for help but who have not consciously thought about psychoanalysis and who hardly know anything about it. How to get a psychoanalytic process going in our everyday encounters with ordinary patients is thus an important question.

This book has arisen out of such concerns. As both its title and the name of the working party behind it suggest, the central preoccupation is with 'initiating psychoanalysis', i.e. with opening up a meaningful and specifically psychoanalytic process in various settings including not only preliminary interviews for psychoanalysis, but also consultation work and the early stages of psychotherapy. As will be evident on reading many of the papers presented in the following pages, this central theme of initiating psychoanalysis is linked to general problems of psychoanalytic theory and technique, as well as to the overarching issue of how to make the best use of the potentials of psychoanalysis.

The idea of publishing this collection of papers arose in the context of efforts to address these issues. The team of psychoanalysts behind this book, the Working Party on Initiating Psychoanalysis (abbreviated as WPIP) of the European Psychoanalytic Federation (EPF), was set up in 2004 as a part of the EPF's much broader Ten-Year European Scientific Initiative launched in 2002 under the impetus of David Tuckett, then EPF President, as a constructive way to confront the challenges facing psychoanalysis (Tuckett, 2002, 2003, 2004).

According to the thinking behind the Initiative, these challenges are not only 'external', with tough competition and criticism from other therapeutic methods, as well as justified demands that we validate our discipline. They are also 'internal' to a demoralised and divided psychoanalytic community in which doubts about our work have put us on the defensive. A basic working hypothesis of the Initiative is that one way out of this impasse is methodological. New methods for grounded investigation into psychoanalysis are needed, as are new ways of working together to put these forms of investigation into practice (Tuckett *et al.*, 2008). Like all Working Parties set up under the Initiative, one of the aims of the WPIP is to pursue this dual-track process of investigation and dialogue.

A corollary hypothesis, which is particularly relevant to the WPIP and to the issue of initiating psychoanalysis, is that the 'internal' difficulties impact on the 'external' ones. Psychoanalysts who doubt their work may become less able and less motivated to involve their patients in full psychoanalysis, or alternatively they may be tempted to take on patients who are not likely to benefit from it, both extremes resulting in a vicious circle of insufficient experience, poor outcomes, discouraged practitioners, poor science and a sceptical public. We could hopefully try to replace this by a 'virtuous' cycle in which more understanding of the process of initiating psychoanalysis can lead to more meaningful beginnings, more experienced clinicians, more opportunities for clinical research and a better-informed public.

In this context, the WPIP was given a general mandate to explore all questions associated with the overall theme of starting new psychoanalyses. Two aspects of the mandate are particularly relevant to this book:

1. To explore and understand the different ways in which psychoanalytic treatment is perceived, understood and offered in the various psychoanalytic subcultures, including routes of referral, outpatient clinics offering psychoanalytic treatment, the work of psychoanalytic contact centres and research carried out in connection with such projects.
2. To share and develop expertise among psychoanalysts about how to convey to a patient something of the experience of psychoanalytic treatment and the specific opportunity it can offer, as well as how to describe this expertise in clinical and theoretical terms across different psychoanalytic cultures and to integrate it in the training curriculum of future analysts.

In practice, and in keeping with the general aims of the European Scientific Initiative, the WPIP was built up of members chosen by the EPF component societies not only for their interest in the work of assessment and initial consultation, but also to represent a wide scope of linguistic and psychoanalytic cultures: currently the WPIP comprises members from Australia (which has an EPF member society), Austria, Belgium, Denmark, France, Germany, Italy, Sweden, Switzerland and the United Kingdom. When they began to meet, they soon found that they worked in contrasting institutional and/or private settings; referred to diverse theoretical and clinical models; and had in mind very different basic references on their subject, be it from their national or from the international literature. And yet, encouragingly albeit somewhat unexpectedly, they found that despite (or because of) their differences they could actually agree on some of the basic dynamics at work in the clinical material that they were led to examine. One of the problems was then to find ways to describe such commonly recognised clinical realities.

The clinical material in question derives from clinical workshops that the WPIP has conducted every year at the EPF conferences since 2005, as well as at International Psychoanalytical Association (IPA) conferences in 2007 and 2009. Simply stated, the aim of these workshops is to bring psychoanalysts from different backgrounds together in small groups to discuss case material from preliminary interviews and to find out what goes on in such interviews when they lead to full psychoanalysis. Using both free-associative and semi-standardised discussion procedures, the workshops examine the special dynamics of these interviews, how experienced analysts from different backgrounds work with them, how the patients respond, and what kind of process ensues that leads to full analysis (or works against it). The same clinical material together with the workshop proceedings is then re-examined by the WPIP and compared to other workshop cases, in the hope that this combination of in-depth study and comparison across very different cases can allow us to derive more precise ideas about what is specific to initial psychoanalytical contacts and what competent analysts do in them to allow a psychoanalytic process to get under way. A preliminary report of this work is published in the *Bulletin of the European Psychoanalytic Federation* (Reith *et al.*, 2010).

Our findings to date have influenced our choice of papers for this book. Without going into a detailed description, some salient points are worth mentioning. Foremost is the power of the unconscious dynamics in all the preliminary interviews that we have studied. The closer one examines them, the more one sees going on, the higher the stakes being played out seem to be, and the better one understands how both patient and analyst can feel at the brink of both great possibilities and great dangers. Bion's (1979/1994) expression of a 'storm' that takes places whenever two people meet for the first time seems particularly apt to describe this situation. By this term we do not mean a conscious or manifest emotional 'storm' of the kind that can also be observed in some clinical encounters, but an unconscious one. This can take place even in encounters that appear calm and straightforward, or even *too* calm, and can profoundly influence both participants in the relationship without their realising it.

Next, but just as important for us analysts, is the special burden that this places on the mind and capacities of the analyst. The analyst can feel vaguely ill at ease, or more disturbed or even overwhelmed, or find him/herself caught up in transient enactments. If he/she can bear such situations and the sense of surprise, not understanding or confusion that can come with them, there can come a point when they can tell the analyst something about the dynamics that are at stake. Alternatively, the analyst may unconsciously defend against the 'storm' for a while and find him/herself caught up in more collusive dynamics with the patient, of varying strength and duration, until he/she realises what is going on. Often the analyst finds that in such a situation it helps to have not just a theoretical template to fall back on, but also a collegiate structure providing opportunities for consultation with other analysts.

Third, what the analyst seems to explore in such situations is not so much the patient's psychodynamic structure and 'analysability', as has often been thought in the past, but *the ability of the analytic couple to 'face' the 'storm'* instead of hiding away from it. The analyst is not unaware of the patient's structure, but is more concerned with whether the patient and analyst are able to work together. This seems to be an important factor not only in private settings where the interviewing analyst will continue with the patient, but also in consultation settings where the patient will be referred to someone else: a main concern in the latter situations is to judge, on the basis of first-hand experience, how the patient can use an analyst and analysis. Thus 'analysability' seems to be subsumed under 'ability to use analysis', at that point in time.

Last but not least, the analytic couple's ability to face the 'storm' may give the patient a sense that one doesn't need to be quite so frightened of the unconscious: this may be the significant experience that makes the project of an analysis possible, as compared to other treatment methods that are more based on avoiding the 'storm' or keeping it under control.

When the WPIP team looked into the psychoanalytic literature for papers that dealt with their field of investigation, perhaps the most striking discovery was the relative paucity of publications on the subject of first consultations that were not centred on the question of indications for psychoanalysis in terms of the patient's analysability. Relatively few papers actually address the patient–analyst dynamics that seem so important. One research tradition reached significant conclusions about the importance of the patient–analyst match (Kantrowitz *et al.*, 1989, 1990; Kantrowitz 1995), but with the exception of one study in some ways similar to our own (Bellanova *et al.*, 1981), to our best knowledge the unconscious dynamics of initial encounters have mainly been addressed in clinical papers and book chapters by analysts writing from their own experience in private or institutional practice.

It is such mainly clinical and sometimes more theoretical papers, based on psychoanalytical experience, that the WPIP team has ended up choosing for this volume. We began with papers that had helped or inspired us in our own clinical work in initiating psychoanalysis, in institutional and/or private practice. From these, we chose those that we think best address significant complementary aspects of the issue of initiating psychoanalysis as we have come to understand it, and that describe them in ways that seem representative of diverse psychoanalytic cultures yet potentially meaningful to all analysts.

The title of this collection: *Initiating Psychoanalysis: Perspectives* is meant to reflect this unity in diversity. Apart from the concentration on initiating psychoanalysis and the wish to bring together what we feel to be a diversity of useful perspectives, the choice of papers is multi-determined by several underlying lines of development.

One dimension is historical, with no ambition to cover the entire history of psychoanalytic thinking on initiating psychoanalysis, but with what we do feel to be a sense of continuity in the evolution of the psychoanalytic interview from Freud to the present day. Some of the papers can be considered to be landmarks in this development; others provide good reviews of the relevant literature. Part I also contains a short overview of some key steps in the evolution of ideas since Freud, with reference to some classic papers on the subject of indications for analysis.

As already mentioned, another main dimension is multicultural. Papers from different European psychoanalytic traditions and from North America have been included and French, German and Italian papers have been translated into English for the purpose of this book, in the hope of allowing a wider audience to become acquainted with local developments in psychoanalytic thinking and showing parallel movements in fundamental ideas in psychoanalytic subcultures that are normally separated because of language barriers. As the reader will see, differences in how theory and clinical observation are talked about and combined are an integral part of these differing traditions, and we have decided to respect this diversity. But this is also a biased book, with inevitable limitations: the choice of original languages is necessarily limited to those mastered by the WPIP team, meaning that important work in other main languages, such as Spanish and Portuguese, is not included here, such as that of our European colleague Antonio Pérez Sánchez (Pérez Sánchez, 2006; Cabré, 2007), or the classical paper in Spanish by José Bleger (1971). Chapters 2 to 6 of Horacio Etchegoyen's book, *The Fundamentals of Psychoanalytic Technique* (1999), provide an excellent overview of Latin American and other literature on the subject; we can also heartily recommend these chapters as a useful general introduction to the basic concepts involved.

A third criterion in the choice of papers has been to look for good descriptions of how the psychoanalytic process is conceptualised in the new millennium. The WPIP's own findings seem to be part of a more general shift in perspective not only from a one-person to a relational psychology, but also from positivism to phenomenology, from objectivity to subjectivity and intersubjectivity, and from analytical data to be uncovered to analytical data that are created in the analytical interaction. This does not mean that it becomes irrelevant to consider the patient's psychological functioning, but it does transform the assessment of the individual and the decision to recommend analysis into a different undertaking. It becomes more complex, perhaps, but is based on a grasp of the situation that is more in accordance with its nature. The main clinical focus in the selected papers is on the unconscious transference and counter-transference dynamics that are relentlessly at work in and around the consultation: from before the actual meeting, through scenic factors at play during the encounter, and right into the act of treatment recommendation.

Finally, we have tried to choose papers that reflect the differing private and institutional settings in which initial interviews take place. Each setting has its specific possibilities and constraints, and may require specific theoretical tools to capture these aspects. We have tried to choose papers that cover this range of environments.

Part I, 'Are you a doctor, Sir?' goes back to the beginning of psychoanalysis with Freud's meeting with Katharina in the 'Ottohaus' in the Austrian Alps during a summer holiday in the early 1890s. It is a marvellous demonstration of how the patient in a first contact is given the experience of what psychoanalysis is. Freud's description of this first meeting is set in context with his early views on indications and contraindications for psychoanalysis. Next is a paper by Hermann Argelander, who shows how the unconscious dynamics of the encounter are revealed not only by Katharina's associations, but also by the whole scenario in which Freud and this young woman find themselves caught up.

This sets the stage for Part II on 'Consultation and referral', which focuses on the context of initial interviews and on the practical, technical and ethical concerns and considerations involved in the analyst's day-to-day work to meet the patient's needs and capacities. The papers in this section address issues like the difference between assessment and consultation; working in institutions; preparing patients for psychoanalysis or psychoanalytic therapy; and especially the very specific work involved in referral. This latter, very important subject tends to stir up strong emotions in analysts when it is discussed in WPIP clinical workshops and panels. Apart from legitimate debates about the management of the transference relationship and the content, timing and phrasing of interventions, this controversy might also express differing views about the personal role of the analyst. In our own study of material from both private and institutional settings, we have found it helpful to regard what is done in initial interviews as helping the patient to find *psychoanalysis* or *an* analyst, and not necessarily *this* specific analyst. Many of the papers in this section explicitly or implicitly make this distinction. Thus, although referral to another analyst acts like a spotlight revealing the powerful human, ethical and technical difficulties of consultation work, in fact, as the reader will be able to judge, these concerns are relevant to all settings where an offer of psychoanalysis is made (or withheld).

After this review of context, aims and technique, Part III on 'The analyst's struggle with the experience of a first meeting' delves more deeply into the unconscious dynamics of initial interviews. Here, we have grouped together papers that deal primarily with transference and counter-transference dynamics and with the borders between subjectivity and objectivity. These papers show, in different ways, how an analytic consultation is an extremely intense and complex experience in which the analyst is always immediately and very deeply involved. As a result it cannot only be conceptualised in terms of assessment and analysability, but must also be understood in terms of the subjective abilities of the analyst to sustain more primitive counter-transference reactions and to elaborate them.

The last section of the book, Part IV, entitled 'Daring or reluctance to start analysis?' builds on the preceding sections to examine the internal factors that can help or hinder the analyst in his work to initiate psychoanalysis. After a succession of papers showing how and why initiating psychoanalysis can be challenging but also definitely interesting and feasible, the papers in this section explore the sources of the analyst's failure to live up to his task. Here the responsibility for empty couches is placed on the analyst and not on the patient nor on society. All these papers explore aspects of the analyst's reluctance to work analytically, demonstrate how they can be understood as 'counter-resistances' to the patient's transference resistances, and show how they can prevent psychoanalysis from getting started. The papers in this section come from Belgium, France, Switzerland and the United States and they are written from Freudian, Kleinian, Bionian and ego-psychological perspectives, but they all clearly converge on the same psychoanalytical realities.

The initial interview is unlike any other. It is neither a normal meeting nor yet psychoanalysis. The unconscious expands into this uncharted territory, revealing both the possibilities and limits of psychoanalytic understanding. Antonino Ferro's paper in this volume, for example, contains many metaphors for unconscious contents overflowing and jumping out of bounds. This requires the interviewing analyst to exercise his/her professional responsibilities in particularly challenging circumstances. He/she is involved as a whole person, and simultaneously must strive to achieve a third-person perspective allowing him/her to reflect on the meaning of this unusual situation. Such work calls on the analyst's capacities for receptiveness to primary identification, keeping in mind sophisticated conceptual tools, and tolerating anxiety and not understanding.

We have found all the papers in this book to be meaningful and useful in our own efforts to understand these problems of initiating psychoanalysis. Although the central concern is with opening up opportunities for full psychoanalyses, there are papers in all four sections that also address the more general problem of how to launch the psychoanalytic process in any professional context where patients can be helped by the psychoanalytic approach. Some papers may make for more challenging reading, while others may seem deceptively simple. This reflects the complexity of the field, as just described. It also reflects the diversity of the linguistic traditions that govern the structure of thought and its logic of exposition. This is an aspect of psychoanalytic diversity in unity that it is worthwhile to respect, because each perspective brings in its own specific contribution. Translation should not attempt to obliterate these differences.

Each part has an introduction and we have added a short reading guide before each paper to orient the unprepared reader. We hope that analysts at all levels of experience, from analysts in training to senior colleagues, will find something useful in this book that they can keep to enrich their own practice and strengthen the field.

References

Bellanova, P., Amati Mehler, J., Argentieri, S., Batini, M., Calvesi, A., Cargnelutti, E., De Lauro, L., Giannitelli, S., Merendino, R., Paulin, P., Tappa, G., Vergine, A., Zerbino, E. (1981). Formazione della coppia analitica e identità dello psicoanalista. *Rivista di Psicoanalisi* 1: 99–121.

Bion, W. R. (1994). Making the best of a bad job. In Bion, W. R., Bion, F. (eds), *Clinical Seminars and Other Works* (pp. 321–331). London: Karnac. (Originally published 1979.)

Bleger, J. (1971). La entrevista psicológica: su empleo en el diagnóstico y la investigación. In: *Temas de psicologia. Entrevistas y grupos.* Buenos Aires: Nueva Vision.

Cabré, L. J. M. (2007). Book Review of *Entrevista e indicadores en psicoterapia y psycoanalysis* [*Interview and indicators in psychotherapy and psychoanalysis*] by Antonio Pérez Sánchez (2006). *International Journal of Psychoanalysis* 88: 1094–1096.

Etchegoyen, H. (1999). *The Fundamentals of Psychoanalytic Technique* (revised ed.). London: Karnac.

Kantrowitz, J. (1995). The beneficial aspects of the patient–analyst match. *International Journal of Psychoanalysis* 76: 299–313.

Kantrowitz, J. L., Katz, A. L., Greenman, D. A., Morris, H., Paolitto, F., Sashin, J., Solomon, L. (1989). The patient–analyst match and the outcome of psychoanalysis: A pilot study. *Journal of the American Psychoanalytic Association* 37: 893–919.

Kantrowitz, J. L., Katz, A. L., Paolitto, F. (1990). Follow-up of psychoanalysis five to ten years after termination: III. The relation between the resolution of the transference and the patient–analyst match. *Journal of the American Psychoanalytic Association* 38: 655–678.

Pérez Sánchez, A. (2006). *Entrevista e indicadores en psicoterapia y psycoanalysis* [*Interview and indicators in psychotherapy and psychoanalysis*]. Valencia: Promolibro.

Reith, B., Boots, J., Crick, P., Gibeault, A., Jaffe, R., Lagerlöf, S., Møller, M., Skale, E., Vermote, R., Wegner, P. (2010). The specific dynamics of initial interviews: Switching the level, or opening up a meaning space? Report on Phase 1 of the WPIP Study of Initial Interviews. *Psychoanalysis in Europe: Bulletin of the European Psychoanalytic Federation* 64 (Suppl.): 57–80.

Sandell, R., Blomberg, J., Lazar, A., Carlsson, J., Broberg, J., Schubert, J. (2000). Varieties of long-term outcome among patients in psychoanalysis and long-term psychotherapy: A review of findings in the Stockholm Outcome of Psychotherapy and Psychoanalysis Project (STOPP). *The International Journal of Psychoanalysis* 81(5): 921–942.

Tuckett, D. (2002). Presidential Address: The new style conference and developing a peer culture in European psychoanalysis: Prague. *Psychoanalysis in Europe: Bulletin of the European Psychoanalytic Federation* 56: 32–46.

Tuckett, D. (2003). Presidential Address: A ten year European scientific initiative. *Psychoanalysis in Europe: Bulletin of the European Psychoanalytic Federation* 57: 7–22.

Tuckett, D. (2004). Presidential Address: Building a psychoanalysis based on confidence in what we do. *Psychoanalysis in Europe: Bulletin of the European Psychoanalytic Federation* 58: 5–20.

Tuckett, D., Basile, R., Birksted-Breen, D., Böhm, T., Denis, P., Ferro, A., Hinz, H., Jemstedt, A., Mariotti, P., Schubert, J. (2008). *Psychoanalysis Comparable and Incomparable. The Evolution of a Method to Describe and Compare Psychoanalytic Approaches.* London: Routledge.

Part I

'ARE YOU A DOCTOR, SIR?'

I 'ARE YOU A DOCTOR, SIR?'

Introduction

Sven Lagerlöf and Elisabeth Skale

Slightly taken aback at first by the sudden demand for a consultation on top of the Rax mountain, Freud becomes more and more interested in the story of the daughter of the landlady who runs the mountain refuge hut. As the interview proceeds Freud finds that he gains a deeper understanding of the young woman just by listening and letting her find her way through her own reminiscences and associations. As Argelander (1978, and this volume p. 26) points out: Freud starts to listen more as an analyst, not so much to explore like a doctor. When Katharina understood the connections she felt much better and this unique consultation ends: 'I never saw her again.' Because of the special circumstances her 'first interview' becomes an analysis.

So, Katharina becomes one of the women – together with Anna O., Emmy von N., Lucy R. and Elisabeth von R., who took part as patients and educators in the early development of psychoanalysis. This is 1893, and still a few years before the publication of 'Studies in Hysteria', where the Katharina episode is one of the case histories, and it is an example of the relation between hysteric symptoms and underlying repressed emotions.

According to a recent overview of the records in his practice (Tögel, 2009), there are indications that Freud – in his daily time schedule – made a clear distinction between 'consultations' and the one-hour psychoanalytic sessions. The 'consultations' were short and used to give clear instructions about the conditions to be respected before beginning analysis, about the beginning itself and the setting. He advised against doing psychotherapy during the consultation period, and referred to the importance of the beginning of an analysis by comparing this initial part of the psychoanalytic process with the opening of a chess game.

In 'On Psychotherapy' (1904), a lecture originally read to an audience of Viennese physicians, Freud's early views on indications for analysis are restricted to the field of neuroses but he puts a particular stress on the personality and motivation of the patient:

> One should look beyond the patient's illness and form an estimate of his whole personality; those patients who do not possess a reasonable degree of education and a fairly reliable character should be refused . . . Nor is the method applicable

to people who are not driven to seek treatment by their own sufferings, but who submit to it only because they are forced to by the authority of relatives.

(Freud, 1904, p. 263)

The most important qualification is that the patient is 'educable'. Psychoanalysis can be understood as an 'after-education in overcoming internal resistances' (ibid.).

A few years later, in his paper 'On Beginning the Treatment' (1913) Freud recommended that:

> . . . when I know little about a patient, only to take him on at first provisionally, for a period of one to two weeks. If one breaks off within this period one spares the patient the distressing impression of an attempted cure having failed. One has only been undertaking a 'sounding' in order to get to know the case and to decide whether it is a suitable one for psychoanalysis. No other kind of preliminary examination but this procedure is at our disposal; the most lengthy discussions and questionings in ordinary consultations would offer no substitute. This preliminary experiment, however, is itself the beginning of a psycho-analysis and must conform to its rules.
>
> (Freud, 1913, p. 124)

Freud also recommends this short trial of analysis as a way of detecting more severe psychiatric conditions. When Freud writes here about 'ordinary consultations' he might be thinking about an ordinary psychiatric consultation and he stresses the superior knowledge gained through a shared psychoanalytic experience, even a relatively short one:

> Lengthy preliminary discussions before the beginning of the analytic treatment, previous treatment by another method and also previous acquaintance between the doctor and the patient who is to be analysed, have special disadvantageous consequences for which one must be prepared. They result in the patient's meeting the doctor with a transference attitude which is already established and which the doctor must first slowly uncover instead of having the opportunity to observe the growth and development of the transference from the outset. In this way the patient gains a temporary start upon us which we do not willingly grant him in the treatment.
>
> (Freud, 1913, p. 125)

The Katharina case from 1895, primarily meant as a consultation, can also be seen as a very short analytic treatment, insofar as the observed relief did follow from the working through of repressed memories.

Beside the recommendations above, Freud was rather pessimistic about the diagnostic value even of a 'trial analysis' when he wrote:

> Our diagnoses are very often made only after the event. They resemble the Scottish King's test for identifying witches that I read about in Victor Hugo. This

> king declared that he was in possession of an infallible method of recognizing a witch. He had the women stewed in a cauldron of boiling water and then tasted the broth. Afterwards he was able to say: 'That was a witch', or 'No, that was not one.' It is the same with us, except that we are the sufferers.
>
> (Freud, 1933, p. 155)

After the decisions made at the beginning of an analysis, the analyst, just like the chess player, cannot influence the development of the game very much during its main course. Following the recommendations for the preliminary conditions, for the setting and the rules for the psychoanalytic technique, the analyst:

> . . . sets in motion a process, that of the resolving of existing repressions. He can supervise this process, further it, remove obstacles in its way, and he can undoubtedly vitiate much of it. But on the whole, once begun, it goes its own way and does not allow either the direction it takes or the order in which it picks up its points to be prescribed for it.
>
> (Freud, 1913, p. 130)

According to the detailed notes now available from the Rat-Man case, it is obvious that Freud lays out the conditions of the setting, number of sessions, finances and use of the couch in the first session, after the patient gave a vivid description of his symptoms, so that the analytic process within this frame of the setting can be observed from the first moment.

Perhaps we should also bear in mind that this was a time of relatively short psychoanalytic treatments:

> To speak more plainly, psycho-analysis is always a matter of long periods of time, of half a year or whole years – of longer periods than the patient expects. It is therefore our duty to tell the patient this before he finally decides upon the treatment.
>
> (Freud, 1913, p. 129)

So, at that time in the history of psychoanalysis, one year is a long time. As time went on, more and more patients, of which quite a few needed more than one year, underwent psychoanalysis. Many of those were not classical neurotic patients of the kind that Freud described together with the Katharina episode in *Studies on Hysteria*. The scope of psychoanalysis widened and the average time span of a psychoanalytic treatment increased.

Later on Freud regrets that, out of consideration for the patient, he had to mask the Katharina case history so much. In a later footnote added to the text in 1924 he corrects the historical record with the following information:

> Katharina was not the niece but the daughter of the landlady. The girl fell ill, therefore, as a result of sexual attempts on the part of her own father.
>
> (Freud, 1893, p. 134, footnote added 1924, and this volume p. 23)

Katharina, whose real name was Aurelia, was born in Vienna in 1875. After her encounter with Freud at the Ottohaus Rax, she consulted him on account of her own children, but never again had the symptoms that originally brought her into contact with Freud. She married a German forester and went with him to Hungary where he managed the forests of a great estate. The marriage did not turn out very well and she eventually returned to Vienna with her six children. She died prematurely from a heart attack in 1929 in Reichenau (Fichtner & Hirschmüller, 1985).

References

Argelander, H. (1978). Das psychoanalytische Erstinterview und seine methode. Ein Nachtrag zu Freuds Fall 'Katharina' [The psychoanalytic initial interview and its method: A postscript to Freud's case 'Katharina']. *Psyche* 32: 1089–1098.

Fichtner, G., Hirschmüller, A. A. (1985). Freud's Katharina – Hintergrund, Entstehungsgeschichte und Bedeutung einer frühen psychoanalytischen Krankengeschichte. *Psyche* 3/85: 220–240.

Freud, S. (1893). Katharina, Case Histories from Studies on Hysteria. *SE* 2: 125–134.[1]

Freud, S. (1904). On Psychotherapy. *SE* 7: 263.

Freud, S. (1913). On Beginning the Treatment (in Further Recommendations on the Technique of Psycho-Analysis I). *SE* 12: 121–144.

Freud, S. (1933). New Introductory Lectures On Psycho-Analysis. *SE* 22: 1–182.

Tögel, C. (2009). Sigmund Freud's practice: Visits and consultation, psychoanalyses, remuneration. *Psychoanalytic Quarterly* 78(4): 1033–1058.

[1] Throughout this volume references to *The Standard Edition of the Complete Works of Sigmund Freud*, Jones, E. (Ed.). London: Hogarth Press (1950–74) are abbreviated to *SE* followed by the volume number and, if applicable, the page range.

1 KATHARINA

Case histories from *Studies on Hysteria* (1893)

Sigmund Freud

In the summer vacation of the year 189- I made an excursion into the Hohe Tauern[1] so that for a while I might forget medicine and more particularly the neuroses. I had almost succeeded in this when one day I turned aside from the main road to climb a mountain which lay somewhat apart and which was renowned for its views and for its well run refuge hut. I reached the top after a strenuous climb and, feeling refreshed and rested, was sitting deep in contemplation of the charm of the distant prospect. I was so lost in thought that at first I did not connect it with myself when these words reached my ears: 'Are you a doctor, sir?' But the question was addressed to me, and by the rather sulky looking girl of perhaps eighteen who had served my meal and had been spoken to by the landlady as 'Katharina'. To judge by her dress and bearing, she could not be a servant, but must no doubt be a daughter or relative of the landlady's.

Coming to myself I replied: 'Yes, I'm a doctor: but how did you know that?'

'You wrote your name in the Visitors' Book, sir. And I thought if you had a few moments to spare . . . The truth is, sir, my nerves are bad. I went to see a doctor in L about them and he gave me something for them; but I'm not well yet.'

So there I was with the neuroses once again, for nothing else could very well be the matter with this strong, well-built girl with her unhappy look. I was interested to find that neuroses could flourish in this way at a height of over 6,000 feet; I questioned her further therefore. I report the conversation that followed between us just as it is impressed on my memory and I have not altered the patient's dialect.[2]

'Well, what is it you suffer from?'

'I get so out of breath. Not always. But sometimes it catches me so that I think I shall suffocate.'

1 [One of the highest ranges in the Eastern Alps.]
2 [No attempt has been made in the English translation to imitate this dialect.]

This did not, at first sight, sound like a nervous symptom. But soon it occurred to me that probably it was only a description that stood for an anxiety attack: she was choosing shortness of breath out of the complex of sensations arising from anxiety and laying undue stress on that single factor.

'Sit down here. What is it like when you get "out of breath"?'

'It comes over me all at once. First of all it's like something pressing on my eyes. My head gets so heavy, there's a dreadful buzzing, and I feel so giddy that I almost fall over. Then there's something crushing my chest so that I can't get my breath.'

'And you don't notice anything in your throat?'

'My throat's squeezed together as though I were going to choke.'

'Does anything else happen in your head?'

'Yes, there's a hammering, enough to burst it.'

'And don't you feel at all frightened while this is going on?'

'I always think I'm going to die. I'm brave as a rule and go about everywhere by myself, into the cellar and all over the mountain. But on a day when that happens I don't dare to go anywhere; I think all the time someone's standing behind me and going to catch hold of me all at once.'

So it was in fact an anxiety attack, and introduced by the signs of an hysterical 'aura'[3] or, more correctly, it was a hysterical attack the content of which was anxiety. Might there not probably be some other content as well?

'When you have an attack do you think of something? And always the same thing? Or do you see something in front of you?'

'Yes. I always see an awful face that looks at me in a dreadful way, so that I'm frightened.'

Perhaps this might offer a quick means of getting to the heart of the matter.

'Do you recognize the face? I mean, is it a face that you've really seen some time?'

'No.'

'Do you know what your attacks come from?'

'No.'

'When did you first have them?'

'Two years ago, while I was still living on the other mountain with my aunt. (She used to run a refuge hut there, and we moved here eighteen months ago.) But they keep on happening.'

Was I to make an attempt at an analysis? I could not venture to transplant hypnosis to these altitudes, but perhaps I might succeed with a simple talk. I should have to try a lucky guess. I had found often enough that in

[3] [The premonitory sensations preceding an epileptic or hysterical attack.]

girls anxiety was a consequence of the horror by which a virginal mind is overcome when it is faced for the first time with the world of sexuality.[4]

So I said: 'If you don't know, I'll tell you how *I* think you got your attacks. At that time, two years ago, you must have seen or heard something that very much embarrassed you, and that you'd much rather not have seen.'

'Heavens, yes!' she replied, 'that was when I caught my uncle with the girl, with Franziska, my cousin.'

'What's this story about a girl? Won't you tell me all about it?'

'You can say *anything* to a doctor, I suppose. Well, at that time, you know, my uncle, the husband of the aunt you've seen here, kept the inn on the – kogel[5]. Now they're divorced, and it's my fault they were divorced, because it was through me that it came out that he was carrying on with Franziska.'

'And how did you discover it?'

'This way. One day two years ago some gentlemen had climbed the mountain and asked for something to eat. My aunt wasn't at home, and Franziska, who always did the cooking, was nowhere to be found. And my uncle was not to be found either. We looked everywhere, and at last Alois, the little boy, my cousin, said: "Why, Franziska must be in Father's room!" And we both laughed; but we weren't thinking anything bad. Then we went to my uncle's room but found it locked. That seemed strange to me. Then Alois said: "There's a window in the passage where you can look into the room." We went into the passage; but Alois wouldn't go to the window and said he was afraid. So I said: "You silly boy! I'll go. I'm not a bit afraid." And I had nothing bad in my mind. I looked in. The room was rather dark, but I saw my uncle and Franziska; he was lying on her.'

'Well?'

'I came away from the window at once, and leant up against the wall and couldn't get my breath, just what happens to me since. Everything went blank, my eyelids were forced together and there was a hammering and buzzing in my head.'

'Did you tell your aunt that very same day?'

'Oh no, I said nothing.'

'Then why were you so frightened when you found them together? Did you understand it? Did you know what was going on?'

4 I will quote here the case in which I first recognized this causal connection. I was treating a young married woman who was suffering from a complicated neurosis and, once again [cf. p. 112n.], was unwilling to admit that her illness arose from her married life. She objected that while she was still a girl she had had attacks of anxiety, ending in fainting fits. I remained firm. When we had come to know each other better she suddenly said to me one day: 'I'll tell you now how I came by my attacks of anxiety when I was a girl. At that time I used to sleep in a room next to my parents, the door was left open and a night-light used to burn on the table. So more than once I saw my father get into bed with my mother and heard sounds that greatly excited me. It was then that my attacks came on.' – [Two cases of this kind are mentioned by Freud in a letter to Fliess of 30 May 1893 (Freud, 1950a, Letter 12). Cf. also Section II of the first paper on anxiety neurosis (1895b).]

5 [The name of the 'other' mountain.]

'Oh no. I didn't understand anything at that time. I was only sixteen. I don't know what I was frightened about.'

'Fräulein Katharina, if you could remember now what was happening in you at that time, when you had your first attack, what you thought about it, it would help you.'

'Yes, if I could. But I was so frightened that I've forgotten everything.'

(Translated into the terminology of our 'Preliminary Communication' [p. 12], this means: 'The affect itself created a hypnoid state, whose products were then cut off from associative connection with the ego-consciousness.')

'Tell me, Fräulein. Can it be that the head that you always see when you lose your breath is Franziska's head, as you saw it then?'

'Oh no, she didn't look so awful. Besides, it's a man's head.'

'Or perhaps your uncle's?'

'I didn't see his face as clearly as that. It was too dark in the room. And why should he have been making such a dreadful face just then?'

'You're quite right.'

(The road suddenly seemed blocked. Perhaps something might turn up in the rest of her story.)

'And what happened then?'

'Well, those two must have heard a noise, because they came out soon afterwards. I felt very bad the whole time. I always kept thinking about it. Then two days later it was a Sunday and there was a great deal to do and I worked all day long. And on the Monday morning I felt giddy again and was sick, and I stopped in bed and was sick without stopping for three days.'

We [Breuer and I] had often compared the symptomatology of hysteria with a pictographic script which has become intelligible after the discovery of a few bilingual inscriptions. In that alphabet being sick means disgust. So I said: 'If you were sick three days later, I believe that means that when you looked into the room you felt disgusted.'

'Yes, I'm sure I felt disgusted,' she said reflectively, 'but disgusted at what?'

'Perhaps you saw something naked? What sort of state were they in?'

'It was too dark to see anything; besides they both of them had their clothes on. Oh, if only I knew what it was I felt disgusted at!'

I had no idea either. But I told her to go on and tell me whatever occurred to her, in the confident expectation that she would think of precisely what I needed to explain the case.

Well, she went on to describe how at last she reported her discovery to her aunt, who found that she was changed and suspected her of concealing some secret. There followed some very disagreeable scenes between her uncle and aunt, in the course of which the children came to hear a number of things which opened their eyes in many ways and which it would have been better for them not to have heard. At last her aunt decided to move with her children and niece and take over the present inn, leaving her uncle alone with Franziska, who had meanwhile become pregnant. After this, however, to my astonishment she dropped these threads and began to tell me two sets of older stories, which went back two or three years earlier than the traumatic moment. The first set related to occasions on which the same uncle had made sexual advances to her herself, when she was only fourteen years old. She described how she had once gone with him on an expedition down into the valley in the winter and had spent the night in the inn there. He sat in the bar drinking and playing cards, but she felt sleepy and went up to bed early in the room they were to share on the upper floor. She was not quite asleep when he came up; then she fell asleep again and woke up suddenly 'feeling his body' in the bed. She jumped up and remonstrated with him: 'What are you up to, Uncle? Why don't you stay in your own bed?' He tried to pacify her: 'Go on, you silly girl, keep still. You don't know how nice it is.' – 'I don't like your "nice" things; you don't even let one sleep in peace.' She remained standing by the door, ready to take refuge outside in the passage, till at last he gave up and went to sleep himself. Then she went back to her own bed and slept till morning. From the way in which she reported having defended herself it seems to follow that she did not clearly recognize the attack as a sexual one. When I asked her if she knew what he was trying to do to her, she replied: 'Not at the time.' It had become clear to her much later on, she said; she had resisted because it was unpleasant to be disturbed in one's sleep and 'because it wasn't nice'.

I have been obliged to relate this in detail, because of its great importance for understanding everything that followed. She went on to tell me of yet other experiences of somewhat later date: how she had once again had to defend herself against him in an inn when he was completely drunk, and similar stories. In answer to a question as to whether on these occasions she had felt anything resembling her later loss of breath, she answered with decision that she had every time felt the pressure on her eyes and chest, but with nothing like the strength that had characterized the scene of discovery.

Immediately she had finished this set of memories she began to tell me a second set, which dealt with occasions on which she had noticed something between her uncle and Franziska. Once the whole family had spent the night in their clothes in a hay loft and she was woken up suddenly by a noise; she thought she noticed that her uncle, who had been lying between her and Franziska, was turning away, and that Franziska was just lying down. Another time they were stopping the night at an inn at the village of N–; she and her uncle were in one room and Franziska in an adjoining one. She woke up suddenly in the night and saw a tall white figure by the door, on the point of turning the handle: 'Goodness, is that you, Uncle? What are you doing at the door?' – 'Keep quiet. I was only looking for something.' – 'But the way out's by the *other* door.' – 'I'd just made a mistake' . . . and so on.

I asked her if she had been suspicious at that time. 'No, I didn't think anything about it; I only just noticed it and thought no more about it.' When I enquired whether she had been frightened on these occasions too, she replied that she thought so, but she was not so sure of it this time.

At the end of these two sets of memories she came to a stop. She was like someone transformed. The sulky, unhappy face had grown lively, her eyes were bright, she was lightened and exalted. Meanwhile the understanding of her case had become clear to me. The later part of what she had told me, in an apparently aimless fashion, provided an admirable explanation of her behaviour at the scene of the discovery. At that time she had carried about with her two sets of experiences which she remembered but did not understand, and from which she drew no inferences. When she caught sight of the couple in intercourse, she at once established a connection between the new impression and these two sets of recollections, she began to understand them and at the same time to fend them off. There then followed a short period of working out, of 'incubation',[6] after which the symptoms of conversion set in, the vomiting as a substitute for moral and physical disgust. This solved the riddle. She had not been disgusted by the sight of the two people but by the memory which that sight had stirred up in her. And, taking everything into account, this could only be the memory of the attempt on her at night when she had 'felt her uncle's body'.

So when she had finished her confession I said to her: 'I know now what it was you thought when you looked into the room. You thought: "Now he's doing with her what he wanted to do with me that night and those other times." That was what you were disgusted at, because you remembered the feeling when you woke up in the night and felt his body.'

'It may well be,' she replied, 'that that was what I was disgusted at and that that was what I thought.'

'Tell me just one thing more. You're a grown-up girl now and know all sorts of things . . .'

'Yes, now I am.'

'Tell me just one thing. What part of his body was it that you felt that night?'

But she gave me no more definite answer. She smiled in an embarrassed way, as though she had been found out, like someone who is obliged to admit that a fundamental position has been reached where there is not much more to be said. I could imagine what the tactile sensation was which she had later learnt to interpret. Her facial expression seemed to me to be saying that she supposed that I was right in my conjecture. But I could not penetrate further, and in any case I owed her a debt of gratitude for having made it so much easier for me to talk to her than to the prudish ladies of my city practice, who regard whatever is natural as shameful.

Thus the case was cleared up. – But stop a moment! What about the recurrent hallucination of the head, which appeared during her attacks and struck terror into her? Where did it come from? I proceeded to ask her about it, and, as though *her* knowledge, too, had been extended by our conversation, she promptly replied: 'Yes, I know now. The head is my uncle's head – I recognize it now – but not from *that* time. Later, when all the disputes had

[6] [Cf. below, p. 134.]

broken out, my uncle gave way to a senseless rage against me. He kept saying that it was all my fault: if I hadn't chattered, it would never have come to a divorce. He kept threatening he would do something to me; and if he caught sight of me at a distance his face would get distorted with rage and he would make for me with his hand raised. I always ran away from him, and always felt terrified that he would catch me some time unawares. The face I always see now is his face when he was in a rage.'

This information reminded me that her first hysterical symptom, the vomiting, had passed away; the anxiety attack remained and acquired a fresh content. Accordingly, what we were dealing with was a hysteria which had to a considerable extent been abreacted. And in fact she had reported her discovery to her aunt soon after it happened.

'Did you tell your aunt the other stories – about his making advances to you?'

'Yes. Not at once, but later on, when there was already talk of a divorce. My aunt said: "We'll keep that in reserve. If he causes trouble in the Court, we'll say that too." '

I can well understand that it should have been precisely this last period – when there were more and more agitating scenes in the house and when her own state ceased to interest her aunt, who was entirely occupied with the dispute – that it should have been this period of accumulation and retention that left her the legacy of the mnemic symbol [of the hallucinated face].

I hope this girl, whose sexual sensibility had been injured at such an early age, derived some benefit from our conversation. I have not seen her since.

Discussion

If someone were to assert that the present case history is not so much an analysed case of hysteria as a case solved by guessing, I should have nothing to say against him. It is true that the patient agreed that what I interpolated into her story was probably true; but she was not in a position to recognize it as something she had experienced. I believe it would have required hypnosis to bring that about. Assuming that my guesses were correct, I will now attempt to fit the case into the schematic picture of an 'acquired' hysteria on the lines suggested by Case 3. It seems plausible, then, to compare the two sets of erotic experiences with 'traumatic' moments and the scene of discovering the couple with an 'auxiliary' moment [cf. p. 123f.]. The similarity lies in the fact that in the former experiences an element of consciousness was created which was excluded from the thought activity of the ego and remained, as it were, in storage, while in the latter scene a new impression forcibly brought about an associative connection between this separated group and the ego. On the other hand there are dissimilarities which cannot be overlooked. The cause of the isolation was not, as in Case 3, an act of will on the part of the ego but *ignorance* on the part of the ego, which was not yet capable of coping with sexual experiences. In this respect the case of Katharina is typical. In every analysis of a case of hysteria based on sexual traumas we find that impressions from the pre-sexual period which produced no effect on the child attain traumatic power at a later date as memories, when the girl or married woman has acquired an understanding of sexual life.[7] The splitting-off of psychical groups may be said to be a normal process in adolescent development; and it is easy to see that their later reception into the ego affords frequent opportunities for psychical disturbances. Moreover, I should like at this point to express a doubt as to whether a splitting of consciousness due to ignorance is really different from one due to conscious rejection, and whether even adolescents do not possess sexual knowledge far oftener than is supposed or than they themselves believe.

A further distinction in the psychical mechanism of this case lies in the fact that the scene of discovery, which we have described as 'auxiliary', deserves equally to be called 'traumatic'. It was operative on account of its own content and not merely as something that revived previous traumatic experiences. It combined the characteristics of an 'auxiliary' and a 'traumatic' moment. There seems no reason, however, why this coincidence should lead us to abandon a conceptual separation which in other cases corresponds also to a separation in time. Another peculiarity of Katharina's case, which, incidentally, has long been familiar to us, is seen in the circumstance that the conversion, the production of the hysterical phenomena, did not occur immediately after the trauma but after an interval of incubation. Charcot liked to describe this interval as the 'period of psychical "working-out" ' [*élaboration*].[8]

The anxiety from which Katharina suffered in her attacks was a hysterical one; that is, it was a reproduction of the anxiety which had appeared in connection with each of the sexual traumas. I shall not here comment on the fact which I have found regularly present in a very large number of cases – namely that a mere suspicion of sexual relations calls up the affect of anxiety in virginal individuals[9] [cf. p. 127, *n*. 1.].

Reference

Freud, S. (1893). Katharina, Case Histories from Studies on Hysteria. *SE* 2: 125–134.

7 [Freud had discussed this at considerable length in the later sections of Part II of his 1895 'Project' (Freud, 1950a) and expressed the same view in Section I of his second paper on 'The Neuro-Psychoses of Defence' (1896b), Standard E., 3, 166–7 *n*. It was not until some years later that he came to recognize the part played in the production of neuroses by sexual impulses already present in early childhood. Cf. the Editor's Note to the *Three Essays* (1905d), *Standard Ed*., 7, 127–9.]

8 [See Charcot 1888, 1, 99. Cf. also Breuer's remarks on the subject on p. 213 below.]

9 [*Footnote added* 1924] I venture after the lapse of so many years to lift the veil of discretion and reveal the fact that Katharina was not the niece but the daughter of the landlady. The girl fell ill, therefore, as a result of sexual attempts on the part of her own father. Distortions like the one which I introduced in the present instance should be altogether avoided in reporting a case history. From the point of view of understanding the case, a distortion of this kind is not, of course, a matter of such indifference as would be shifting the scene from one mountain to another.

2 THE PSYCHOANALYTIC INITIAL INTERVIEW AND ITS METHOD

A postscript to Freud's case 'Katharina' *by Hermann Argelander*

Commentary

Elisabeth Skale

Hermann Argelander (1920–2004) was a member of the German Psychoanalytic Association, trained at the Berlin Psychoanalytic Institute (1951 to 1957). He was Professor and Research Scholar at the Sigmund Freud Institute Frankfurt and Director of the Institute from 1983 to 1985.

A group of psychoanalysts working at the institute in Frankfurt were very impressed by the fact that in their first interviews with outpatients they regularly came across the complex dynamics of an unconscious phenomenon. In evaluating these observations they were amazed by the abundance and numerous layers of data. A research group of relatively inexperienced investigators (students, trainees at the Sigmund Freud Institute, and general practitioners) was formed to discuss the verbatim protocols of first interviews in order to develop a method for rendering the data obtained in a first interview.

In 1967 Argelander published a series of papers about this research project. It could be confirmed that at a crucial point in the initial interview the unconscious conflicts seemed to converge into a focused conflict due to the spontaneous transference developing in the doctor–patient relationship. Another result of this investigation was that a process determined by analysable elements could be discriminated, when the actual unconscious dynamics found in the interview were related to the patient's personality structure. This brought about the conclusion that since patients will shape the interview situation in a typical way (which is connected to their unconscious motivations or expectations), predictions about the possibility of treatment and predictions about the outcome could be inferred on the basis of these observations.

The author's paper 'The Scenic Function of the Ego and its Contribution to Symptom and Character Formation' (1970) refers to the capability of the Ego to turn a situation into a 'scene', that is, into an appropriate representation of an unconscious, infantile configuration, which is relatively stable and personality bound. This unconscious, infantile configuration has the status of latent dream-thoughts, and the transformation into a 'scene' appropriate to the situation, like the production of a manifest dream, is the only way to bring its content to the surface. The same process is found in the transformation of a neurosis into a transference-neurosis – only then can it be approached by analysis.

The concept of 'scenic understanding' was introduced by Alfred Lorenzer (1970/1971) when he followed the question: 'What is the analyst doing during the session?' He argued that only 'scenic understanding' can reach the patient's unconscious, that neither logical comprehension, i.e. explanation, nor empathy can do so. Alfred Lorenzer was a psychoanalyst and social psychologist working at the Institute of Alexander Mitscherlich. His view on psychoanalytic theories was influenced by the critical theory of the Frankfurt School and their research on the interaction between the structure of society and that of personality (Schaffrik, 2002).

Argelander further developed the concept of 'scenic understanding' and maintained that 'scenic and situational information' provides the interviewer with invaluable tools for a psychoanalytic understanding of personality structure during the first interview, so that this kind of information should be included in the assessment evaluation as equivalent to the personal (subjective) information given by the patient and observed (objective) data found by the 'doctor' interviewer.

In his papers of 1976 and 1978 Argelander points out that Freud's 'Katharina' is the very first psychoanalytic interview and – due to the particular circumstances – Freud has to apply his method of 'free association' in order to evoke memories for the first time. With this 'secondary' analysis of the process of this case history, the author shows that Freud described 'objective' data about Katharina, listened carefully to 'subjective' information given by Katharina, but succeeded in uncovering the incident which had triggered the patient's hysterical symptoms because the interview situation permitted a partial scenic reproduction of that very incident.

References

Argelander, H. (1970). Die szenische Funktion des Ichs und ihr Anteil an der Symptom- und Charakterbildung [The scenic function of the ego and its contribution to symptom and character formation]. *Psyche* 24: 325–345.

Argelander, H. (1976). In a walk-in interview with Freud: Technical considerations concerning Freud's case 'Katharina'. *Psyche* 30: 665–702.

Argelander, H. (1978). Das psychoanalytische Erstinterview und seine methode. Ein Nachtrag zu Freuds Fall 'Katharina' [The psychoanalytic initial interview and its method: A postscript to Freud's case 'Katharina']. *Psyche* 32: 1089–1098.

Lorenzer, A. (1970). *Sprachzerstörung und Rekonstruktion. Vorarbeiten zu einer Metatheorie der Psychoanalyse*. Frankfurt a.M. Suhrkamp, 1971.

Schaffrik, T. (2002). *The Work of Alfred Lorenzer. An Introduction*. © Tobias Schaffrik 2002 (bidok.uibk.ac.at/library/schaffrik-lorenzer-work-e.html).

2 THE PSYCHOANALYTIC INITIAL INTERVIEW AND ITS METHOD

A postscript to Freud's case 'Katharina'[1]

Hermann Argelander

The objective significance of information

In general, a first interviewer has his own method to reach the goal of obtaining as much information as possible from the patient about the illness. In the end, the indication for therapeutic procedure is derived from this information. The information has an objective character because it deals with statements about relationships to family members and general life events, as well as happenings in the family which could be verified and which are recognized as connected to the illness. This sort of method was adopted in the anamnestic enquiry as it has been practised in medicine for centuries. The information gained obtains its value through the expertise, which makes it into relevant statements about the illness and its psychological nexus. Because the interviewer alone ascertains the value of the information, he is also responsible for actively guiding the interview in an exploratory way. During this process the patient merely delivers information and, being a layman, does not penetrate its relevance for understanding his illness. Should he offer his own insights on his illness, these are inferior to the interviewer's critical expertise and for the most part are discarded as subjective.

In the exploratory process, where important standardized questions can be allowed, one uses a personality theory and illness theory to explain the interrelated complexities of the illness. When Freud published his first free interview in 1892, he also initially applied a technique based on this method of interviewing. In the piece 'In a Walk-In Interview with Freud' (1976) I dealt extensively with this unique exchange between the 18-year-old Katharina and the then 39-year-old Freud. Using this historic protocol, I would like to present the development of the psychoanalytic interview in its most important phases.

It was probably in the year 1892, as Freud was on a hiking tour in the Hohe Tauern, when after he had rested and eaten at a mountain hut, he was

[1] Originally published as: Argelander, H. (1978). Das psychoanalytische Erstinterview und seine methode. Ein Nachtrag zu Freuds Fall 'Katharina'. *Psyche* 32: 1089–1098.

approached by the daughter of the hut's landlady as he was pausing at a nearby vantage point. Under the circumstances – being addressed as a doctor while in contemplation of the beautiful landscape – Freud needed a moment to bring his attention as a doctor to the task at hand. I shall first deal with the interview as an anamnestic enquiry and give an account of the information, which is relevant for this method. It will later become apparent that when there is a change in the method, different correlating information must be drawn from the protocol.

The exploratory interview begins with Freud's question, 'Well, what is it you suffer from?' Katharina answers with a description of her symptoms: shortness of breath, feelings of suffocation, constriction of the throat and chest. She ends her account with the spontaneous remark 'I always think I'm going to die . . . I think all the time someone's standing behind me and going to catch hold of me all at once.' With his specialist's know-how Freud accordingly states, 'It was a hysterical attack the content of which was anxiety.' (S.F., *SE* 2, p. 126)

Freud subsequently asks about the specific circumstances of the hysteric fits. There can be no doubt that Freud is led by his theoretical knowledge of the illness 'hysteria' in his questions or that he perceives the answers only in this context:

> 'When you have an attack do you think of something . . . or do you see something in front of you?'
>
> 'Yes. I always see an awful face that looks at me in a dreadful way, so that I'm frightened.'
>
> 'Do you recognize the face?'
>
> 'No.'
>
> 'Do you know what your attacks come from?'
>
> 'No.'
>
> 'When did you first have them?'
>
> 'Two years ago . . .'
>
> (S.F., *SE* 2, p. 127)

After this exploration Freud formulates a hypothesis, which complies with his theory for hysteria. Given the circumstances, he did not dare to employ the technique of hypnosis, which he was still using at that time. In order to get an answer to his question other than the 'no' the girl had given him, he had to, as he expressed it, 'make a lucky guess'. The 'guessed' hypothesis goes as follows:

> I had found often enough that in girls anxiety was a consequence of the horror by which a virginal mind is overcome when it is faced for the first time with the world of sexuality.
>
> (S.F., *SE* 2, p. 127)

This hypothesis forces the presentation of the symptoms into a context of its own and declares components such as 'I always think I'm going to die' or 'I think all the time someone's standing behind me and going to catch hold of me all at once' to be merely subjective accessories to the information which draws its relevance only from a theoretical understanding of the illness and not from the subjective form of the presentation. The focus of the hypothesis on the horror of sexuality as something new and unknown introduces a topic that had not yet been expressed directly in the presentation of the illness. At this point of his exploration Freud therefore employs his hypothetical knowledge of the cause of the illness and says:

> 'If you don't know, I'll tell you how I think you got your attacks. At that time, two years ago, you must have seen or heard something that very much embarrassed you, and that you'd much rather not have seen.'
>
> 'Heavens, yes!' she replied, 'that was when I caught my father [uncle in Freud's paper[2]] with the girl, with Franziska, my cousin.'
>
> (S.F., *SE* 2, p. 127)

Then she gives an account of what had happened two years earlier. At that time two men came up and asked for something to eat. Katharina had to go look for Franziska, who always did the cooking, and caught her and the father [referred to as 'uncle' by Freud, see editor's footnote] in flagrante in his room.

> 'I looked in. The room was rather dark, but I saw my father [S.F. uncle] and Franziska; he was lying on her . . . I came away from the window at once, and leant up against the wall and couldn't get my breath – just what happens to me since . . .'
>
> (S.F., *SE* 2, p. 128)

Freud's hypothesis is amazingly and immediately confirmed when Katharina reports these facts, and the consequences of that event confirmed her information: after hearing about the adultery from Katharina, her mother divorced her father and moved up to the hut in the mountains where Freud later stopped for a bite to eat. Her father married the pregnant Franziska and remained at the other hut where the events described had taken place.

Katharina had thus, confirming Freud's hypothesis, literally taken a virginal look into the world of sexuality and immediately reacted with a first hysterical fit.

[2] Editor's note: In quoting from Freud, Argelander has substituted 'father' where Freud wrote originally 'uncle'. We have retained Argelander's decision here.

The subjective meaning of information

This interesting piece of information becomes the subject of a dialogue, which, however, jumps the rails because Freud wants to see the particulars of the symptoms explained exclusively in connection with the concrete event. In answer to Freud's first question asking why she was so frightened, Katharina has nothing to say, she has forgotten everything. To his second question – if the head, which she always sees when having difficulty breathing might be Franziska's head as she saw it that day – Katharina has a clear answer at hand:

'Oh no, she didn't look so awful. Besides, it's a man's head.' To the third question, 'Or perhaps your father's [S.F. uncle's], Katharina answers quite decidedly, 'I didn't see his face as clearly as that. It was too dark in the room. And why should he have been making such a dreadful face just then?' Freud acknowledges this convincingly logical answer with the remark, 'You're quite right.' (S.F., *SE* 2, p. 128)

This last attempt to clarify the described facts and circumstances using the hypothesis again failed and so Freud decided to broaden the exploratory method and had the desired success with this:

> 'But I told her to go on and tell me whatever occurred to her, in the confident expectation that she would think of precisely what I needed to explain the case.'
>
> (S.F., *SE* 2, p. 129)

Impressed by his experience with the 18-year-old girl, Freud gave up the exclusive use of the exploratory method for the interview in 1892 and supplemented it with spontaneous dialogue in which the patient takes the lead by following the completely subjective free flow of his or her thoughts. Here the information no longer obtains its relevant significance from the specialized knowledge used to elicit it. Instead, the new pieces of information coming from the spontaneous thoughts of the patient obtain their relevance for the psychical disturbance from the subjective meaning, which the patient gives them in the form of his or her spontaneous presentation.

The important pieces of information were not only the interesting facts and the ones which confirmed the hypothesis, but also their subjective meaning for Katharina. Freud was able to discern this after the girl spontaneously related how the father ['uncle' in Freud's original text] had made sexual advances to Katharina herself and how she had later noticed the beginning of his affair with Franziska in suspicious details. This is the point where we are first able to imagine what went on inside the young girl at the time of the first event related: disappointment in her unconscious incestuous love of the father in the face of this rival as well as feelings of guilt for betraying the 'clandestine love play' to the mother. Katharina's face reflects the subjective significance of the situation, i.e. its interpretation on the subjective level, during her conversation with Freud. At first sullen, after her spontaneous account she is 'like someone transformed. The sulky, unhappy face had grown lively, her eyes were bright, she was lightened and exalted' (S.F., *SE* 2, p. 131).

The exploratory interview method was expanded in 1892 and made space for another methodological component, which culminated in the spontaneous dialogue in which the patient, following his thoughts, takes over the leading role. The central focus of this enhanced method was no longer solely on the significance the interviewer, in applying his know-how, assigns to the facts. Instead, the material is also interpreted using the subjective meaning the patient gives it. Thus the subject matter of the method has also changed. The patient is no longer merely the supplier of information whose significance is not known to him, he is also the warrantor that the subjective significance the information holds for him is correctly understood. With this the patient becomes an essential partner in the dialogue. Here we are dealing with a fundamental step taken in the interview method, one implemented by Freud himself, even if he did not concentrate on the interview method at that time as his interests were still solely focused on methodological problems of psychoanalytic treatment.

The scenic significance of information

To bring the interview method into line with insights already won from classic analytical treatment, the information conveyed in the current relationship needed to be relevantly evaluated. I would like to retrospectively demonstrate this further development using protocol material from the exchange between Freud and Katharina.

In this phase in the development of the interview method the patient is no longer merely the source of information and guarantee for the correct interpretation of the subjective meanings of the content he reports to us, he is a partner in the relationship as well. The insights psychoanalysis has won into the unconscious relationship with its phenomena of transference, counter-transference and defence are also valid for a single or several interviews, if not always in the unique form which they take on in a continuing long-term relationship.

Psychoanalysts had reserved these phenomena for treatment, and had not considered that they also play a role in short encounters, as any life experience shows. Indeed, for a long time the first interview remained a step-child of psychoanalysis so that the interesting question of how many seconds, minutes or hours it actually takes until phenomena of the unconscious relationship noticeably emerge as transference or counter-transference did not arise.

If we look at the interview protocol between Freud and Katharina under this aspect we will see it with entirely fresh eyes. We must get to the bottom of the conditions of the manifest relationship and first read the inconspicuous, subjective remarks in the protocol as pieces of information about a different context: the unconscious.

Freud was at that time 39 and, as we know from pictures, a good-looking man whom Katharina had obviously already observed during his meal. There is no question that he interested her for she had looked in the guestbook and seen what his profession was. When she ascertained he was a doctor she probably made up her mind to speak to him about her illness and after the meal followed him to where he was sunk in contemplation of the view nearby the hut. For his part, Freud had registered her sulky face when she served him but he also realized that 'to judge by her dress and bearing, she could not be a servant, but must no doubt be a daughter or relative of the landlady's' (S.F., *SE* 2, p. 125). So each of the two partners in the dialogue had already wondered about the other before they actually spoke. As is so often the case, the relationship begins long before the actual exchange, thus the course of the conversation is determined by factors which completely escape the observer of objective givens and factual information. In addition, let us give our attention to the mood and the feelings accompanying the dialogue. To this end, we shall look at the introduction of the protocol, which we had previously overlooked as an unimportant accessory.

> 'Feeling refreshed and rested, I was sitting deep in contemplation of the charm of the distant prospect. I was so lost in thought that at first I did not connect it with myself when these words reached my ears: "Are you a doctor, Sir?" But the question was addressed to me, and by the rather sulky-looking girl of perhaps eighteen . . .'
>
> (S.F., *SE* 2, p. 125).

Of course Katharina already knew the gentleman was a doctor for she had, curious as she was, looked it up in the visitor's book. So the question served purely to make contact and was consciously accompanied by the motive to consult the doctor about her illness. Freud's reaction: 'So there I was with the neuroses once again – for nothing else could very well be the matter with this strong, well-built girl with her unhappy look.' Thus Freud's interest in her was also accompanied by his interest in neuroses. But let us look at his own postscript: 'I was interested to find that neuroses could flourish in this way at a height of over 6,000 feet' (S.F., *SE* 2, p. 125). A truly superfluous ironic remark for a scientific protocol, nevertheless something resonates in this almost poetic utterance, which characterizes how he experienced this unique relationship. After this quite personal description of its prelude, the conversation became factual when it came to the symptoms of the illness. But immediately afterwards there again emerges a passage which, when looked at it in terms of the relationship, earns our increased attention. Earlier, when the focus was on other contexts, I omitted the following passage as unimportant:

> 'Was I to make an attempt at an analysis? I could not venture to transplant hypnosis to these altitudes, but perhaps I might succeed with a simple talk. I should have to try a lucky guess.'
>
> (S.F., *SE* 2, p. 127)

As is well known, it was following this that Freud formulated his hypothesis. Of course it was not the altitude which kept Freud from applying his tried and tested hypnosis technique, it was the inner and the outer circumstances of the situation. How should we imagine this situation? Could the mother see the two from the hut? Or might her mother come to get Katharina because some guests wanted their meal? What would the mother have thought if she had surprised them during hypnosis? With our questions into the meaning of the relationship under the given circumstances of the situation, we evoke the 'avoided' scene of the 'discovery' situation, which was the central point in Katharina's account, where she begins with:

> 'This way. One day two years ago some gentlemen had climbed the mountain and asked for something to eat. My aunt wasn't at home, and Franziska, who always did the cooking, was nowhere to be found. . . . We looked everywhere, . . . I saw my father [S.F. uncle] and Franziska; he was lying on her.'
>
> (S.F., *SE* 2, p. 127)

Wasn't Freud also a gentleman who had climbed up and asked for something to eat? Mustn't that fact have evoked the memory? Now the context of the scene gives new meaning to the protocol. We directly experience the course of events in the situation and recognize how the participating persons are enmeshed in its context. We see how Freud here abandons his tested method, attempts to free himself, tries to avoid ambiguities with his justification of the 2,000 meter altitude, and in doing this he makes a decisive, but up to now underappreciated, discovery for psychoanalysis.

Thus the multi-layered meaning of the 'scene of the discovery' is the unconscious topic at the core of this interview and so also logically determines the succession of the conversation quite independent from the misunderstandings following in its wake, which I previously described. First the father ['uncle'] is discovered in flagrante with Franziska. Then, as Freud augments his method, after great and understandable resistance this event is 'dis-covered' to the mother. Let us take a look at the following passage to see how, in its ambiguous choice of words, it also includes the scene going on between Freud and Katharina at this very moment:

'Well, she went on to describe how at last she reported her discovery to her mother, who found that she was changed and suspected her of concealing some secret.'

(S.F., *SE* 2, p. 129)

These words are an exact description of the situation with Freud. Freud saw Katharina's sulky face and suspected the secret of neurosis behind it, and Katharina 'dis-covered' it to him by beginning to describe her real discovery. When Freud finally let her spontaneously tell her account further 'dis-coveries' followed. Freud comments on this passage with these words:

'After this, however, to my astonishment she dropped these threads (the 'dis-covery' of her experience to her mother) and began to tell me two sets of older stories.'

(S.F., *SE* 2, p. 129)

These deal with the 'dis-covery' of her unconscious love of the father in the topic of his 'sexual advances' and the 'dis-covery' of the father's secret love affair with Franziska.

'At the end of these two sets of memories she came to a stop. She was like someone transformed. The sulky, unhappy face had grown lively, her eyes were bright, she was lightened and exalted.'

(S.F., *SE* 2, p. 131)

Katharina had now 'dis-covered' herself to Freud.

'Thus the case was cleared up. – But stop a moment! What about the recurrent hallucination of the head, which appeared during her attacks and struck terror into her? Where did it come from? I proceeded to ask her about it, and, as though her knowledge, too, had been extended by our conversation, she promptly replied: 'Yes, I know now. The head is my father's [S.F. uncle's] head – I recognize it now – but not from that time. Later, when all the disputes had broken out, my father [S.F. uncle] gave way to a senseless rage against me. He kept saying that it was all my fault: if I hadn't chattered, it would never have come to a divorce. He kept threatening he would do something to me; and if he caught sight of me at a distance his face would get distorted with rage and he would make for me with his hand raised.'

(S.F., *SE* 2, p. 132)

Katharina's understanding had increased to such an extent by the end of the conversation that she was able to definitely identify the head which appeared during her attacks as the head of her father, with, in fact, the same threatening facial expression as when he persecuted her after she had 'dis-covered' her observations to her mother. Her remark 'but not from that time' marks a turning point in the relationship to her father. Up to this point he persecuted her in a sexual sense, afterwards he persecuted her out of revenge.

I shall here summarize the three phases in the development of the psychoanalytic method of the interview where in each case the subject of the method changed: first the subject was the information about the objective facts and circumstances of the case, whose connection to the course of the illness is established by the interviewer's expertise; then the information about the subjective meaning of facts and circumstances from the case, whose relevance for the course of the illness is demonstrated by the patient in her spontaneous presentation; and finally the information from the situation, whose significance arises out of the context of unconscious occurrences in the psychoanalytic relationship and which thus represents a product of the participation in an unconscious relationship. These three phases followed one another historically in becoming components of the method, but they stand in a continuous complementary relationship to each other in its application. The integration of the three dimensions, which can only come about through a flexible interplay of inner attitudes, facilitates the specific psychoanalytic statement we expect from a psychoanalytic first interview.

If we ask ourselves what justifies this claim to integrate three dimensions of understanding, we must answer that the interview, aside from its advantage of allowing us to study the interplay between these dimensions in an assessable situation, also facilitates a decisive fundamental experience which allows us to intuitively anticipate the process of future treatment with the persons participating in it. We can well imagine how the process of treatment would have continued between Freud and Katharina had a treatment taken place. The pieces of information which come by their emphasis out of the situation's lively interplay, allow themselves to be decoded into the indication criteria, i.e. motivation, psychological strain, constancy of object relationship, insight, and so on. One must take stock of how rich the information from an interview actually is when it can be viewed in the context of the three dimensions. It contains, like a microcosm, all kinds of possibilities, which in the subsequent treatment unfold and develop.

What such an interview holds in therapeutic possibilities of its own remains to be discovered by further research. Regrettably, we will never know how Katharina, after her interview with Freud, later fared.

References

Argelander, H. (1976). In a walk-in interview with Freud: Technical considerations concerning Freud's case 'Katharina . . .' *Psyche* 30: 665–702.

Freud, S. (1893). Katharina, Case Histories from Studies on Hysteria. *SE* 2: 125–134.

3 A SHORT OVERVIEW OF THE DEVELOPMENT OF IDEAS ABOUT 'FIRST INTERVIEWS' AFTER FREUD

Sven Lagerlöf

If you suffered from neurotic symptoms around 1895 you turned, as did Katharina, to a somatic doctor, preferably a neurologist, not a psychiatrist. Her consultation marks the beginning of a development where the analyst's decision to offer psychoanalysis or not and the way to reach that conclusion was made more and more outside the traditional frame of medicine. Questions about nosology, which occupied academic psychiatry, were not central to psychoanalysis, and within psychiatry, psychological treatment was of secondary importance.

During the first decades of the nineteenth century the interest in Freud's new psychological treatment increased. In Berlin in 1920 and in Vienna in 1922 clinics were opened to the public offering psychoanalysis at low cost. London followed in 1926. These were pioneering activities at the time and, at least in Berlin and Vienna, psychoanalysis was seen as part of a general movement towards social and political change (Danto, 1998, 1999).

Following the Second World War, mental health organizations and clinical psychiatric services went through a period of great development and extension, offering consultations and treatment as normal health-care procedures outside the stigmatizing world of the asylums. The mental-health movements in the USA and northern Europe were strongly influenced by psychoanalytic thinking.

With membership in the American Psychoanalytic Society limited to medical doctors only, psychoanalysis was transplanted right into American clinical psychiatry, and, as a rule, psychoanalysis was practised by specialists in psychiatry. So, the method and science of psychoanalysis were amalgamated with the professional and therapeutic worldview of psychiatry to a greater extent than in most European countries.

The Widening Scope of Indications for Psychoanalysis was the title of a symposium arranged by the New York Psychoanalytic Society in 1954, with Leo Stone, Anna Freud and Edith Jacobson as participants.

Stone's paper (1954), with the same title as the symposium, has been known as the paper that opened the door for psychoanalytic treatment of a wider range of diagnostic categories than the classical neurotic disturbances.

Contrary to the expectations that a modern reader might have, it is not a revolutionary pamphlet but a reasoned and thorough overview at a time when 'the generally expanding scope of psychoanalysis . . . is now on a sort of peak plateau'. He starts by giving a definition of the concept of psychoanalysis to be able to proceed to the central discussion about modifications and parameters and how much an analyst can modify a treatment and still call it psychoanalysis. Stone wants to think in terms of 'modified psychoanalysis', not psychoanalytic psychotherapy. 'For without these important processes, the profound reorganization of the personality which we associate with analysis, and in which the cure of illness is, in a sense, an incidental part of general economic change, cannot occur' (p. 577).

He then discusses some examples of diagnostic categories that have benefited from a modified analytic treatment, such as borderline disorders, narcissism and severe character disorders. He concludes that the effect of psychoanalysis does not have a simple relation to diagnosis: 'The "borderline" patient under certain special conditions may be a better patient in the long run, for all of the intrinsic difficulties, than the hysteric whose epinosic gains are too great' (p. 591).

Diagnostic labels, even if they are newly minted ones, do not give any certain prediction about the success of psychoanalysis.

> Nowadays, we are groping toward recognizing and regrouping such problems in such conceptions as the 'borderline' case or the 'latent psychosis.' This would still be an essentially (although improved) nosological approach. However, it is my feeling that there are elements of great importance which, while they may come to play a role in nosologies of the future, remain for the moment in a different sphere. I have in mind personality traits and resources, which we may try to assess from careful historical and cross-sectional evaluation of the personality.
>
> (p. 590)

Stone sets his hope on more careful assessment procedures and increased diagnostic precision but at the same time – and because of the scope and depth of his discussion – the reader feels that there must exist better ways to understand what happens between analyst and patient when they decide about starting an analysis. He turns to the analyst factor as being undervalued in relation to the patient. But in the hope for a possibility of prediction of outcome the light is still on the analyst or on the patient, not so much on the interaction between them.

The catchy title of the symposium; Stone's balanced and thoughtful treatment of a number of topics that engaged psychoanalysis for many years to come; and most importantly his optimistic appraisal of the possibilities of the 'widening indications', if only the analyst was good enough: all made this paper one of the most influential papers of the time.

Anna Freud commented on Stone's paper and expressed her worry that psychoanalysis was spreading its resources too much on conditions where therapeutic advances were uncertain and that more would be gained by concentrating forces on the development of the analysis of neurotic suffering. This is a discussion that returns later on, especially in the continued discussion about the relationship between psychoanalysis and psychoanalytic psychotherapy.

Thirteen years later, the International Psychoanalytical Congress in Copenhagen in 1967 arranged a symposium called *Indications and Contraindications for Psychoanalysis*. Even if indications now refers also to characteristics or resources of the patient, which are more or less independent of the diagnostic classification, time is ripe for the new concept of analysability, which now more and more comes into use. If indication refers to categories of mental conditions that can be treated with psychoanalysis, analysability refers to the ability of the actual patient or categories of patients to derive benefit from psychoanalysis.

The most well known of the contributions at the Copenhagen symposium in 1967 was Elisabeth Zetzel's paper, 'The So Called Good Hysteric' (Zetzel, 1968), which offered advice on how to differentiate between patients who shared a diagnosis of hysteric neurosis but had very different prospects as analysands. One finding was that cases diagnosed as hysteric turned out either very well or very poorly, and Zetzel's paper seemed to explain how this could be predicted from an initial interview. Typically it centres on the qualities of the patients as they are revealed by the assessment. The 'not so good' of the literary allusive title refers to a lack of analysability in the patient.

Beginning in the early 1960s, a number of papers were published with experiences from psychoanalytic clinics at universities or psychoanalytic training institutes. These clinics as a rule were assessing patients for subsequent referral to psychoanalysis with candidates under supervision. At this time a lot of people looked for low-fee psychoanalysis through the institute clinics, and the relatively larger number of applicants in relation to the limited number of treatment options made for a sellers' market. This situation seemed to call for objective measures of analysability that could ensure that the patients with the greatest chance of benefit from the psychoanalytic treatment were selected. Reports from the Philadelphia Psychoanalytic Institute and Society Clinic (Lower, Escoll, & Huxster, 1972; Huxster, Lower, & Escoll, 1975) showed that practising analysts who interviewed and screened people who applied for psychoanalysis at the Clinic were far more positive to the patients' demand for analysis than the Clinic Committee, which decided about acceptance to analytic treatment from the written reports of the interviewers. The researchers concluded that this was because the screening analysts were subjected to a pressure emanating from strong unspoken psychological currents in the meeting with the patient and so were prone to become too subjective and intuitive in their judgements, whereas the committee made decisions founded on a more objective appraisal of the applicant. This pressure inherent in the face-to-face interview is at this time and under these circumstances regarded only as a disturbance to the objective assessment. Lazar (1976) quotes similar conclusions from other psychoanalytic clinics in the USA and recommends a more careful evaluation of ego functions. For the interviewer that means judging social adaptation, object relationships, job and study performance of the applicant within a frame of ego psychology and against some private normative scale of the interviewer, and without taking transference and in particular counter-transference much into consideration. The kind of moralistic stance that can emerge within 'the assessment culture' has been strongly criticized by Rothstein (1994, this volume, p. 281).

A number of researchers at psychoanalytic institute clinics in the USA tried to establish a relation between outcome of psychoanalysis and initial assessment of analysability, drawing on the great number of analytic treatments done by candidates at the institute clinics. On the whole this research did not give the hoped for confirmation of the hypotheses, that assessment could foresee the outcome of psychoanalysis. For an overview see Bachrach and Leaff (1978).

Between 1986 and 1990, Judy Kantrowitz and colleagues (1990) made a follow-up study of a number of psychoanalytic treatments with a special interest in the influence of 'the analyst factor' and the match between analyst and analysand. They found that both these factors influenced outcome. This points to the importance of transference and counter-transference factors in the first interviews.

At the same time as the American institute clinics struggled with the problems of objective assessment, analysts in many countries, including the USA, began exploring the dynamics of the first interview, which is the main topic of this collection.

In the development over time of the understanding of the nature and possibilities of first interviews, a number of discussions are intertwined: the changing needs of the patients; the relationship between psychoanalysis and psychotherapy; the role of diagnosis; the dynamics of the first interview; and the role of the economic and institutional frame of the interview. All these factors have to be made visible, discussed and evaluated according to their importance for the individual patient.

References

Bachrach, H. M., Leaff, L. A. (1978). 'Analyzability': A systematic review of the clinical and quantitative literature. *Journal of the American Psychoanalytical Association* 26: 881–920.

Danto, E. A. (1998). Freud's Free Clinic in Vienna. *International Journal of Psychoanalysis* 79: 287–300.

Danto, E. A. (1999). The Berlin Poliklinik: Psychoanalytic innovation in Weimar Germany. *Journal of the American Psychoanalytical Association* 47: 1269–1292.
Huxster, H. K., Lower, R. B., Escoll, P. J. (1975). Some pitfalls in the assessment of analyzability in a psychoanalytic clinic. *Journal of the American Psychoanalytical Association* 23: 90–106.
Kantrowitz, J. L., Katz, A. L., Paolitto, F. (1990). Follow up of psychoanalysis five to ten years after termination: III The relation between the resolution of the transference and the patient–analyst match. *Journal of the American Psychoanalytical Association* 38: 655–678.
Lazar, N. D. (1976). Some problems in faculty selection of patients for supervised psychoanalysis. *Psychoanalytic Quarterly* 45: 416–429.
Lower, R. B., Escoll, P. J., Huxster, H. K. (1972). Bases for judgement of analyzability. *Journal of the American Psychoanalytical Association* 20: 610–621.
Stone, L. (1954). The widening scope of indications for psychoanalysis. *Journal of the American Psychoanalytical Association* 2: 567–594.
Zetzel, E. R. (1968). The so-called good hysteric. *International Journal of Psychoanalysis* 49: 256–260.

Part II

CONSULTATION AND REFERRAL

II CONSULTATION AND REFERRAL

Introduction

Penelope Crick

In this section, the papers we have selected concern the psychoanalytic interview where a potential patient meets with an analyst in order to be referred on to the treatment of choice, which may, or may not, be psychoanalysis. These are not the 'first meetings' of a potential psychoanalysis, but are the 'assessment interviews' or 'consultations' commonly carried out with patients in psychoanalytic institutions, and also in the private practice of analysts who elect to work in this way to guide or 'ferry' (Bolognini, 2006, this volume p. 148) would-be patients for whom it is appropriate towards analysis by referral to colleagues. These are not, then, the 'two-person' situations where analyst and future patient meet and perhaps ignite between them the fuse of an analysis, but are by contrast, 'three-person' scenarios: you, me and the potential other, absent, as yet unknown, future analyst.

In the former, we can assume to some extent at least that both analyst and future patient come to it in the expectation that some form of treatment with the interviewing analyst is what is sought – even if this does not turn out to get initiated by that meeting. In the latter, the expectation is that a referral on to another clinician is the most likely outcome. But for both, at this starting point, the consultation is an open-ended situation: the person may not know what they want, they may not know if they wish to become 'a patient', or 'an analysand', or know very much at all about what psychoanalysis may involve psychically, emotionally and practically, or even if it is the approach they want to take. The consultant analyst equally may not at the outset know much, if anything, about the person at all, let alone whether the person is going to be able to make use of analysis, whether it would be the treatment of choice that they would recommend or whether some other form of treatment would be more appropriate.

Whatever it is that goes on in the process of a psychoanalytic consultation-for-referral is no doubt very similar in many respects to what goes on in a first interview of a potential analysis, and it is this 'something' that the EPF Working Party on Initiating Psychoanalysis (WPIP) is exploring (see General Introduction; Møller, Lagerlöf, & Reith, this volume, p. 1). However, the 'setting' for a consultation which is conducted with the intention of then making an appropriate referral on for treatment, is a *distinct* one which has implications for the rationale, expectation and technique of consultation. In examining examples of both 'types' of consultation in the WPIP research work, we have found that there is a lot to be learned from the 'three-person', referral on, consultation scenario which can usefully inform thinking about the 'two-person' consultation.

Not only will the analyst's 'internal' setting be significantly different and distinct if they are seeing someone that they know they will not be taking into treatment, but also the external setting may be different, the work may be carried out in or on behalf of a clinic, other professionals and reports and letters of referral may be involved.

Such meetings are often referred to as 'assessments', and behind this is often the assumption that the consultant analyst will 'assess' the patient, much as a doctor will make an assessment of the condition and symptoms of an unwell patient, in order to be able to 'prescribe' appropriately. Literature on the subject will discuss the 'suitability' of a person for analysis, the factors in a person that are thought to make them more likely to be 'analysable', and would, it follows, predict 'a good outcome'. Cases for candidates to see as training patients are generally selected on this model. However, analysts universally will testify to the fact that many a prospective 'good case' has turned out to be very complex and technically demanding once the process of analysis is underway, and equally that many cases felt to be more dubious as far as 'suitability' is concerned, turn out to do very well in analysis and to be rewarding patients.

The inadequacy of a simple 'patient factor' approach to 'assessment for psychoanalysis' is well illustrated in a recently published study in the USA (Caligor *et al.*, 2009). The decision to recommend analysis, or not, was made on *some* basis, but not, it was found, one that was captured by standard tests tapping patient factors. In practice the variables leading to a recommendation for analysis seem to be more implicit to the particular individuals involved and not accessible to conscious conceptualization.

So, if there is no convincing clinical evidence to suggest that there are assessable variables in prospective patients that predict a positive outcome in psychoanalytic therapy, why do we have such systems of consultation and assessment? Why not just offer an analysis to anyone who thinks that they would like to work in that way and see how it goes? Why not just start straight in with the two-person situation of analyst and patient, as recommended by Rothstein (1994, this volume, p. 281) and avoid all the complications of the assessment, referral and 'three-person' scenario?

In the context in which many such consultations may take place, one important reason is that first and foremost the assessment will need to take sufficient account of the patient's clinical needs in terms of whether a psychoanalytical therapy is the treatment of choice. In public health and other services where people who are very troubled or disturbed may be seen, perhaps referred by mental-health professionals out of desperation or optimistic lack of knowledge about the scope of psychoanalysis, perhaps self-referred for similar reasons, the psychoanalytic consultant may need to make an initial judgement about how much at risk the patient might be as a result of embarking on a psychoanalytic exploration. This may well be beyond the normal level of a basic 'psychiatric screening' and, indeed, not be related to the presence or absence of obvious psychiatric symptomatology, but be more something that arises out of the person's initial response to the psychoanalytic setting in a consultation. Milton (1997), in a very helpful paper entitled 'Why assess? Psychoanalytical assessment in the NHS', describes how, once the consultant is reasonably satisfied that the prospective patient will not be at physical or mental danger from this form of treatment, the level of the consultation can deepen towards a more complete exploration of whether this approach would be likely to suit them. She gives vivid clinical examples illustrating how a sensitive consultant can pick up when a patient's response to the psychoanalytic setting in the consultation indicates that their safety may be put at risk as a result of becoming involved in an analytic process.

It can also sometimes be very helpful to the person to have something of a psychoanalytic consultation to help them to find out enough about the process to see that psychoanalytic treatment would not, in the longer term, be something that they are in a state to be able to manage. Some individuals can be relieved to be able, with the help of a psychoanalyst, to acknowledge and thus begin to face up to the extent of their disturbance and to relinquish the defensive fantasy that the idealized 'psychoanalysis' would resolve or remove their pain.

Another and perhaps more ethically complicated reason is to do with the economics of limited resources. If a person is seeking treatment that is to be funded by the state or by a charity, then this 'setting' will dictate criteria that need to be met before treatment can be provided. The organization concerned will almost certainly have limited resources and have an ethical duty to ensure that these are allocated in the most equitable way; that is, to the people who are most likely to be able to make use of and benefit from the available treatment vacancies. This of course highlights one aspect of the 'assessment' component of psychoanalytic consultation: the psychoanalyst must, in the broadest terms, assess the capacity of the patient to make use of psychoanalysis, and in particular the psychoanalytic setting that would be available to be allocated. For example, in the case of organizations where patients can receive low-fee treatment from candidates in training, then it is in the interests of both candidate and prospective patient that the assessment has taken account of the relative inexperience of the candidate, and perhaps also the advantages of the analysis being contained within a training and supervisory structure.

Psychoanalytic consultation gives the prospective patient the opportunity to make their own assessment of whether this is an approach that they feel interested in and able to work with. All the papers in this section emphasize the value and importance of the patient having an experience in consultation which allows them to make as informed a decision as possible about embarking on a future analysis.

The papers by Klauber and Bolognini in particular emphasize the value for the individual of being able through consultation to explore and understand something of the *motivation* for seeking treatment now. What is the person's desire to communicate, and can communication develop to a deeper level in response to interpretation? Or, as the consultant may learn from the person's response to exploratory interpretations, is this something that their defensive organization cannot accommodate? Does the person want to explore and face painful feelings? Until someone has experienced something of the process, has found out experientially about what is involved in the analytic process, their motivation may well be unrealistic. For example, the person may be keen to come along provided s/he can remain passive while something is done to her/him. Having some interpretive work can give a much better idea of what is going to be involved and thus allows the real motivation to emerge. Not just the consultant but also the potential patient may learn a great deal from this and thence have a good basis for being able to make a decision about next steps.

The question of what and how much is interpreted about what can be discerned about the patient's discourse presents itself at once: in psychoanalytic consultation, is interpretation offering containment through understanding or does it run the risk of being unhelpfully intrusive? Klauber warns against the temptation to attempt a 'mini analysis' and suggests that what should be offered is: 'enough tentative explanation and interpretation to give the patient a glimpse of the emotional and intellectual processes involved without unduly seducing him'. A trial interpretation also gives the patient the sense that they are understood, or at least that the consultant is making an effort to try to understand them. And this can, in itself, help the person in getting to deeper and more meaningful areas.

There are those who argue against the use of trial interpretations – on the grounds that it makes the patient feel as if they have opened up to the interviewer and have got close to them through having gone a long way towards being understood by them. However, this does not need to be a negative experience for the patient: the impact of a first consultation on someone who may never have really spoken about themselves in such depth, and perhaps not had the opportunity before to discover the meaning of what has been incomprehensible or disturbing, can be profound and significantly therapeutic in its own right. Interpretation does not, of course, have to be verbalized to the patient and a thoughtful and sensitive consultant will be judicious in what they decide to share with the patient and what they keep in their minds and find more tangential ways to explore other than through direct interpretation.

But if a 'psychoanalytic experience' is to be offered in consultation with an analyst who will not go on to be the analyst for this patient, then what of the transference that is stimulated by the analytic setting and inevitably becomes part of the currency of the interaction? What kind of technique is used in such meetings to both evoke the material and emotional experience that makes them 'psychoanalytic' and yet also protects the would-be patient and their defences from potentially unhelpful or even traumatic intrusion? How should a genuine but highly limited psychoanalytic experience be offered so that, while it may be quite challenging, it is more likely to be experienced as helpfully containing rather than damagingly intrusive? Most who advise on the conduct of psychoanalytic consultation suggest that two meetings are most helpful – to give both the individual and the analyst the opportunity to digest their experience, to dream, associate and think about their response and to bring this back to learn from in the second meeting; and for there to be a proper 'leave taking' and ending of the intense, potentially very meaningful and yet constrained process.

This implies a potentially considerable degree of involvement by both parties; Donnet and de M'Uzan are among those in the papers that follow who advise against the analyst getting 'too involved' by which they mean that the analyst should retain a receptive stance, not being too active but rather observing relatively silently how the patient responds to the setting. However, this does not mean that the analyst is not internally very involved, and Bolognini and Klauber in particular stress the demands that this particular sort of work places on the analyst. Being receptive in the intensive and condensed situation of consultation, whatever the setting, is hard work, requiring a lot of energy and a different sort of perhaps more active concentration to that of an ordinary analytic session.

For example, the intensity of the consultation can result in the consultant getting unconsciously drawn in to an enactment of the patient's internal object relations or identification with some aspect of the patient so that their judgement about the recommendation is influenced in a way that might only be perceived by the external 'third' of the Institution. At the London Clinic of Psychoanalysis, for example, consultations are often discussed in work groups and recommendations reviewed with the Clinical Director, before a final decision about what to offer to the patient is made. In this way, blind spots or enactments can sometimes be identified, which helps to refine or more thoroughly understand some important aspect of the potential patient. Inevitably such enactments are liable to take place whether it is a first interview or a consultation for referral on – in the former, there is the rest of the analysis ahead in which this can be understood and worked through, but in the consultation, the perspective made possible by the consultant having the 'third' in mind, be it institution, clinic or prospective referred-to analyst, can be very helpful to the consultant's thinking as well as clinically very valuable in ensuring the best care of the prospective patient at that point in time.

Donnet and de M'Uzan, and also the other French papers, put special emphasis on the three-person nature of consultation and how the experience of this constellation can in itself be made a valuable aspect of the assessment of the capacity of the patient to use analysis. They note that a very positive indication of a person's capacity for analytic treatment will be present when it is clear that the future patient recognizes that the transference belongs to him/herself and is not specific to the consultant.

The consultations that are discussed in this section are often carried out within an institution: a prospective patient may well elect to seek consultation and advice from an institution or intermediary with a good and trusted reputation, allowing them to have time and opportunity to think about and decide what they want to do rather than going direct to a potential analyst and feeling that they have started right in on a two-person relationship without having had a mediating stage. Of course much may be learned about the person, their motivation and the nature of their anxieties from their choosing to approach an institution and their fantasies about it as revealed in their communications around the setting up of a consultation.

The crucial role of the institution in giving space through psychoanalytic consultation for the fostering and development in an individual of an internal therapeutic arena is highlighted in some of these papers. The individual's decision to become 'a patient' may be relatively straightforward, or, as illustrated in the clinical material in the paper in this section by Bronstein and Flanders, the decision to commit may arise out of an appetite for analysis being stimulated by the consultation process, where it could truly be said that a psychoanalytic process has been initiated in the patient as a result of the consultation work.

The institution which provides the consultation can have a number of important roles, not least in the patient's fantasy, where it may be the institution which is the third object, perhaps helpfully facilitating the relationship with the consultant, perhaps rather seen as cruelly and bureaucratically preventing the relationship from continuing. It may also be the continuing and more 'neutral' link that holds the patient between consultation and eventual referral on to analysis or other recommended treatment of choice; in which case it may be that for the patient the institution is the constant, facilitating object, helping them through the process of detaching themselves from the consultant who they may experience as having 'rejected' them in their fantasy of being able to continue into treatment.

The consultation will, ideally, come to an end with the consultant having discussed with the prospective patient what will be the next step in terms of treatment. There may be a referral on to a colleague or the person may be placed on a waiting list managed by the institution. Or some other form of treatment may be proposed. Whichever of these, the consultant is carrying a considerable responsibility, which they may or may not be in a position to share with the potentially containing institution. Bolognini makes a particular point about the demand on the consultant who has to find a way of supporting 'handing over' the patient whilst at the same time renouncing the status of having been the important and significant other. The community of colleagues or more specific institution into which one is 'referring' can at this point provide a very particular support.

But what of the patient, left waiting, perhaps for some months, only to have to form a new relationship with someone else altogether? The transition to the future analyst can be very difficult and unless handled with care may result in the person breaking off treatment early on. Klauber observes that the patient will be sensitive to whether the referral on is made with the personal qualities of both patient and future analyst in mind or whether it is the result of some more random or routine process. However, if the 'ending' with the consultant is worked on and made part of the consultation experience, then the positive aspects of the good relationship will have more of a chance of being internalized and kept safe to remain as a helpful reference point later when on the waiting list or when treatment has started. The consultant and the consultation can become a valuable object in difficult times in the analysis in the future, the one who can usefully stay in the patient's mind as a trustworthy 'midwife' to whom gratitude is due for having aided in the initiation of an idea of what they might get from analysis.

References

Caligor, E., Stern, B. L., Hamilton, M., MacCormack, V., Wininger, L., Sneed, J., Roose, S. P. (2009). Why we recommend analytic treatment for some patients and not for others. *Journal of the American Psychoanalytic Association* 57(3): 677–694.

Milton, J. (1997). Why assess? Psychoanalytical assessment in the NHS. *Psychoanalytic Psychotherapy* 11(1): 47–58.

4 WELL, THEN, ANYTHING NEW?

What that 'first' interview can teach us

by Evelyne Kestemberg

Commentary

Alain Gibeault

Evelyne Kestemberg was a clinical psychologist and training analyst of the Paris Psychoanalytical Society. In 1975 she became the Director of the Centre for Psychoanalysis and Psychotherapy of the Mental Health Association of the 13th arrondissement of Paris. Amongst her functions, she did all the first interviews with the patients who were referred to the centre by different intermediaries: psychiatrists, general practitioners, social workers, police, etc. This practice, in which the director functioned as the only initial consultant, was not only created for practical reasons, but also corresponded to a specific conception of the patient's mental functioning.

The Centre for Psychoanalysis and Psychotherapy was founded in 1974 by Evelyne Kestemberg's husband, Jean Kestenberg, a psychiatrist and also training analyst of the Paris Psychoanalytical Society; she took over after his sudden death in 1975. Over the next 15 years, she initiated important investigations into the theory and practice of the various psychoanalytic treatments of borderline and psychotic patients, with a focus on the importance of first interviews as a decisive encounter for initiating a psychoanalytic treatment. The centre was later renamed the Jean and Evelyne Kestemberg Centre for Psychoanalysis and Psychotherapy, after its two leading founding figures.

Psychopathological considerations have had a significant influence on how the centre operates: from the start, the idea was to facilitate a new relationship between psychiatry and psychoanalysis, one in which psychoanalysis would not be subservient to psychiatry nor psychiatry restricted in its development. There were two possible choices: either to integrate psychoanalysts as staff members in psychiatric units, or to create a Centre for Psychoanalysis and Psychotherapy as a separate venue. The latter solution was chosen as it allowed patients to make a clear distinction between the complementary functions of psychiatrist and psychotherapist, and better protected them against any threat of being overwhelmed by a single object. This 'third-party' function of the institution would not, however, have been enough in itself; what was required in addition was the third-party function represented by the role of the director (for more on the concept of third-party function, see the introduction to the paper by Jean-Lois Baldacci and Christine Bouchard, on p. 108 below). Although the director does not have patients in treatment him/herself, he/she conducts the initial assessment interviews with patients referred to the centre in the presence of a small number of colleagues who do not intervene directly in that discussion. The specific nature of this kind of setting enables the patient – often acutely anxious at the idea of a one-on-one relationship – to feel supported by the presence of the director's associates, thus alleviating the emotional impact of the encounter. After the first interview, which is usually not repeated, the patient may be sent to one of the 50 psychoanalytic psychotherapists of the centre, all of whom work on a part-time basis.

Patients who find the group procedure of the first interviews too upsetting can meet the director on an individual basis. Patients can also arrange to see him/her individually at any time, either during or at the end of their treatment. Experience has taught that the more the patient's psychological disposition is psychotic in nature, the less he or she will be upset by the presence of other people – quite the contrary: indeed, this may even prove helpful at times. Conversely, in more neurotic states, a one-on-one dialogue is required.

With the patient's consent, all initial interviews are recorded on audio cassettes, transcribed, and placed in the patient's file. Once a month, an initial interview, chosen for its teaching and research potential, is both recorded and relayed live to an audience of health-service professionals, again with the written consent of the patient concerned.

Thus the structures of the institution illustrate how the third term, as Baldacci and Bouchard underline (in this volume, p. 111), 'is thus not the patient but the audience (*l'assistance*), whose anonymity virtualizes a third reference. Through the reversibility of functions that it permits, this setting guarantees objectification, as distinguished from reification.' (See also the introduction to their paper, p. 104.)

In this setting, the director's third-party role is a guarantee for the present and for the future. It is important for patients whose psychotic mental states are complex to be able to meet the director at crucial moments in their life or at significant turning points in their treatment. This helps them to deal with the anxiety that is inherent in every individual psychotherapy.

In her paper, Evelyne Kestemberg reflects on the psychic processes involved in the first interview, through her description of the importance of what has been going on *before* the meeting, what happens *during* the evolution of the interview according to six parameters, and the results *after* the encounter with regard to the beginning of psychoanalytical treatment. She particularly stresses the importance of the period prior to the first interview. It could take several months before a patient can be given an appointment for an initial interview. However, once the interview has taken place, the psychoanalytic treatment can begin promptly, either in the centre itself or with a colleague in private practice if that is thought to be preferable. Having to wait for an initial interview does not necessarily have a negative impact. In the interval between making an appointment and the actual interview, patients often do a significant amount of thinking through certain issues as the idea of meeting a psychoanalyst takes shape. The patient is often helped in this by the psychiatrist who referred him or her and who will continue to work with the patient in providing on-going support.

Evelyne Kestemberg was also very interested in promoting psychoanalytic treatment with patients presenting psychotic mental functioning and she introduced, with her husband Jean Kestemberg, the concept of *cold psychosis* (Kestemberg, 1981/2001). This can be compared to borderline states and is her attempt to describe forms of non-delusional and auto-erotic psychotic functioning, as distinct from delusional and allo-erotic forms.

The aim of these initial interviews is to assess the psychic economy (Freud, 1915, p. 181) of each patient, taking into account the fact that the patient will be referred to another analyst after the first interview. The issue is to evaluate the patient's mental functioning without involving him or her too much through transference interpretations. For example (Gibeault, 2010), a schizophrenic patient who felt much persecuted before a first interview at the centre was more confident during the interview, because of the possibility he found there to speak about his annihilating anxiety and his violent experiences. At the end of the interview the analyst asked the patient if he could remember his dreams. He told the interviewer about a traumatic and repetitive pre-psychotic dream of his childhood and stressed the fact that as an adult he had many nightmares which he could not remember. However, with much insight, he wondered if these nightmares had something to do with what he feared, for example coming to see an analyst for a first interview. When the analyst then asked him what he thought about this first interview, he answered: 'It is an encounter', stressing the fact that it was an encounter even if it was not 'an acquaintance'. This interview showed that even if he did not know the interviewer before, he felt recognized narcissistically with regard to his psychotic anxiety and without feeling intruded on by the analyst. The patient was then able to accept the offer to begin a psychoanalytic treatment.

This clinical vignette shows the interest of Evelyne Kestemberg's technical approach as she describes it in her paper on the first interview. She was less concerned about assessing and making a diagnosis, than about involving the analyst in a *process* that would give him or her the possibility of understanding the patient's psychic functioning and of helping the patient to feel the possible benefit of psychoanalytic work, taking the economy of his affects into account.

References

Freud, S. (1915). The Unconscious. *SE* 14: 166–204.

Gibeault, A. (2010). Schizophrenia and soul murder. Psychoanalytic psychodrama with 'John' the man 'saddled with that/the Id'. In: Birksted-Breen, D., Flanders, S., Gibeault, A. (eds), *Reading French Psychoanalysis* (pp. 752–764). London and New York: Routledge.

Kestemberg, E. (1981). 'L'appareil psychique' et les organisations psychiques diverses ['The psychic apparatus' and the various psychic organisations]. In: *La psychose froide* [*Cold Psychosis*]. Paris: Presses Universitaires de France, 2001.

4 WELL, THEN, ANYTHING NEW?

What that 'first' interview can teach us[1]

Evelyne Kestemberg

> Heaven or Hell, does it matter?
> To the depths of the Unknown to find something new!
> Baudelaire, *The Flowers of Evil*

The very title of this chapter[2] makes clear the general direction I intend to follow in this discussion. I have no wish to outline some kind of theory and technique of the initial interview, the virtues of which are a fairly recent discovery – to such an extent, indeed, that the manner in which it unfolds and its technical aspects are now part of various university curricula – but I would like to explore its unique or at least eminently transitory character, one that is not repeated and, in the best of cases, is not repetitive.

As one might suspect, this 'first' interview is never really the inaugural one. It may, however, in certain cases be a 'first' in the sense that something new emerges from it: for the patient, of course, first of all – and to that extent it will undoubtedly be of some therapeutic help to him or her – but perhaps also for us, in that it may help us to see things in a different light or hear them with a different ear and therefore learn something that we did not already know. In that sense, it will without doubt be useful on a didactic level.

[1] The original version of this chapter was a paper read during an international symposium on 'Psychiatry and Psychoanalysis' held in Montreal, Canada, 5–8 September 1984. It was thereafter published [in French] – but without the clinical material presented at that Symposium – in Amyot, A., Leblanc, J., Reed, W. (eds), *Psychiatrie–psychanalyse. Jalons pour une fécondation réciproque* [*Psychiatry–Psychoanalysis. Some reference points for reciprocal fertilization*]. Chicoutimi: Gaëtan Morin éditeur, 1985, pp. 11–20.

[2] What follows is significantly different from the paper I read at the symposium. This is because it is necessary to ensure the confidentiality of the interview with the patient about whom I spoke on that occasion. I was able then, of course, to share with the other participants what I had learned from that interview. It is unfortunate that, in the present text, I have to put the actual material to one side, because the manner in which the dialogue between the patient and me unfolded was no doubt much more eloquent than the somewhat 'paler' version I am giving here.

To summarize very briefly, the patient was a young man in his late twenties who spoke at some length about a highly active obsessional symptomatology about which he complained a great deal but which failed significantly to express and 'counterbalance' his deep-rooted feeling of malaise. There were many hysterical and hypochondriacal components present too, together with – at least in the recent past and perhaps also still active at that time – an interesting but somewhat unstable delusional configuration.

Of course, by definition, every one of these interviews is new for both participants. Up until then, neither of them had met nor listened to the other. Yet that *de facto* novelty is soon pushed into the background when, in both protagonists, the ordinary way of discussing clinical matters takes over – though reassuring, this does tend to cloud the issues. After more than thirty years of clinical work, I would say that, if we begin by looking out for nosographical[3] benchmarks or *a priori* proof of our own theoretical standpoint in what is said or understood, it is very easy to learn nothing at all from these first interviews. On the other hand, if we are prepared to do so, we can always find some new element to interest and perhaps even to surprise us.

As I say, that interview is never really the 'first' one. Yet the effort we put into it could well, in some way, turn it into something inaugural, in that it could open up a new way of looking at the situation.

How could we describe the usual turn of events? In my own experience over the past ten years, patients make an appointment with me at the *Psychoanalysis and Psychotherapy Clinic*. The great majority of them have been referred by a consultant psychiatrist (group A), by their family doctor (group B), by friends who know of the clinic's existence or because of some information that they themselves have gleaned from sources which they can no longer recall (group C). For those in groups A or B, it goes without saying that the interview they will have with me is certainly not their 'first' one. They will already have discussed at some length their difficulties and symptoms with the medical practitioner treating them, and often indeed will have obtained some relief from the distress and anxiety that accompany these problems as they affect their lives and their thought processes. We might well expect that this would not be the case for those in group C, but this is not entirely true, because we soon come to realize that they have already discussed their problems and their distress with friends or at the very least have 'talked' about them within their own minds. Thus it is that, even when patients consult in a crisis, they have already 'prepared' in their head the discussions we will have with them.

It would therefore be quite legitimate to assume that this 'first' interview has three phases: 'before', 'during' and 'after'. As such, each of these phases should be thought about and evaluated in terms of any novelty aspect that it might contain.

Perhaps I should make it clear why I think that discovering something new in these interviews is of such importance. It could possibly take a whole book in itself to answer that particular question, or perhaps it could be dealt with in just a few lines. In the present chapter, of course, I shall try to give an adequate answer in the following few pages.

[3] The nosographical benchmarks to which I am referring could be either psychiatric or psychoanalytic. I do not mean that nosography is of no use – on the contrary, I would argue that knowledge of this kind is indispensable, as long as one can put it to one side as and when the occasion requires.

The reader would, I imagine, agree with me that the repetitive aspects of mental functioning *per se* have not only a pleasurable element to them but also an impact on that functioning which could prove disastrous. I would therefore argue that the possibility of alleviating or loosening that repetition even for a short time, temporarily, during an interview is of interest in itself and may even represent a glimmer of hope. This is the hope that is present in every patient when he or she comes to the interview; our task is to use all the sensitivity and precision of which we are capable in order to try to grasp the potentiality for change encapsulated in that hope.

As Angelergues put it in an earlier Symposium[4], we have some grounds for arguing that the opposite of depression is looking ahead expectantly; in addition the status, outcome and handling of depression by patients and by those treating them could be seen as being vital for the outcome of psychic disorganization or mis-organization. That being so, we can immediately see, I think, just how important is this 'moment of hope' that is always a prelude to the initial interview; sometimes, indeed, it is so important that its effects can be felt while the actual interview is still ongoing, i.e. in the 'during' and 'after' phases.

I suggest, then, that we examine under those three headings ('before', 'during' and 'after') the content, the movement (or inertia) and the outcome of this particular interview, which ought to be different from what went before and from what will happen next.

I. 'Before'

I have already quite naturally made some reference to this phase – when I mentioned the 'hope' which this interview *a priori* carries with it. The paradox, of course, is that we know nothing of this 'before' phase until we are actually *in* the interview itself (the 'during' phase). Only the patient him or herself will be able to tell us how that interview 'existed' before it actually took place. Even then, we ourselves have to find that aspect interesting and be able to understand what the patient says about it. To put it simply, we should not content ourselves merely with the letter that the referring colleague addresses to us – the patient will either give it to us or it may have arrived shortly before by some other means – nor with the few sentences in which the patient tells us how he or she came to make the appointment.

In the overtones of what the patient says, even though this may appear to be purely informative – even in states of major mental disorganization – we should be able to assess the relative importance of passivity ('Mr X said I should come', for example, is a pretty standard way of putting it), of repeated despair (the impression we have is that, running through the entire interview,

4 'The Notion of Depression', Symposium of the Mental Health Association of the 13th *arrondissement* of Paris, 3–4 March 1984.

there is the idea of 'None of this is going to be of any use') or of remaining glimmers of hope, even if they are brushed aside ('Well, after all, you have come here; nobody, except perhaps yourself, forced you to do so'). That statement – rarely explicit and perhaps indeed always implicit – represents to my way of thinking something that is very close to the famous, 'Well, you're the one who had the dream'. In other words, the very fact that the patient comes for the interview and that it can take place (even though, as sometimes happens, he or she remains silent) bears witness to the existence of a sufficiently active wish which is present at that point in time. That wish obviously has to do with change – at least in part – even though it may well be thwarted to some extent by the parallel wish to go on repeating.

The present state of the patient's psychic economy thus falls to be assessed from the very beginning of the interview: this involves all that is said or remains unsaid in the patient's to-and-fro struggle between inertia and despair on the one hand, and, on the other, change and hope. With that as a baseline, the variations in psychic economy, of which we initially make a mental note, are in my view a crucial element in assessing the present state of the patient's mental functioning (and *in fine* in reaching a tentative diagnosis and prognosis). I shall come back to this point later, for it is particularly relevant to the 'during' phase.

To return to the 'before' aspect, I should point out that the particular circumstances that surround such interviews in the clinic helped me to learn a great deal about that phase, or at least to pay close attention to it as regards my working hypotheses. The waiting period for an appointment can be really quite long (sometimes several months), except in special circumstances in which there is some 'urgency'. The idea of 'urgency' is almost always emphasized by the patient's psychiatrist who feels that the time is ripe for envisaging a new kind of assessment and perhaps even treatment procedure.

The length of the waiting period and the fact that the interview does take place in spite of it are factors which in themselves speak volumes about the patient's desire for an 'encounter of a [new] type' and about the economic importance of that desire in his or her mind. To put it slightly more theoretically, this is a clear manifestation of the possibilities available to the individual for dealing with a new object of cathexis. The forthcoming meeting with the analyst is pre-cathected with enough intensity and sustainability for the interview to take place.

The relative proportions of auto-erotic and allo-erotic cathexes in the individual's present psychic economy are, to my way of thinking[5], a decisive

[5] I explored these ideas in almost all of the papers I wrote in the 1980s, for example 'Le personnage tiers, sa nature, sa fonction' ['The Third Party: Nature and Function'], in *Les cahiers du Centre de psychanalyse et de psychothérapie* (Association de Santé Mentale du 13e arrondissement de Paris [Mental Health Association of the 13th *arrondissement* of Paris]), 1981, 3: 1–55. That paper was published also as a chapter in my book, *La psychose froide* [*'Cold' Psychosis*]. Paris: Presses Universitaires de France, 2001, pp. 145–177.

element as regards diagnosis. That anticipatory cathexis may however dry up or even find itself disorganized and broken up by the interview itself; this would seem to indicate either the inability to cathect an object different from the one that was being cherished deep inside (in a 'cold' psychosis, for example, in which auto-eroticism predominates), or the dread of being overwhelmed by a 'palpable' object if I can put it thus (in schizophrenia, for example). On the other hand, it can happen that the object has been cathected with enough resonance and flexibility for the interview to have inspired a dream that defines it or, more usually, precedes it. The negation that usually accompanies this – 'I had a dream, but it has nothing to do with . . .' – is thus not so very important, except insofar as it bears witness to the considerable psychic work that has been done with respect to the anticipated encounter.

To my mind, then, this 'before' phase, implying that we take into account in our thinking what may have been 'anticipated', its economic importance and the dynamics to which it gives rise (with respect to the depression and inertia that may also be present), constitutes the first lesson that the 'initial interview' can teach us – an original, new quality of which we must take note.

II. 'During'

In the interview itself – whatever the specific external parameters such as the presence of colleagues sitting in on it, or the fact that the patient has agreed to the interview being recorded – the rhythm will be either unchanging or variable. What the patient says may be entirely preordained, a kind of 'carbon copy' of what he or she has recited on many earlier occasions, to other specialists or to him or herself. Any comments we may make, with the idea of changing this, may go unheeded; the pre-existing hopefulness may weaken little by little and disintegrate so that all that is left is a kind of 'mechanical' unfolding of something that resembles a pre-recorded message. On the other hand, it may happen that the analyst's few comments become integrated into what the patient says, into the silences that occur and into the changes which, in the patient's view, it is important to make known.

For example, during the patient's report on his or her symptoms, with its repetitive 'off by heart' quality as regards 'how it all came about', a new element may suddenly emerge – probably peripheral and apparently irrelevant, but in fact something new that opens on to the way the patient's mind works. Often it will be a sudden but fleeting resurfacing of something from the patient's past, or perhaps a comment that has an identificatory quality to it (for example: 'My father used to do that too'), or again a new meaning acquired by some habitual form of behaviour. It may also be an absorption of the analyst into what the patient says: 'Of course you'll say . . . You'll think

. . .', etc. These new glimmers may turn out to be lifeless inclusions or, on the contrary, may influence the remainder of what the patient has to say, bring about a new dialogue-oriented monologue or even a true dialogue and, in the best of cases, lead to the patient's having a changed picture of him or herself. For example, a patient suffering from obsessional symptoms may talk about them at some considerable length, and then manage to see his or her distress and isolation in terms of the alpha and omega of some unbearable anxiety against which anything and everything has to be tried out, including delusional phases and repeated suicide attempts.

In this situation, in spite of everything, the capacity to cathect an object is still present, the work of mourning for the loss of an object is still possible and the patient's psychic economy is still alive and mobile. That economic flexibility, to which the dynamics of the interview bear witness, augurs well for a beneficial recourse to preconscious functioning. In a case like this, we would pay particular attention to the patient's capacity for free association as regards what is said, as well as to his or her fantasy or oneiric creations which, in this kind of interview, are almost always communicated to the analyst.

Also, the individual's own past may be reported in a lively way, 'romanced' differently, as though he or she could find in it some new personal significance as well as the idea that someone else might well find it interesting. The opposite, of course, may also occur: the same old story told over and over again bears witness to the defensive nature of such a construction – which, indeed, may well be of crucial importance when it comes to represent the only skeletal structure that keeps the patient going. The very need for such dryness and inflexibility proves that the patient's psychic economy is, for the moment, extremely fragile in spite of its austerity, to such an extent that he or she is unable to maintain a proper internal 'protective shield against stimuli'. The object's presence (that of the interviewer, in the present case) and very existence constitute a 'thorn in the flesh' and could well prove dangerous if the patient's inflexibility, spiritless and prepared in advance, did not act as a blanket in much the same way as the sea rolls over the sand. This is, of course, a very important element for diagnostic purposes with respect to the defensive modalities to which the patient has recourse (denial rather than repression, for example).

Other patients, in the course of the interview, become more and more excitable – their thoughts and the events they are reporting may start to 'jostle' one another, so that the end result becomes almost chaotic. Here too, the fragile nature of the patient's psychic economy – experienced almost as being under attack simply because of the interviewer's presence – gives some indication, at least initially, of his or her capacity to tolerate or otherwise the object and the novelty of the situation; that in turn indicates a prognosis and the kind of follow-up that may be suggested as a result of the interview.

Thus the 'novelty' of the situation and the idea that this is a 'first' interview may give rise to various manifestations and ways of dealing with it; the accurate evaluation of these enables hypotheses concerning diagnosis and prognosis to be adumbrated, and these, in general, will have a solid foundation.

Each of us, I imagine, can recall with some feeling of despair patients whose interviews – perhaps with different colleagues and over some time – have remained almost exactly the same throughout the whole procedure, no matter who the interviewer may have been. For as long as that kind of immobility is maintained, it is absolutely futile to attempt any new therapeutic approach, even in cases where the diagnosis itself poses no problem at any level – economic, dynamic or topographical/structural.

It can of course happen that the analyst's or psychiatrist's attitude during the interview turns it into something 'humdrum' and therefore unproductive. I cannot, of course, draw up a list of the kinds of conduct that may bring about such an outcome; similarly, space prevents me from going into any detail about the virtues and vicissitudes of the counter-transference and of counter-attitudes[6].

I shall simply say that interviews of this nature are a particularly apposite breeding ground for helping both of these aspects to come to fruition. It is obvious that the analyst cannot take refuge in an attentive but prudent silence. This is not, after all, an analytical session; the analyst has to make some comment from time to time in order for the interview to take on the quality of being 'new' and thereafter, perhaps, lead to some productive outcome or other. However, the idea that 'something *must* happen' may turn out to be a trap and lead in fact to the opposite result – perhaps the analyst's attitude, too intrusive, gives rise either to monotony or to excitement, causing the patient to back off; or perhaps he or she is too distant, too neutral, so that the patient just 'gives up' internally and falls back on already well-known material.

Each time, then, there are new issues to be dealt with. The vicissitudes of the situation for the analyst could perhaps be summarized in just a few phrases: the wish to succeed, to draw the patient in, to control, to dictate, to understand too much and too quickly. If I may say so, the highly schematic nature of the terms I have just used hardly does justice to the sheer complexity of the whole undertaking or to the tact that it requires.

[6] In my opinion, a distinction must be drawn between the two. A seminar I conducted on that theme in 1983–1984 fully justified what I consider to be the advantages of such a distinction. For a more general discussion of the counter-transference, see 'Le contre-transfert en psychanalyse d'aujourd'hui' ['The counter-transference in contemporary psychoanalysis'], *IVièmes journées occitanes de psychanalyse*, Toulouse, 20–22 May 1982 and the chapter I wrote for *Le psychanalyste et son patient* [*The psychoanalyst and his/her patient*], Toulouse: Editions Privat, 1982.

III. 'After'

If the encounter passes off well enough, the possible outcomes can be summarized as heading in one of the following three directions:

1. The interview did indeed turn out to be 'something new' – a new event in the patient's life, shall we say, but he or she does not yet feel quite up to dealing with it.

   Apparently, then, nothing happens – or, more exactly, it is almost as though nothing had happened. Yet some weeks, months or even years later the interviewee asks for another appointment, another interview, and wants to work through certain issues: the 'novelty' aspect of that initial interview and the memory the patient has of it – deeply buried perhaps, but still alive – gives him or her the impression of being able to go through with it. Something new might well take place in the future, which thus begins to exist on the basis of that 'project'. It is perhaps hardly necessary to point out that the very idea of a 'project' opens up a fault-line in the sheer massiveness of depression, in the dense blackness of despair and distress. The 'novelty' of that interview is transformed first into a memory then, gradually, into a project – looking therefore towards the future.
2. The interview did resonate with a new tone, but the sheer novelty of it was terrifyingly discouraging. Shelved, the memory of it deteriorates and loses all colour – back to square one. Any stirring up of internal forces that may have taken place has proved incapable of undermining the sheer weight of the deadly but reassuring pleasure that repetition offers.
3. The 'novelty' of the interview proves to be truly productive. Thanks to his or her ability to face up to a new kind of relationship with the object, the patient's narcissistic continuity finds itself reinforced. The situation is felt to be sufficiently advantageous in giving the patient enough auto-erotic and allo-erotic unconscious pleasure for self-confidence to be restored. That achieved, he or she may then be able to have confidence in some other person.

There will then be a shared decision to try out some form of therapy – psychoanalytic psychotherapy or perhaps even psychoanalysis – the outcome of which is not, of course, cast in stone, although the possible benefits can already be sensed by both protagonists. Some patients are especially frightened by what goes on inside themselves; they are to some extent phobic as regards the workings of their own mind – yet, with some considerable courage, they can accept the idea of this new project. It can happen that, from time to time, this kind of patient needs to be comforted and strengthened by the person to whom he or she spoke in that new 'first' interview.

In an earlier paper[7], I pointed out how important such an approach might be and how it could, in my view, be understood; I shall therefore refrain from going into more detail here on that topic.

For the great majority, therapy and analysis will go on, with the vicissitudes and fruitful moments that are part and parcel of such an endeavour, for as long as may prove necessary. We could therefore say that, for them, the 'first' interview was indeed 'a first', in that something entirely new opened up at that moment for them. The pleasure of something new replaced that of mere repetition – or, to put it more modestly, the patient was able to discover that he or she could feel pleasure other than in mere repetition. That, of course, is a *sine qua non* of any therapeutic endeavour.

Therefore, if we take into account the 'novelty' aspect that I have now discussed in some detail, I would suggest that what we may learn from this 'first' interview can be summarized as follows:

1. The extent to which the patient feels free to enter into a significant relationship with an analyst and, therefore, with him- or herself (personal request or following a suggestion).
2. What may be mobilized in the patient in the context of the interview situation, with its specific attentiveness – in other words, the changes that occur in what the patient says and in his or her self-presentation throughout the interview, as exemplified or not in the analyst's comments.
3. The quality of the patient's account of his or her past history – dry and lifeless, as though it were just tacked on, or able to be taken up again in a new light.
4. Fantasy and oneiric creativity – still present or perhaps jeopardized.
5. The manner in which auto-erotic and allo-erotic cathexes are distributed will enable a more accurate diagnosis and prognosis.
6. The counter-transference elements that come to the fore impact positively or negatively on the interview and influence in a more or less subtle manner the way in which the situation unfolds and any potential therapeutic project.

The absence or presence of any of these factors can give us an initial assessment of the patient's psychic economy as it stands; it may also help us to reach some kind of prognosis, as long as we have sufficient grounds for going that far. The importance of these elements, communicated in an interview that can

[7] Kestemberg, E. 'Le personnage tiers, sa nature, sa fonction' ['The Third Party: Nature and Function'], in *Les cahiers du Centre de psychanalyse et de psychothérapie* (Association de Santé Mentale du 13e arrondissement de Paris [Mental Health Association of the 13th *arrondissement* of Paris]), 1981, 3: 1–55. Also in Kestemberg, E., *La psychose froide* [*'Cold' Psychosis*]. Paris: Presses Universitaires de France, 2001, pp. 145–177.

shed only a partial and temporary light on the issues involved, emphasizes to some extent the vicissitudes of the undertaking.

These interviews are without doubt thought provoking. All the same, we have to be able to stand back somewhat, as regards any possible margin of error, so as not to be caught up in errors of prognosis – simply because they would, in themselves, lead to mistakes as far as the therapeutic outcome is concerned.

5 PERSONAL ATTITUDES TO PSYCHOANALYTIC CONSULTATION *by John Klauber*

Commentary

Penelope Crick

Klauber (1917–1981) originally wrote this paper for Giovacchini's (1972) *Tactics and Techniques in Psychoanalytic Theory*. It was later republished in 'Difficulties in the Analytic Encounter', a collection of his papers (Klauber, 1986). Klauber was an active member of the British Psychoanalytical Society, of which his Presidency was cut short by his sudden death. He had worked closely for ten years with the London Clinic of Psychoanalysis where, as now, as part of the charitable work of the Institute of Psychoanalysis, a large number of people are seen for consultation and either offered low-fee analysis, some with candidates in training, or referred on for appropriate treatment elsewhere. Although he does not say so, I think he must have drawn considerably from his experience as a clinic consultant for this paper, as he is specifically describing consultation where the aim is to establish, for both the prospective patient and for the consultant, whether psychoanalytic treatment is the treatment of choice for an individual and to advise and help towards finding a suitable analyst or other form of help.

In this very clearly written paper, Klauber carefully considers what is required for a successful psychoanalytic consultation, in terms of structure, content and process. While he weaves in considerable detail about the characteristics of potential analytic patients and the sorts of factors that it is advisable to observe and take into consideration, he avoids any attempt at listing criteria for 'selection for suitability' for analysis, an exercise which he warns can result in 'an unpleasant combination of the dogmatic and the banal'. His focus is very much on the interaction between the consultant and the patient and how this unfolds in the analytic setting of the consultation.

Klauber sees the aim and essence of consultation to be for a person to get an *experience of psychoanalysis* within this specific framework so that a successful consultation will 'offer enough tentative explanation and interpretation to give the patient a glimpse of the emotional and intellectual processes involved . . .' As analysis works by giving access to unconscious emotions, an intellectual understanding of psychoanalysis is insufficient if someone is to be able to make an informed choice about it as a treatment. If a potential patient is to be able to have a genuine idea about what they may be embarking upon, they need, says Klauber, to also have *experiential* understanding of psychoanalysis.

He recommends a particular and broad exploration of the person's motivation for seeking treatment, their desire to communicate and capacity to develop communication to a deeper level. This requires the consultant to create the conditions for the patient to be able to communicate to the best of their ability. He discusses the demands that working in this time-limited and specific way places on the analyst, who has to listen attentively and intelligently, to put forward trial interpretations, and to assess their impression of the patient in a balanced way, neither seducing nor being seduced.

As Klauber points out himself, given the 'great responsibility' that a psychoanalyst takes in making the recommendation to an individual to embark on psychoanalysis, it is remarkable that there has not been more written about psychoanalytic consultation. What is perhaps more remarkable is that this paper has remained unique for over thirty years in its detailed and thorough guidance to psychoanalysts on the subject of this very specific aspect of psychoanalytic work, requiring what Klauber describes as a 'distinct' technique.

References

Giovacchini, P. L. (Ed.) (1972). *Tactics and Techniques in Psychoanalytic Theory* (Vol. 1). USA: Science House Inc.

Klauber, J. (1986). Personal attitudes to psychoanalytic consultation. In: *Difficulties in the Analytic Encounter* (Chapter 9). London: Free Association Books, Maresfield Library.

5 PERSONAL ATTITUDES TO PSYCHOANALYTIC CONSULTATION[1]

John Klauber

Psychoanalysis seemed often to be recommended without the patient understanding fully what he was embarking on. For instance, some analysts started an analysis before the end of the first consultation hour. This paper was designed to draw attention to some of the pitfalls in consultation, such as the tendency to lay the blame for the ill success of previous treatment on the therapy rather than on the patient's capacity to use it. My emphasis is on a clear understanding between consultant and patient about what is involved, taking full account of the patient's history and the difficulties of analysis. I also emphasize the importance of some trial during the interview of the patient's ability to use interpretation. My ethos of consultation assumes that analysis acts by fostering development not transformation.

To recommend a patient to psychoanalysis is a great responsibility. It implies an enormous investment of hope, often of family involvement, money, and time. Analysis will dominate the patient's psychic life for several years, and he may become more depressed or disturbed and will certainly become more dependent in the course of treatment. The analysis, and the powerful effects of the transference, may seriously affect marital relationships or the choice of a partner or a career. An underlying conflict of value systems between patient and analyst may cause a permanent discontent which the patient is unable to articulate and which may force him to make painful psychic adjustments that can only gradually be thrown off after the analysis is ended. Failure of the analysis may result in the impoverishment of the personality of the patient and, if too often repeated, of the analyst. Similarly, if the analyst, confronted with what appears to be a stalemate, forces termination before the patient is fully ready and willing, this can also be destructive to both. The psychoanalyst is left with a sense of failure and guilt, the patient feels the rejected victim of a broken home. In some cases analysis lasts for twenty years or more, usually

[1] Klauber, J. (1986). Personal attitudes to psychoanalytic consultation. In: *Difficulties in The Analytic Encounter* (Chapter 9). London: Free Association Books, Maresfield Library. First published as Psychoanalytic Consultation. In: Giovacchini, P. L. (Ed.) (1972), *Tactics and Technique in Psychoanalytic Therapy* (Vol. 1, Chapter 5). USA: Science House Inc.

with the patient changing analysts several times. Successfully analyzed patients not uncommonly want to return, and no one knows in what proportion of cases the habit of analysis, once established, cannot be permanently broken. It is remarkable that so little attention has been paid in the psychoanalytic literature to the criteria on which analysis is recommended.

When a patient seeks a psychoanalytic consultation, he presents the analyst with a problem at the centre of his life. He comes in a crisis in his relationship to his life, whether he brings this overtly as the final instance of a repetitive failure or as a self-critical depression, or in the guise of symptoms, which are the acute expression of permanent unconscious conflicts. Since only a partial understanding of a life problem can be reached at consultation, since the concept of cure for problems rooted in the character structure is only partially applicable, since psychoanalysis is not an entity in itself, but a complex relationship between two individuals whose understanding of one another will inevitably also be partial, it is clearly inappropriate that it should be recommended like a medicine. Recommendations of this kind are not infrequently made however, especially by doctors who are not psychoanalysts or by inexperienced analysts.

If someone' s difficulties are rooted in his life and character more than a recommendation will be needed for him to understand how psychoanalysis can help him. Here a problem arises. He will need discussion of his situation and of what may or may not be expected from analysis. But as analysis works by giving access to unconscious emotions, this understanding cannot be given by intellectual means alone. It can only be fully grasped by the actual experience of analysis, but at this point the patient comes only for consultation. He has therefore to get an experience of analysis within the framework of the consultation. This is the essence of consultation, and achieving it is a delicate procedure. The consultant cannot and should not conduct a miniature analysis. If he did, it would either overwhelm the patient or attach him too much to his person at the expense of the smooth evolution of the transference to his eventual analyst. But successful consultation can offer enough tentative explanation and interpretation to give the patient a glimpse of the emotional and intellectual processes involved without unduly seducing him. It is primarily the quality of the rapport formed as a result which will enable patient and consultant to judge if the patient can make further use of this type of experience.

How is this experience to be given? The technique of analysis and the technique of consultation are not the same. The aim of analysis is to free the patient to make his own decisions. Consultation inevitably has more of an advisory role, however much we may try to bring the patient to his own point of decision. After all, even the consultant's recommendation to another analyst is loaded with control on the basis of his assessment of factors of which the patient has little or no awareness, such as his assessment of prognosis or of the capacities of other psychoanalysts. Its aim is a plan of action to be discussed in rational terms at the end of the sampling procedure of consultation. Consultation must therefore be directed primarily to the functioning ego. So in a sense must analysis. But there is more than one psychoanalytic technique and a considerable variation in the degree to which different psychoanalysts approach problems from the standpoint of the id or of the ego. If the patient is to commit himself to a procedure lasting an indeterminate number of years, after which, for better or worse and sometimes both, he may never be the same, it is only fair that he should do so with his powers of judgment as fully in operation as possible. He will greatly appreciate the care which is taken to ensure that he makes his decision without being pressured. This is especially important as the power of the transference, once analysis is started, to hold the patient in an unsatisfactory situation is not to be underrated. This attempt to give the patient as full a freedom of choice by rational means as possible is in fact the first way in which he glimpses the ethos and method of psychoanalysis. The difference is that the aim of consultation demands that this emphasis on the conscious functioning of the ego should be sustained and paramount. Even more than in analysis there should be no playing of the doctor game or any of its variants, like the silent analyst.

This orientation toward the ego also enables another aspect of psychoanalysis to be demonstrated. The patient needs to know that psychoanalysis is sensible and that decent analysts are sensible, not mad. Even more, he needs to understand that psychoanalysis can make good sense of what he feels as madness and that it will not at the first breath compound the madness with the omnipotent symbolic or 'deep' interpretations which he may expect or consciously hope for.

All this implies that if something of the function of the symptoms in preserving the stability of the patient can be grasped by the consultant and communicated, this will be the best demonstration of all of the rationality and depth of insight of psychoanalysis. To take a simple example, a woman architect in her late twenties broke down with crying attacks and psychic paralysis when insufficiently supported by her male superior. She had a good personality and was successful in her work, but she had got where she had in order to personify her father's ideal of his own father. The question was 'Where is she now?' It is surely better to verbalize this to the patient and to discuss her need for emotionality, which her parents suppressed in her, than to interpret the contributions to her breakdown from the Oedipus complex. This I take as obvious. But it is in practice the hardest test of a consultant to wrest the contribution of the ego regularly and clearly from the disguises produced by the patient's fear of his own unconscious aspirations. It is not merely the emotional difficulty involved in sustaining the attempt to obtain the rational and human from people who occasionally present themselves in a bad light. There may also be a difficulty in combining a capacity to listen, to respond appropriately, and to observe with the intense intellectual activity necessary to construct a coherent picture of the patient's life pattern and to formulate it, or at least begin to formulate it, as a living response in the time available – as may sometimes be necessary. However, I believe that with time and a capacity to wait it is possible in most cases for a consultant to gain enough information without undue effort for a fairly convincing understanding of the patient's presenting problem in the context of his life from childhood to the present day.

This poses an administrative and technical problem of how much time it is necessary to allot for a consultation. To some extent this must depend upon the taste and temperament of the consultant and, to a lesser extent, upon the capacity and needs of the patient. A few patients are too inhibited to make use of an extended first interview, but this will not occur very frequently with an experienced interviewer. Whatever the time, it must obviously be enough for the patient to feel that some contact has been made, otherwise the consultation may not be continued. To set aside a session may be enough for a first interview in some instances, but it is dangerous to allow a period which may prove frustrating or in some cases may be too short to deal with unexpected developments. The aim should rather be to give the patient time to state his problem fully enough to be able to wait peacefully for the next interview, if another interview is necessary. The majority of patients come to consultation in a state of anxiety and tension. The functioning of their ego has been impaired by regression, so it tends to operate under increased pressure from the primary process, that is, on an all-or-none basis. Behind their politeness, their unsatisfied fantasies, libidinal or aggressive, contribute to the events of the interview. This means that for the patient to feel really satisfied with the consultation, he must have discharged his tension and reached the feeling that he has said all that he needed to say at that particular time and that what he has said has registered. This needs a good deal of time. For my own speed of working, fifty minutes is rarely adequate, though to allot longer may on occasion be a counsel of perfection for a busy psychoanalyst. I cannot agree with the view (Glover, 1949) that a longer period than an hour imposes an excessive strain on the patient, except in the rare cases already mentioned. The vast majority of patients come with a great load of accumulated tension and do not find that time spent talking about their problems passes slowly, as later analysis shows. On the other hand, the consultant has to consider himself too, and he should not become the masochistic victim of compulsive delayers. I find that if I allow an hour and three quarters, I can complete most consultations or at least reach a satisfactory stage for breaking them off. To allot two hours allows ample time for making a few brief notes at the end. When I review the information I have gleaned in this time, however, I frequently find important gaps, and I may have to see the patient a second or third time to continue the assessment and think over my recommendation in the light of further developments. After the initial consultation it is usually possible to fit the patient into a fifty-minute schedule.

A consultation, then, is an extended private talk between analyst and patient in which the analyst tries to get the feel of the patient's personality and to give him the feel of the character of psychoanalysis and of how a psychoanalyst may employ his personality to enrich his professional role.

How the patient judges this may be revealed in his subsequent analysis. A good consultation should stimulate as little as possible the feeling that the patient who is referred to a second analyst is being fobbed off with second best, but allow the analysis to get under way without impediment. However, the personality of the consultant should make a sufficiently positive impression to be valued for future reference if difficulties occur. It may well be, however, that the immense initial transference of the patient to the consultant in fact makes a more lasting imprint than we usually allow for in our egocentricity when we analyze patients who are referred to us.

Advising patients who have already had one or more analyses is an important and difficult part of a consultant's work. The deficiencies of the earlier analysis are always consciously or unconsciously exposed, and the consultant's feelings of professional rivalry are easily stimulated. It is important not to be too easily drawn in to criticisms of the previous analyst, even when a gross failure seems to have occurred. What is more relevant is to disentangle the repetitive elements in the patient's history (without using them to blame the patient for the analyst's failure) and to assess the significance of the patient's attitude to his previous analyst for the aims of the present consultation. For example, a patient may present criticisms, perhaps valid, of an analyst who has helped him considerably and whose advice he is using in coming to the particular consultant. Interpretation of these positive elements may clarify the degree of the patient's confusion of feeling in his present crisis or be the indicator of a possible underlying paranoid process.

I shall try to outline some of the main criteria which a consultant can use, or try to use, in making referrals and some of the pitfalls he may encounter. In this attempt I know that I shall not succeed in giving more than a sketchy and personal presentation. Worse, much of it may turn out to be an unpleasant combination of the dogmatic and the banal. My excuse is that it has taken me a long time to orientate myself to the tasks of consultation and that my most common mistakes are of an elementary kind.

The first thing I set out to do is to make contact with the patient about his problem. I regard psychoanalytic consultation as a traumatic event in a patient's life, and I do not think he should be further traumatized by being left almost entirely on his own to make a start, frightened and sometimes ashamed. Some sort of bridge to shared experience is usually possible without guiding the patient's responses. This can be quite slight, such as 'I have heard a bit about your problem from Dr. So-and-So, but I would like to hear about it directly from you.' The quicker the patient is put at his ease, the freer the communication and the fuller the consultation. This also is obvious, and I would not stress it unless I believed that the ethos of the detached analyst – or the analyst as a mirror – were sometimes used as a cover for sadism.

The consultation inevitably starts with certain preformed ideas in the consultant's mind. He may have had telephone contact with the patient. Probably he has already had experience of the sort of cases the referring doctor sends: he starts with some suspicion of the general practitioner who tends to send cases on his own rather than the patient's initiative or with confidence in the woman gynaecologist, in some trouble herself, who makes her cases sound worse than they are, and he knows the reliable colleague who may want a considered opinion on the relative of one of his patients with a difficult character problem. Above all, he gets certain impressions as the patient enters the room and begins to talk. None of these impressions or preliminary ideas are to be discounted. But it is even more important that they should be carefully balanced in the consultant's mind in the light of the total interview. He must beware of judging by impression, even though he will rightly sometimes allow his impression to overrule his judgment. One sometimes is convinced of the correctness of a feeling when one's apparent reason urges one differently. Nonetheless, to rely too much on impression is to ask for difficulties. Perhaps the most common pitfall is to blame the ignorance or ineptitude of other doctors for the failure of previous treatment and instead to believe the patient's assurances of his serious intentions. So equally, patients who present themselves poorly may demonstrate by their history that they have a greater reliability than they allow themselves to show.

A consultation is an interaction between two personalities, previously unknown to each other, in which the patient is trying to express himself on topics of great emotional resonance. There is therefore scope for the unpredictable to occur and for errors of judgment to be made – that is, for irrational response to the patient's transference. I believe that it is wise for any psychoanalyst to remember this before accepting a patient for analysis, no matter who the consultant has been. This contrasts with the advice sometimes given to make the preliminary interview as short as possible or even to convert it into an analytic session. It does however have the advantage of ensuring from the start that the analyst acts on his own judgment and that this can be seen by the patient.

What is to be evaluated at consultation, and how is this to be done? But first is there any need to evaluate a great deal at consultation? If the patient has 'a fairly reliable character', can respond with non-delusional transference, wants psychoanalysis, and has the money to pay for it, can the decision not be left to him? On this view psychoanalysis is the treatment of choice for the moderately ill, and consultation consists largely in excluding psychosis and in subsequent referral. This comes near to the view of psychoanalysis as a medicine which I have already criticized. Psychoanalytic diagnosis must of necessity be more sophisticated than psychiatric diagnosis. It depends upon a complex assessment of defences and motives and reaches a richer, and deeply relevant, picture of the personality stretching far back into the patient's history. Most importantly, it recognizes the strength of the compulsion to repeat patterns of relationship inside and outside analysis and can therefore make some attempt at a prognosis of how an analysis will run. This attempt may be inexact, but at least it alerts the potential analyst to some of the possible complications. Besides, the patient knows too little of such possible impediments and needs and deserves the opportunity to interact with the consultant's experience, for instance, to discuss his difficulty in making full use of opportunities he may value. If he is to embark on analysis, or to decide against it, or to begin a course of analytic psychotherapy with full conviction of the wisdom of his choice, he needs to have defined as far as possible the nature of his crisis and its place in his life history.

It follows that the essential factor to define at consultation is the nature of the patient's motivation in its widest sense. His sustained and realistic engagement with analysis is clearly the most important requirement for success. In fact, however, the patient's motivation, even at a conscious level, is the factor most consistently overlooked in making a referral to a consultant. What commonly brings the patient is the pressure of his immediate suffering, usually on himself, but not infrequently on his doctor or his family. But in any case his conscious motivation, whether for analysis or against it, is only a partial indicator of his unconscious motivation. It is his unconscious motivation which has to be determined – the repressed wish, so to speak, behind the manifest content of his presentation and the relevance of this wish to the present crisis in his life. Ideally, therefore, the whole illness must be scrutinized to elicit and make clear to the patient the nature of the motive which has brought him. This is, of course, an impossible task, requiring not merely a whole analysis but subsequent reflection on it. It may well be that the consultant may suspect motivation which he may think it unwise to communicate – say, the desire to become acceptable to a mother for whom the child was fundamentally unacceptable. But if he attempts the task of a thorough assessment, the whole quality of the consultation will change, and what can be communicated to the patient will emerge more clearly for instance, the possible difficulties that a woman may have to guard against in sustaining a marriage or in becoming a mother in view of the history of her own relationship with her mother.

To reach such an assessment clearly requires success at a number of stages. The first requirement is to assess the patient's desire to communicate and his capacity to develop communication to a deeper level. The emotional level of what he says must be compared with the emotional level which the consultant infers for his illness. The 'illness' is of course essentially the product of a character problem, and the evaluation of the symptoms can be made accurately only on the basis of the evaluation of the character defences. A successful professional man comes to consultation on his wife's initiative. He does not feel any need of it. His complaint is that her constant criticism is getting him down. He adds that he has even come to believe that he has 'feet of clay' professionally and he recognizes that he is being overtaken by younger men.

It emerges that his wife is a substitute for his father, who was literally and metaphorically a wholesale butcher, and that his professional self-doubt has become accentuated since his wife has had quarrels with a professional adviser in a field symbolically related to his own. In considering this man's problem, it will be necessary to evaluate the total extent of the masochism in his character and not merely the sexual masochism which made him marry her. Only when the relative balance of his justified self-criticism, of his turning of his aggression against himself, and of his sexual masochism are determined can the danger of a serious depression be estimated.

Some of the patient's character defences – such as turning of aggression against the self, or of denial, or isolation of affect – can be interpreted immediately and the patient's response noted. The discussion of the life pattern also affords an opportunity for pointing out some of the patterns of repetition or unconscious equations and identifications, and observing the nature of the analytical engagement which usually follows. In this connection the significance of organic illness is not to be neglected, either as an indicator of psychological crisis or for the evaluation of fixation points. Such comments or interpretations as are made can still be general in nature and within the capacity of the conscious ego to appreciate. If they are not too 'wonderful' or startling, they need not interfere unduly with a subsequent analysis by another analyst. If the patient's power of communication is blocked, even transference interpretations can be given provided they are made in general terms not designed to rape the patient for analysis (and for the consultant) by overwhelming his ego with unconscious impulse. A woman, married to a perpetually tired man with a low sperm count, presents with depression because she has not conceived a second child. It is not necessarily traumatic to relieve her hesitation in speaking by telling her that it may be difficult for her to discuss her sexual problems with her husband with another man. On the other hand, she might be disturbed in a way she might find difficult to control if she were told that she could not speak to the consultant because she was afraid of falling in love with him.

The overall concept of motivation represents the final availability of motive after the inhibiting forces of the illness, notably rigidity of defences and degree of traumatization, have been allowed for.

The indications for the future also depend on another balance of forces. If the motivation is to be assessed primarily on the history of past struggles against regression, then the potential outcome has to be assessed in terms of the feasibility of change within the patient's life situation. Failure to recognize the difficulties of the life situation sufficiently is in fact one of the important reasons for which the final therapeutic results of analysis sometimes disappoint when contrasted with the analytic results in terms of illumination of psychopathology. Is a full analysis really indicated for the woman, married to her tired husband, when she does finally conceive her second child and still complains of depression? Other balances may require more subtle decisions:

for instance, the need of analysis of an émigré with a possibility of continuing to work in the country for some years, but under the thumb of a discontented wife who looks forward to their return to their own country – and so on.

I will list a few of the types of patient and situations of which I am wary. I am deliberately suspicious of charming patients, and even of 'very good cases for analysis.' If one is charmed, one's critical judgment is lulled. Besides, the ability to charm in a state of distress may indicate either excessive narcissism or despair, and how often can one really meet a very good case for analysis? When we really achieve splendid results, what was the trick? While the quality of the analysis in these cases was usually good, the result may well have been facilitated by a considerable rapport. I hesitate with patients who try to make unrealistic arrangements, and I do not think that analysts should compound arrangements which will turn psychoanalysis into a burden, or to break down, or cause the patient to hate it. A young mother in the suburbs should not be expected to park her baby five times a week to come to town. An analyst who encourages a patient to change his place of residence and work for analysis is either brave or foolhardy. An analyst who charges the patient more than he can afford for four or five 'necessary' sessions a week instead of adjusting his therapy to what the patient can pay misses the wood for the trees. Psychoanalysis (as it seems to me) is a way of understanding people, and whether the patient sits or lies or takes a walk round the town like Gustav Mahler is to some extent peripheral. Similarly, the analyst who consents to treat a patient out of his diminishing capital is onto a bad bet, especially with a masochistic patient. What a temptation to express his resentment by not getting better, until all his capital is exhausted! I do not like patients with only one symptom: the lack of capacity for varied forms of displacement implies a near delusional mechanism. Similarly a psychosomatic complaint without adequate additional conflicts or anxieties makes me suspicious of the patient's power to sustain analysis. I do not believe all that has been written about the relationship of ulcerative colitis to psychosis, but I am inclined to believe with de Boor (1966) that it is characteristic of bronchial asthmatics to hold their love objects at an intermediate distance, neither allowing them to come close nor to go, and I do not welcome this form of transference. Like others I regard hypochondriasis with suspicion. While hypochondriacal patients clearly have serious problems with projected and reintrojected aggression and may have great difficulty over making stable love relationships, including analytic relationships as a result, I do not regard hypochondriasis as necessarily an indicator of near psychosis. I will end this list with the most dogmatic statement of all. While I believe that patient psychotherapeutic work can greatly help severely disturbed patients and not infrequently transform their lives, I believe that the greatest pitfall of analysis is an excessive belief in our power to reconstitute the character. The best results are still generally to be obtained with those who, in Freud's description, 'have a fairly reliable character' to start with.

There remains a class of patient who 'needs' analysis, because he is making someone else's life or analytic treatment impossible, but cannot see it. Very occasionally there may seem to be no alternative but to send them to analysis as the older child analysts tended to send a child. An example would be the husband in a double second marriage characterized by constant rows which were provoked on each side. The rows often centred on the husband's sexual seduction of his children, all of whom required psychiatric help. In spite of her propensity to provoke rows the stepmother's concern for the children was genuine, but she could not get her point of view through to the perverse father. In general such solutions do not work. As soon as the second analysis begins, a surprising amount of projection on the part of the spouse who advocated it becomes revealed. Besides, to persuade someone into analysis by telling him what a mess he is in when he does not quite believe it provokes profound resentment and resistance.

However, a more common problem than that of pitchforking patients into analysis is the question of how to keep them out of it. They feel ill and ask for treatment, and if one analyst does not provide it they can go to the next. It may be agreed at once that a person in distress, or suffering from a psychiatric illness, who asks for help has to be helped, and that in general, for the type of patient who consults a psychoanalyst, some deeper understanding of his illness is the help he needs. In this sense he needs psychoanalysis as I have already defined it: a particular way of understanding people. But in a technical sense this definition is not discrete enough. Patients are differently treated if they discuss their problems, or sit in a chair and engage in an analytic exchange twice a week for a year or two, or lie on a couch three, four, or five times a week for years on end while their unconscious fantasies about the analyst sitting behind them are consistently explored and related in detail to the totality of their problems in life. It is difficult to define the difference, but perhaps one valid generalization is that patients in skilled psychotherapy seem to be spared a great deal in suffering and in regression and to do remarkably well on it. In Freud's day there was no acceptable alternative to full psychoanalysis. Today, with a greatly extended social and possibly psychological range of patients, psychoanalysts are experienced in applying analysis to groups and individuals. It is also a naive analyst who does not bear in mind that therapies not based on interpretation also have their successes and will never consider recommending them.

The main object of consultation therefore defines itself as making a tentative estimate of a feasible aim for treatment. To do this it attempts to answer a series of questions.

First: Is this a patient who ought to have a full analysis from the start, or is he someone who may not be able to use this fully, and with whom, therefore, either some completely different form of therapy is indicated (like relaxation therapy for a tense, elderly obsessional of limited intelligence with a history of depressive breakdown), or a form of analytic psychotherapy which does not prejudice later analysis should this be found to be indicated?

Next: Who is the sort of analyst who will be able to understand this patient's problem? The answer here must be intuitive, but some similarities of character agree and some do not. It is not implied that an inhibited violinist has to be recommended to an intensely musical analyst who may share in some degree a virtuoso's obsessionality. But the perverse husband who seduced his children might have been considered suitably placed with an experienced woman analyst with special experience of child analysis.

Thirdly: How can the patient's needs be matched with his financial resources? How can the dilemma be resolved of the young academic (say) with a transvestite perversion who rightly feels he needs a full analysis in spite of his slender means? Should he be allowed to go to a clever but newly qualified analyst four or five times a week at a low fee, or should he be sent to someone more experienced.

The answer to this must depend very much on individual judgment and the availability of analysts. But with cases of unusual difficulty it seems to me justified to remember that no analyst did his best work with his first set of patients and that intractable cases will adversely affect his morale for many years. This of course raises the question of what is psychoanalysis in another form. Clearly a patient may get more psychoanalysis in the sense of analytic understanding sitting in a chair twice a week with someone who understands him easily than lying on a couch five times a week with an analyst who is hard put to it to grasp the continuity.

The consultation is at an end when I feel satisfied that I have a reasonable grasp of the patient's problem and when I feel that he can feel satisfied with what I have to tell him. Since a whole analysis is not enough to understand a person's problems, this point is determined by affective indicators. But affects are, after all, the arbiters of all our judgments. Having formed a judgment, I like it to be shared with whoever else may be involved – certainly with the patient's doctor wherever possible. He can be of great help to patient and analyst in a crisis and, especially, at holiday time. If one gives a patient the name of a colleague, the colleague may be inhibited and chary of offering interpretations, or he may give interpretations, in which case he is liable to become the object of the patient's transference fantasies. If one is lucky in finding a friendly general practitioner, who is in no sense a rival, he may be able to handle the patient on common sense lines without undue transference complications. Moreover, the reputation of psychoanalysis will not be damaged by his subsequent discovery of crises handled without his knowledge. The general practitioner can also be of great help in illuminating the family background or even in bringing medical information which the psychoanalyst may find of importance in his assessment.

The other people involved may be relations. If a relative pays for the treatment, he deserves to know a little of what he is paying for. I ask a wife who cannot pay out of earnings to discuss it with her husband. With a young adult (I do not see children) I sometimes ask for permission to discuss at least the general nature of the problem and its implications with the parents.

Finally, I do not think that the patient should have to commit himself under pressure. If the potential analyst is oneself, it is especially important to make as sure as is possible without driving the patient away that he can have a graceful way out of it.

References

de Boor, C. (1996). *Zur Psychosomatik der Allergie insbesondere des Asthma Bronchiate.* Bern: Huber; Stuttgart: Klett.

Glover, E. (1949). *Psycho-analysis.* London: Staples Press.

6 THE DEVELOPMENT OF A THERAPEUTIC SPACE IN A FIRST CONTACT WITH ADOLESCENTS

by Catalina Bronstein and Sara Flanders

Commentary

Penelope Crick

Both of the authors are training analysts at the British Psychoanalytical Society, Bronstein a Kleinian and Flanders a Freudian. They both have extensive experience of working with adolescents at the Brent Centre for Young People, a part public and part charitably funded free walk-in service in North London for 14- to 19-years-olds, founded by Moses Laufer (Laufer & Laufer, 1984).

They describe how adolescents are seen for therapeutic consultation, which may go on over several months, prior to being referred for the treatment of choice, be it psychoanalysis or another appropriate form of treatment. Their paper specifically discusses the rationale and technique for this particular form of consultation work with adolescents, giving some rich and vivid clinical material. However, their thinking about the creation of a therapeutic space is also entirely relevant for working with adults in psychoanalytical consultation.

The paper is in two sections, with Bronstein first giving an account from a theoretical perspective of adolescence, highlighting the particular characteristics of this developmental stage that come to the fore where there is a need, in the mind of the adolescent or, more usually, in that of their parents, school, general practitioner or probation officer, for a therapeutic intervention. In the second section, Flanders describes in very helpful and clear detail the consultation work she carried out with two adolescents, showing through comparisons of the differences between the two, ways in which preparatory work for later therapy or analysis was achieved and also illuminating how earlier developmental experiences result in different capacities for self-reflection at adolescence.

Bronstein and Flanders, both theoretically and by clinical examples, convincingly show how important it is for the adolescent to be helped to identify for him or herself the problems that need to be tackled and to establish an internal therapeutic space within which to work analytically. The extended consultation process, which they describe, aims to address the particular anxieties about analytic treatment that are specific to adolescent experience. To simply 'assess and refer' a troubled adolescent for therapy would be unlikely to result in an engagement with the therapeutic process, they contend. It would rather be to risk enacting the typical adolescent anxiety of being passively overwhelmed, due to a threatened loss of the omnipotent defence, which has been established in the first place to cope with adolescent change.

The role of the institution in the consultation process, as a third object in the intensively charged field of the transference and counter-transference, is emphasized. The immensely important impact of a first therapeutic contact is vividly illustrated in this paper and, through the intensification of adolescence, valuably draws our attention to the processes that go on in first encounters with potential patients of any age and invites us to give serious consideration to the very specific technique of psychoanalytic consultation.

Reference

Laufer, M., Laufer, M. E. (1984). *Adolescence and Developmental Breakdown.* London: Yale University Press.

6 THE DEVELOPMENT OF A THERAPEUTIC SPACE IN A FIRST CONTACT WITH ADOLESCENTS[1]

Catalina Bronstein and Sara Flanders

Introduction

This paper is based on work developed at a walk-in centre for adolescents. We see adolescents between the ages of 14 and 21 who either refer themselves or are referred by their doctors, members of their family, teachers, social workers, probation officers, etc. They are seen initially either once a week or fortnightly until we reach a decision together with the adolescent, and after discussing the case at a weekly meeting with other members of staff, on the kind of help they need, whether it be psychoanalytic psychotherapy, psychoanalysis, hospitalization, attendance at a day-unit, and so on. All members of staff have had a psychoanalytic training. The process that develops in this first contact with the adolescents we call 'interviewing', though it could also be described as 'psychotherapeutic consultations'. It may involve a few interviews or many months of work, depending on the individual case.

The adolescents who come to our centre are usually in a state of crisis. They may be suicidal or feel compelled to behave destructively towards themselves or others; may feel total despair or hopelessness; may be terrified at the prospect of exams which will determine whether or not they can leave home and go to university; may feel overwhelmed by the feeling that something is wrong with their bodies; may hear voices and feel they are going mad. Many adolescents, however, are unaware of their need for psychological help and feel that their problem lies with their family, friends, teachers or even with their bodies.

It is often the case that they come to see us under pressure from parents, schools, social workers, probation officers or general practitioners. Many others who refer themselves insist that there is nothing wrong with them, that their problems will be solved through some concrete 'solution' such as moving away from home, going abroad, changing career, becoming pregnant

[1] *Journal of Child Psychotherapy* (1998). 24(1): 5–35. First presented as two papers at the Second European Conference on Child and Adolescent Psychoanalytic Psychotherapy, Stockholm, September 1996.

or changing the way they look by reducing their weight or having plastic surgery. If we were to try at this stage merely to make an assessment and refer them for therapy, most of these adolescents would not understand what therapy entailed and why we were suggesting such a thing and would either leave prematurely or passively accept the recommendation only to drop out later. Anybody who has experience of working with adolescents will agree how difficult it is to help adolescents to seek psychotherapeutic help and then be able to sustain it. We will begin by addressing this very specific issue of the first therapeutic contact with adolescents.

PART I ADOLESCENCE BY CATALINA BRONSTEIN

The period we call adolescence starts with puberty and is characterized by the different tasks and needs that the individual has to face in order to move into adulthood (Blos, 1962). According to Freud (1905) 'with the arrival of puberty, changes set in which are destined to give infantile sexual life its final . . . shape'. The pre-pubertal child's image of himself has to give way to take into account a changing body, a mature sexual body that heralds the arrival of a new identity, new freedom and new responsibilities.

Irreversible sexual development and the accompanying physical changes give rise to a changing image of themselves as well as a changing image of the parents in the minds of adolescents. The capacity to face these changes will be greatly influenced by specific psychological characteristics established in childhood, developed in accordance with the early relationship with the parents and modified by the child's own unconscious phantasies. Anxieties aroused in relation to the early relation to parental objects are reactivated in adolescence and revived in a radically new setting, that of their sexually mature bodies.

According to M. E. Laufer, 'the manner in which [the adolescent] is able to relate to [his/]her body in this new role is determined by [his/]her existing psychic reality within which these changes have to become integrated' (Laufer, M. E., 1995). The need to reconcile infantile omnipotent phantasies and desires with the current reality thus comes to the fore (Bronstein, 1993). The adolescent is confronted with the reality of the passing of time and the inevitability of death. Puberty also re-awakens early Oedipal phantasies and anxieties, matched now by the vivid awareness of the sexual relationship between the parents and contempt for, as well as hatred of being excluded from it. These anxieties are the same paranoid and depressive anxieties that were experienced in the early relationship with the primary objects, as described by Melanie Klein (1946). These now become more intense under the strain imposed by pubertal changes and the phantasies accompanying sexual development, with the possibility of their being enacted through the use of the adolescents' own bodies as well as external objects.

According to Melanie Klein, the baby's experience of frustration leads to an early splitting of the ego into a libidinal and a destructive part, corresponding to the perception of a similarly split object. There is splitting and projective identification of the baby's hostile impulses as well as parts of the self 'into [the] mother's body, which then becomes identified with those projected parts' (Segal, 1979). In phantasy, there can be projection of the whole self into another object leading to total identification, a taking over of the other's personality. Segal (1979) described how 'schizoid mechanisms, starting with the relation to the breast, continue to operate in relation to the mother's whole body'. She states that Klein describes how

> the mother's body becomes a source of terror at the time of the primitive Oedipus complex . . . She related [this] to the sadistic attacks the child makes in his phantasy. [These attacks] are carried out by means of projective identification, so that the mother's body is phantasied as full of and identified with the child's projected parts.
>
> (Segal, 1979)

The operation of such projective identification can give rise to paranoid anxieties, such as the fear of retaliation by the object, as well as the fear of being controlled by it. The resolution of the Oedipus complex goes together with the lessening of these paranoid anxieties and the development of a capacity to integrate love and hate and the capacity for symbolic functioning.

Puberty is a crucial time when Oedipal conflicts have to be re-worked. It seems to me that those adolescents who have failed to negotiate the early splitting of the ego into a more integrated ego may experience a breakdown with the arrival of puberty. Excessive projective identification may lead to the adolescent's dread of 'becoming' like the parent of the same gender, and of being unable to sustain a sense of identity. It may also promote the repudiation of the adolescent's own gender or attacks on his/her body. It may provoke delusional phantasies of being the subject of the parent's, or friend's envy and attacks. Early splitting mechanisms may also lead to a manic denial of reality and to sustaining a phantasy of an idealized object that could provide a magical solution to the adolescent's conflicts.

Concurrent with the physical changes, the adolescent is left with the feeling that both sexual and violent feelings could be now enacted, that is, that the omnipotent phantasies about themselves and about their internal parental objects that felt moderately safe during childhood can now lead to action. Being driven into action is often experienced as an exciting and dangerous possibility leading to the emotional experience of feeling out of control, with a body that can no longer be used as a means of safely containing sexual and violent phantasies.

Most adolescents who come for help feel overwhelmed by the intensity of their feelings, as well as by the anxiety that accompanies the different ways in which they attempt to deal with them and which often leave them even more anxious and depressed. The inability to think at these times is quite marked, with many adolescents being driven into compulsive action as a defence from these anxieties. Such action, according to Hyatt Williams (1978), might be

> 'of a token kind used as an announcement of distress and as a plea for help' but might also be aimed at destroying the object and themselves. This action makes them feel active and in control compared to the experience of being passively overwhelmed, as well as obtaining 'gratification to some degree without the conscious experience of guilt'.
>
> (Schachter, 1986)

One adolescent, Mary, described how she felt after her boyfriend rejected her:

> She felt fat and ugly anyway, but then, after the phone call, she felt so bad that she had to do something. She made herself sick, but this did not bring the relief she had hoped for. She felt like cutting herself and, while she spoke to the interviewer, she was scratching her arms. She then said she needed a cigarette, she felt such tension she just had to do something.

The overwhelming power of paranoid anxieties in relation to the maternal object and the move towards enactment as a defence can be seen in a 16-year-old girl, whom I will call Penny, who came to our centre saying she was being attacked everywhere by voices shouting at her that she was a 'bitch'. These accusations developed not long after her first sexual intercourse. She was living with her mother, who was a chronic schizophrenic and with whom she had shared the bed as a child. As a child, she had often thought her mother was going to stab her in the middle of the night. She also said that her mother had become mad when she was pregnant with her. Penny now thought she should stab herself in her belly and confirmed my interpretation that she thought there was a very bad baby inside her belly that she had to get rid of.

Early anxieties about having destroyed her mother and driven her mad by her own badness and her expectations of her mother's retaliation (which, of course, also matched her mother's psychotic state) had been more or less contained during childhood. She was a bright girl, good at her studies and had many friends. Her pubertal changes made her feel she was now a sexual woman, like the mother she hated and felt hated by. Her search for a solution through sexual intercourse was probably an attempt to find a man who could separate her from her mother.

This, however, left her feeling more trapped in her identification with her mother, sustaining the belief that she had now actually become the mad-bad-bitch-mother containing the bad-baby-her. In her attempts to deal with the anxiety of being driven to kill herself (and to kill both the baby and the mother at the same time), she ran away from home several times before her doctor realized how ill she was.

Resorting to action is one of the ways in which adolescents deal with persecuting and depressive anxieties. Defence mechanisms such as splitting, projective identification and dissociation also become intensified and determine complex symptomatic behaviours that usually start in adolescence – eating disorders, self-harm, promiscuity, compulsive gambling, drug addiction, truanting, suicide attempts – and contribute to the shame, humiliation, despair and hopelessness attached to them.

Despair and hatred of themselves and of the parental objects make some adolescents feel intensely mistrustful of any adult who is seen in a parental position. Reluctance to seek help from an adult can also be compounded by the relief, gratification and triumphant feelings that the adolescent feels in connection with his compulsive actions, such as bingeing or drug taking. Intensification of the claustrophobic–agoraphobic syndrome described by Rey (1979) can then be easily seen: adolescents may alternate between feeling oppressed by the adult from whom they are trying to separate in order to deal with their hostile and sexual phantasies and feeling abandoned and left to struggle on their own.

An adolescent girl, Jane, told the interviewer how she found herself in the kitchen, crying, at two in the morning. She hoped nobody could hear her but suddenly her mother was there and got her back in to bed. Jane said that in the kitchen she had found herself staring at the floor and thinking about the knives in the drawer beside her. She added that her mother had stopped her from killing herself and she was furious about it. However, next morning, she got up early and worked hard at her studies. This was not the first time she put herself at risk and was about to attack herself when she was surprised by her mother. It was clear that she desperately wanted her mother to save her from the hatred she felt towards her mother and the aspects of herself she identified with her mother but she could not bear the knowledge that this was what she longed for as it would imply recognizing her need for her mother which in itself triggered more violent feelings.

Given their intense ambivalence about asking for help, these adolescents' first therapeutic contact with us is therefore of great importance, in that their anxieties about being mad or very bad, and the speed with which the therapist is going to be felt as accusing, attacking, humiliating, being indifferent to, and not caring about them, are in play from the very first moment of their contact with the worker.

The need to provide empathic understanding is of fundamental importance but it is not enough. Assessment and quick referral can produce initial relief, but, if not accompanied by some understanding of the underlying anxieties, this frequently ends up with the adolescent running away, feeling they have submitted to another adult who has failed them again by not providing them with the 'magic solution' that they were expecting.

It is therefore, I believe, of crucial importance to work with these adolescents to enable them to own their need for help, by helping them develop some understanding that their behaviour is symptomatic of something else; that feeling compelled to cut themselves, to binge and vomit or to drink has a meaning which is specific to each of them. What seems obvious to us is not for many adolescents who come to a walk-in centre and who have been referred by concerned adults.

Therapeutic space

Having described some of the difficulties inherent in work with adolescents, I should now like to explore what I understand by the notion of 'therapeutic space', which is, basically, the possibility of enabling the development of a space for thinking. In his 'Two principles of mental functioning', Freud (1911) talks about 'thinking' as a process which 'was endowed with characteristics which made it possible for the mental apparatus to tolerate an increased tension of stimulus while the process of discharge was postponed'. Bion developed this further by stating that it is the capacity for tolerating frustration that enables the psyche to develop thought and, if the 'toleration of frustration is inadequate', the psyche is confronted with the need to 'decide between evasion of frustration or its modification'. He adds that this incapacity for tolerating frustration 'tips the scale in the direction of evasion of frustration . . . What should be a thought . . . becomes a bad object, indistinguishable from a thing-in-itself, fit only for evacuation'. This leads to excessive use of mechanisms such as projective identification and difficulties in the development of a capacity to think. He adds that, if intolerance of frustration is dominant, steps are taken to 'evade perception of the reality by destructive attacks'. At other times, he says, this is dealt with through 'omnipotence' (Bion, 1962).

We can infer from this that we are not talking only about frustration of physical needs such as eating or sleeping but also about frustration in early experiences with an external object, initially the mother and, later the father. These early experiences have a unique and personal quality as a result of the unconscious workings of a child, modified by the mother's capacity to accept the child's projections and to convert these 'sense-data from the child into [what Bion called] alpha-elements and thus provide the psyche with the material for dream thoughts'. The mother's capacity to be open to the baby's projections, Bion called a capacity for 'reverie'. This is the basis of the notion of 'containment' (Bion, 1962).

'Therapeutic space' suggests a relationship which enables and promotes inquiry and a desire to know about oneself through being able to tolerate the psychic pain involved in exploring and learning about one's psychic reality, without having recourse to omnipotence, evasion or destructive attacks against either others or oneself. This space, to use Bion's terms, 'would allow the self to be conscious of itself in the sense of knowing itself from experience of itself', that is, being able to think but not compelled to act.

We all know this is the final aim of therapy and/or analysis and that it can take years to achieve this. However, I think that, in the case of adolescents, unless there is preparatory work of this kind done prior to therapy, there are great risks that this process might never get started, let alone completed.

Interviewing

What, then, would be the aim of our first contact with these adolescents? It is, I think, to put the adolescents in touch with their anxieties and primarily, at this stage, with those that are closer to consciousness (such as feeling out of control and wishing to destroy themselves, feeling they are going mad, being afraid of being deserted by everyone if people knew what they did in private with their own bodies or if they knew how murderous they felt, etc.), as well as understanding their despair and hopelessness. This takes time and cannot be achieved in two or three interviews.

It took one adolescent boy, Tom, seven interviews during which he said almost nothing to me and just sat, passively waiting for me to provide him with something, before he could let me know of his worries about himself by describing a dream which had woken him up. In this dream, he said 'he knew he was hallucinating and he saw himself looking at the mirror and blood coming out of his arms and legs'. But he relieved his anxiety about his wish to attack himself by saying it was not real, he would not do that, it was a hallucination. At the same time his other anxiety was that he was being driven mad by his sexuality. But again, he felt more in control because, as he said, he 'knew' he was hallucinating. This was an important moment in my contact with him as he could acknowledge his own worry but also do some work with me, feeling that his dreams and symptoms meant something to both of us.

Transference and countertransference

As in every psychotherapeutic process, the transference sets in from the very beginning and most of us would probably agree that this is the analyst's main tool in his work with patients. Being in touch with the patient's anxieties and their enactment in the transference is certainly of fundamental importance in our work, enabling the analyst to understand and to help create a space for thinking, as mentioned before in connection with the mother's capacity for reverie.

When I describe the work we do in our first contact with adolescents, a very familiar question arises: what happens in the development of a transference relationship? It might be thought that the development of the transference would be counterproductive at this stage, considering that we end up referring the adolescent to somebody else at the end of the period of interviewing. This is the most frequent reservation brought up by workers who think that a very short assessment period would pre-empt difficulties when the adolescent is referred on to therapy.

Awareness of movements in both transference and countertransference are, of course, of vital importance in understanding the nature and dynamics of the psychic conflict that the adolescent holds with his internal objects. It is important to discriminate here between understanding what is being transferred to the therapist from the use we can make of that knowledge. We might understand the movements in the transference as a communication from the adolescent – as in the case of Tom, described above, who sat passively waiting for me to 'act'. I felt in the countertransference pressure to follow him and become too active as the result of his projection on to me of the more active aspects in himself that he had to get rid of in order to avoid anxiety (we may remember here that in his dream activity might be felt as linked to violence and was probably also associated with sexual phantasies). I used this knowledge to interpret to him how he wanted me to take the initiative in the interview and spoke of his anxiety in thinking about his own difficulties. I also made a link with the dream. I took up his anger that he had to do some work here in these consultations to help me work out what was going on with him. Therefore, the dream, which might be understood as a transference dream, was of great use in helping us to show Tom his anxiety about his state of mind in relation to violence towards himself.

Interpreting the transference is not the central aim in interviewing as it is in therapy or analysis. However, we do follow its development very closely and this enables us to understand why, for example, after a specific interview, the adolescent will not turn up for the next appointment, or suddenly decides to leave home, or gets pregnant. With the passage of time, and usually after we have worked out with the adolescents what kind of ongoing help they need, it becomes more relevant to take up the anxiety and the phantasies involved in the oncoming change, such as the pain and resentment about feeling let down and having to change therapist, the anger that we have not colluded with their omnipotent denial of their difficulties and that we might have 'not eased their anxiety about madness'. At the same time, adolescents may also feel relieved and grateful that we have recognized there is something wrong with them and take it very seriously without giving up hope.

Understanding the transference and being receptive to it, without necessarily interpreting it consistently in a direct way, allows the interviewer to become a more active participant when and where this is needed. These adolescents come in off the street to ask for help. Very few of them are in touch with their own psychic pain. Many come from very different cultural backgrounds and are terrified of being perceived as disloyal by their families. In many cases they feel 'made' to come by somebody else or are searching for a very concrete solution to their problems. Therefore, meeting with their parents or social workers, always in the presence of the adolescents, referral to hospitals, liaising with probation officers, writing to general practitioners, teachers or other professionals are all tasks required of the interviewer prior to the referral for psychotherapy or psychoanalysis.

Understanding and bearing the countertransference is a very difficult task when working with disturbed adolescents. The intensity and sometimes persecutory quality of their projections can make the analyst feel either frightened, or very anxious, or experience a feeling of rejection and the wish that some adolescents would not come back. The interviewer is frequently subjected to periods of waiting for an adolescent who has not turned up, not knowing whether he/she is dead or alive. Some adolescents make suicide attempts, leaving the interviewer feeling confused and very guilty about not having been able to prevent them. Similarly, having to witness adolescents' repeated attacks on themselves and on others can be overwhelming. It is very important then for the interviewer to be able to understand and think about what is going on, that is, to have developed his or her own internal 'therapeutic space', as well as to rely on the help provided by the institution.

Psychotherapy

This brings us to explore some of the differences between the process of interviewing, or prolonged psychotherapeutic consultations, and psychotherapy. I have already explored some of the differences in relation to the interpretation of the transference.

As mentioned earlier, these consultations do not have a time limit and, at the end of each session, the analyst and the adolescent decide when the next appointment is going to be. This allows for flexibility and, in contrast to a fixed contract, makes the adolescent feel more secure, less anxious about being trapped in a claustrophobic situation with the interviewer but also sufficiently looked after. Many adolescents decide after a number of interviews that they do not need or want help and leave, but also many of them return to us after a gap of some months. They leave with a different feeling from the one they would have experienced after leaving therapy in that they do not feel they have attacked or destroyed the setting, or that the attack on the object-interviewer is one that would prevent them from coming back.

So, interviewing acts as a preparation for psychotherapy in that its aim is the development of some capacity to bear mental pain, to think about themselves, to own the need for help. But it is not psychotherapy. The interviewer might also need to become involved in meetings with members of the family or with other professionals. The adolescents know from the very beginning that at the end of this process they will be referred and this knowledge is one that is kept alive and borne in mind throughout the period of consultations.

The institution

The role played by the institution is, I think, akin to the role played by the third object in the Oedipal situation. This affects both the interviewer and the patient.

The interviewer

Many adolescents who come for help feel inundated with anxiety and prone to destructive and self-destructive actions. The intensity of the projection of psychotic anxieties can be overwhelming for any therapist working on his/her own. For example, in Penny's case I had to decide whether it was safe to allow her to go home rather than hospitalize her straight away, whether she would leave the room and try to stop the voices calling her 'bitch' by stabbing herself.

My capacity to work this out, to feel able to think and make a decision, that is, to contain this girl's anxiety and my own while retaining my own space for thinking, had to be enabled by both internal and external circumstances. The internal ones have to do with the analyst's resolution of his/her own conflicts and the quality of the relationship to the therapist's internal objects. The external ones have to do with the supporting environment of an institution which promotes understanding and shares the anxieties brought up by these adolescents. The institution, therefore, provides a third space for thinking, and does not function only at the meetings when the case is being discussed. Even while the interviewer is talking to the patient, there is an unconscious use of the institution in this capacity. The staff meetings at which a case is discussed make manifest a mechanism which is already operating.

However, there are times when the institution might become unable to help the interviewer with a particular adolescent. Certain patients might stir up different thoughts and feelings in other members of staff who might lose their capacity to listen to different ideas and entertain some flexibility when thinking about these patients. This may be compounded by feelings of jealousy, rivalry and competition that may be operating already in the institution. It is therefore important that the staff meetings are chaired in such a way that these issues can be talked about and understood rather than enacted, in order for the staff group to regain its capacity to contain and go on helping the interviewer.

The adolescent

For the adolescent, transference to the institution operates from the very beginning. The institution provides them with the security that boundaries will be respected, that there is another 'parent' there, perceived as solid and stable in a very concrete way, who will protect the interviewer from their sexual and violent phantasies. It therefore eases anxieties about their destructiveness as well as paranoid anxieties about being taken over by the therapist. The institution also eases the anxiety about being abandoned. During summer breaks, for example, the adolescents know they can telephone the centre and that somebody will answer the phone. If the person who is seeing them is away, somebody else will phone them back. Even if their own interviewer is not available, they are left feeling they have not been completely deserted and left with their mad thoughts for a month.

If referral for psychotherapy is made to somebody who works in the same institution, the interviewer will introduce the therapist to the adolescent. It is frequently the case that patients who are referred for therapy and/or intensive psychoanalytic treatment will be treated in the analyst's private consulting room. But it is still very important for these adolescents to feel there is a connection between the interviewer and the therapist, that we introduce them and that they know that the institution is still in the background.

According to Britton, the 'closure of the Oedipal triangle by the recognition of the link joining the parents provides a limiting boundary for the internal world' (1989). It creates what he called a 'triangular space', that is a

> space bounded by the three persons of the oedipal situation and all their potential relationships. It includes, therefore, the possibility of being a participant in a relationship and observed by a third person as well as being an observer of a relationship between two people.

This provides the individual with a capacity for seeing himself in interaction with others and for reflecting on himself. Britton states that the analyst's capacity to think may be experienced by some patients as a form of internal intercourse which corresponds to a parental intercourse and is felt by these patients as immensely threatening.

It seems to me that this threatening Oedipal situation, that can awaken extreme persecutory anxiety, may sometimes be seen in some disturbed adolescents who experience the interviewer's wish to know and think as threatening and his link with the institution as potentially dangerous. They can become very anxious as to whether anybody else knows about them and may interpret any comment that the receptionist makes as proof that the interviewer is not reliable enough. For most adolescents though, the institution may be concretely experienced as a reliable and necessary 'third' object.

There is a sense of urgency in working with these adolescents, as Laufer reminds us when he says that, if their difficulties are left free to take their own course, they

> can destroy the person's emotional future, with the result that adult life becomes, at best, a compromise which has as its purpose fighting the unknown enemy who is housed in one's mind and who may destroy one's adult life.
>
> (Laufer, M. 1995)

Negotiating this first therapeutic contact with adolescents, enabling them to develop some capacity to think about themselves, is a very difficult task, but it is a crucial one for the many desperate adolescents who are on the verge of giving up hope.

PART II CASE STUDIES BY SARAH FLANDERS

The second part of this paper will look in detail at material from two adolescent patients who attended the walk-in centre. Sasha, after nine months of interviewing, entered once weekly psychotherapy, while Stephen, after a similar period, entered psychoanalysis. In both cases, the process of interviewing developed into a preparation for further treatment, although the material will show a qualitative difference in both their individual capacities for self-reflection and the therapeutic potential of the space for thinking achieved in interviewing. In spite of the individual differences, Sasha and Stephen share anxiety about therapy or analysis which is specific to adolescent experience, particularly fears of being passively overwhelmed due to the threatened loss of a defence established to cope in an omnipotent way with adolescent change.

Sasha

With Sasha, a girl from an ethnic minority, the absence of a space for thinking constituted the main problem of the interviewing work. The struggle to create such a space proved as difficult for me as allowing it to evolve was terrifying for her. I found the confusion and frustration in my own mind, the usual effect of my interviews with Sasha, quite painful, and I sometimes experienced my colleagues' rightful insistence on helping her to think more persecuting than encouraging. For her part, Sasha found the effect of her struggle for understanding disturbing enough to take an overdose of a dangerously potent medication in the middle of interviewing. She did so when the effect of our meetings was to challenge the omnipotence of her fixed ideas, or obsessions, which had become her desperate defence against developmental imperatives she could not adapt to in any other way. After nine months of interviewing, during which time we met usually on a fortnightly basis, she was finally able to own and articulate her state of 'confusion' to me and to her baffled parents, and was able therefore to justify her own wish for treatment and to win their approval for embarking on psychotherapy.

Initial encounter

From the very beginning the problem of making contact was evident. Sasha had a quality of unreachability, even inscrutability, which I associated with her very controlled manner, her graceful way of moving and perhaps also with the clearly foreign culture from which she had come. While her physical appearance spoke clearly of her foreign background, her clothes told a different story. Plain, clean and sexually neutral, she wore trainers, tee shirt and jogging trousers throughout the interviewing period, standard school clothes for any child from the age of 5 or 6 onwards. I never saw any other kind of dress or look, a remarkable consistency for an adolescent. Dramatic changes are more common, an actualization of the changes taking place inside.

In a childlike style for a girl of 17 she explained that she had been referred by her school, where she was studying for three A-level examinations, the teachers having become aware that she was not working. She explained that this was indeed so, she did not want to take A-levels, and she was not studying because she was 'stubborn', she wanted to leave school and perhaps work, but above all, go to America, where she might choose to study if she so wished. She explained that she had a friend at a different school, a girl from the same ethnic background, who had conceived the idea to go to America. It quickly emerged that she had had almost no contact with this friend since the summer, and it was now already January of the following year. It was apparent then, at this first meeting, that what looked like poise or self-containment was in fact Sasha holding herself together with the help of a fiercely held fantasy. This was her *omnipotent defence*, which would be challenged in interviewing.

She was slightly more forthcoming about her family life. She said she was the youngest of two children; she had an older brother who agreed with her that her father was impossible. There was, she said with a confiding air, a long history to the present situation, which she could not go into but assured me it was all written down in a diary. She would, she promised, bring it next time. The diary never materialized. Her father, she told me, was diabetic and volatile, and she was very angry with him. He was at the moment unable to work as a driver because 'two poles came through the cab of his bus last year'. No details to place this event in a shared conception of reality were made. The stark and bizarre intrusion into ordinary life, the attack upon her father's identity and authority cut through the otherwise opaque material of the interview. I now consider this image a piece of information about Sasha's inner world, depicting a terrible traumatic violation of the boundaries, linked to anxieties about intercourse, but also about information, thoughts coming from a dangerous external world, one conceived in paranoid terms. The violated bus represents, I now think, this disturbed adolescent's conception of the changes taking place in her body at puberty, experienced as an intrusion on an unconscious phallic narcissistic sexual identity. To this intrusion, Sasha was saying 'No'. Hindsight is illuminating.

In the interview, I was more taken up with the striking fixity of what I perceived to be an unrealistic plan to go to America. I asked if she felt in danger of being forced into something, like an arranged marriage. In her response, she managed to say 'no' but to imply 'yes' in a way that seemed to close off thinking but awaken doubt simultaneously. She sounded firm, marriage was not on the agenda, but mentioned a contradictory view from a relative. Yet she sounded as if this muddle was clear: it was I who was confused. This became my familiar countertransference state. It was necessary for me to bear the confusion for much of the time, and I found it very uncomfortable. In the notes I kept of this first session there is much puzzled rumination in which I ponder the few bits of information I had gleaned. I seemed mostly to be asking myself questions, some of which touch on a paranoid conception of the situation: Did she suspect that her parents wanted her to get a degree so that she could be more marriageable? Did she think her only chance to choose her own future would be to go to America? Why America? Was there already transference reference to my accent? Was there any reality sense or testing going on in her mind at all? Was my doubt explicable as cultural difference? Why did she make me think of a very small child packing her bags? She had none of the force of a rebellious or streetwise adolescent, and she showed me no capacity even to be in touch with the friend with whom the plan to go to America had been hatched.

Establishing a partnership in the exploration

At the second interview, one week later, she came in distress, because of a meeting she had had at her school with her parents at which her father, sounding quite normal to me, had said that there was no point in her continuing her studies if she was not committed or involved in her work. It was a waste of everyone's time. She was shocked by this statement, a contradiction of her fixed perception of his obsession with her education. When asked by the teacher if she wanted to continue the course she said she had answered 'in a very quiet voice, "yes" '. Why the quiet 'yes'? Again, I had the sense that there was meaning here, but I could not make it out. When I told her that I was quite confused myself about her true feelings, she smiled demurely, added 'yes' again and further acknowledged we were having difficulty communicating. I think it was probably at this point that I managed to make a working alliance with Sasha which sowed the seeds of her continued work with me and the hope for help which allowed the transfer to psychotherapy later. Probably it was my tolerance for my own confusion coupled with willingness to find meaning in it, that at that moment gave her some hope or faith in a struggle for understanding which would not be a violent intrusion. However, we were far from that here, and I was working hard with little certainty of any constructive work being achieved.

My confusion then emboldened her: she told me with gathering excitement that her father had rounded on her violently at Christmas time the year before last, that he had been intermittently violent with her, which I believe meant occasionally striking her in a temper, since secondary school, which would mean since puberty. To my question she answered that her father had never been violent with her mother in her memory, but when she was small her mother told her of her father's violence when she had been pregnant. Again I picked up threads to indicate her destiny as a woman was terrifying her, her father becoming violent with her after puberty, when she, in principle, could become pregnant. I again, with Western prejudice, pursued the question of anxiety about an arranged marriage, as if this was the dreaded submission she was warding off. She answered in terms of her studies, she had felt less anxious when studying for GCSE exams (normally taken at 16) by which I believe she meant, still not threatened with adulthood. A-levels were something else, a trap, a threatened submission to be avoided. (A-levels, taken at 18, mark not only a level of academic achievement, but an age of consolidation of the adolescent process.) She came much more alive as we talked, slightly at cross-purposes, I pursuing marriage, she sticking to studies. Containment was provided here, I think, by conveying to her my own awareness of a fundamental adolescent fear of feeling trapped and pressurized into an unliveable submission to a terrifying sexual reality (Laufer, M.E., 1996) but, at the same time, I was slightly missing the point about the meaning of her studies, through which she was putting the brakes on the discourse as she was putting the brakes on her development. She was not exposed to too much understanding, she was not invaded by too much truth, and so we could carry on together. Following research done at the centre, I am now much more aware of how frequently a compulsion to fail, frequently at A-levels (in England), represents an attempt to take hold of fate and dictate the terms of time, to stop the hated sexual development which is provoking overwhelming anxiety, threatening a loss of life or mind, certainly destroying whatever *modus vivendi* the adolescent utilized in latency to get on with the business of living. When Sasha stated categorically at our fourth meeting that she was desperate not to be controlled by her father, not to have her life dictated to by him and ruined as her mother's life was ruined, at the same time showing no capacity whatsoever to place herself in relationship to any reality in the world, either at school, at potential work or in relationship to peers, she disclosed how desperately cornered she experienced herself to be. In fact, there was not any space for any potential resolution in her mind, because Sasha was at war, fundamentally, with the reality of her sexual development, which she experienced as a terrifying takeover. Situated in the external world between the Scylla of what was in fact a weakened patriarchal authority (her father from a superior family, was now unable to work at his relatively humble job) and the Charybdis of the sexually alive world of peers, school, individual responsibility, she fastened on a compulsion to fail and an almost unthinkable trip to America as a way of warding off reality, inner and outer.

Time and space for thinking

In the third month of interviewing, I noted how I was often alarmed by Sasha's references to a timeless state of mind. I tried to bring to her awareness a passing reference to something taking place 'two years ago, no yesterday', probably a reference to her father's behaviour. We embarked on some consideration of Sasha's ways of experiencing time, her ways of registering events. I could understand her sense of hopelessness in relation to A-levels, particularly in history. How could she ever make sense of events taking place in time? In fact, the reality of time had become her enemy. Time, changes which take place in time, changes in the body, growth, development, this is what she was trying to avoid.

Spatiality also constituted a threat: space implies separateness, boundaries, physicality and, finally, the possibilities of intercourse. Unconsciously, intercourse was an enemy, both realistically and symbolically. Her mind was armoured against the penetration of thought almost as much as her image of her developing female body was armoured against the thought of a sexual penetration. And yet, she persevered, and I persevered. She never missed an interviewing appointment. I never stopped trying to bring some illumination. She was able to recognize some truth in my observation that her head was frequently full of ideas which went round and round, but it was almost impossible to conceive of trying to think things through, to puzzle out a problem, to put one and one together. (I had not yet articulated the concept of establishing a point of view, of trying to locate her point of view within a context of others, the conception which drove her, I believe, to a suicide attempt.) Sasha was able to reflect a little on my observations, to note that there was always a point in her reading when she stopped, put up the barriers to thought. I saw a pattern in her reaching such a point with me, often at the point of hypothesizing her life were she to go ahead and give up on A-levels. She could not enter into this imaginative hypothesis except to picture it as a mindless action. With a terrible courage, she would be able to 'stick it out' or 'get through it'. I used to picture this slim, pretty girl with her severe plait donning a helmet and running an invisible gauntlet. This, my image and not hers, held no nuance of containment or therapeutic space. In fact, I could not really picture her in any space at all, but armoured as she entered a void. My image was probably linked to the father's accident, which I now think had such specific resonance with her internal situation. As we struggled towards understanding, I noted that in some material relating to her present life, she began to locate herself in specific spaces, articulating some awareness of boundaries. She described coming home from school and going to her room. She described an altercation with her father when she was standing in the kitchen, a specificity unusual enough that I noted it, despite its apparent banality.

I believe my recognition of the great difficulty in imagining a present or a future began to get through to Sasha, and met with her own dawning awareness of the true state of her despair. This was useful, but also dangerous. She acted out her fury at home and became openly argumentative again. When her father berated her for not knowing the dates of her term at school, persecuting her with his anxiety about her refusal to know her own time and space, she angrily threw a cup and walked out of her house at 10.00 in the evening, went to the corner shop, and then telephoned home. For her, this was daring. At the same time, her achievement pointed out the true limits of her horizons, the absurdity of her making her way to America. However, this exit from home did constitute a shift, a small reality test. She had got herself to a corner shop and back again. She had survived. Her parents had survived.

Another event followed. She took a portable radio belonging to her father into her room after ringing a radio station and asking for them to dedicate a song, any song, to her, on the eighteenth day of the month in which she turned 18. A strange but not entirely magical link with the outside world was established, provocatively, because there was a rule against moving this portable radio. A mad scene ensued, with Sasha stubbornly staying in her room listening for the hoped-for dedication while her mother tried to break down the door and take away the radio. Sasha described this event as convincing her that she must move out. By now, I understood this as something for a distant future. Instead, I tried to explore with her the meaning to her of turning 18, her desperate attempt to establish a relationship to the world outside the family, her anxiety about being controlled but an equal and less well-articulated terror of being abandoned in a void, which is the world devoid of meaningful relatedness (Green, 1975).

Her worried father rang the centre. I had begun to feel that there was a need to establish some contact with the family, especially if I was to try to work with Sasha to establish psychotherapy. I was particularly concerned about the need to accommodate a potential cultural problem, although it was clear that the family had not interfered with Sasha getting to the appointments with me, which she attended unfailingly.

The suicide attempt: Recourse to omnipotence

In the sixth month of now twice monthly contact we planned a family interview. Sasha expressed an expectation that I would be telling her father how things were, in a rather controlling way. Instead, I emphasized a need for understanding his point of view, particularly in relation to a future therapy. The projected meeting frightened Sasha in ways I had not foreseen. She became more agitated about how in reality she felt controlled by her parents, who kept her bus pass, who minded very much when she stayed in the library to produce a drawing for the firm where she was doing 'work experience', thus getting home slightly later than usual. She described her mother in tears because of her lateness, and informed me that her family belonged to a strict religious sect, which I had not known. Nor had I an inkling that this meeting would in fact be preceded by a suicide attempt, that the threat of meeting together, my stated intention to 'establish points of view', would be understood by Sasha as a threat sufficient to justify taking an overdose. Although the possibility of adolescent suicide is at the forefront of concerns at the centre, I missed it.

Having said that she would like to delay the meeting with her parents, she came to the next interview full of a saga about losing first one, then another of her father's bus passes which she had been given to use. She complained about feeling out of control, and wondered if she was mad; she could not understand how she had lost these passes. Unusually, she described a two-week period in which her father had been kind to her, and she even did well in an English exam. Such complexities disturbed her, more than I fathomed. Quietly, she continued, 'I didn't think I could live'. She took an overdose of a prescribed medication for asthma. She fell asleep, and had a dream, which she reported. Her dream was that she was lying in bed, there was a slit in her wrist and there was an enormous amount of pus coming out. Eventually she was dead in the dream and she was relieved by it, until the alarm clock woke her up. The only symptoms she recalled having had upon waking were strange physical sensations, weak legs.

Establishing a therapeutic space

Confronted with an encounter with her parents in a meeting where points of view might be established, her own potential success even noted, she was compelled to go on the attack, to take omnipotent control. I believe the prospect of her own mind in interaction with the minds of her parents shattered her obsessive sense of omnipotent control, her poor substitute for secure mental and physical boundaries. I believe she was terrified of both the parents who would come dressed in the projections of her inner terrors, as well as the parents who might be able to think, and so leave her, as at the school meeting, disclosed to be the mad one. In addition, the prospect of her parent's physical presence in the interviewing space highlighted, I believe, her own terror of her physical reality. The helpless panic with which she must have realized that I too was proving unreliable, un-holding, un-containing, being out of her control, drove her to take the overdose. In turn, she drove me to step up the pace at which we had been making our way towards a firm commitment to psychotherapy. I found myself promising to see her on a weekly basis for the short time before a coming August break, at the same time telling her of my own and the institutional concern for her, the recommendation for long-term treatment, and the necessity of meeting with her parents, who needed now to know of the overdose. The containing space became less a space for holding and exploring Sasha's confusion than a firm boundary to counter her potential destructiveness in recognition of the seriousness of her suicidal feelings, ultimately the despair with which she experienced herself trapped in her woman's body, her woman's place. Confirming the seriousness of the suicidal act became the necessary new basis of the work.

It might be possible to imagine that this 18-year-old was responding to the potential tyranny of arranged marriages, and the contradictions resulting from growing up with conflicting familial and cultural influences. But a limited cultural focus was belied by the sad, befuddled concern of the couple who came with their baffling daughter to the adolescent centre. This meeting disclosed the vulnerability of the parents, where the mother lapsed into a lament about her own need for counselling she foreclosed on her thought in the mindless way that might have informed Sasha's despair: 'We are all needing counsellors', she said sadly, and then stopped the initiative with, in the circumstances, the absurd observation that 'the family's the best counsellor', implying that she looked for counselling not only from her husband, but also from her children. She betrayed at this meeting a great helplessness in her ability to stay in touch with what was going on, and it appeared to me that she mentally lapsed, with a serene smile, for much of the time to some other plane of reality. In a significant way she disclosed herself to be quite unavailable to her daughter, although generous in her declaration of love for her. Sasha, on the other hand, appeared far less remote, more immediate, attached and alive. In fact, in this meeting Sasha challenged her parents in a heartfelt way about their intentions for her. She was able to talk of the suicide attempt, express her great anxiety about destroying the parents, at pains to tell them that she had not come to the centre in order to hurt them. The possibilities for impasse in this situation were starkly disclosed by the previously hidden fact that Sasha and her older brother, who continued to take and fail A-level exams, had not spoken for two years. Out of the mixed picture of confused concern and misplaced tenacity I actually felt more hope, as I saw for the first time the lively, emotional attachment which underlay Sasha's confusion and helplessness and desperate opaque defensiveness with me.

In this meeting Sasha showed something of a precarious capacity to think, when she was able to say, regarding the A-levels, that nothing seemed like a good solution, because withdrawing from the course actually caused her some alarm, there was some security that had grown up in the school even though she did have the conviction that she would fail her exams because she would not be able to work. Here she showed herself able to own some conflict, to name her conflicted feelings. She was no longer sticking to an omnipotent claim that, if she were to leave school, everything would be all right. Something was wrong inside her, and she was able to hazard minimal recognition of this fact, indeed, to acknowledge something of the belief in the safety of an institution, a containing space, here, the school. At the same time, she acknowledged her great difficulty in actually *using* it.

My task then moved to supporting this new capacity for awareness, helping Sasha with the thinking which might support her choosing to embark on long-term psychotherapy in order to help her to think more clearly about her fears and her desires. She was in less danger of experiencing a commitment to therapy as a submission to me because she had developed some belief in a benign and potentially helpful space, container, institution. She was able to articulate a conflict, and a sense of worry, a feeling worthy of exploration. She was willing to think about the meaning of her wish to go to America; I was glad that she did not give it up. This was something to take from interviewing into therapy. She cried about the change, in the ninth month of interviewing. At the same time she acknowledged a changed state of mind which she struggled to articulate: she used to feel terribly trapped at home, then when she came to the centre, in her words, 'the circle widened'. This widening circle could be traced in incidents which marked the interviewing process: the journey down to the corner grocery store and the telephoning home, the request for the dedication of a song on the radio. In all these actions she took an initiative and created some kind of exchange between herself, her home and the world outside, establishing links that widened, as she put it, the circle which marked her growth. There is aggression associated with these moves, and there *is* survival, as the aggression proves less destructive than feared (Klein, 1930) and the boundaries prove to be more permeable and less fragile.

At a last meeting with her parents, where I worked to establish with them some support for the beginning of regular psychotherapy, here paying attention again to the facts of cultural difference, she was able to say to her father, who projected his own depression on to her, that she was 'more confused than depressed'. Here was the result of interviewing: she could own her own disturbance, which was different from his, though surely informed by his own confusing mixture of depression, kindness, desperate helplessness, rage. His poignant response to his daughter was: 'And are you ready? Do you want to live your own life?'

In the space of the consulting room, he was able to show his own understanding, which was here acutely in touch with his daughter's difficulty.

Sasha was, of course, not ready, but she was ready to start to work at it, and she had found a space in which to bring the anxiety which she had begun to own. She was not very able to acknowledge the end of interviewing as such, a task of mourning taken up by some adolescents, who have moved further in their recognition of the experience of separation.

Stephen

Stephen, at 19, a little older than Sasha, had been advised to get help one year before his arrival at the centre, when he had seen a counsellor at his secondary school where he had broken down while studying, again for the crucial A-level exams. In many ways he was very different from Sasha. He was English, articulate, expressive, if eccentric, not nearly so isolated. He had friends. He walked with an awkward, hunched-over gait, revealing, rather than hiding, his discomfort with his body. Bubbling over with anxiety, his speech was full of what seemed like little verbal tics, some that must have belonged to his parents, 'Oh goodness me', and others, which sounded more adolescent. His presence palpably illustrated his floundering struggle towards adulthood, as he seemed in his speech to make visible the active chaos of identifications, with parents or peers, with which he tried to bind his confusion and anxiety. His aim was consistently communicative, and, unlike Sasha, he therefore brought an expectation of my capacity to receive or contain his anxiety. He certainly inspired my wish to help him own his good looks, not totally camouflaged, and his intellectual capacity, also evident.

Stephen described his breakdown at our first meeting. Following an impulsive declaration of love to a girl he had been chatting to for months in an A-level class, she responded with surprise, 'That's an awful thing to say'. He reacted with shock, then withdrawal into reading about Buddhism, Shamanism, as he put it, elevating himself into another state of mind out of his body, until he woke up one morning feeling 'terrible'. The devastation of that moment, his state of extreme anxiety, depression and depersonalization, was still vivid in his presentation to me two years after the event. He told his teacher and she in turn directed him to a counsellor, and it was she who helped him to begin to think about his state, to believe that it was meaningful, and could be communicated. This put a frame around the terror, and he managed to finish his studies, though not to do well enough to leave home and go to university. This counsellor gave him his first taste of therapeutic help; it was she who suggested he come to the centre when he left school. It took him eighteen months to do so.

Meanwhile, although he had not done well enough at A-level to go to university, he had not stood still: when he came to interviewing, he had already taken one more A-level and done well, and he was studying to do another. He was in a state of prolonged preparation to separate; he had not given up, and, unlike Sasha, he had stopped attacking his capacity to think and was realistically involved with studying a subject to which he was committed. He had been told by tutors he had a reasonable chance for university now, so he came to interviewing with the possibility of a future more realistically established. He also brought, along with his dread, a concerned curiosity about his internal world, a sense that the problems, however exacerbated by intrusive factors in his home life, were internally driven.

The home he was preparing to separate from consisted of a mother and father whom he always presented as very loving, if possessive, but also as reluctant to see him go from home as he was desperate but also terrified to do. His father, like Sasha's, had lost his position in the world. Once admired as a successful professional, he had turned to selling fabrics in a shop with his wife. It was a family affair. They all worked there. Stephen expressed a great dread of getting stuck there, buried under bolts of fabric.

It took, however, a panic attack to bring Stephen to the adolescent centre, brought on by an encounter with a girl his age. He had no way at all to cope with the virulent anxieties which overwhelmed him when he registered the proximity of an attractive girl. His charm covered the intensity of his misery, but there was no mistaking the extremity. His only defence was avoidance, which he practised with obsessional rigour. He felt that, if he went to university, girls would be impossible to avoid. His panic, in effect, trapped him at home. When he described the panic overtaking him in the proximity of a girl, he similarly conveyed a feeling of entrapment, overwhelmed and paralysed with anxiety, yet gripping the chair in order to hold on to some reality. He made vividly clear the experience of entrapment within the family from which he dare not separate, and the entrapment within his sexual body, which terrorized him. Like Sasha, he was stuck, although he was much more able to articulate his dilemma and was living much closer to overwhelming anxiety.

This anxiety, identified with an experience of entrapment, kept Stephen in interviewing as long as Sasha, even though I felt from the first interview that what he was asking for was psychotherapy. In fact, he started five times weekly psychoanalysis, a more ambitious therapeutic commitment, but only after he had managed to take several real steps towards actual separation, which relieved some of the fear of helpless submission (Laufer, M.E., 1996). He used the period in interviewing to support these moves, to facilitate his passing another crucial examination, to apply to university, to get accepted by a university near both home and psychoanalysis, where he could live separately but within easy access to his parents. Stephen was encouraged by these achievements, often, I think, into believing with a part of himself that he was only short of a little push towards a girl, and he would be no different from the average young scholar. Because I found Stephen very appealing, I must have colluded with this fantasy. Such a collusion often lies behind a failure to establish a therapeutic space with an adolescent. Included in such a shared resistance is a response to the adolescent's wish for recognition of the healthy side of himself and his despair of losing it in treatment. This anxiety needs to be met in interviewing, and is modified by its acknowledgement, as well as, in Stephen's case, by simultaneous gains made in reality.

The parents

Stephen's anxiety about being a 'nutter' was often projected on to the father, who carried much of the doubt about stigma. I did not doubt that the father had set up a small campaign of ridicule, not wanting his son to be in need of therapeutic help. His mother, as he described her, the daughter of a vicar and very religious herself, wished that he could find the answers to his problems in religion. Both his parents came over as loving, indeed, he seemed hunched over carrying the burden of a love that made him guilty about wanting to separate. Perhaps, more accurately, he wanted to *want* to separate. Both Stephen and Sasha had a very powerful sense of the damage they would do to their parents as well as to themselves if they committed themselves to treatment, imagining that, in so doing, they were attacking the structure of a home which was dependent on them. Because Stephen was so much more richly communicative about his parents, it was possible to work with him on these fears, and to help him understand some of these projections. At no time did I feel the need to have a meeting to establish the parental perspective, which Stephen convincingly carried around inside him, alongside the more primitive internal images. Although his parents did not actively support Stephen seeking psychotherapeutic treatment, and though he displayed much anxiety about their response, I have no reason to believe they actively tried to stand in his way. This was then true in both cases.

Alongside the anxiety about damaging the parents were they to separate from them, both Sasha and Stephen disclosed a terrible panic about becoming entrapped, specifically within the world of Stephen's mother's religion and Sasha's father's patriarchal attitudes. The siren call of Stephen's mother's religion was clearly projected on to me and treatment, and was disclosed in a number of dreams of sexualized entrapment, anxieties which it was necessary to identify and articulate, rather than provoke by a rush to intensive treatment. As far as I could understand, his mother's actual attempts to take her son to church with her were honest attempts whose failure she reluctantly accepted. Therefore, neither of these cultural matrices emerged as being as controlling in reality as they were in the minds of the adolescents. Indeed, if the parents in reality were as controlling and as needing of control as the inner parents, it would have been doubtful that any therapy or analysis could have been established, at least at this point in the lives of these adolescents.

The body

Stephen, whose anxiety was palpably erupting much of the time, was able to bring his anguish about his body into the interviewing much earlier and with a good deal more trust than Sasha. By the third meeting he came with a deeply worried and never articulated history of childhood masturbation, memories of childhood fantasies, some of which he found terrifyingly violent. A few details he let me know about, including images of rooms covered in faeces, cannibalistic attacks, dead babies. Stephen's anxieties obviously had a history, one which could usefully be explored in analysis. With relief he said he now masturbated regularly, later he would acknowledge with some shame, compulsively, but with more normal fantasies. In the interviewing, he was able to hypothesize a link between these past fantasies and his present panics, and he was aware that he was disclosing an anxiety about having some very bad stuff inside. For Sasha, such a revelation was disclosed in her dream of the slit in the wrist out of which the pus poured, but she displayed no concerned interest in her dream, no capacity to own consciously the anxiety expressed in it. She had much more successfully cut herself off from her body, but paid the price of much greater inhibition in thought and achievement, a devastating inability to make links. Stephen's ability to articulate a fear about therapy or analysis related to his articulated sense of a constant danger of being sucked into a 'vortex' of overwhelming anxiety; as he put it, so overly conscious of himself, his own body, that he wanted only to escape from it. Therapy, and analysis even more, represented a closing off of an escape, again the claustrophobic anxiety of entrapment, although it also represented a way out of his inhibitions. Stephen's articulation shed light on Sasha's more opaque wish to go to America, to get away to some place as far from the impinging physical and mental reality and, ultimately, problematic sexual development as she could imagine.

The limits of interviewing

As stated before, one of the reasons that psychoanalysis often fails with adolescents is that they experience it in very paranoid terms, as if being taken over, as they fear they have been in puberty, by the changes which take place in their bodies, changes which colour their experiences of their inner objects, which erupt as primitive and primitively sexualized. In interviewing, some of this anxiety about being taken over is mitigated by the fact that each meeting is arranged from one week to the next, or from meeting to meeting, and this helps to protect the process from the fears of submission and conversion. As an arrangement it helps to create trust in a therapeutic space which then loses some of its overpowering associations. The adolescent is part of the process of establishing the *boundaries* of the interviewing situation. He or she learns the experience of establishing boundaries; this makes commitment to a treatment less threatening. At the same time an adolescent like Stephen has time to voice anxieties, to have them recognized and contained.

Like Sasha, Stephen never missed one of the interviewing sessions which were always booked at the end of the previous meeting. This is a very strong indication of the adolescent's attachment not only to the interviewer, but also to the developing dependency on a reliable therapeutic space. I believe for Stephen, as well as for Sasha, there was some disillusionment which had to be faced. I believe Stephen was disappointed that his problems, his panic before an eligible girl and his compulsive masturbation, did not disappear following his confession. I believe he was hoping that, between him and me, he would master the anxieties, however overwhelming, and he was in fact alarmed at my taking him seriously, as well as relieved by it. Unlike Sasha, he was able to tell me this, rather than show it in a suicide attempt. In order to be able to transfer from interviewing to psychoanalysis in such cases, this disillusionment needs to be faced, and for the adolescent, this is very painful, as the anxiety of being for ever abnormal is devastating and is implied by the acknowledgement of the problem. In the case of Stephen, this was added to by the fact that the treatment he was considering, indeed the treatment which colleagues at the centre insisted upon, was psychoanalysis. His interpretation, like that of many outside the analytic world, was that this recommendation confirmed the severity of his disturbance. I could not shirk from this, as my colleagues in discussion were helpfully certain. This was a very disturbed boy, although the other side was also true, he would be able to use an analysis. For my part, I sometimes found myself wishing that his acute anxieties were less severe, and in supporting him in his strengths, of which there were many – his intellectual capacities as well as his ability to imagine himself living away from home were very strengthened in interviewing – I would actually need reminding myself of the preoccupations and panic which did not go away.

From interviewing to treatment

One of the aspects of interviewing that is most anxiety provoking to the interviewer is the worry about creating a situation where the adolescent feels betrayed by the loss of the interviewer. Because it is always presented as a task-oriented involvement, which is to say, interviewers reiterate the task of exploring the problem with a view to finding the best sort of help, there is always an end in sight for the project, even though sometimes no real end is reached. This helps to mitigate the anxiety about being taken over, and it also means that a goodbye is implicit from the very beginning. I would have to say that my experiences with this aspect to the work are variable, and I have had the experience of a transfer to psychotherapy breaking down because the loss of me, the trusted interviewer, was too great. However, usually, by the time an adolescent has owned the need for treatment, this recognition, with the hope it implies, very much outweighs the loss, which in itself links to normal adolescent loss.

Sasha came to her last session in an atmosphere of more confusion than usual, referring to a feeling of sadness associated with a story from school she was unable to link to any feelings about ending with me. I noted that she turned her attention very much to the projected responses her parents would have to her starting therapy, and I simply tried to take them back to her own anxiety throughout the interview. As it happens, I know from her subsequent therapist that Sasha suffered a prolonged and still mysteriously understood separation from her mother when she was an infant, and then a subsequent and extremely sharp separation from the grandparents who had looked after her, and no doubt the armoured defensiveness she so commonly presented, only more so in the last meeting, was a product of this formative experience. Stephen, who was much more in touch with his feelings, brought a genuine expression of gratitude to his last meeting, which he also used to get support for his decision to enter psychoanalysis in the autumn, which he thought his parents continued to lament. Interestingly then, though the atmosphere was so different, both focused at their last meeting on their parents' response to their embarking on treatment, those parents from whom it would be their task to give up an outgrown and now profoundly distorted dependency. Therapy, or, in Stephen's case, analysis, had become identified with that struggle. The dread of dependency on the treatment was countered by the extent to which each adolescent was able to own it as an active choice rather than a passive submission.

Summary of Part II

The interviewing of two adolescents, with their very different character structures and histories, shows anxiety about therapy or analysis specific to adolescent experience, particularly fears of being passively overwhelmed due to the threatened loss of an omnipotent defence which had been established to cope with adolescent change. Interviewing, in form and intent, aims to address such fears and to counter the omnipotent adolescent defences with the establishment of a therapeutic space and the development of commitment to its use in tackling problems the adolescent has been helped to identify in him or herself.

References

Bion, W. R. (1962). A theory of thinking. *International Journal of Psychoanalysis* 43: 306–310. Reprinted in *Second Thoughts*. London: Heinemann, 1967.

Blos, P. (1962). *On Adolescence: A Psychoanalytic Interpretation.* New York: The Free Press.
Britton, R. S. (1989). The missing link: Parental sexuality in the Oedipus complex today. In: Britton, R. (Ed.), *The Oedipus Complex Today* (pp. 83–101). London: Karnac.
Bronstein, C. (1993). *Working with Suicidal Adolescents.* Public lecture, British Psychoanalytical Society.
Freud, S. (1905). Three Essays on the Theory of Sexuality. *SE* 7: 135–243.
Freud, S. (1911). Formulations on the Two Principles of Mental Functioning. *SE* 12.
Green, A. (1975). The analyst, symbolization and absence in the analytic setting. *International Journal of Psychoanalysis* 56: 1–22.
Klein, M. (1930). The importance of symbol formation in the development of the ego. In: *Love, Guilt and Reparation.* London: Hogarth Press, 1975.
Klein, M. (1946). Notes on some schizoid mechanisms. In: *Envy and Gratitude.* London: Hogarth Press, 1980.
Laufer, M. (1995, October 28). *Adolescent Breakdown and Beyond: Detecting and Responding to Present and Future Risk.* Brent Adolescent Centre Conference, London.
Laufer, M. E. (1995). *Psychic Reality and the Menarche.* IPA Conference, San Francisco.
Laufer, M. E. (1996). The role of passivity in the relationship to the body during adolescence. *Psychoanalytic Study of the Child* 51.
Rey, J. H. (1979). Schizoid phenomena in the borderline. In: Le Boit, J., Capponi, A. (Eds), *Advances in the Psychotherapy of the Borderline Patient.* New York: Jason Aronson.
Schachter, J. (1986). *Action Without Understanding: Pitfalls in Working with Troubled Adolescents.* Paper read at conference organized by BCC.
Segal, H. (1979). *Klein* (pp. 112–121). Glasgow: Fontana.
Williams, A. Hyatt (1978). Depression, deviation and acting out in adolescence. *Journal of Adolescence* 1: 309–317.

7 THE ANALYTIC ENCOUNTER

A historical and process-oriented perspective *by Jean-Louis Baldacci and Christine Bouchard*

Commentary

Alain Gibeault

Jean-Louis Baldacci and Christine Bouchard are training analysts of the Paris Psychoanalytical Society. They work at the Jean Favreau Centre for Psychoanalytic Consultations and Treatments (CCTP; *Centre de Traitements et de Consultations Psychanalytiques*), which is the outpatient clinic of the Paris Psychoanalytical Society. They have been much involved in doing first interviews at this centre and in reflecting on the theoretical and clinical issues of the first interview, both in general and more specifically within institutions.

Their paper exemplifies how the French psychoanalytical approach to the first interview is determined by 'the question of the third'. They show that three poles, 'evaluation, treatment and knowledge', have to be taken into account in order to consider the first interview as a *process*. They relate this perspective to the Freudian definition of psychoanalysis, which inspired a specifically French way of understanding any psychoanalytic issue.

Jacques Lacan (1955/2006) played an important role in the history of French psychoanalysis when he recommended that 'the meaning of a return to Freud is a return to Freud's meaning' (p. 337); since then, French psychoanalysts have found it important to refer to Freud's metapsychology in order to understand clinical material. Moreover, in introducing his distinction between the Real, the Imaginary and the Symbolic, Lacan promoted a way of thinking systematically in terms of a triadic structure and perspective, and criticized psychoanalytic theories that favoured a dual approach in terms of the mother–infant relationship as a model of the analytic encounter.

This perspective was elaborated further by André Green (2002) when he introduced his concept of 'thirdness' as 'a theory of a generalized triangular structure with a variable third': this meant for him 'to envisage triangular relations in which the third term would not represent the paternal function' and 'not to let oneself be imprisoned by the dual relation' (p. 267). From this point of view, the reference to the third also has to do with the absent object. It means that any psychic structure or event is characterized not only by the two polarities of the subject and the object, but also includes the connotation of the absent object, the 'other of the object'. Language shows this reference to the third, when the 'I' and the 'you' are related to the 'he' or 'she'. In this sense, 'thirdness' would thus be a form of relationship in itself, the third term that relates the other terms with each other; as Green (1990) writes, 'the reference to the mediation' is 'an opening to thirdness' (p. 261).

The distinction made by Baldacci and Bouchard between the *objectification* of the third and its *virtual* reference is fundamental for understanding the French approach to first interviews and its development as it is recapitulated in their paper, and exemplified by the other French papers published in this book. They stress that with patients who have a non-neurotic organization, it is necessary to objectify the third in order to help them not to be engulfed by the dual relationship. Indeed, many of the French analysts who have written on first interviews have been influenced by their work in psychiatric or psychoanalytic institutions, like the authors' own Jean Favreau Centre for Psychoanalytic Consultations and Treatments, or the Jean and Evelyne Kestemberg Centre for Psychoanalysis and Psychotherapy, which is described in the introduction to Evelyne Kestemberg's paper earlier in this book (p. 51). These institutions have permitted French analysts to see many patients in first psychoanalytic interviews and to reflect on their practice.

The Jean Favreau Centre for Consultations and Psychoanalytic Treatments was created in 1954 by the Institute of Psychoanalysis, the Training Institute of the Paris Psychoanalytical Society, thanks to Sacha Nacht and René Diatkine, two important training analysts who contributed to the revival of psychoanalysis in France after the Second World War. Originally it was a sort of people's dispensary, conceived along lines similar to the Berlin Institute set up by the rising psychoanalytic movement at the time of the First World War. These treatments were carried out by psychoanalysts who were not paid, but who received supervision from an experienced analyst by way of remuneration. This arrangement made it possible to explore the effects of free treatment on the analytic process and to facilitate the access of analytical practice to lay analysts.

At a time when many psychiatric institutions were inspired by psychoanalysis, the centre found its specificity in proposing the experience of classical analysis three to four times a week on the couch. This was considered as the most efficacious treatment when applied advisedly. It was also seen as the best professional training for the practice of face-to-face psychoanalytic psychotherapy at one or two sessions per week. Later on, other treatments were gradually developed to deal with demand: individual psychotherapies, individual and group psychodramas, group psychoanalysis. However, these other treatment modalities are derived from the model of the classical setting, with a strong link between method, setting, and process of change: they are all based on the understanding and the interpretation of the transference.

There are currently about 50 analysts, including some candidates, who work on a part-time basis and who may or may not exercise the function of consultant in preliminary interviews. From the outset, the function of the consultant who conducts the first interviews was separated from the function of the analyst who carries out the treatment. This centre is thus an exceptional place for the evaluation of first interviews and for research on indications for psychoanalysis and their predictive value, as well as on the pertinence of the different forms of psychoanalytic treatment.

The paper by Baldacci and Bouchard is illustrative of the research on first interviews carried out at the Jean Favreau Centre. They offer a critical discussion of the theory of the analytical encounter. Instead of considering the encounter either from the point of view of the assessment, or from that of the beginning of the treatment, they broach them dialectically by interweaving the three levels of the Freudian definition of psychoanalysis, i.e. *investigation, treatment*, and *knowledge*.

According to the authors, certain modes of psychic functioning require *objectification* by a third party (an institution, public welfare services, separation of the functions of the consultant and of the psychoanalyst) to facilitate the movements of identification and dis-identification that are necessary for psychic triangulation; in other cases this reference to a third party can remain *virtual*. The authors therefore describe the value of having other colleagues participate in such a consultation in a psychoanalytic institution. They describe two phases: the individual consultation proper, followed by a discussion in the absence of the patient with other colleagues who represent a third party. After this discussion the consultant sees the patient again with the task of formulating the indication and referring him to another analyst. This triangular setting is particularly helpful with patients who have difficulties with symbolization. It facilitates the transformation of a symmetrical relationship during the interview into an 'announced dissymmetry' necessary for the development of a psychoanalytic process, and so promotes a process during the encounter that will result in proposing psychoanalytic treatment. Indeed, the analytic process requires an ability to identify with the analyst's function, as opposed to a desire to identify with the analyst as a person. This also requires the renunciation of immediate gratification. Both can be made impossible by the patient's paradoxical narcissistic demands.

This paper reflects the choice made by French analysts to take into account many possible settings for the development of an analytic process, as described above. It is interesting because it shows how French analysts conceptualize the dynamics and economy of the first encounter and of the different psychoanalytic settings, taking into account the reference to the capacity for representational work and the importance of the third-party dimension as linked to the internal and external setting. It is a good example of how setting and process are involved already in the first encounter without being based exclusively on nosographical issues like the opposition between neurosis and psychosis. The paper contains many references to other French authors who have written on the first encounter: Sacha Nacht, Serge Lebovici, Conrad Stein, Nicole Berry, Jean-Luc Donnet, Pierre Marty, Francis Pasche, Evelyne Kestemberg and Piera Aulagnier. It gives a good idea of how French analysts who have been working with non-neurotic patients have been driven to reflect on the theory and clinical experience of the first interview. It is illustrative of the French point of view on how to promote a process in the first interviews in order to initiate a movement of identification and 'a passage from the demand for help to the demand for meaning', which is eventually a passage from working face-to-face to working on the couch.

References

Green, A. (1990). De la tiercéité [On Thirdness]. In: *La psychanalyse: questions pour demain* (pp. 243–277). Monographies de la Revue Française de Psychanalyse. Paris: Presses Universitaires de France; In: *La pensée clinique* (pp. 259–308). Paris: Odile Jacob, 2002. [*Psychoanalysis: A Paradigm for Clinical Thinking* (pp. 233–277). London: Free Association Books, 2002.]

Green, A. (2002). *Idées directrices pour une psychanalyse contemporaine* (400 pp.). Paris: Presses Universitaires de France. [*Key Ideas for a Contemporary Psychoanalysis* (321 pp.). London and New York: Routledge, 2005.]

Lacan, J. (1955). La chose freudienne ou sens du retour à Freud en psychanalyse. In: *Écrits* (pp. 401–436). Paris: Editions du Seuil, 1966. [The Freudian Thing, or the Meaning of the Return to Freud in Psychoanalysis. In: *Ecrits* (pp. 334–363), trans. B. Fink. New York: Norton, 2006.]

7 THE ANALYTIC ENCOUNTER

A historical and process-oriented perspective

Jean-Louis Baldacci and Christine Bouchard

The dilemma: Investigation and transference

Regarding the analytic encounter, Freud (1913, p. 125) suggested that it was better to avoid repeating preliminary interviews because they would interfere with the emergence of the transference: 'the [patient meets] the doctor with a transference attitude which is already established and which the doctor must first slowly uncover instead of having the opportunity to observe the growth and development of the transference from the outset'. A trial analysis could be considered but its failure would confront the analyst and the patient with the problem of interruption and with the potentially iatrogenic disappointment associated with it. Between these two poles, it therefore seems advisable to develop a sufficiently brief method of evaluation. But the problem is paradoxical, since it would be necessary to measure an aptitude for transference whose emergence would simultaneously have to be limited. . . . What theoretical references and technical rules should then be used? These issues link up with those concerning the nature of analytic knowledge and its transmission. With extreme caution, Freud warns us against the risk of turning knowledge into a fetish, and the illusion that this would help us out of the dilemma. He emphasizes the importance in this connection of direct exchange between analysts. This is what he writes to his pupil Blanton: 'I do not believe one can inculcate technical principles through written texts; it can only happen through direct teaching. Obviously, beginners no doubt need a minimum to begin with, otherwise they would have no basis on which to proceed; but if they follow directives too conscientiously, they will soon meet with difficulties so they must above all learn to develop their own personal technique'[1].

In their 1955 paper, 'Indications et contre-indications de la psychoanalyse [Indications and contraindications for psychoanalysis]', Nacht and Lebovici (1955) tackle the problem from the standpoint of evaluation and the possibility

[1] Quoted by Alain de Mijolla, 23e séminaire de perfectionnement, 1981. (Translator's note: our translation.)

of prescribing analysis within a range of therapeutic strategies. They link analysability with establishing a diagnosis and prognosis in a classically medical model. The diagnosis is based on a structural evaluation, which should enable the analyst to appreciate how the Ego can be modified by transference interpretation and by the lifting of resistances. The prognosis raises the question of the *a priori* representation of criteria for treatment termination, which would make it possible to assess retrospectively the pertinence of the original evaluation. Two sets of criteria thus seem to be introduced: first, a psychoanalytic nosography, based on a structural perspective; and, second, criteria for ending the treatment. This double reference to the structure and history of the future treatment would thus be the starting point for psychoanalytic clinical work. The encounter is thus presented as the establishment of a project, i.e. of a prediction in relation to a standard. This historicizing dimension of prediction is found in the proposed clinical approach, in which considerable emphasis is placed on history, biography and the study of personality. Even if it seems partly in contradiction with the need to maintain a dialectical understanding of the relationships between the universal and the singular, this model perhaps prefigures a view in which the history of the encounter itself represents, in a condensed form, an encounter between the analytic project for the future and the patient's past, and so reveals, in a specific clinical situation, the rudiments of a possible de-condensation.

But the medical model, with its clear differentiation between diagnosis, prognosis and treatment, is not so easily transposable because the diagnostic evaluation concerns the patient's ability to use the proposed therapeutic method. Diagnosis coincides with prognosis and treatment in a sort of specific condensation, the result of which is the analytic project. Their differentiation thus seems difficult, even impossible.

This is hardly surprising if we refer to Freud's (1922) definition of psychoanalysis, which distinguishes three levels:

1. a procedure for the investigation of mental processes;
2. a therapeutic method based upon that investigation; and
3. a collection of psychological conceptions gradually being accumulated into a new scientific discipline, that is, a body of knowledge that is both constituted and still in the process of being constituted.

What seems to be specific, then, is the indissoluble link between these three levels, which means that, contrary to the medical approach, to investigate is already to treat in terms of an evolving body of knowledge. This is where the analytic encounter differs from both the consultation and the preliminary interview, and appears as an exercise that must seek to preserve not only the heterogeneity but also the interlocking nature of these three levels and their internal logic.

This text by Nacht and Lebovici seems to emphasize the first level of the definition (i.e. investigation). It seeks in fact to free itself from the therapeutic (or iatrogenic) aspect of the encounter by developing the third term of the definition, namely knowledge, seen as the basis for a specific psychoanalytic clinical practice interested in the patient's personality and Ego strength. In the discussion which follows the paper, Held compares this aspect of the consultation with the intrusive violence of projective tests, due to their objectifying and anticipatory character, which short circuit the second aspect of the consultation, i.e. the transference/countertransference axis. He refers to the need for the subjective dimension, for a moment of intuitive understanding, which alone can provide a sense of conviction about the indication or at least about a trial treatment. As can be seen, his criticism gives greater importance to the therapeutic pole, to the detriment of the evaluative pole. Faced with this conflict, Nacht and Lebovici evoke the advantage of the dichotomy between the consulting (medical) and therapeutic (strictly psychoanalytic) functions. They write: 'It is possible that this latter situation is more favourable to the evolution of the analysis and to the establishment of the transference' (p. 165). This implicitly introduces the problem of the third term in the encounter, as a condition for the emergence of the transference.

This conflicted relationship between evaluation and treatment (i.e. establishment of the transference) is at the heart of the problem of the psychoanalytic encounter, of that which is at stake from the very outset. At this stage of the discussion, the different contributions generally favour one or the other of the terms of this relationship.

Conrad Stein (1971), for example, in his text 'La double rencontre [The double encounter]', tries to preserve a double reference which allows each of the protagonists to be both an incestuous object and a separating third party for the other. But this ambiguity remains exclusively intersubjective, and its abandonment, which dispels the illusion, would risk inducing a sort of paranoiac reification or acted-out seduction. Furthermore, how can we assess the patient's potential tolerance for this ambiguity?

In her article 'Entrer en analyse [Entering analysis]', in *La Nouvelle Revue de Psychanalyse*, Nicole Berry (1974) continues along the same line of thinking. For her, the establishment of a psychoanalytic process imposes an exclusively dual relationship and the first interview is presented as being a homogeneous and integral element of the evolving treatment. The history of each treatment – by analogy with the history of psychoanalysis (from the theory of seduction to that of fantasy) – consists, from this perspective, in a movement from the outside to the inside (from events to fantasies); any reference to a third person is *a priori* excluded because it is liable to give rise to a reification which will restrict the possibilities for interplay between the regressive movement of the dream and the progressive movement of mourning that characterize the analytic process. It is through the experience of the transference and its interpretation that the pairs cathexis/decathexis and identification/de-identification can eventually be rearticulated.

In the above perspectives, the patients in question are those for whom the indication of analysis presents no difficulty, because they are able to tolerate and make good use of the ambiguity that is necessary for establishing the transference. In other words, the fact that the contraindication is not taken into account implies that the problem is, as it were, considered as resolved, which takes us back implicitly to the use of the provisional treatment discussed by Freud in his papers on technique.

The question of the third

In *L'enfant de Ça*, Jean-Luc Donnet and André Green (1973), describing their practice of consultation and differentiating it from the preliminary interview, revisit the conflicts inherent in the Freudian definition of psychoanalysis. In the chapter entitled 'Une consultation psychanalytique [A psychoanalytic consultation]', they demonstrate the fundamental entanglement of the three poles of the definition (evaluation/treatment/knowledge) during a public psychoanalytic consultation in a psychiatric setting. All three terms are important. The poles psychiatry/psychoanalysis/public, in fact, reduplicate the three poles evaluation/treatment/knowledge of the definition and can thus serve as a model for reflecting on the psychoanalytic encounter. The therapeutic aspect is present in the emergence and admission into consciousness of the unconscious processes brought to light during the investigation. The investigation itself cannot be conceived of as pure observation in pursuit of knowledge, but is part of a transformational project that involves the activation of a process and is based on an interview analogous to an analytic session. In the particular setting they describe, the analyst may appear as a 'super-consultant' contributing supplementary elements to the diagnostic evaluation, while the psychiatrist remains responsible for the treatment; the analyst may also represent the treatment pole, in which case the psychiatrist then embodies the reference to the diagnostic evaluation. This objective reversibility of their functions, which resists any form of fixed reification, presupposes the reference to a third term, namely, the encounter between different bodies of knowledge. The topographical, economic and dynamic aspects at stake in this encounter are carried by the audience: the third term is thus not the patient but the audience (*l'assistance*[2]), whose anonymity virtualizes a third reference. Through the reversibility of functions that it permits, this setting guarantees objectification, as distinguished from reification. The consultant's

2 Editors' note: There is a pun here on three meanings of the French noun 'assistance': (1) help; (2) public welfare; and (3) audience. The consultation took place in a publicly funded setting, where the audience is composed of health-care specialists.

opinion is discussed, his power is limited by the audience, and there is no indication or contraindication emanating from a private process that he cannot account for. Listening and countertransferential affects are articulated with nosography, with established knowledge, and with the discussion with the audience. This triangular situation, which confirms the possibility of error, makes it possible for the analyst, through the complex interplay of the identifications/de-identifications and cathexis/decathexis specific to each person, to be in turn master, carer or pupil, or even father, mother or child vis-à-vis the patient, and so to offer the conditions for the representation of the primal scene.

The interest of this model is that it emphasizes the importance of this triple reference, a triangular reference echoing the Oedipal situation and defining, from the outset, the specificity of psychoanalysis. But its limit, of course, is that it is designed for patients whose insufficient symbolic capacities make this objectification of the triangulation necessary; in other cases the triangulation can and must remain an inter-subjective reference, i.e. held within the dual relationship.

Pasche (1975) has showed that even when the encounter is exclusively dual, it implicitly imposes a reference to two distinct phases corresponding in practice to the face-to-face phase and to the couch phase. He sees these as a phase of presence/seduction and a phase of withdrawal/castration, which are accompanied by a double dynamic marked by the perception of the reality of the analyst and its necessary denial. These two phases are separated by an act which is in a way foundational: recognizing the admissibility of the request and the possibility of a refusal both structure the encounter and constitute, as such, a triangular situation.

This issue of the third term, considered from the standpoint of its objectification or as a virtual reference, and linked to an act that establishes a differentiation between two phases, had already been brought up in Pierre Marty's (1963) introduction to *L'investigation psychosomatique* [Psychosomatic investigation]. Although it is situated in another context, and with different patients, his argument overlaps in some ways with *L'enfant de Ça*. We have identified four main points:

1. First, investigation and transference are not opposed but articulated: Even when applied to an object outside the usual field of psychoanalysis (psychosomatics), the investigation is psychoanalytic and its specificity is to use the transference. It encourages the emergence of the transference through an interview technique derived from the basic rule of free association. But it is an adaptation of the basic rule that takes into account the face-to-face situation and the patient's sensorimotricity, and which does not preclude possible interventions aimed at injecting fresh impetus. To qualify the orientation of the interview, Marty utilizes the term 'associative anamnesis' borrowed from Deutsch (1939).

2. This articulation of the investigation and the transference gives the consultation its therapeutic character. It is because the situation is disconcerting and traumatic that it permits the emergence of elements that are indispensable for understanding the patient. The core of the investigation concerns the nature of the patient's object-relations, making the process of the consultation the basis of the evaluation. The consultant is caught in a dilemma because he finds himself oscillating between a regressive identification with the patient – Marty speaks of the risk of absorption – and the need to maintain the appropriate distance required by the investigation. So, he will sometimes have to resort to interpretation as a means to overcome this situation.
3. It is here that a new risk arises – namely, of premature engagement in the analytic treatment, at a point when the consultation has not yet said its last word. This problem is all the more difficult in that the consultation applies to an 'object' outside the field of classical psychoanalysis, outside the field of an established body of knowledge, whose investigation would require precisely the conceptual references that still need to be developed.

   Three technical elements are necessary to prevent this risk: an audience, the involvement of this audience[3], and the patient's prior informed consent to these procedures.
4. This involvement of the audience objectifies the deficiency of analytic knowledge, which corresponds to the symbolic deficiency of the patient. While Donnet and Green speak of 'blank psychosis', Marty speaks of a 'blank relationship' to qualify this inability of established knowledge to capture this new field of experience, homologous to the patient's symbolic void, or rather the failure of the theory to articulate with effective practice. As a result, the group ritual, as witness to the reversibility of identifications and evidence of the renunciation of omnipotence, compensates for the double deficiency: a symbolic deficiency in the patient, and a deficiency of knowledge in analysts.

Thus the exploration of the opposition between evaluation and treatment was nourished during this period by reflections on the third party, as a third term that might make it possible to go beyond the impasse. As we have seen, the authors chose situations where the need for objectification of a third party makes it possible to measure the importance of the third term.

[3] The consultation takes place in two phases: the consultation proper, followed by a discussion with the audience in the patient's absence; then, on his return, the indication is formulated together with an eventual referral to one of the members of the audience.

In 1981, Kestemberg added to the complexity of these investigations in an article entitled 'Le personage tiers, sa nature, sa fonction [The nature and function of the third person]'. Underpinning her considerations is not 'blank psychosis', or the 'blank relationship', but 'cold psychosis'. In this particular case, she points out the interest of the consultant/analyst dichotomy, which allows the patient to compensate for his/her symbolic deficiency by resorting to the consultant as the fetish-like support for a pre-transferential cathexis as the guarantor of the patient's narcissistic continuity through the magical power conferred on him, and as the intermediary between the patient and the therapist. In other words, the proposed third-person function is used in a fetish-like manner by the patient. One could say, following Winnicott (1951), that the found object is not lost, because its fetish-like use makes it possible to maintain the illusion that the object is found and created.

Because they permit analysts, whatever their position in the setting, to identify and dis-identify in turn with the consultant, with the future analyst, and with the patient, the involvement of the audience, together with the consultant/therapist dichotomy, highlights the complexity of the identifications that are at play in the encounter. No sort of reification is involved since none of the protagonists present is assigned to a fixed function, in relation to a given body of knowledge defined once and for all. The function of the third term remains virtual and emerges thanks to the reversible identifications permitted by the setting. It corresponds to the possibility of challenging knowledge, as demonstrated by analysts' need to exchange ideas, in settings ranging from simple discussions to full-fledged clinical case-review meetings.

The objectification and the reversible identifications that it entails allow us to circumscribe more clearly this function of the third, which is indispensable to the process and corresponds to the ambiguity of the relation between knowledge and ignorance: we may suppose that, when this objectification is not necessary, and an exclusively dual encounter is possible, it is because both sides simultaneously recognize a reference to knowledge as a tradition that can be challenged[4]. Hence the famous term '*supposé savoir* [supposed to know]', in all its ambiguity, may be pertinent here because it expresses the idea that the analyst, in spite of the asymmetry of the situation, is not an embodied fetish, but introduces the element of illusion that is necessary for symbolization and subjectivation.

The upshot of these investigations into the third, then, is that the encounter seems to provide an opportunity to evaluate the state of the reference to the third and the quality of the identifications that it allows. The degree of objectification and the more or less necessary recourse to exchanges with other analysts, as well as the possibility of bringing both these parameters

[4] For neurotic patients consulting an analyst in private practice, we may suppose that the unavoidable reference to the real or imaginary discussion with colleagues constitutes an equivalent.

into play, make it possible to establish the indication – a 'standard' or modified one – or a contraindication.

The aim of the treatment and the possibility of refusal

These studies give greater place to the superego and the structural model: in this change of orientation, the – even implicit – reference to psychoanalytic nosography becomes secondary. Progressively, more importance is given to drive dualism and to evaluating the potential effects of lethal forces, as well as the subject's ability to oppose them by tolerating his sexuality and its conflicts. Character, moral masochism, hypochondria, and somatic disease, on the one hand, and desire, motivation, and more or less eroticized suffering, on the other, are taken into account.

As a result, there is a general consensus about the very serious ethical dimension involved in the decision to take someone into analytic treatment. The negative therapeutic reaction, interminable analysis, and existential catastrophe all prey on the consultant's mind.

In 1984, Piera Aulagnier published a very fine text entitled 'Les entretiens préliminaries et les mouvements d'ouverture [Preliminary interviews and opening moves]', which gives a good idea of the prevalent concerns at that time about the analytic encounter and indications. She proposes transcending classical nosographical references, in particular the demarcation between neuroses and psychoses. According to her, the question of indication or non-indication does not coincide with this differentiation, which refers only to the need for different opening moves. On top of unconscious conflict and suffering, the determination of analysability is based on the aims of analytic treatment which she links to the relationship between the life and death instincts. 'My aim or my hope', she writes, 'is that once his analysis is over, the subject will able to put what he has gained from that experience at the service of aims that are still chosen as an expression of his own specific difficulties, his psychic alchemy, and of course his history, but aims which, however different they may be from mine, are in harmony with the same ultimate purpose, that is, to reinforce the action of Eros at the expense of that of Thanatos' (p. 177). From the outset, she thus raises the problem of the use that the subject will be able to make of his analysis. Indeed, the renunciation/decathexis that the analysis necessarily brings about will temporarily give more freedom to the death instinct. What will the patient and analyst then be able to do with it? 'Not only', she writes, 'will we be unable to avoid it, but Thanatos will have to find some targets within the experience that force it to drop its mask so that the analysis of its instinctual movements can permit the work of re-fusion' (p. 179). So, the issue is to manage to confine death not only within symbolic realizations, but also within living human relationships. But this is not always possible (defusion), so that for her the presence of this danger of the working with the death instinct can constitute a contraindication, even if nosographical considerations were to lend support to an indication for analysis.

But how is this risk to be evaluated? For the examination of the issue of thirdness – from its reification to its virtuality, via its objectification – has shown that it is in fact closely linked to that of the setting: the classical setting, a modified setting, or even a combined setting (in institutions). But there are cases where the tolerance of the most orthodox setting paradoxically allows the development of the most deadly forces, that is to say, where the acceptance of the cultural conditions of triangulation comes at the highest price: destruction, defusion, and death.

Transferences and identifications

A classically discussed topic is the analysis of the treatment request or, for Anglo-Saxon authors, the analysis of motivation. Thus, for example, during a conference on the first interview in Montreal in 1993, Dufresne (1994) tried to describe the clinical evidence of motivation. This was to be measured by the relationship between self- and object-representations. On the side of self-representations, he takes into account the desire for change, the severity of the Superego, which is likely to hinder eventual improvement, and finally the more or less projective or introjective character of the subject's own explanatory theory. As for object-representations, he identifies the way in which the other is evoked – for instance, as severe, narcissistic, or omnipotent – and above all the way in which the patient manages – or fails – to express his therapeutic expectations, owing to the narcissistically intolerable character of a potential refusal – and, we would add, of an agreement.

But the problem is more complex. Indeed, in a paper entitled 'Demande et Identification [Request and Identification]' (1986) – a paper, moreover, that was widely taken up and discussed by the participants at the above-mentioned Montreal conference – Piera Aulagnier shows, through the dialectic confrontation of the offer and the request, that by 'asking', the patient also offers himself, and so confirms the analyst's position of one who also makes a request. Thus the patient's request unveils that of the analyst, his desire, his transference according to Lagache, or the precedence of his countertransference according to Neyraut (1980). The encounter is thus based on the possibility of sharing, a coincidence of desires and a mutual choice. And since this is about analysis and speech, the decathexis that this shared encounter imposes, the renunciation that it confirms, turn it into an encounter through identification. The request becomes linked to identification. What is relinquished in the treatment request, because this necessarily involves the recognition of differences, is partly compensated for on the level of identification through crossed identifications, a shared sense of community and kinship; what is left over can be deposited in the cathexis of the analytic frame.

But are these reciprocal identifications and mutual desires symmetrical? On the patient's side of the encounter, it is his unconscious Oedipal conflict and history that are reactivated. On the analyst's side, it is his relationship to knowledge and to the meaning that emerged from his own analysis that are at stake. But in this meeting of strangers, everything vacillates and, as if for the first time, knowledge and tradition are embodied, as it were: they each become the analyst's analyst, master, father or mother, and something else which takes them still further and which Freud called the 'primal father', with whom they identify, impelled once again by incestuous desires. The relationship is symmetrical here, the seduction is mutual and, in its regressive potentialities, can sometimes go beyond the pleasure principle and evoke 'the community of denial' referred to by Michel Fain (1982) in *Le désir de l'interprète* [*The Interpreter's Desire*]. But with secure roots in his own analysis and in the aims of analysis, the analyst has the means to extricate himself from this and so to establish the analytic process and its dissymmetry. The analytic encounter thus seems to be a symmetrical relation waiting for an announced dissymmetry, a programmed refusal. This ambiguity underlying the encounter is hysterical in nature, and stems from a reciprocal hysterical identification.

But there are many cases in which this reciprocal identification process does not work. If so, what is the situation with regards to identification? It oscillates between maintaining cathexis and refusing to let go of the object, on the one hand, and on the other hand a forced idealization which puts off indefinitely the possibilities of fulfilment: 'Once I am grown up, when I am an analyst, for example, then I will get involved; but in the meantime I am going to hold on to what I already have and I don't need anyone else'. But the dependence imposed by this postponement of any need for identification is often refused because it is incompatible with the demands of narcissism. The patient's paradoxical request for help and his own moral masochism have the effect of confining the analyst, giving him the feeling of being captive, in an impasse, and of having to find an impossible solution. The encounter can turn into a duel, dragging the protagonists into a sadomasochistic regression, which becomes the most intolerable compromise between the requirements of narcissism and sexuality, but in which the central role of projective identification is evident. It can also happen that the patient shows a 'white paw'[5], as it were, accepting to fall in with all the simulacra of analysis in order

[5] Editors' note: The French original is '*le patient monster "pâté blanche"*', in reference to a fairy tale: A ewe has to go out and warns her lambs not to let anyone in unless the visitor can show a white paw through a crack in the door to prove that he/she is a bona fide sheep. The wolf tricks them by dipping his paw in flour. They let him in and he eats them all, except one who manages to hide in the grandfather clock. '*Montrer patte blanche*' can mean 'to show one's credentials' in a positive sense, but more negative connotation of dissimulation is never far off. . . . There is also a word play between the 'white' of the paw and the 'blank' of '*psychose blanche*' and '*relation blanche*'.

to preserve a link, a 'stop-gap', a fetish. In such cases we can see the unaccomplished variants of the identification process at work: mimetic, narcissistic and projective, which lead back to an initial disorder, a disturbance of the very first encounter, one which, before all the others, left traces of a fundamental antagonism between being cathected by the first object and the possibility of identifying with it in order to be able to turn one's desire elsewhere. It is especially important to recognize this form of distress because the forces of life will need to be sufficiently powerful to overcome its deadly effects. What, in such cases, will be the analyst's response?

The act of the response

When shared identifications mark the encounter, the 'passage' from the armchair to the couch – as a renunciation – will offer a solution. It is a passage, an act of passage, and not a *passage à l'acte* [an acting out], an inaugural act that expresses the renunciation of action, according to Donnet (1995), and commemorates – through the hallucinatory regression induced by analysis, the requirement to put things into words and the experience of the transference – the separating and unifying power of speech at the origin of the human family. At the other pole, when the identificatory dynamic is degraded to the point of expressing merely the refusal to make any renunciation, there may be a complete refusal of any form of psychoanalytic treatment, or at least a refusal of 'classical' analysis. But that does not mean exclusion or banishment, for if another setting provides the help and cathexis that are required, the patient may meet a psychoanalyst without being threatened by the narcissistic paradoxes of his need. Here the distinction proposed by André Green between psychoanalysis and the work of a psychoanalyst takes on its full meaning. Between these poles, all possible adaptations have been tried, ranging from interpreting the specific difficulties of the passage[6], to prescribing a face-to-face setting, which would be limited to listening and to the possible elaboration of a separation, as well as the face-to-face situation as a deferred passage to the couch. In these last cases, it is perhaps a matter of rediscovering with the subject what the circumstances were that led him/her to withdraw before the challenges of culture and of enabling him/her to regain sufficient self-confidence.

Incest . . . murder . . ., 'in the beginning was action', Freud tells us. As we have seen, all possible analytic responses refer to the act and its renunciation, as the reawakening of a common origin. It is probably this vertiginous plunge into our beginnings that is experienced when one simply asks someone to talk about themselves, and which led Winnicott (1971, p. 4), who was

[6] That is to say, the passage from cathexis to identification; from clinging to separation; from the request for help to a search for meaning; and from the armchair to the couch.

surprised by the degree of confidence that children showed him during the first interview, as well as the depth of what was involved, to say: 'it has made me use the term "sacred" '.

References

Aulagnier, P. (1984). Les entretiens préliminaires et les mouvements d'ouverture. In: *L'apprenti historien et le maître sorcier.* Paris: Presses Universitaires de France.

Aulagnier, P. (1986). Demande et identification. In: *Un interprète en quête de sens.* Paris: Ramsay.

Berry, N. (1974). Entrer en analyse. *Nouvelle Revue de Psychanalyse* 9: 93–103.

Deutsch, F. (1939). L'anamnèse associative. *The Psychoanalytic Quarterly* 8: 354–381.

Donnet, J.-L. (1995). *Le divan bien tempéré.* Paris: Presses Universitaires de France.

Donnet, J.-L., Green, A. (1973). *L'enfant du Ça.* Paris: Editions de Minuit.

Dufresne, R. (1994). Colloque de Montréal, *Le premier entretien et l'écoute analytique.* Communications de J.-L. Donnet, R. Dufresne, I. Lasvergnas, W. Reid, B. Tanguay. Montreal: Editions du Méridien.

Fain, M. (1982). *Le désir de l'interprète.* Paris: Aubier-Montaigne.

Freud, S. (1913). On beginning the treatment. *SE* 12: 123–144.

Freud, S. (1922). Two encyclopaedia articles. *SE* 18: 235–259.

Kestemberg, E. (1981). Le personnage tiers. In: *Cahiers de Psychanalyse et de psychothérapie du Centre du XIII*, autumn.

Marty, P., David, C., M'Uzan, M. de (1963). *L'investigation psychosomatique.* Paris: Presses Universitaires de France.

Nacht, S., Lebovici, S. (1955). Indications et contre-indications de la psychanalyse. *Revue française de psychanalyse* 19: 135–204.

Neyraut, M. (1980). *Le transfert.* Paris: Presses Universitaires de France.

Pasche, F. (1975). Perception et déni dans la relation analytique. *Revue française de psychanalyse* 39: 565–568.

Stein, C. (1971). La double rencontre. In: *L'Enfant imaginaire.* Paris: Denoël.

Winnicott, D. W. (1951). Transitional objects and transitional phenomena. In: *Collected Papers: Through Paediatrics to Psycho-Analysis.* London: Tavistock, 1958. Second edition London: Hogarth and the Institute of Psycho-Analysis, 1975, pp. 229–242.

Winnicott, D. (1971). *Therapeutic Consultations in Child Psychiatry.* London: Hogarth Press and the Institute of Psycho-Analysis.

8 THE ANALYTICAL ENCOUNTER
by Jean-Luc Donnet and Michel de M'Uzan

Commentary

Alain Gibeault

This paper is a dialogue between two senior training analysts who were consultants for 35 years at the Jean Favreau Centre, the outpatient clinic of the Paris Psychoanalytical Society. This is another example of first interviews done by analysts who were not taking the patient in analytic treatment themselves. The functioning of the centre has been described above (p. 104) in the introduction to the paper written by Jean-Louis Baldacci, the Director of this Psychoanalytic Centre since 2000, and Christine Bouchard.

Jean-Luc Donnet was the former Director, from 1989 to 2000, and has contributed much to the centre's research on the process of first interviews. He has initiated twice-monthly working sessions, which are a privileged opportunity for analytic exchanges, during which it is possible to evaluate and discuss the function of consultation, its predictive aspects, and the suitability of indications for psychoanalysis. Generally the method of these meetings has been to explore a present moment in a treatment, and then to go back to the first interview with the consultant, in order to reflect on the original prediction. The work of the group has helped to differentiate three positions, i.e. that of the consultant, that of the analyst conducting the treatment, and listening by the group. Each can function as a third party with respect to the other, thereby introducing a reciprocal third dimension. Jean-Luc Donnet has written extensively on the issue of process and setting, and is very interested in the theory of the relationships between the different psychoanalytic settings and their impact on the mental functioning of the patients.

Michel de M'Uzan was a consultant at the Centre Jean Favreau from the early 1970s until 2007. He has particularly studied the question of how a process can be induced in the first interview that gives the analyst an opportunity to understand the patient's defence mechanisms and resistances during the consultation, and to use this understanding to initiate a psychoanalytic treatment. He is very interested in reflecting on the specific technique and the psychic economy of first interviews with patients who have psychotic or psychosomatic modes of mental functioning. Michel de M'Uzan is one of the French analysts who have been involved in the study of psychosomatic patients and, with Pierre Marty, he introduced the concept of *operational thinking* in the 1960s. Many of his writings deal with the study of the psychoanalytic process as the co-creation of a *chimera*, in which the analyst shares something of the patient's experience, and which is made possible by the analyst's particular predisposition to primary identification and his capacity to tolerate experiences of depersonalization. He has continued his study of first interviews since 2008 at the Mental Health Association of the 13th arrondissement of Paris, in collaboration with the E. and J. Kestemberg Centre for Psychoanalysis and Psychotherapy and the Institute of Psychosomatics (IPSO).

The dialogue between these two experts is interesting as it shows the similarity of their approach as well as some differences within the same Freudian and French perspective. They have similar points of view with regard to the conceptualization, the practice and the ethics of the first encounter, in situations where the analyst considers himself to be *a priori* excluded from any later therapeutic engagement. They both consider the consultation as an attempt to promote an analytical event: the success of this attempt is the best sign for an indication. They also agree on the need to distinguish the psychoanalytic preliminary interview from a medical and psychiatric model of assessment.

However, they differ on some issues:

1. Michel de M'Uzan favours a widening scope of indications for analysis and considers that we can always modify the setting later on if necessary: to deprive someone from doing an analysis is more damaging than making a wrong indication. He is in favour of proposing only one interview, to ensure that the analyst becomes as little involved as possible as a person, and thus to preserve analytic neutrality. He follows Maurice Bouvet's recommendation that the analyst might eventually propose a second interview, but certainly not more, because then he would risk manifesting himself too much as a person in this face-to-face position.

   In opposition to this, Jean-Luc Donnet is more restrictive about the indications for analysis, because he is sensitive of the fact that if a change of setting later proves to be necessary, this can provoke a narcissistic wound. At the same time, he is aware of the dilemma between the wish to do a more precise evaluation and the need to stop the process of the preliminary interviews as quickly as possible. The more the analyst sacrifices his analytic function to make the encounter possible, the more difficult the evaluation becomes, because the analyst's seduction as a person comes to predominate over the 'seduction' of the analytic situation and of the method. In French thought, 'seduction' in the latter sense means the libidinal investment by the patient of the method's potential. However, Jean-Luc Donnet thinks that initiating a treatment involves a temporal perspective within a fixed number and duration of sessions; as a result, without neglecting the disadvantages of this approach, he favours the possibility of having more than one preliminary interview (eventually four to six). The proposal of a provisional time setting corresponds, in a minor way, to the Freudian idea of a *trial treatment*.
2. Michel de M'Uzan prefers to limit his interventions in the interview to the interpretation of the patient's resistances to the project of analysis.

Jean-Luc Donnet sees the patient's difficulties in accepting the project of analysis as a crisis in 'the setting of the setting' and considers the first interview to have a particular function of explanation and elaboration. They both consider what is at stake in the refusal of analysis by a patient or in eventual failures.

This paper is interesting because it shows the confrontation of two experienced analysts over the development of the first interview, its metapsychology and what is at stake in this experience. It also shows their differing conclusions concerning the indications of analysis.

Bibliography

Donnet, J.-L. (1985). *Le divan bien tempéré* [*The Well-tempered Couch*]. Paris: Presses Universitaires de France.

Donnet, J.-L. (2005). *La situation analysante* [*The Analysing Situation*]. Paris: Presses Universitaires de France.

M'Uzan, M. de (1977 and 1994). *De l'art à la mort* [*From Art to Death*]. Paris: Gallimard.

M'Uzan, M. de (1994). *La bouche de l'inconscient* [*The Mouth of the Unconscious*]. Paris: Gallimard.

8 THE ANALYTICAL ENCOUNTER

Jean-Luc Donnet and Michel de M'Uzan

Interview by Christine Bouchard and Jean-Michel Porte [March 1997]

Introduction by Christine Bouchard and Jean-Michel Porte

A dialogue between Jean-Luc Donnet and Michel de M'Uzan on the subject of the analytical encounter seemed to us to be particularly apposite. They are both consultants in the Jean Favreau Centre and although their practice of public consultations may appear very similar, there are nonetheless differences that are well worth thinking about and attempting to clarify.

Their discussion – which deserves to be pursued further – leads to the conclusion that there is considerable agreement between them as to the conception, practice and ethics of the analytical encounter, particularly as regards the work of consultation, which in itself is highly specific in that the psychoanalyst conducting that interview is *a priori* excluded from any potential therapeutic involvement that may follow on from it. Donnet and de M'Uzan are in complete agreement as to their conception of the consultation in terms of an attempt at psychoanalytic intervention, the success of which is by far the best indication of what therapeutic action should thereafter be envisaged.

There are, nonetheless, important differences between them:

Michel de M'Uzan argues in favour of broadening psychoanalysis, even if this entails modifying the setting whenever it is found to be inappropriate. Jean-Luc Donnet emphasizes the fact that any proposal to begin psychoanalytic treatment includes the perspective of its duration within the setting that is decided upon; at the same time, he argues in favour of prolonging where necessary the preliminary work, without ignoring the disadvantages that this may involve.

The reader will observe that de M'Uzan prefers to limit himself to individual interpretations of the resistances that create obstacles for a treatment proposal. Donnet sees in problems of feasibility the sign of a crisis in the 'set-up of the setting'; in his view, the preliminary consultation can give rise to explanations that make for some degree of working-through.

Q:[1] *As an introduction to this discussion, could you tell us how, in your experience, you see the development of the analytical encounter?*

J.-L. D.: Personally, I had no real experience of an analytical encounter before being myself on the couch, after a series of rather formal pre-selection visits. Basically, I began without any kind of introduction and it was on the couch that I discovered psychoanalysis. In the context of the end of the 1950s, that was probably the case of quite a lot of people.

M. de M.: As far as I am concerned, I have the impression that the analytical encounter occurred in my very first interview. There was something very persuasive about it that made me feel absolutely convinced deep inside myself that it was with that particular analyst that I wanted to continue. It was a unique experience that I had never before had in any other situation, and it did have something almost uncanny about it. For you, it was on the couch; for me, it was the initial encounter.

J.-L. D.: Well, there is probably some degree of repression about this, some erasing as it were of what was in those first interviews. With hindsight, all the same, they seem to me to have been infiltrated by the pre-selection situation in which the aim was to assess the solidity of the candidate's ego and capacity for sublimation rather than encouraging a complete freedom to say whatever one wanted; that indicates right away that there are variations not only as far as individuals are concerned but also with respect to the actual context . . .

Q: *Given the history and evolution of psychoanalysis, could you say something about the features that you think have changed not only in your thinking about psychoanalysis but also in the way in which you yourself conduct initial interviews?*

M. de M.: It's hard to know quite how to answer that question. It is obvious that there has been a development not only as to the principles and practice of the analytical encounter but also as regards the people concerned – they have changed quite a bit. People like Parcheminey and Schlumberger were highly cultivated and gave the impression that, for them, psychoanalysis was something of a passion. That was immediately obvious to anyone who discussed analysis with them. I would be inclined to say that that element features less nowadays. I do not see so much of that passion which could in those days go beyond the setting and the objectives of psychoanalytic treatment – always assuming, of course, that such

[1] Throughout the dialogue that follows questions (Q) by Christine Bouchard and Jean-Michel Porte are set in italics, while replies by Jean-Luc Donnet (J.-L. D.) and Michel de M'Uzan (M. de M.) are in Roman type.

objectives do exist. In those days, it was seen as somewhat surprising if a house doctor in psychiatry was not on some analyst's couch. There were others, of course, who undertook analysis because of some internal necessity; they did not need the excuse of wanting to train as psychoanalysts in order to give themselves the benefit of analytical treatment – that was much more the case later on. So, where is the passion in all that? *Cherchez la passion*!

J.-L. D.: The first models that I had of the analytical encounter were those of certain consultants in the Saint-Anne Hospital. The contrast – but also the continuity – with psychiatric consultations was something that impressed me considerably. Consequently, the effort to differentiate between them was an invaluable feature of the situation. I was, for example, struck by André Green's capacity to tolerate prolonged silences, even when there were 30 people present at the open consultation. When the patient began to say something, it was not at all the same thing as a response to 'questioning'.

M. de M.: I have come across something that, on a formal level, is not unconnected with what you say about the psychoanalytic dimension being detached from its psychiatric counterpart. I experienced that on the medical side. The contrast in some ways was all the more striking, because there is a huge gap between medical interviews and psychoanalytic ones. It is at that point that we can take into consideration the idea of distancing oneself: when I was working in a gastroenterology unit, I was both inside and somewhat apart from it.

Q: *How did that situation develop?*

M. de M.: The whole atmosphere changed, psychoanalysis became more popular – in the positive sense of the word. The stakes are no longer quite the same: the artistic vision of psychoanalytic treatment has gradually given way to much more serious dimensions.

Q: *Such as?*

M. de M.: Taking suffering into account is not quite the same as in earlier days; suffering is perhaps more intense nowadays, we feel more concerned by it and it demands of us adjustments that may well be far-reaching.

J.-L. D.: There have indeed been developments: psychoanalysis has become more popular, society's representations of psychoanalysis and psychoanalysts have changed, and this has had an influence on the request for analysis and on the way in which the initial encounter is perceived. An evolution that is undeniable, although I find it difficult to describe and to grasp fully. To supplement what you have just said, I would emphasize the fact that, as far as

I recall, thirty-something years ago the issue of indications was expressed in terms that had much more to do with medical aspects. We could say that the conjunction in the interview between its value as an event or as an encounter and its usefulness as regards assessment was not highlighted to the same extent; the idea of a diagnosis as to psychological structure was often enough to warrant an indication for psychoanalysis, with a kind of disjunction between the moment when a diagnosis was reached and that of actually beginning the treatment. That, I think, has faded away somewhat.

M. de M.: That is not quite my own feeling. You were telling us about how impressed you were by the kind of silence that André Green could deal with. I was already familiar with that kind of thing in the 1950s – and, what is more, in a context of somatic illnesses. My own experience, all the same, is too much of a personal one to be of general significance.

J.-L. D.: Since we are dealing here with diversity, it is very difficult to paint a coherent picture.

M. de M.: Coherence comes from the fact that several aspects or facets can be brought forward.

Q: *Could it be said that, on the one hand, the purpose of such an interview is to set out a treatment indication after bringing together anamnestic data and nosographical factors, while, on the other, the issue seems to be for the patient to have some experience of the analytical situation through that initial encounter?*

M. de M.: Don't they both go together? Ideally, if there has been a true 'encounter', then we can be more sure of the fact that the assessment will be correct.

Q: *Given the idea of listening in an interpretative manner to what the patient says, could the initial encounter be seen as a 'fragment of analytical treatment' even though the setting has not yet been defined and the patient does not know whether that analyst will indeed be the person with whom the treatment will continue? Is there not a contradiction between the offer to say whatever comes into one's mind and the absence of any proposed setting (the fundamental rule, no date being fixed for the end of the treatment . . .)?*

J.-L. D.: I would agree with that way of putting things insofar as the initial encounter is not a psychoanalytic one – it has to become so. In that sense, it could be compared to what Freud called 'trial treatment'. There is, therefore, an attempt at doing things psychoanalytically, and the most reliable indication, afterwards, depends on how we think that attempt worked. In setting up that encounter, i.e. the kind of situation that the psychoanalyst proposes (a particular way of listening, the implicit offer to the patient of saying whatever he or she wants), there is a 'simulation' of the psychoanalytic situation. There is all the same a gap between that situation and the analytical situation in the strict sense of the term (the classical form of treatment or psychotherapy): the setting is not explained, nor is it established as a reciprocal commitment with no defined temporality as regards the duration of treatment. The patient is thus in a situation in which any difficulties encountered follow on not only from his or her own resistance as regards talking about things – the internal 'threat' – but also from what may be a much more important issue: that each protagonist consents to the other. It is problematic issues such as these, which involve both the search for meaning and the search for a setting, that I consider to be the crucial, 'epistemological', aspect of the encounter.

Q: *The search for a setting?*

J.-L. D.: Insofar as the fundamental issue in this retroactive assessment procedure is what underpins the decision as to the future work setting upon which patient and analyst may or may not agree, the anticipation of that decision will be a factor in the conflicting tensions that act on the various modes of listening and of talking that are prevalent in the interview.

M. de M.: There are indeed two aspects to this, but I would say that, thanks to the possibility of a psychoanalytic approach in that initial encounter, the patient can experience something that is quite exceptional – indeed, unique; like it or not, patient and analyst have to some extent 'embarked' on something, even though the analyst is in a better position to stand back somewhat from it. When, after our interview in public, I meet patients again for a brief encounter, they often already have the idea that something will follow on from that initial discussion. When I say that things will be different all the same, because any follow-up will be with someone else, there is always some degree of surprise. It would seem, therefore, that presenting an offer of self-expression in a psychoanalytic frame of mind tends to propel the patient in that direction in a way that he or she imagines to be what is actually going to happen in reality. It is perhaps worth exploring that further. Could it be said that there is some cheating involved? Was that offer of self-expression too important, given what will thereafter take place?

Q: *You are speaking here of the situation in the Jean Favreau Centre. Are things different in your private practice?*

M. de M.: I do things in the same way. I strongly believe in the setting we propose and on how we carry things out. The underlying essence is the same; the stringency with which it is put into practice takes on different forms, depending on the situation. The fact that there are other people present at the interview, with the idea of conveying something to them, means that there will always be something demonstrative about the whole procedure, and that may distort the situation a little. We are in a kind of arena, and the message must get through. I would even go as far as to say that, in such circumstances, my concern will at some point be to set up the situation in a way that is almost theatrical.

J.-L. D.: Like a soufflé, then, perhaps?

M. de M.: Yes. And when it has risen properly, I cannot see myself trying to make it rise again in a second or third interview. . . . Basically, it seems to me that we generally get a fairly quick idea of what is going on. I am therefore somewhat against repeating interviews. Bouvet used to say that we could perhaps have a second interview but not too many; in his view, it was not advisable for the analyst to reveal any personal features.

Q: *Would the fact that several meetings might enable us to observe and evaluate any dynamic changes not be an argument in favour of such a procedure?*

J.-L. D.: It is important that the person who has asked for the appointment knows that he or she will be talking to an analyst as an initial consultant, whether the meeting takes place in the analyst's private practice or in the Jean Favreau Centre: it is quite natural for that 'setting' to structure the encounter, at least to some extent. Some patients are very forgetful of that aspect – while others do not forget it enough. Although it is true that the processual development of the encounter provides by far the most solid basis for 'prediction', we must take into account the potential impact of that setting. It is worth noting that those patients who have a gift for psychoanalysis, even though they may regret not being able to 'continue' with the same consulting analyst, do accept that situation without too much difficulty; it is as though they realized that their transference belongs to them and that their new analyst will be able to be integrated into their family romance.

As for the matter of the number of interviews, it is clear that there is a contradiction between the wish to fine-tune one's assessment and the requirement to call a halt to it as quickly as possible. There are two diametrically opposed kinds of patient with whom closure is quick: on the one hand, 'natural' analysands with whom there is no reason – other than that of teaching the other participants – to postpone offering an appropriate setting; and, on the other, obvious contraindications that lead to the decision to refuse analytical treatment. Between those two extremes, the whole thing is about as clear as mud. The more the analyst gets involved in order to bring some life to the encounter and make it somewhat more dynamic, the less clear is the assessment, because it has more to do with the attraction exerted by the analyst than that of the situation and the analytical method themselves. Given the evolution in pathology and in the requests for analysis, it is difficult for us to reach that inner core of firm belief upon which some decision can be based as to the potential suitability of a given setting. The risk is that we find ourselves in ambiguous situations that just go on and on. That is why I personally find it a good idea to suggest a provisional setting, limited in time (say from four to six sessions); this corresponds, in a minor way, to Freud's initial idea of trial treatment. The significance of creating such a possibility, limited in space and in time, comes from the fact that the deadline for taking a decision is both postponed and fixed; appropriate listening and talking may thus be able to find a more solid basis on which to build than that afforded by a single encounter. Of course, the impact that the postponed decision may have could be all the more tricky to negotiate.

It is in fact a matter of principle for me to offer a second meeting: it allows me to assess the effect, the deferred impact, of the initial encounter and to work dispassionately, in a different dimension of reality, on the problem of the 'feasibility' of treatment. The important thing is to give time to the perplexity that may remain; if the interview was properly handled, this will be seen as meaningful.

M. de M.: I agree completely. There are people who impress us very quickly as being of the *homo psychoanalyticus* sort.

J.-L. D.: 'Natural analysands' (in the same way as we speak of 'natural athletes').

M. de M.: Then there is the vast domain in which things are not quite so obvious. I myself do not propose several meetings before taking a decision. In that single encounter, I focus on trying to assess the density of preconscious functioning, to use Pierre Marty's term. If my assessment is sufficiently positive, I would not hesitate on that basis to propose psychoanalysis, because I think that it is less detrimental to make a mistake and propose psychoanalysis than to refuse a psychoanalysis when it would be a potentially justifiable option. We can be really surprised at how things turn out sometimes, and it is always possible to introduce more or less important technical variations, and perhaps even to find oneself practising psychotherapy if it comes to that. I would therefore tend to be generous as regards the indications for psychoanalysis; when, in my private practice, I do not propose analysis immediately, it happens almost without thinking – as though there were some obvious sign that the person involved could not work with me in the way that I feel is absolutely essential: in other words, the manner in which his or her preconscious functions seems inadequate. Such cases usually have some kind of psychosomatic dimension to them.

Q: *Could that intuition that you spoke of not interfere with the way in which you listen attentively to the patient's free associations? That could perhaps be an argument in favour of having several meetings with the patient in order to mitigate that effect.*

M. de M.: Bouvet used to say that intuition is more trustworthy when it is based on a rational representation of its object. I am more concerned with how things function than with actual meaning. I would even go as far as to say that, to a certain extent, bringing unconscious representations into consciousness seems to me to have more of an instrumental value than a teleological one, in the service of modifying psychical economy.

J.-L. D.: For me, the fundamental issue is to perceive what transpires between that kind of functioning and the manner in which something becomes meaningful on the level of drive-related introjections – because some things can be made meaningful without bringing about any economic or dynamic change. To come back to your idea of being somewhat generous as to treatment indications, since it is always possible later to introduce variations if need be, I would say that the characteristic feature of a decision about initiating treatment is that, from that point on, many things depend on how it works out over time: we may indeed be pleasantly surprised (although there may be some unpleasant surprises too – interminable treatments and disorganization). Of course, the analyst's own personality plays a part in all this. There is also a certain logic of the psychoanalytic situation, which assumes that we put our trust in the dynamics of the process within the agreed setting. I find it somewhat paradoxical to refuse any further exploration in a face-to-face setting in favour of setting up a psychoanalytic form of treatment the parameters of which we would quite willingly change after a very short time. In addition, when a patient is moved from the couch to the armchair, this can be very hurtful even when the situation is handled by an analyst as experienced as yourself.

Q: *This may be a good moment to discuss what is at stake in the analytical encounter. How would you define these issues and the technical modalities that in your view are more likely to make a success of it? Is there such a thing as a 'classical' encounter, in the sense in which we speak of the 'classical' form of psychoanalytic treatment?*

J.-L. D.: I like to compare the psychoanalyst's technical procedure to the navigational manoeuvre that sailors call 'berthing': this means coming alongside in a rounded approach, acknowledging that there will be a bump even though the line of approach follows a curve. The patient should be allowed to 'bump into' the psychoanalytic method (the analyst's silent listening, benevolent neutrality) in such a way that drives and defence mechanisms are stimulated; above all, insofar as the setting is neither explicit nor agreed upon, there should be no reciprocal 'accreditation' – the principle of elasticity (Ferenczi) has its place here. The difficulty lies in the fact that the psychoanalyst's adjustment to the 'requirements' of the dynamics of the interview has to take on an *essential* quality in order to reflect, as far as possible, the patient's structural constraints and room for manoeuvre. In order to do this, the 'readjustments' with respect to the initial analytical position *sensu stricto* must correspond to a countertransference mourning process *a minima* and be initiated at the behest of the psychoanalyst, who must not simply be subjected to them.

To give a very simple example: at the beginning of an encounter, the person who asked for the appointment becomes tongue-tied at the idea of saying whatever comes into his or her head and wants the analyst to ask questions. There are three possible responses that can be made, and the analyst *must* choose which one to follow: (i) give no answer at all – this might bring about an increase in anxiety, and also a way of resolving it; (ii) ask questions based on the analyst's intuitive grasp of the small amount of meaningfulness in the situation or even of the threat of its being interrupted; or (iii) 'interpret' *a minima* ('Perhaps you prefer other people to take the lead?' for example) – this may open things up somewhat or be a complete failure: both aspects are part of the process of the encounter and have prognostic value.

M. de M.: I would say that my first aim would be to mobilize the patient's drive-related aspects and, in parallel if not correlatively, his or her projections, given the frustration. My second aim would be to identify the extent to which, at some point or other in the discussion, what the patient is saying includes 'meaningful representations', i.e. what some would call signifiers. Taking up these representations can sometimes change the nature of the discussion quite radically. It is at such moments that I find myself best able to assess the patient's preconscious functioning. This therefore implies a twofold approach: a frustration, a discreet relaunching by means of an association and the identification of a signifier that I can then stimulate. Those would be my main guiding principles, together with, at the very end of the interview – a supplementary feature, something that I do not do systematically – exploring the patient's capacity for representation by asking some questions.

J.-L. D.: What I find extremely important is the way in which the patient cathects the situation. When patients let themselves be carried along by what they are saying towards some unknown destination, when they show surprise ('Oh! I wasn't expecting to say that'), when they see that they have made a slip of the tongue, when they appear to discover by themselves what thinking in a freely associative way is all about ('Well, that makes me think of . . .') – these are undeniable indications. Another landmark is the way in which the following aspects are mixed up together or are evoked one by one: the process of the encounter, the manner in which the history of how the patient came to be there (the 'history of the illness' in medical terms) is expressed, and the patient's childhood past as it takes shape through the emergence of parental and other family figures. There is also a countertransference element, the importance of which can never be over emphasized: the length of time during which the analyst is able to put completely aside his or her purposive ideas with a view to assessment, a time in which there is a true 'immersion' in the temporal dimension typical of attentive analytical listening. That said, the specific attributes of the temporality of the encounter lie in the conflict concerning the point at which time is up – when begin to emerge questions relative to what I call 'touchdown', the point at which we wonder what we are going to say 'in conclusion'.

Q: *Could we say that, for patients, one of the aspects of the encounter has to do with becoming aware both of the new quality of communication and of its repetitive nature?*

J.-L. D.: For both patient and psychoanalyst, I think it essential that they have the feeling of having 'accomplished' or 'created' something, as Conrad Stein puts it, that something has been constructed. That is the best foundation for any decision that leads to further treatment.

M. de M.: I would say that patients have the feeling that they have experienced something unique and exceptional which was constructed with them, that something was accomplished together. The awkward thing is that the psychoanalyst is involved in that, participating in the construction even though he or she knows very little about many important things that are part of that construction. In my view, the analyst may participate a little too actively in it – but perhaps it is well-nigh impossible to avoid doing so, for reasons that have to do with the kind of construction it is and the uncertainties it involves. Similarly, there must obviously be something to do with seductiveness, an inevitable consequence of inviting someone to say whatever he or she may want. The psychoanalyst participates in that construction, just as there is a whole facet of the transference neurosis that is the outcome of the encounter between the unconscious of each protagonist.

J.-L. D.: To add to what you say, the assessment of the initial interview has to take into account the analyst's participation in that construction – we could perhaps look at it in terms of his or her countertransference involvement. As we have said, one typical feature of 'natural analysands' is that, to some extent, while experiencing disappointment, they are able to take their transference with them and re-transfer it onto someone else. If the consultant were to participate to too great an extent, such patients would be left with a feeling of having been abandoned, they would feel puzzled, and that could affect their capacity to cathect a therapeutic situation with their 'second' analyst. That seems to me to be a problem situation of which the practice of consultation work can make analysts more aware.

Psychoanalysts have a natural tendency to believe a little too quickly that, since they were the chosen object of the initial transference, they are in a better position to deal with whatever becomes of it in an analysis. Consultation work teaches you not to think of yourself as indispensable; and that experience is true also of private practice, when the analyst is his or her 'own' consultant.

Q: *Is there any room in preliminary interviews, as is sometimes said, for interpretations in the true sense of the word?*

J.-L. D.: Not only is there room – sometimes it is absolutely necessary to interpret.

M. de M.: On that point, I have changed somewhat. I used to think that interpretations in that context ought to be rather low key. The more I think about it, the more I would say that there is certainly room for interpretations – and, indeed, that they have an important role to play. As long as we do not do too much, the fact of offering an interpretation makes it possible to render the ongoing process more dynamic and to ensure that it goes on developing satisfactorily.

Q: *Could it be of value from a demonstrative point of view, showing patients almost immediately what the psychoanalytic process is all about?*

M. de M.: The risk would be that it might create a misunderstanding, such that the patient could not even envisage the idea of continuing with someone else.

J.-L. D.: We could also argue, *a contrario*, that an interpretation – if it comes at the right moment – creates a certain distance with respect to the present, unbinds it in a way, by introducing a third-party dimension. The way in which a patient understands and makes use of an interpretation – or an intervention that amounts to an interpretation – is a fundamental aspect of the assessment procedure (cf. the example previously given). I would say that an interpretation can compensate for the ambiguity created by the fact that the setting is not explained in detail (the fundamental rule).

M. de M.: Would you agree that we have to take into account the pleasure (and its vicissitudes) which, at that point, is shared by both participants?

J.-L. D.: Well, fundamentally, an interpretation creates a separation between analyst and patient, insofar as the latter can identify the element upon which it was based. It is therefore a 'component' of the analytical process, of its intelligibility and its sublimated pleasure.

M. de M.: We have slightly different views on that point. Even though you may theoretically be correct, I would argue that we have to investigate the pleasure that may result from that, in both analyst and patient. Interpretations have narcissistic implications too, in that, in a way, they extend the empire of the ego and thus may open on to other aspects.

J.-L. D.: Winnicott emphasizes the fact that transference interpretations can give rise to a kind of hiatus when he says that he makes an interpretation in order to show the patient that he has been able to understand up to a certain point. We could of course offer many interpretations to 'natural analysands', but in fact we do not do so, simply because they do not need them. On the other hand, interpretations are highly relevant in interviews where there is no feeling of deep-seated consistency or coherence, because they help us to see if the patient understands their nature, if they are in any way meaningful.

Q: *Now that you have mentioned the technical variations of the encounter, how do you react when some misunderstanding or other persists, when the patient seems not to cathect the psychoanalyst's offer of complete freedom of speech and an interpretative way of listening, when, to the latter's proposition 'tell me about it', the patient response with a 'cure me of it'? Should some technical adjustments (which ones, in what way, how far) be introduced, as long as they do not endanger the very consistency of the analytical method?*

M. de M.: The first question that I would ask myself is: is the presentation that the patient offers us not simply a resistance and does he or she not expect that we will in fact not be taken in by it? I would tend, in some ways, to treat what the patient says as credible, but if the overall picture is as gloomy as you seem to think, that would give rise to some perplexity on my part and make me wonder what we are doing together. Since I do not have within myself a tremendous urge to cure my fellow man – and that is even more the case given that I am not at all sure that I would be helping him if, by chance, such a desire did take hold of me in a megalomaniac way – I would wonder how best to extricate myself from such a tight spot.

J.-L. D.: Michel de M'Uzan implicitly agrees with what you say about the consistency of the psychoanalytic method. He has not adopted the point of view according to which psychoanalysis would be forever relevant and extensible, and a perfectly analysed psychoanalyst would be suitable for every patient who happens to contact him or her. When the relevance of psychoanalysis comes up against some kind of restriction, the functionalization of the countertransference is also limited, so that we then have to deal with the delicate issue of non-indications and contraindications. Certain adjustments and inventions are, of course, possible (with adolescents or psychosomatic patients, for example), but the problem of refusal nonetheless exists, and there is a point at which the idea of renunciation does emerge. At that point, the main issue becomes how we reach that decision, work on it, inform the patient of it or, on the contrary, dodge the whole question.

M. de M.: What you are saying has to do with the standpoint that I was arguing in favour of earlier: depriving someone of analysis is more serious than making a mistake as to the indication. But that does not mean that I am adopting an 'analysis-for-all' approach! There are, in my view, indications and contraindications, but the one group is more extensible than the other. For example, when patients whom we might possibly think of as contraindications, because they do not stop complaining about those in their immediate circle in an instrumentalist way that leaves no room for interpretation, keep on coming very regularly and take pleasure in our discussions, they must be getting some benefit out of these.

J.-L. D.: That example is a good illustration of the specific issues involved in cathecting the analytical situation. Some patients become attached to it in such a very static and non-specific way that they raise the problem of what we could call psychoanalytic 'assistance'. I now distance myself somewhat from the standpoint we shared some twenty-five years ago in the Paris Psychoanalytical Society, according to which, if a patient attended regularly and paid for his or her sessions, then something must be happening. Firstly, because it is not true to say that the frustration of having to pay always has a dynamic value to it; and, secondly, because we cannot avoid thinking about that other aspect of the question, the 'interminable' factor. It is obvious that that concern has a retroactive impact on the decision to initiate psychoanalysis.

Q: *As regards what has been called the 'indication for a given psychoanalyst', would you say that, leaving aside contraindications and non-indications, there is always a solution or always an analyst for any given patient?*

M. de M.: My off-the-cuff response would be that if there is an indication for a specific analyst, I would tend to think that that implies that there is no indication for psychoanalysis.

J.-L. D.: I wonder if there is not a contradiction between what you have just said and your position as regards 'broader' indications for analysis. We could say that a particular analyst is advisable in the sense that, for a given patient, a specific kind of competence is required in the analyst. I personally use that approach in cases where the initial encounter does not lead to a precise form of treatment (psychoanalysis, psychotherapy, etc.); the indication then becomes one in which there is a commitment with an analyst, after mutual co-opting and with no defined setting. An appropriate setting may eventually emerge from the dynamics of regular sessions and the analytical work done in them. The fairly wide application of that approach to the patient's request runs the risk of merely obeying the laws of supply and demand, of levelling out the various possible sites to the detriment of the analytical situation – the most demanding of all, but also the most effective.

Q: *In addition to that first definition of an 'indication for a given analyst' – chosen because of his or her specific competence – could it be said that in some cases the transference will unfold only with a specific analyst?*

J.-L. D.: It is true that it would be paradoxical to ratify the patient's fantasy according to which only one analyst could possibly be suitable. This applies mainly to training analyses, with the fantasies of filiation that underpin or even precede them. We should remember that, from a Freudian point of view, analysis of the transference supposes that the analyst is 'non-specific'. This, of course, is not the same problem as arises when the patient is referred directly or indirectly to that second analyst by the first one he or she encountered.

Q: *Does the psychoanalytic way of listening to the patient exclude any reference to nosography and a diagnosis as to structure? If that is not the case, how do you reach some kind of compromise between the analytical dimension and that of consultation in the initial encounter?*

J.-L. D.: Nowadays, nobody would say that the aim of that encounter is to reach a diagnosis as to structure, which in turn would be sufficient to give an adequate indication of the prognosis. When Michel de

M'Uzan says that borderline states are often better indications for analysis than the neuroses, he emphasizes the fact that both prognosis and indication are based essentially on a precise assessment of what actually does transpire in the encounter. On the other hand, I would argue that an attempt at nosographic classification is interesting on both theoretical and didactic levels. And when the material is looked at again for assessment purposes, I believe in the countertransference hygienic value of the attempt to identify clinical types, i.e. with reference to non-specific structures – whereas the encounter has basically to do with particularities and with the inter-transference. Taking nosographic references into account is one way of distancing oneself, of adopting an inter-analytical approach, with its objectivizing clinical dimension, and as such is well worth preserving.

M. de M.: Yes, I would say that thinking in terms of nosography does encourage us to go more deeply into what is taking place, not only in discussions with colleagues in the case of open-to-others interviews but also within ourselves, because it does protect us from adopting too readily an impressionistic approach. As long as we are not taken in by it, the effort to think along nosographic lines can be very hygienic.

Q: *How do you react in practical terms to the gap that might open up between the 'promise' of analysability that arises in the initial encounter and the obstacles that the patient raises when the proposed treatment is about to be set in motion?*

J.-L. D.: There always has been a certain gap between the momentum of the encounter and a commitment to a project, with the necessities of time and money that the latter implies: patients who seemed to have made up their mind but who do not come back or come back much later on, etc. It is much more frequently the case nowadays, as though the patient's resistances were taking support from the realities of modern life and, on a deeper level, from the particular development of collective, social and cultural resistances (with respect to cost, the demand for an immediate response, the difficulty of having enough time available).

When we look back, we can see how the cultural values and customs of thirty years ago contributed to the patient's agreeing to analysis. It is striking to see how people who, in the course of the initial encounter, show all the signs of a wish and a capacity for analysis, seem to lack judgement when the problem of the feasibility of analysis is raised.

We cannot but wonder what the consequences will be, for the practice of psychoanalysis, of the erosion of the support afforded by superego and sociocultural ideals.

M. de M.: Could we not see that as a resistance in the classical sense of the term, one which comes to the fore as soon as anxiety is generated by what is appearing on the horizon?

J.-L. D.: Resistance has always been a factor. What I am talking about is the kind of mutual support that exists between individual and collective resistances. Twenty-five years ago, when we proposed three sessions per week, that did not give rise to any problems because the cultural vogue of the time was in support of the authoritative nature of the 'prescription' of analysis that 'overcame' all resistances. Nowadays those resistances take support from such elements as the economic downturn and work-related issues. It is an eminently practical problem: how can it be worked on? The advantage that the consultant has over the analyst in private practice – who can merely say 'Well, think about it, and when you're ready come back and see me' – is that he or she can work differently on those resistances in the course of the discussion, while taking on board the idea of representing certain 'values' of psychoanalysis.

M. de M.: When the indication is indisputable and the patient raises difficulties concerning the actual implementation of the planned treatment, I would first of all tend to see it as a kind of last stand; my inflexibility would probably be enough to carry the day. It can, however, happen that, for whatever reason, we would like the patient all the same to do something. In such cases, I would lower my requirements but without going below a certain level all the same.

Q: *That brings us to the question of what, in your view, are the minimum criteria or signs that would be decisive in prompting you to suggest psychoanalytic treatment sensu stricto or psychotherapy, assuming that the latter is not a mere outlet channel for analysis?*

M. de M.: Stating them objectively is somewhat difficult. I would take as my basis the inner belief that there exists in the patient an adequate degree of preconscious functioning; I would not refer at all to semiology or nosographic arguments, which are there only to lend support to our thinking. The minimum requirements – which are also the maximum requirements – are based on the patient's mental functioning in the course of the interview. As for psychotherapy, I would not be in favour of seeing it as an indication by default, because in my view it is more difficult to carry out than a psychoanalysis since it implies a particular kind of activity on the analyst's part. I think that ideally I would be in favour of psychotherapy with a programme – what I mean by that is a psychotherapy which, one hopes, would be short-term and limited to processing the principal conflict that led to the indication in the first place. If we have to accept the idea of bringing the transference into this – and at times we do indeed have to do this – I think we must proceed on the basis of a single position and a single role. Unfortunately, it is not always possible to stay on course, so that sometimes we find ourselves involved in hybrid situations that can last for some time. It is of course somewhat provocative to say that we should not use psychotherapy as an indication by default because, especially in an institutional context, we have a responsibility to offer some kind of treatment. That said, I have the impression that very few psychoanalysts are actually trained to practise psychotherapy.

J.-L. D.: I agree entirely with what you say. On the one hand, the indications for psychoanalysis *sensu stricto* can be fairly extensive – once patients give us the impression that they are capable of cathecting it in an intelligible way, once the analyst has taken into account his or her own personality traits and countertransference capacities, and once the analytical situation includes a commitment to interpret its gridlocks and the potentiality for detecting the shadow it casts.

As for psychotherapy: it is undeniable that highly psychoanalytic psychotherapies do exist in which the transference dynamics are similar to those of the analytical process. The face-to-face setting is not in itself sufficient to indicate that the idea of psychoanalysis has been abandoned. On the other hand, there is what we might call 'psychotherapeutic assistance', with a relationship that has no temporal dimension to it, one that is both essential and supportive.

In the middle of the spectrum, and to avoid the indication of psychotherapy from becoming a dumping ground, there is something I do find interesting: psychotherapies 'of limited duration', in which there is an attempt to make a virtue out of the violence done to the transference. The simple fact of modifying a fundamental element of the analytical or psychotherapeutic set-up – the indeterminate aspect of the succession of sessions – quite often reorganizes the logic of the work being done by bringing some clarification to it (including the style of interpreting). When it is over, it is always possible to look at the problem again; and I am particularly sensitive to treatments that get bogged down and seem to be never ending. It is true that, in dealing with time in this way, we must explore the relationship between action and time; it is a pity that Lacan's acted scansion, given the way it was put into practice, had for us purely negative connotations.

I must also add that other methods, such as psychodrama and group psychoanalysis, are also very interesting, not only, of course, as therapies but also as a 'preliminary' treatment.

Q: *How do you react, afterwards, to failures such as no sequel, early interruptions, etc.?*

M. de M.: Well, what is 'failure'? The fact that patients do not accept an offer of psychoanalysis is not a failure, it is the result of their freedom of action! If we speak of early interruptions then we must speak also of late ones, because the two are indissociable – an early interruption, by definition, means that there will be no late one. What I would call an early interruption is the one that takes place quite specifically when the initial resistances are set up in parallel with a stabilization of the transference. In that sense I am very close to Glover's way of thinking: there is a critical phase that we cannot afford to miss. If the patient's anxiety goes unseen, if the analyst has not managed to intervene effectively when a significant resistance meets up with a transference commitment that was ill-defined but is now becoming more stable, then there will be an early interruption.

J.-L. D.: That is a difficult question. Of course, the patient's freedom is our ultimate reference point. However, when an encounter has taken place and seemed to lead to some kind of sequel or project, it is difficult simply to push aside the word 'failure'. We cannot avoid wondering about what happened, was it inevitable or necessary, etc. It is therefore worthwhile differentiating between the 'assessment' success of the encounter, which is compatible with a no-sequel outcome, and an 'introductive' success thanks to which the wish to continue is stronger than the resistance.

There is one aspect that Piera Aulagnier considered to be particularly important: the possibility that the patient, in all other respects eager and suitable, gives the impression that he or she will use the therapeutic situation for destructive purposes. Aulagnier seemed to think that countertransference intuition has a decisive role to play in such cases.

M. de M.: That raises an almost doctrinal question about the relationship between Eros and destructiveness. It is indeed difficult to decide on a course of treatment in the type of case that you have just mentioned, but I would define such cases differently: I would say that at that point we realize that hate is the only road that love can take in order to be expressed. It's not quite the same thing.

J.-L. D.: Hate is already on the side of projection; I was talking about particularly torpid forms of masochism, of negative narcissism (A. Green).

M. de M.: Personally, I prefer to think in terms of what is called the resistance of the Id . . .

J.-L. D.: All right. But it has happened that I have disregarded my premonition, and have subsequently regretted having done so.

To come back to the question of 'failure', I would say that it comes very much to the fore in the Jean Favreau Centre when, after the patient is put on a waiting list, nothing happens as it should: the patient makes no reply when contacted, or has changed his or her mind, etc. It is therefore with respect to our demand for prediction that there is a failure, a mistake, and the need for retrospective assessment. The same applies if the intended treatment setting turns out to be inappropriate or even calamitous.

You are absolutely correct about an encounter that, by mutual agreement, is a one-off venture (with, ordinarily, 'the door remaining open' for further developments). Given that the encounter is an attempt at psychoanalytic activity and that, as we know, even a single encounter can be therapeutic (cf. Winnicott), that situation should not be looked upon as a failure, as a 'refusal' (whatever its motivation), as an encounter without an outcome. A one-off encounter could in some way be thought of as accomplishing the optimum form of analytical treatment for that particular patient at that time in his or her life: it bears witness to the invisible and above all imperceptible unity of accepting or refusing psychoanalysis.

M. de M.: I agree entirely.

Q: *Could we come back to the consultation, a topic that has not been developed in any detail?*

J.-L. D.: I have given some considerable thought to the ethical and analytical status of the consultant; this, to a great extent, was due to the situation at the time in the Jean Favreau Centre. The then medical director was 'against' consultations because, in his view, when someone gives a patient an appointment, he or she should be prepared to undertake any follow-up treatment. I have studied in some depth what, in that standpoint, is analytically well founded and also what can be seen as an improper use. My conclusion was – and this is now part of the principles upon which the centre functions – that the duality consultant/treatment analyst has symbolic value. Patients who make an appointment with the centre and go on to have treatment there must know from the outset that they will be seen by (at least) two psychoanalysts; the inter-analytical link between them, which exists from before the patient came to the centre, is a constituent part of that centre, a part that is 'already-there'. It is with respect to that reality that the patient's transference is structured. That feature is not necessarily more of an encroachment than the phenomenon of 'referring' the patient to someone in private practice.

The existence of a psychoanalyst-as-consultant is not without its drawbacks but it has also certain advantages: the consultant accepts the ambiguity of speaking in his or her own name and in that of the institution, i.e. in the name of an instituted competence, psychoanalysis. Consultants, as I have said, have the experience of a particular kind of tension between, on the one hand, the wish to take their time in order to gather more support for a decision that is all the more difficult to take in that the consultant is not the only person involved, and, on the other, their wish to call a halt 'as quickly as possible' to the procedure in order to allow the follow-up to be set in motion if such an indication is indeed made. In addition, consultants are less involved and can more easily discuss with the patient the various problems in reality that are consequent upon the treatment project. In particular, they can discuss financial issues more freely than a potential analyst in private practice can, since the latter is both judge and judged.

M. de M.: I would be somewhat more hesitant about that because the consultant's more relaxed position seems to me to depend really on the psychological structure of the patient involved.

J.-L. D.: I probably did not make myself clear. When we are in private practice, the only choice we have is to say, 'Think about it and let me know'. The consultant, on the other hand, has, given his or her position, the possibility of encouraging some explanation of the patient's resistances; that opens up the discussion in a way that does not compromise anything because, by definition, the consultant will not be the patient's future analyst. That space for discussion is made necessary because of what psychoanalysis is in relation to society. It would of course be superfluous if the analyst has a waiting list or too many clients as it is!

Q: *Although you have already answered the question, we will put it to you again, differently this time, so as to make sure that there is no fundamental divergence of opinion between you. Does refusal enter into your practice as psychoanalysts and do you consider it to be a feature of the analytical field? Would a refusal that is not based on countertransference reasons be considered to be a 'misuse of power'; when a patient is making some request for help, should we not go along with that, at least with an 'adapted' form of psychoanalytic treatment?*

J.-L. D.: What I call the 'problem situation to do with refusal' coincides with what, in objectivizing language, we would bring together under the heading non-indications and contraindications. There is of course a whole gradient from psychoanalysis to psychotherapy but, if we look at it from a subjective point of view, the person who asked for the appointment is someone who, after the initial encounter, the analyst hopes will not come back.

In cases like this, what usually happens in private practice is that analysts very diplomatically say that they are unavailable or refer to their personal limitations. Over and beyond the disagreeable nature of the situation, there is a matter of principle involved in that avoidance: it would seem that when an analyst takes the decision to refuse treatment, he or she has the impression that explaining the refusal is not a psychoanalytic act. *A contrario*, it would seem that, after a successful initial encounter, when the analyst proposes psychoanalytic treatment to the patient, he or she has the impression that the analytical process that has been initiated can be prolonged quite naturally by the adjunction of a setting in which the work will then take place. The gap between the two dimensions is erased, whereas a refusal tends to make it disproportionate. I would say that this corresponds to what divides psychoanalysis itself, between analysis in practice and 'applied' analysis: when the initial encounter ends in failure, the psychoanalyst, through and beyond his or her countertransference, can account for that failure, but it does reveal a discrepancy between the theory and practice of psychoanalysis.

Once that unease is acknowledged, it becomes more possible in a certain number of cases to put that 'refusal' to work: it can happen that the person being interviewed can get in touch with the inadequate nature of his or her request for help, and reach the point where it is he or she who refuses analysis or the analyst. Here again, that kind of work is easier to undertake with a consultant.

M. de M.: I would say that, ideally, a psychoanalytic refusal ought to exist, an original kind of work with someone for whom there is no possible indication for analysis or psychotherapy. The theoretical references for this are not for the moment very clear, but I am sure that they do exist.

J.-L. D.: We could say that the fundamental issue for that kind of work would be to succeed in dissociating, for the patient, the refusal resulting from some mismatch as regards the method from the meaning that it might well seem to take on, that of refusing the patient as a person.

M. de M.: Just as in an indication for psychotherapy, which, as I have said, must be positive, here what we propose must not be thought of in terms of 'this is not what . . .' but rather 'this is what . . .' – in other words, we should not be putting the accent on the refusal but on what we are proposing in its stead.

Q: *How is an initial encounter brought to a close?*

J.-L. D.: This is the 'decision about the setting'. At that point, what we say is not in itself psychoanalytic, but something along the lines of, 'Well, I agree with the idea of working with you; here is what I suggest . . .'. How are we to bring together this change in the level of discussion with what went before, in order to respect the heterogeneity of the realities with which we are confronted? The encounter is a practice of what is heterogeneous.

M. de M.: You are talking here of the hiatus between what structured the interview and the point at which we shift to another level, that of reality in the most basic sense of the word. The final statement, which is impossible to eradicate, constitutes a loss for the patient, the loss of what did indeed structure the whole encounter.

J.-L. D.: And the touchdown is somewhat bumpy.

M. de M.: Yes: 'It will cost you such-and-such, any missed sessions . . .'. We can come out of it in my opinion with a good response: 'You can think about it and let me know'. At that point, the loss is to some extent cancelled out by the '. . . and let me know'.

J.-L. D.: But what if you think it better not to undertake something with that person and you do not want to refer him or her to anyone else? Do you say: 'I do not happen to have any time available right now'?

M. de M.: I do not say that I do not have time when I do have time. But since I never have time, it is, alas, easy for me. [*Long silence*] A silence heavy with meaning.

J.-L. D.: There is a real evasiveness concerning the problem of refusing, as if there were something improper about it. I think we make the patient feel this, we arrange things in such a way that we meet with a refusal. I, for example, have a way of becoming unpleasant . . .

M. de M.: That's correct. We have ways of making the patient feel that this is not the right track.

J.-L. D.: There are people who are attracted by that kind of attitude – and who want you all the more, in a masochistic way.

M. de M.: So that, by accepting, you risk having to carry a cross for the next twenty years . . .

Q: *Would you say to a patient, using the appropriate words of course, that what he or she is asking for has nothing to do with psychoanalysis and that there is nothing more that you can do?*

M. de M.: Do you think that there are cases for whom it is impossible to propose anything at all? In my opinion, that is a rare occurrence.

J.-L. D.: Rare, yes, but it can happen. For example, there are all the cases in which the initial encounter reveals the fact that the request the patient is making is not his or her own but comes from some other person who is suffering because of the patient.

What is important is that the possibility of a refusal is not simply pushed aside – it may be possible to do some useful work on it.

M. de M.: It is very difficult to say to someone that he or she is not a 'human being'.

J.-L. D.: As though the 'analytical' refusal implied a refusal of the other person's humanity. . . . I think that when we uphold the idea that issues concerning failure or a possible refusal are an intrinsic part of the encounter itself, we are then in a position to break free of that equivalence.

Our idea in asking two psychoanalysts – each of whom has considerable experience of the practice of analysis and the desire to pass on what he has learned – to confront their points of view on what transpires in an initial interview, its metapsychology and the issues involved in it was to enable them to explain why they sometimes reached completely different conclusions – for example, on the indications for psychoanalysis – even though the technique that they employ in public consultations seemed to us to be quite similar.

Conclusion by Christine Bouchard and Jean-Michel Porte

Having reached the end of the discussion, we would argue that the sheer quality of the topics that they discussed and the subtleties of their points of view would have warranted a continuation – and perhaps an indefinite one – of the debate. There were of course many points of agreement on such fundamental issues as the conditions under which psychoanalysis can be initiated, the role of predictive assessment in the dynamics of the encounter, the potentiality for and limits of adjustments in technique, and what becomes of inaugural interpretations; but there were also differences of opinion as to the possibility of refusing – or of adjourning – the patient's request for help.

9 THE PROFESSION OF FERRYMAN

Considerations on the analyst's internal attitude in consultation and in referral *by Stefano Bolognini*

Commentary

Ronny Jaffè

Over the last thirty years, Italian analysts have accumulated experience in first interviews from a vast number of analytic consultations offered by the different psychoanalytic consultation services all over Italy. Thus, the initial interview as a first step towards an eventual referral to analysis has been especially carefully examined by Italian analysts. The following paper by Stefano Bolognini also links to this tradition, and he reminds the reader of the many psychoanalytic centres in Italy that offer psychoanalytic consultations.

As in other papers in this section, Bolognini focuses his attention on first interviews performed by an analyst who will not take the patient into analysis himself but will refer the patient to a colleague. Sending a patient to a colleague requires good psychoanalytical cooperation in the psychoanalytic community based on trust, appreciation, respect, mutual knowledge and a shared training. Within such a thoughtful frame, an analyst can reflect on who could be the right analyst for that specific patient.

The analyst – the ferryman – is aware, together with the patient, of a fixed time: a dense and condensed time where the analyst has to understand and deepen the request for help and where he/she is requested to give a recommendation and the name of a colleague.

Though the analyst will not take the patient into treatment, the fundamental functions of his or her curiosity, and the awareness of desire as well as fear, are strongly implicit in the first encounter with a stranger. Two strangers meet for the first time. But one stranger – the ferryman – must have a receptive and 'concave' function in order to create space for the patient and allow him to reflect on himself. This is possible if the analyst has acquired a sense of 'social responsibility' towards the other and has internalized such a psychoanalytic frame thanks to his own personal and analytical background.

Every first interview is a challenge for the analyst, as his meeting with an unknown person can also awaken unexpected and forgotten parts of him/herself. Every new encounter is an original event created by the specific unconscious identifications and projections between two minds.

In this situation the analyst must be able to oscillate between the capacity to maintain 'a sort of partial and conscious trial identification' (in Italian '*immedesimazione*') with the other, and the need to monitor his own internal feelings during the interview. There is a fundamental difference between the ordinary psychoanalytical concept of identification and 'this particular partial and conscious trial identification'; the first has an unconscious character whilst the second is based on a conscious and pre-conscious level; the analyst has to work on this pre-conscious level to avoid a splitting between conscious and unconscious.

This kind of analytical approach is defined by Bolognini as an experience and a work of the self, an emotional experience of contact with the patient and with the analyst's internal objects, which goes along with the work of the Ego of the analyst.

At the end of the paper Bolognini illustrates his theoretical paradigms through a very interesting case, showing step by step the evolving communication between the patient and himself.

Bolognini is the current president of the Italian Psychoanalytic Society and he is a training and supervising analyst. He is a member of the European Editorial Board of the *International Journal of Psychoanalysis*.

9 THE PROFESSION OF FERRYMAN

Considerations on the analyst's internal attitude in consultation and in referral[1]

Stefano Bolognini

This paper presents a very specific aspect of the analyst's professional activity: interviewing a patient who will not be taken for treatment by the consultant analyst – mostly due to lack of time, although not only for this reason – but sent on to another colleague after one or two assessment sessions aimed at clarifying the patient's suffering, needs, ways and levels of functioning, difficulties, fears, motivations, expectations and real possibilities for change. In this paper, then, 'consultation' means an encounter in which both parties, analyst and patient, have accepted the idea of devoting a fixed amount of time (which can be prolonged in the case of further necessary investigation) to the 'staging' of the request, subsequently proceeding to an assessment, technical choices and to sending the patient on to a specifically chosen, presumably definitive, analyst.

In recent years, this practice has grown in importance in our scientific-professional community for at least two main reasons: (1) the increasingly common creation of specific consultation centres, managed by members, within the centres and institutes of many psychoanalytic societies. Patients received ask initially for undifferentiated help; some of them may benefit from psychoanalysis; and (2) recognition that even the phases of the first contact and referral to a colleague are the object of theoretical-clinical study and reflection, given their importance for the patient's path towards the help requested.

This significantly concurs with the 'Working Party on Initiating Psychoanalysis' of the European Psychoanalytic Federation, set up to look into *intake issues*, which the scientific community is increasingly aware of and which are often crucial to the concrete aspects of analysts' professional activity. This phase of elaborative reflection still appears to be in its infancy, despite various study groups in recent years in numerous centres (e.g. London, Milan, Lyon and Rome) connected to the regular work of the consultation services set up by psychoanalytic centres (Jaffè, 2004b; Landoni, 2004).

[1] Bolognini, S. (2006). The profession of ferryman. *International Journal of Psycho-Analysis* 87: 25–42.

Generally, in fact, the majority of consultations still seem to be requests *ad personam*, rather than to an institutional structure, representing a partial obstacle to a common process of elaboration for psychoanalytic groups (Berti Ceroni, 2004), and a partial explanation for the relatively sparse literature on the subject. This paper proposes a number of focal points to introduce the subject, following personal choices and with no claim to any systematic treatment or rigid organization. I point out, therefore, various aspects chosen specifically as being highly characteristic, which, while not foreign to the normal work of analysis, are particularly accentuated by the consultation situation. A concluding clinical description reports passages from a consultation interview, with essential links to what has been set out in the first part.

A necessary premise: Curiosity

Society owes a lot to man's capacity to usefully exalt his instinctual fixation components which would otherwise end in neurosis or perversion. We know that our category too uses various primitive components which, suitably transformed, help our work: curiosity definitely plays a fundamental role in consultation. It combines and blends with other components (repair requests, a tendency to reconcile and recover parts of the self that are recognizable in the other, a renewal of treatment paths, a sharing of group objectives, and so on), contributing to the analyst's 'desire' and forming a useful instrument of interaction with the other's request.

During a debate among the members of the mailing list of the Italian Psychoanalytic Society, Mori (2004) wrote, referring to his personal reasons for actively participating in the 'institutional' consultations of his Florence Psychoanalytic Centre:

> What interests me especially are the possibilities I am offered through participating in this service: (a) for knowing this person; trying to understand with him his difficulties and problems; what we can do together to see them more clearly; what path can be taken to face them; and perhaps resolve some of them and tolerate others better; and (b) for dealing with everything that I feel in this encounter, my emotions, my ideas, and how it would be possible to use all this to know this person and myself better; to put this person and myself in the condition of being able to be in greater contact with himself even when he is with others.
>
> (Mori, 2004)

Even in its range and apparent generalization, this formula successfully synthesizes the happy coincidence of professional motivation and attitude, leading to a sufficiently harmonious personal solution.

In proceeding with these reflections it will be seen how the analyst's internal attitude in the consultation can be based on (and influenced by) extremely complex internal motives, some of which are not necessarily part of such a harmonious self-representative picture. To free the field of possible conciliatory idealizations, I will immediately mention how an efficient complex motive can, in certain cases, include the universal, obscure, profound 'Dionysian' aspects of the analyst, provided they are transformed and directed (not merely repressed) towards technique. I must in fact acknowledge that in some specific, though not frequent, situations, for example before rather arrogant and complacently inhuman narcissistic patients on first meeting, I know I have *converted into a project and technique* part of my personal reaction (which included the feeling of having been used badly during the interview), knowingly implementing the subtlest of vendettas: starting them off on analysis, in the clear knowledge of seeing them one day *presenting themselves with their plate of reckoning*, in painfully acquired, responsible and integrated awareness.

Curiosity is a powerful motivational motor, about whose origins much has been written, so I will not enter into the complex aspects of it. I would like to recall, though, at the bottom of the desire linked to curiosity, the unavoidable jump in facing the unknown of the first consultation. It is an obscure subterranean thrill that vaguely relates to a challenge: having accepted to meet an unknown person who might place us in difficulty, who could potentially place us before the equivalents of 'difficult' objects from our own past and who might also give back to us unexpected and unacceptable remains of ourselves, coming from who knows where: a disturbing 'who knows where' that might concern us.

In a letter dated 17 April 1921, Freud described the *unconscious* as 'the gentleman in the havelock whose face I cannot see distinctly' (Groddeck, 1977, p. 58), an exquisite representation of the *heimlich/unheimlich* that attracts and intimidates us at the same time. I would definitely include the more profound desire/fear conflict implicit in curiosity among the known stress factors of a consultation: the need for great concentration, rapid memorizing of data, a 'wide-angle' cognitive synthesis of the clinical situation, intense contact with another's experiences, operative solutions and rapid leave taking. I also believe that some corner of our minds harbours the phantasy of meeting the 'intolerable' patient, the one we cannot succeed in truly accepting and understanding: the unanalysed 'remainder' of ourselves. This underground phantasy clashes with our need to maintain sufficient and constant trust in our professional self, measuring ourselves against the reassuring 'already known', and with our megalomaniac residues that desire us to be invulnerable and intrepid explorers of the unknown. Consequently, when also sustained by desire, consultation anticipates a possibly difficult challenge with an unknown and perhaps little accessible object, *the patient we cannot understand* nor, as a consequence, help. Our curiosity is not therefore free from conflicts, fears or costs to pay, if it drives and energetically sustains us in consultation.

Naturally this is true when meeting every new patient, including those we have not excluded *a priori* from being taken on for direct treatment. However, it is probable that the idea of a presumably intense and profound encounter, in which parting and referral are declared objectives, stimulates further specific phantasies and fears: suffice to recall the possibility that the patient might feel refuted and harbour resentment, despite having accepted the consultation knowing he would not be taken on by the same analyst (Semi, 1985; Racalbuto, 2004); this is something that an instinctive part of us can certainly not ignore, despite possible technical solutions.

Phantasies, desires and fears can create a complex game of starts and stops, sudden investments and equally abrupt withdrawals, which mean too much work for the defensive ego at great economic cost.

Undoubtedly, taken as a whole and from personal experience, consultation is a stimulating professional activity, but it calls for an enormous amount of energy, much more than for a normal analytic session with a patient in treatment for some time.

Concavity and/or convexity

The analyst's initially receptive function is one of the cornerstones in our discipline: the analyst welcomes the patient's communications in much the same way he welcomes the patient into his room, starting with the consultation. So, once the person has been received respectfully and comfortably, analysts really do remain silent for quite a lot of the time, without becoming those paradoxical mute stereotypes depicted by cartoonists. This does not aim to arouse persecutory feelings nor make an idealized narcissistic inaccessibility weigh on the patient, but rather to create space, to let the other's thoughts and words find – even in an inevitably conflictual way – a path towards internal growth, and subsequently expression. I like to call this the analyst's opportunity for creating an *aspirated vacuum*.

Normally the patient notices whether the analyst's silence is a sadistic act equivalent to shutting the door in the face of a needy pilgrim, or the interpersonal equivalent of an open, welcoming place. The analyst can propose this *interpsychic place* (Bolognini, 2004b) if he really does have this inner space available, and the inclination to receive and accommodate through listening. This can be true in a concrete way too: as Semi (1985) writes, the situation of a therapist whose diary is overflowing with engagements, and – by chance – has one hour free the next week, is very different from that of another who has a lot of free time. The concept of 'inner space' is naturally understood by analysts in a mainly dynamic sense, not as static space such as a container, connected, for example, to the inescapable fact of 'having hours free', but rather as the potential freedom of a living organism that can let himself go to welcome or spastically contract according to relational developments.

In communications to a generically 'non-psychic' public it is usually effective to point out how, in requests for help and expressions of suffering, the person requesting help is soon halted by his interlocutor, who hurries to 'advise' him after a few utterances, 'telling' him what he should do, just as he (the interlocutor) had done on that particular occasion, in which . . . and so forth. This is immediately followed, like military fortifications, by an overwhelming story of his own personal experience, already organized and categorized by the interlocutor himself. The latter, unable to tolerate the inner experiential contact with suffering or with the anxiety communicated by the petitioner, stops him immediately with suggestions and advice in order to pack him up and send him back to wherever he has come from, with his baggage of pain and conflict intact, within a picture of real impermeability.

The interlocutor soon assumes a rather rigid *closed and convex form*, aimed at returning to the sender (complete with all interest, that is the premature narration of his own story, as an example) what he has not been able to contain: with all the vicissitudes of the evacuation as described in detail by the English School, especially Rosenfeld and Meltzer. Due to his training the analyst has a *capable basic attitude*, which may be described as *concave*. He is not an inert container but has a proven capacity for suspension, for waiting, for inner transformation, including the 'negative capability' that Bion (1970) spoke of, after Keats, which Giaconia *et al.* (1997) and Racalbuto (1994) come close to in the interesting formula of 'representational abstention'.

In any case it is all to do with configurations of inner attitude characterized by suspension, not by closure or spasticity. Ferro (2002a, 2002b) has given us the best descriptions of the transforming functions that can be progressively exercised by a living dynamic container. The ways and even the amount of receptive openings of the container/analyst must, however, be the object of a specific modulation if it is a consultation, as shown later. I recall that Etchegoyen, for example, emphasizes 'the prudence with which we should receive information (if not confessions) and gather data from one who, by definition, is not going to be our analysand' (1991, p. 58).

Responsibility

How did we arrive at our analytic experience? I believe that in the private safe that conserves our most intimate memories there are a number of certainties regarding the fact that our personal story, well before our professional one, would have been very different if someone had not given us the right 'tip', had not sent us to a reliable and competent analyst, if – as in the film *Sliding doors*[2] – even a series of casual circumstances had not given us a hand to hit on a fruitful growing path.

Erikson's historic description of the 'generativity vs. stagnation stage' [the seventh in a series that goes from evolutive immaturity to the highest levels of inner growth in human development (1964, pp. 266–268)], based on the care taken in creating and bringing up a new generation, provides theoretical direction. But, to be effective, it cannot be separated from the personal memory of having received direct help from someone more expert, more informed and more responsible, who directed us to analysis. The work of consultation, with an important mandate of a superegoistic or ideal stamp, can be arrived at (and I hope it is very clear that I do not belittle, *a priori* or from preconceived ideas, either of these). However, I believe that – subject to due respect for the conscious separateness and differentiation between analyst and patient – the best fuel for our 'motivational motor' is the very human memories of ourselves, and in some cases of our analytic brothers and sisters, in our search for a path, a useful object, a competent interlocutor who truly offered us a hand in the darkness. That said, the social responsibility analysts bear, which goes beyond our community as single individuals and subjects, should be recognized: analysts represent at least a category, and in certain instances also a precise institution, the one of psychoanalytic belonging – local, national and international. This strengthens analysts' ethical standards as much as it credits and sustains our community as objective confirmation of achieved professional credibility and competence. Once again, I am referring specifically, above all, to analysts' internal attitude; it would be misleading to consider this independently from these institutional premises.

Certainly, one can unauthentically camouflage and hide behind institutional belonging, 'dressing as an analyst', and a pathological attitude of this type needs no comment. On the other hand, I believe that the system of values and rules common to a group or psychoanalytic institution often plays an immediately fundamental and responsibilizing role during consultation, and that it is often perceived in a precise way also by the patient. This system of values and rules helps to positively structure the analyst's 'working ego' (Fliess, 1942), making him more articulate and complex, adding group responsibility to the more strictly individual one. Schafer's (1983) classic subsequent definitions of 'second self' and 'working super-ego' are essentially quite similar, but the first appears terminologically too dated compared to recent developments of the concept of self. These developments propose

[2] The film *Sliding Doors* (1998, director: Peter Howitt, with Gwyneth Paltrow and John Lynch) depicts a young woman taking the London underground. In a subsequent scene, in fact parallel and alternative to the first, the same young woman does not succeed in taking the same tube, by a fraction of a second. So two destinies of the same person start. If she had taken that train, what would have happened? Consequently, there are two possible stories: one finishes well, with a new boyfriend; the other finishes badly, in a striking narrative experiment.

more primitive and intimate dimensions compared to the 'third' and to the professional 'ensemble', already implicitly present to some degree in the idea of referral.

Empathy and identification

Even if necessarily brief, the consultation certainly does not spare the analyst from the possibilities, vicissitudes and risks of the countertransferential experience. Indeed, I believe the degree of exposure is particularly high, because of the expectations, phantasies and tensions that precede the encounter and that are concentrated in it. Regarding this, Jaffè (2004b) rightly refers to Green's (2005) conception of 'pretransference'. Very often, the consultation, apart from the difficulties and reticences, is an event of potentially high investment for both interlocutors. It would be as though the expectation of knowing each other was charged with an unconscious accumulation of libido and idealizations (as well as fears). These would be ready to be discharged and/or invested in some way on the object at the agreed time: sometimes with the delicacy and precision of spaceships docking in space; at others, with the effects of a real collision. As analysts we cannot 'ignore how much an *original* event is created in every new encounter' (Racalbuto, 2004), giving rise to a 'complex network of psychic neo-births', in a complex event with a high rate of partially shared regression. Consequently, important projective attributions and passages of un-worked-through elements, via the two mental sets of apparatus, often occur *immediately*, with sudden invasions and unconscious identifications, at the very threshold of the consulting room.

These events are well known to analysts, who tend to remain openly perceptive with regard to their sensations, associations, memories and affects right from the first moment of an encounter, in order to get to know the other without losing their sense of self and their own borders. Unlike certain psychiatrists and almost all neurologists, analysts do not limit themselves to observing patients from the outside, noting their behaviours, dysfunctions, logical inconsistencies, apparent moods and so on. They deepen their recognition of the other by means of progressive empathetic inner contact with the other's subjectivity, on the one hand, and by means of constant and customary monitoring of their own internal conditions during the exchange, on the other.

The topic level radically distinguishes empathy from identification – conscious and preconscious in the first case, classically unconscious in the second (Bolognini, 2001, 2004a). Any difficulty in entering the preconscious can result in a clean split between the conscious and the unconscious experience, thus destined to be lost or acted out. In consultation, analysts quickly enter an *experience of the self* that allows them to perceive and feel others and their worlds, passing through (for example): bright or pale colours; hot or cold temperatures; stable or changeable climates; close or faraway distances; soft or rough contacts; quick or slowed-down rhythms; delicate or violent styles; or fluidity or dryness. What I want to point out are the *direct experiential aspects connected to the contact and passage*. This part of analysts' daily work can be called *work with the self* (Bolognini, 1991, 2004a). In this experiential phase, analysts who are not balanced can lose themselves, through reaction, contagion or perversion; their capacity for representing, remembering, associating and naming can be lost. Analysts can *identify* with the other, and for this reason a *second consultation encounter* is often necessary. This allows them to recover separateness, thought and elaboration with regards to violent or even subtly pervasive collisions.

I certainly do not denigrate the analyst's *work of the ego*. I believe it is absolutely necessary in consultation in order to build a sufficiently realistic representation of a patient's personality, psychic functioning, longitudinal evolutions, needs and possibilities for change. The encounter must not merely be 'tasted', but also thought out in its complexity and prospects. To favour work with the ego or with the self, in analytic work as in consultation, seems to me to be a false problem. It will be an issue of quantity and doses, but it is clear that one can no longer theoretically reason in terms of splitting, as if paradoxically we were listening to talk about what was necessary to make a car: an engine or the *bodywork*.

Slightly more idealistically, it is evident today that there is greater historic continuity and some opportunities for progressive integration between the theoretical-clinical proposals of ego-psychoanalysis and the acquisitions (European as much as American) of the self. Such integrations are in progress between: the Oedipal or the pre-Oedipal focus; the emphasis on representation and emphasis on experiential recovery; and the relative priorities of the intrapsychic and interpsychic. The present age is one of painful anti-narcissistic recognition of complexity, and since Winnicott onwards we have not been able to entrench ourselves securely inside a single castle, avoiding the intermediate areas also in a scientific sense. The North American influence of Mitchell and Aron (1999), Ogden (1994, 2002) and Pine (1998), the post-Freudian, Winnicottian and British neo-Kleinian developments, the wide-ranging and articulated theoretical recognitions of an entire recent generation in Italy, and even the integrative explorations of highly classical French psychoanalysis (Squitieri, 2002), are all unequivocal signs of a recently initiated new integrative process that must surely have suffused and progressive repercussions on the analyst's attitude in the session and in the consultation.

A task has been embarked upon of widening perspectives, connections between theoretical segments, and integrative harmonizing of knowledge and technical possibilities, even in the nuclear distinctions of the different models. So I like to portray contemporary analysts in consultation as sufficiently suspended to experiment with the shared experience of their selves, which 'feel' and perceive. In a similar way, they experiment with the necessary work of their minds, which associate, connect, elaborate in a secondary moment, recognize patients' historic, functional and dysfunctional profiles, and think of something new and forward-looking for them. And it cannot be denied that each patient will arouse complex operations on different levels of depth in the analyst. I believe that in consultation all this is verified, usually, in a particularly accentuated and intense manner, which contributes to the special laboriousness and arduousness of this specific, and very demanding, clinical activity.

Contacting without seducing; restoring without binding

There are ethics and aesthetics associated with 'bridge-functions', the role of 'ferryman' and 'intermediary', the role of *transitory* rather than transitional *object*, capable of referral to another more decisive object in a path from consultation to finally being taken on by another colleague. The aesthetics of these functions and figures is connected in films, in narrative and generally in contemporary myths to a knowingly minimalist, partial and temporary dimension. It can be represented by the humble yet wise boatman who deeply inspires Siddhartha and directs his path, or by the old boxing instructor of a little-known gym in the Bronx who is the first humanly credible interlocutor for the young black delinquent with no family and who then initiates him into the sport and to personal redemption, knowing from the beginning that he must soon renounce sharing the glory of the champion, who other more prestigious trainers will shape. Signs of a moving aesthetics are found in many figures of *necessary, decisive and transitory secondary characters* since this is based in some way on a previous renunciation, on a resigned and aware status of being a minor and momentary character, who moves us for the pain deriving from his narcissistic minimalism. This 'touching' aspect already aesthetically contains an intrinsic 'prize for him/her', in the narcissistic economy of the narrated story, because it forms the basis for the subject's/public's solidarity towards this character, and towards the inner parts of the self that it represents. This role is true compensation for the ferryman's wounded pride, an object destined for fruition and abandonment, an object that 'will be left behind'.

I cite these literary *topoi* because they form a backdrop to the problem of the analyst's narcissistic vicissitudes in consultation. I am referring, for example, to what Semi states regarding 'our *standing aside* to let the patient express himself as best he can' (1985, p. 116), intentionally frustrating our narcissism in favour of the patient, with the neutrality that is truly a result of curiosity, willingness and attention. I am also referring to: Balint's '*unobtrusive analyst*' (1968, my italics), who sacrifices his centrality; Bonaminio's declaration of the risk of '*subterranean erosion, of narcissistic origin on the part of the analyst, of the patient's space*' (2003, p. 45, my italics); and the beautiful image proposed by Chianese of '*exiting the stage*' (1997, my italics), for the analyst who knows how to conclude treatment with a patient humbly. More specifically, I cite Montani (2004), played out in the constant awareness of the *first and last meeting* that contemplates its own dissolution. Referring to the consultation interview in the services of the centre, Montani points out the intrinsic constant of the 'suffering that the analyst has to experience during that encounter due to the inability to take complete charge of its initial and conclusive nature', and states that 'the element of loss (loss of the other) analysts have to face during this particular "first interview" – in which, above all, they make a paradoxical gift of their time – obliges them to depend on ethics in order to sustain and understand it'. Thus, basic *ethics* are necessary for the analyst, together with the self-repairing *aesthetics* I have briefly mentioned.

It is not difficult for me to link these aspects to the fundamental capacity, lacking in so many parents, of renouncing, while continuing to provide affection and support, being the fixed point from a certain moment onwards, the status of 'owner' of their children's lives. In my work on erotic and amorous transferences (Bolognini, 1994), I mentioned the highly symbolic moments of the father accompanying and 'handing over' the bride at the altar, and the suitable narcissistic tribute provided, in the rite of the first waltz, by the 'admiring' and confirming father to his 'debutant' daughter, ceding his place to her future companion. Egon Molinari (personal communication) reported a custom still practised in Albania at the beginning of the 20th century that held similar symbolic values for men in the representation and working through of the Oedipal process. Everyone at the wedding (bride and groom, witnesses, guests) took part in the rite, except for the groom's mother, who stayed at home. Halfway through the ceremony, the groom and witnesses went to the bride's house and the groom slapped her several times in front of his witnesses, signifying the definite and guaranteed break with the bond of dependence. After this, everyone (including the repudiated mother) returned to the ceremony, which could now be 'truly' carried out, thanks to the spectacular renunciation of the previous bond.

We are in the sphere of renunciation and mourning, which is easier for those who have been able to effect a bearable landing, rather than a traumatic collision, during the waning of Oedipus (Kavaler-Adler, 1992). How these arduous Oedipal passages are faced *also* depends on how the separations and mournings in the preceding relational phases were experienced. A capacity for depression and working through separation (strengthened by the habit of clinical *fort-da*) are therefore the necessary bases for being able to carry out sufficiently serenely the work of consultation, which involves a highly concentrated and intense experience of meeting, contact and leaving. Often, in the second part of a deeply lived consultation, it is common to think along the lines: 'How can I send him on to a colleague? *I* would be the right analyst for this patient!!!' Let us remember Molinari's story, and accompany 'our', though now no longer 'our' patient, to the consulting room of our colleague, who will be able to help the subject after us.

In consultation, analysts generally allow patients to perceive the potentials of the analytic encounter through the overall quality of their listening, their recognition, and sometimes even a certain degree of restitution. This occurs in a balanced, unsaturated and discreet way, with a minimum amount of habituation necessary for being ready for the next passages, directed towards another and more long-lasting reference object. In consultation, the analyst avoids *flirting*, while he allows the prospectives of the analytic work to be perceived through a real microexperience of listening and understanding. This *experiential tasting* is useful for giving the patient an idea of what he might receive, but the expert analyst avoids going beyond a certain threshold.

Klauber maintained that some analysts begin analysis even before finishing the first hour of consultation. He did not approve of this way of proceeding, though he believed it useful to make some trial interpretations during the interview, to test the patient's capacity to make use of them. In consultation:

> The consultant cannot and should not conduct a miniature analysis. If he did, it would either overwhelm the patient or attach him too much to his person at the expense of the smooth evolution of the transference to his eventual analyst. But successful consultation can offer enough tentative explanation and interpretation to give the patient a glimpse of the emotional and intellectual processes involved without unduly seducing him.
>
> (Klauber, 1981, p. 143, and also in this volume p. 63)

This last point is absolutely crucial for not complicating the patient's life in detaching himself from the consultant, and for not leaving too idealized a mark inside him, which would be troublesome for his future definitive analysis. Despite this, Klauber, in a very balanced way, agrees that the analyst should give a positive impression in consultation so that he can be trusted as a 'sender on', as well as a possible referent in case of future difficulties.

I agree with this observation: the consultant must appear a reliable 'ferryman', and personally I harbour much gratitude towards those older and more influential colleagues who sent me patients during my first years of professional practice, with the protection and credit deriving from their trustworthiness and experience, which – and this is the point! – had not escaped their patients' attention.

The community of colleagues

Semi (1985) states that whoever works in a good group, with collaborative colleagues he respects, has a clear idea about the real possibilities of treatment for a patient, and it is essential to be aware of these possibilities. Those who work in a group torn by internecine struggle or envy, will instead have a disturbed image of the field, and of what can be offered. I will not dwell on this extremely important theme. I only want to point out that the institutional context in which we are trained and continue to work is decisive for creating basic trust in the possibilities – precisely – of *entrusting* the patient to someone else after consultation, and for having adequate reciprocal knowledge that allows specific and targeted referrals of *particular patients to particular colleagues.*

It is difficult to trust unknown colleagues, and if this might appear obvious I would like to point out that in our field, apart from the valuable members' roster, one gets to know colleagues above all through work done together: the institutional 'siblings' during one's training years, then active participation in the centres (especially presenting and discussing clinical experiences), in multiple seminar work groups, or similar occasions. Colleagues we have never heard utter a word, or who do not participate in scientific-professional exchanges, will not easily inspire our trust and allow us to send them patients in full awareness of what we are doing.

Consultation connects us with a non-bureaucratic and nominal 'network'; it places us in a condition of continual work and representation among ourselves. Jaffè (2004a) has written, 'The consultation service, in my opinion, is a common good for everyone . . . thanks to its institutional nature'. I fully agree with this statement and believe that its function and importance should be understood and valued in those terms.

Referral

The referral phase is extremely delicate due to its intrinsic conditions of separating, and it cannot always be realistically effected with a reasonable degree of success. Racalbuto stresses that:

> If a patient arrives in consultation who cannot, due to his dual narcissistic attitude, accept that the analyst acts the 'third', connecting between two, between the 'here and now' and the 'there and then', it will be more difficult to propose another colleague. How can one propose 'somewhere else' if he needs to be accepted, if it is probable that he will live the implicit affirmation 'I will not treat him' as an unacceptable rejection (Semi, 1985).
>
> (Racalbuto, 2004)

The complexity and delicacy of the narcissistic aspect involved in this procedural phase are evident.

As in many other problem areas in our practice, it is very difficult to set out any general firm guidelines, so analysts must constantly strive to perceive their internal conditions and the other's deepest movements, monitor their future narcissistic equilibrium, and be aware of the vicissitudes of the ephemeral, but powerfully intense, relationship triggered by the consultation.

I would also like to mention a special issue of the referral technique. It has been discussed whether it is preferable to refer a patient, after consultation, to more than one colleague (so that he has more names from which to choose) or only to one, in a certain sense chosen for him by us. Different opinions on this point exist, as both hypotheses have advantages and disadvantages. Liberman (1972) favours providing just one name, so that the patient does not get the idea that he is the one to examine possible analysts. Etchegoyen thinks likewise, adding the colourful anecdote of various interviews with patients equipped with lists, who treated him like someone choosing personnel, adding parenthetically, 'and, even worse, they did so confident of their great psychological ability!' (1991, p. 58). Etchegoyen prefers to leave the possibility open that the patient will return to consult him if he did not like the proposed interlocutor. I would add that patients are often comforted by the idea that the consultation analyst has made a specific choice for them after their interview, and that in that specifically directed choice there is a special phantasy of carefully and attentively conceiving a personalized project. However, it is true that a wider choice avoids the risks of 'combinations' or comparisons; it allows the patient a decent decisional margin; it increases the possibility of finding a colleague who is free; and it provides an institutional background to the whole project. The creation of a *super-personal phantasm* (the society, or group of colleagues) inspires an important portion of *institutional transference* which, at the beginning of an analytic path, assumes a reassuring containing and founding value.

In short, I think that the choice between a specific or a slightly broader referral can be made each time on the basis of the patient's individual characteristics and conditions. As an example, patients that are tendentially ocnophile, dependent or inclined to support, would probably prefer just one name; philobatics, autonomists and narcissists like at least three (and will, as Etchegoyen says, go and 'examine'). However, I believe that in every case patients perceive whether the referral is the result of reflection or merely of routine sorting, and whether the relationship between the referrer and the colleagues chosen is merely bureaucratic or based on significant and pertinent reciprocal professional knowledge.

Clinical material: A taxing consultation

As an example, I report here a recent consultation. I deliberately use a *subjective* style for my narration in order better to render the sensations and atmosphere of the interview, and to allow the reader to travel the inner paths of the analyst at work. Specific and personal references to the environmental context are an integral part of the phantasy-associative fabric shared during the dialogue, in addition to, and to a greater extent than, the external reality of which the two interlocutors are part. Consequently, the references are faithfully reported as being important to the development of the consultation.

My encounter with Mino, a 21-year-old student who moved to Bologna from the south of Italy in order to go to university, begins with two methodological encumbrances. First, the summer holidays are about to start, and due to fatigue accumulated during previous months, I make a few errors – I agree to see him, in fact, at his family's request and not his, something that theoretically should not be done. Second, I already know that I cannot take him for treatment, and tell his parents I could only see him for a consultation. I do not know whether they pass this information on to him: I believe it to be timely and correct to do so. Some of my patients are already on holiday, so I have a number of hours free, and I am happy to see a new patient and possibly to be able to refer him to another colleague.

Mino is a *punkabbestia*[3]. He lets me know this without saying a word. He simply arrives at the front door with a pit-bull (which he hands over to a girl who looks just like he does). He presented himself with hair in a spiky crest; ears and nose with a variety of piercings; long, baggy trousers, the crotch level with his knees, skater-style, dragging along the ground; a mediaeval bag of dark cloth slung over one shoulder, traveller-style; and a dark, crumpled shirt. In short, very, very 'alternative', parading a sense of superiority and self-sufficiency; staring diffident eyes. I can avow that his personal hygiene is decidedly lacking; he gives off a terrible rancid smell, different from the traditional psychiatric one. In a word, I find myself making the same observations and considerations as when I worked 'in psychiatry'. From first glance he gives the idea of a bizarre object, and signals – I don't know how – that this hypermanifest bizarreness must not be talked about.

The premises are not the best for a consultation. In fact, he expresses fundamental doubts about this interview, in a sufficient way and with the classic formula: 'My parents told me to come here'. However, he has in fact arrived, and when I ask if he wants to have an interview he accepts in a way that does not displease me: 'Well, since we're here . . .'. And so we start.

In fact, I do not know how to take him. If I ask him how old he is, by way of a beginning, I might sound like a police officer. I could remain silent, but I feel that that is not right; he has already done a lot in arriving here and I must help him start. I follow my *curiosity*, and ask him what he does.

He assumes a busily important air and answers, 'I'm studying at DAMS [the faculty for performing arts and music]'. (He pauses, not for a short time, resulting in my corresponding protracted tranquil wait . . . *then air fills the vacuum.*) 'I . . . am working on . . . *iconic creativity*.' In the face of my questioning expression (I have no idea what 'iconic creativity' is, but I tread cautiously because today these fields contain a bit of everything), he opens up a bit: 'It's

[3] The *punkabbestia* are a widespread youth phenomenon in Italy (and possibly elsewhere). They are girls and boys dressed as I have described, who leave home and their towns with just one fixed companion: their dog. Conjunction of 'punk' with bestia (animal, beast) gives *punkabbestia*. In actual fact, they then form groups, and their dogs stay together but do not form packs, because they each depend on their individual owner.

. . . *eidetic research*, that is . . . creating unusual mental images, through methods . . .'.

For an instant, I imagine a sort of laboratory halfway between the psychophysiology of perception and Gestalt, but instead he gives more information, this time with an air of partial surrender. 'You see . . . you use various substances . . . you smoke joints, then I lie on my bed . . . and sometimes I see images . . .'.

Little by little, the bleak reality emerges: this boy smokes dope from morning to evening and has withdrawn his investments in the real world. He has not taken an exam for two years; his parents know very little about his life so far from home; they continue to maintain him, hoping for the best.

I note that there is an insidious problem in the air – a problem of category. This is not just a consultation between patient X and Dr Bolognini; two classes are being compared, in a certain sense opposing each other: the *punkabbestia* and the psychoanalysts. These are two subcategories, with strongly specific and divergent characteristics, of the 'children' and 'parents' classes.

The *punkabbestia* try actively and narcissistically to sustain an idea of themselves as intentionally 'eccentric' in order to deny an original experience of decentring and exclusion. They avoid depression with a narcissistic overinvestment in an idealized self-sufficient image, and maybe project the needy and dependent self on to the dog, which follows them like a shadow and depends totally on them. Their *piercings* condense a complex representation that I will not dwell on here.

I will only say that our consultation is really difficult, because the patient is split between suffering and need, and is ready to release the rejection device: Pinocchio's blows to Jiminy Cricket's superego. Inside myself, two corresponding reactive replies are equally ready to burst forth (*countertransference*).

The first, which mirrors his, is that of shutting down in my turn and of taking up a position on the axiom of a principle. If he does not ask, and says he does not need anything, I will not listen to him any more. I will not propose anything and I will send him away. To strengthen this, I also think that he will not pay me. I could swear he has not brought the money, so at least I will not waste time and energy. If, one day, he comes into contact with his needs, then he will be the one to ask. How stupid of me not to have held to the classic precept by which you do not accept appointments made by third parties.

The second: this patient has made a challenge, a narcissistic challenge inside the consultation, making me feel like a hotel waiter who has brought breakfast to the wrong room and who should excuse himself and withdraw, tray in hand. No! I must hand over this 'breakfast' at all costs (frustration of the *analyst's omnipotence*).

Inside myself, an argument is brewing between two obstinate children; I realize this, and this gives me the opportunity to take time and to create space within myself and between ourselves. Who or what is he opposing in this moment? Perhaps me as a paternal equivalent charged with unbearable feelings of Oedipal rivalry and struggle for power? I find it difficult to picture the patient thus richly structured, and connect up with the more serious and disturbing sensations (*analysis with the self*) that he has transmitted to me from the very first moment.

While I think the beginning of this consultation contains, repeats and actualizes early polemics and drama, my phantasy instead leads me towards the reports of mothers relating their newborn's immediate refusal to attach to the breast. This refusal leaves neonatologists and early development stage psychologists full of doubt and confusion, and sometimes raises disquieting hypotheses about the internal attitude with which, quite unconsciously, the child has been contained and then welcomed into the world by the mother. (I have in mind, for example, 1960s super-8 home movies collected by Balconi [1986], now unfortunately lost, in which newborns and breastfed babies were seen to be held in quite different ways. Follow-up films of the 1970s showed the same children, with their respective development towards health or autism.)

I do not think I can interpret what is happening in this way, nor reconstruct his story in these terms (*analysis with the ego*). I am only reporting the associations and configurations that help me, at this moment, give a temporary meaning to what is happening, and which in fact make this encounter liveable for me. Mino, meanwhile, explains, at my gentle prodding, how both parents, coupled together in his picture, are good people, but wrong to worry about him; it's their problem, they should leave him in peace. He reveals a rather evacuative attitude; one senses he is prickly. There is tension in his cutting the subject short, even if he wants to show coherence with himself. Naturally, I think he is telling me, between the lines, to mind my own business, so I shift my interest on to something less specific and less likely to create conflict, and ask him about his village.

He allows himself an amused and vaguely affectionate expression: 'Oh, it's nice! . . . I'm going in August; my friends are there . . .'. Friends belong to a narcissistically less 'other' class. They are the cloned confirmation of the self. They form a more narcissistic and therefore more bearable object-'environment', which allows him to live with a certain amount of affection without feeling himself at war (as happens instead with distinct non-self-objects, from which he wants nothing). The village had got small for him because 'there's nothing there', but he talks about it with pleasure, though with a superior tone.

I feel a partial opening of the libidinal channels (still analysis with the self); we are a little more relaxed; a few colourful expressions succeed in escaping the mesh of withdrawal and denial. I then ask him about the move from his village to Bologna, trying to seem a little more Bolognese than analyst, and how he had got on after his arrival here three years ago. He describes his great expectations and the real difficulties of adapting (the passage from village/home to university city/school comes to mind). Then the gradual losing of himself in what I would call the 'Land of Toys' (of *Pinocchio*) in Bologna, a bit like Barcelona or Berlin for students from the south. These students arrive full of exciting illusions: never-ending nights, clubs, dope, 'alternative' groups, the friends of Lampwick, and so on. Bologna 'offers' too much.

Home, village and family are much more than 1,000 miles away, they are in another dimension. For some minutes, I seem to be with him (*empathy without identification*) in his tale, going about at night from one packed drinking haunt to another in the university district. The people, the noise, the smoke and tables full of glasses, the guitar, the sax and the double bass that raise the volume; and then the Moroccan, outside, who gives you the other 'smoke'. Then off to the disco where you feel like a god with two tabs and stroboscopic lights – light–dark–light–dark, you're out of your mind, and if tomorrow you stay in bed all day well that's just fine, because in the evening you're out again – and so it goes on.

I know these paths and exciting, confused configurations very well. They have nothing to do with discovering the other, or the 'Other', but with the narcissistic 'Alien' imbued with omnipotence and with self-sufficient anti-object polemics, which progressively comes to power in the inner world, bearing the stamp of psychosis. I have already had many consultations like this one, and I now orient myself quite well, even though I end up every time experiencing the immersion with specific differences. Now I think I can give him a hand, *from inside*, to help him 'return home' in a figurative sense.

To cut a long story short: after about 20 minutes of assisting inner contact, the pseudo-intellectual false self gradually leaves room for the *lost* boy. Then it is easy for me to cautiously reconnect with his painful points: his difficulty in being alone; in studying; in sleeping; in eating; in having not 'normal' but simply liveable rhythms. He appears needy and confused, so I propose the possibility of 'putting his drawers in order' and recovering his times and functions. However, he would have to accept the opportunity of working with a colleague of mine who really would be able to help him (I have a very calm and accepting candidate in mind, who would not incite him to rebel).

He seems a little shocked by the momentary re-meeting with a self that he had practically knocked senseless and locked in the cellar, or to a small extent projected on to his dog. I encourage him, telling him frankly that in my opinion he could feel better if he decided to deal with his inner conditions. He makes a few remarks about structuring situations, like 'returning to school' and so on. He takes the name of the colleague and says he will go, appearing, at the moment, tolerably defeated as an 'eidetic researcher' and perhaps retrievable as a possible patient. I think to myself though that it is necessary to see the next encounter, when desperation on the one side, and narcissist-autonomist defences on the other, will have fully engaged again.

He is ashamed to say he has not brought the money; he insists he will bring it tomorrow (not today because he has already used his bank card); we agree and he leaves. The next day, he punctually hands over the money; I thank him but do not add anything, with the feeling that for the moment whatever could have been done has been done. I have many doubts about the relationships of force within him, even if, there and then, the impression is not negative. He appears to communicate some sort of continuity with the day before.

Now, let's see whether he presents to my colleague.

References

Balconi, C. (1986). Communication to the Bologna Psychoanalytic Centre, March 1986.

Balint, M. (1968). *The Basic Fault: Therapeutic Aspects of Regression.* London: Tavistock.

Berti Ceroni, G. (2004). Opening address. Presented at: L'assetto mentale dello psicoanalista nella consultazione [The analyst's mental attitude in consultation], Milan, 8–10 October 2004.

Bion, W. R. (1970). *Attention and Interpretation: A Scientific Approach to Insight in Psychoanalysis and Groups.* London: Tavistock, 144 pp.

Bolognini, S. (1991). *Gli affetti dell'analista: Analisi con l'io e analisi col sé* [*The analyst's affects: Analysis with the ego and analysis with the self*]. *Rivista di Psicoanalisi* 37: 339–371.

Bolognini, S. (1994). Transference: Erotized, erotic, loving, affectionate. *International Journal of Psycho-Analysis* 75: 73–86.

Bolognini, S. (2001). Empathy and the unconscious. *Psychoanalytic Quarterly* 70: 447–473.

Bolognini, S. (2004a). *Psychoanalytic Empathy* (M. Garfield, translator). London: Free Association Books, 191 pp. [*L'empatia psicoanalitica.* Turin: Bollati Boringhieri, 2002.]

Bolognini, S. (2004b). Intrapsychic-interpsychic. *International Journal of Psycho-Analysis* 85: 337–357.

Bonaminio, V. (2003). La persona dell'analista: Interpretare, non-interpretare e controtransfert [The person of the analyst: Interpreting, non-interpreting and countertransference]. In: Fabozzi, P. (ed.), *Forme dell'interpretare. Nuove prospettive nella teoria e nella clinica psicoanalitica* [*Forms of Interpretation. New Perspectives in Psychoanalytic Theory and Practice*], p. 45. Milan: Franco Angeli.

Chianese, D. (1997). *Costruzioni e campo analitico: Storia, scene e destino* [*Constructions and the Analytic Field: History, Setting and Outcome*]. Rome: Borla.

Erikson, E. H. (1964). *Childhood and Society*, 2nd edition. New York: Norton.

Etchegoyen, H. (1991). *The Fundamentals of Psychoanalytic Technique.* London: Karnac, 863 pp. [*Los fundamentos de la técnica psicoanalítica.* Buenos Aires: Amorrortu, 1986.]

Ferro, A. (2002a). *Seeds of Illness, Seeds of Recovery: The Genesis of Suffering and the Role of Psychoanalysis* (P. Slotkin, translator). Birksted-Breen, D. (ed.). New Library of Psychoanalysis. Hove: Routledge.

Ferro, A. (2002b). Superego transformations through the analyst's capacity for reverie. *Psychoanalytic Quarterly* 71: 477–501.

Fliess, R. (1942). The metapsychology of the analyst. *Psychoanalytic Quarterly* 11: 211–227.

Giaconia, G., Pellizzari, G., Rossi, P. (1997). *Nuovi fondamenti per la tecnica psicoanalitica* [*New Foundations for Psychoanalytic Technique*]. Rome: Borla, 208 pp.

Green, A. (2005). *Key Ideas for a Contemporary Psychoanalysis: Misrecognition and Recognition of the Unconscious.* Birksted-Breen, D. (ed.). New Library of Psychoanalysis.

Hove: Routledge, 312 pp. [*Idées directrices pour une psychanalyse contemporaine: Méconaissance et reconaissance de l'inconscient.* Paris: PUF, 2002.]
Groddeck, G. (1977). *The Meaning of Illness: Selected Psychoanalytic Writings, Including Correspondence with Freud.* London: Hogarth. (International Psychoanalytical Library, No. 105). [Freud, S., Groddeck, G. (1973). *Carteggio* [*Correspondence*], *1917–1934*, L. Schwarz, translator. Milan: Adelphi.]
Jaffè, R. (2004a). Contribution to the SPI mailing list, March.
Jaffè, R. (2004b). *Il centro di consultazione* [*The consultation centre*]. Paper presented at: L'assetto mentale dello psicoanalista nella consultazione [The analyst's mental attitude in consultation], Milan, 8–10 October.
Kavaler-Adler, S. (1992). Mourning and erotic transference. *International Journal of Psycho-Analysis* 73: 527–540.
Klauber, J. (1981). *Difficulties in the Analytic Encounter.* New York: Aronson.
Landoni, G. (2004). *Il malato immaginario* [*The Imaginary Invalid*]. Paper presented at: L'assetto mentale dello psicoanalista nella consultazione [The analyst's mental attitude in consultation], Milan, 8–10 October.
Liberman, D. (1972). Evaluación de las entrevistas diagnósticas previas a la iniciación de los tratamientos analíiticos. Criterios diagnósticos y esquemas referenciales [Evaluation of diagnostic interviews, before analytical treatments. Diagnostic criteria and referential patterns]. *Rivista Italiana di Psicoanalisi* 39: 461–488.
Mitchell, S. A., Aron, L. (eds). (1999). *Relational Psychoanalysis – The Emergence of a Tradition.* (Relational Perspectives Book Series, Vol. 14.) Hillsdale, NJ: Analytic Press, 536 pp. [*Psicoanalisi Relazionale.* Turin: Bollati Boringhieri, 2002.]
Montani, L. (2004). Contribution to the SPI mailing list, March.
Mori, F. (2004). Contribution to the SPI mailing list, March.
Ogden, T. H. (1994). *Subjects of Analysis.* Northvale, NJ: Aronson.
Ogden, T. H. (2002). A new reading of the origins of object-relations theory. *International Journal of Psycho-Analysis* 83: 767–782.
Pine, F. (1998). *Diversity and Direction in Psychoanalytic Technique.* New York: Other Press, 242 pp.
Racalbuto, A. (1994). *Tra il fare e il dire. L'esperienza dell'inconscio e del non verbale in psicoanalis* [*Between Doing and Saying. The Experience of the Unconscious and the Non-verbal in Psychoanalysis*]. Milan: Cortina, 187 pp. (Collana di psicologia clinica e psicoterapia.)
Racalbuto, A. (2004). *La consultazione in psicoanalisi e i suoi 'luoghi': Un lavoro di confine* [*Consultation in Psychoanalysis and Its 'Places': Work on the Frontiers*]. Paper presented at: L'assetto mentale dello psicoanalista nella consultazione [The analyst's mental attitude in consultation], Milan, 8–10 October.
Schafer, R. (1983). *The Analytic Attitude.* New York: Basic Books, 316 pp. [*L'atteggiamento analitico.* Milan: Feltrinelli, 1984.]
Semi, A. A. (1985). *Tecnica del colloquio* [*Interview Technique*]. Milan: Cortina, 116 pp.
Squitieri, G. (2002). Tra trasformazione e rappresentazione: Note sul 62° congresso degli psicoanalisti di lingua francese [Between transformation and representation: Notes on the 62nd congress of French-speaking psychoanalysts]. *Rivista di Psicoanalisi* 48: 799–812.

Part III

THE ANALYST'S STRUGGLE WITH THE EXPERIENCE OF A FIRST MEETING

III THE ANALYST'S STRUGGLE WITH THE EXPERIENCE OF A FIRST MEETING

Introduction

Mette Møller

Understanding the first interview as a two-person process is the logical consequence of developments in psychoanalysis towards a relationship psychology. In the following section the shift from assessing the 'analysability of the patient' towards rather an evaluation of the way in which the patient and the analyst use the analytic interaction in the interview is the central focus.

Members of the WPIP have found over the last seven years of participating in the clinical workshops on initial interviews at EPF conferences, that our attitude to the first interview and the way we work with the presented clinical material has changed. Although we started out treating 'the first interview' as the last bastion for the illusion of the possibility of making an objective evaluation, over the years we realized that it was necessary to actually integrate the theoretical conviction shared by most of us: that is, that a forceful transference–countertransference field unfolds from the first contact, and that this matrix of interaction is what the interviewer must try to contain, use and understand in order to eventually reach a recommendation for analysis.

The following section presents papers from five very different authors, who not only all see the first meeting as a direct plunge into a powerful, dynamic interaction, but who also demonstrate ways to use it. The papers show, each in their own individual way, how an analytic consultation must be conceptualized as something quite far from an assessment of the patients' analysability: the meeting is rather seen as an analytic dialogue with two engaged participants. What also emanates from the different papers is that during the last decades a parallel development in the way first interviews are understood has taken place in the different psychoanalytic traditions and subcultures. This sameness found in diversity strengthens the view that there is common ground in psychoanalysis.

The section opens with Ogden's paper on countertransference and transference in the first analytic meeting; here the specific analytic nature of the first contact is brought into the foreground. The suggestion that in the first consultation the analyst shall not explain analysis but instead conduct himself as an analyst, reveals Ogden's basic attitude to the job in hand. The true psychoanalytic technique of the first interview is further stressed by the idea of 'the intimacy of the relationship in the context of formality', and in his conviction that there is no psychoanalytic rationale for trying 'to diminish the anxiety level by putting the patient at ease', even in the first encounter. The psychoanalytic way to deal with anxiety is to find a way to describe it in relation to the analyst and the meeting.

The next two papers are by German psychoanalysts. In his paper Dantlgraber builds on Argelander's way of using 'scenic information' in the initial interview as a starting point for also taking the interaction into account. He expands Argelander's work with an examination of what goes on in the transference–countertransference matrix. Dantlgraber explores both in theoretical and great clinical detail the transference–countertransference positions in the first interview and connects this to the possibility of predicting the patient's ability to make use of psychoanalysis. Although the first interview is seen as different from the eventual next phases of psychoanalysis, the analyst's way of getting a picture of the patient's potential is through considering the quality of the transference pressure, and the countertransference reactions. The patient's way of relating to the analyst is differentiated into two basic forms: making a 'concretized encounter' or 'an encounter in symbolic space', a difference that could help the analyst clarify and predict how the patient will be able to work in psychoanalysis. It is not only a more analytic way of assessing analysability, but also, as shown in the concept 'subjective indication', contains the view that the possibility of a psychoanalysis is as much seated in the ability of the analyst, his capability to sustain more primitive countertransference reactions, as in the psychological function of the patient.

Wegner's paper 'The Opening Scene and the Importance of the Countertransference in the Initial Psychoanalytic Interview' is clearly a continuation of the work of Argelander and Dantlgraber, drawing the special German developmental line from assessing the patient to studying the process between two participants. Moreover the reader is guided through important classic and newer psychoanalytic theory, including important British psychoanalytic works. Wegner's own contribution, also shown through clinical material, is the demonstration of the wealth of information in the subtle cues of the first meeting. From Wegner's point of view the information emanates from psychoanalytic technique, from the analyst's reflection on the countertransference experience, which he describes by an evocative new concept: 'free floating introspectiveness'.

The two Italian papers which follow bear witness to the fact that also in Italy there has been a development in the psychoanalytic thinking about consultations towards more focus on the analytic couple's difficulties with and capabilities of getting into and using an analytic interaction (see also the paper by Bolognini in Part II, p. 148).

The paper by the Italian psychoanalyst Racalbuto is the only paper in this section that uses the fact that the consultation is a *first* contact to contemplate the need of a special psychoanalytic function. He describes a special kind of 'psychic functioning in search for a meaning' a function that can metabolize new experiences, endure an obscure position 'along the border between internal and external, between subject and object and, at an intra-psychic level, between the perception/consciousness system and the unconscious'. Racalbuto thinks the analyst's situation in a consultation can be compared to a crisis, and the function needed to contain this comes close to Bion's concept of 'negative capability'.

In the last paper of the section, Ferro illustrates from his field-theoretic perspective how immediately, in the first meeting, a forceful drama is beginning to unfold. He sees the special task of doing a consultation as resting on four different capacities in the analyst: (1) for staying unsaturated (negative capability); (2) 'for transformation into a dream'; (3) 'for narrative transformation'; and (4) 'the analyst's ability to give himself a consultation'. Through several short clinical vignettes he demonstrates how, from what the patient tells and shows him and from his own reactions, he identifies the figures and narratives that take form already in the first contact; thus he gives new ideas and concepts to how the analyst digests and conceptualizes the complicated interaction that takes place.

Although each paper in the present section has its own individual perspectives, its own theoretically original and new ideas, there is a common underlining of recognizable psychoanalytic thinking and technique. And although the patients who have met these analysts in their first consultations must have had very different experiences according to these analysts' individual styles and personalities, the reader is left in no doubt that what these prospective analysands have found is *an experience of psychoanalysis* and its inherent possibilities; they have not necessarily found their future analyst. This must be the essence of what a consultation should offer: help for the patient to find *psychoanalysis*, not Dantlgraber, Wegner, Ogden, Racalbuto or Ferro.

10 COMMENTS ON TRANSFERENCE AND COUNTERTRANSFERENCE IN THE INITIAL ANALYTIC MEETING

by Thomas H. Ogden

Commentary

Mette Møller

The author of the following paper, Thomas Ogden, is one of the most original and influential American psychoanalysts of the last three decades. Ogden's psychoanalytic thinking is firmly based on the British object-relational theories of Klein, Bion, Winnicott, Fairbairn, Tustin, and Meltzer, to mention some of the most prominent. He has throughout his extended writings constantly reworked, developed and created psychoanalytic theory and technique in a highly innovative and personal way; and at the same time his work is an integration and extrapolation of concepts developed by the analysts that influenced him. His understanding of projective identification (Ogden, 1982), his concept of the autistic-contiguous position, the intersubjective analytic third (Ogden, 1994), the central role of reverie (Ogden, 1997), to name some of Ogden's contributions, is widely known throughout the psychoanalytic culture. In his latest book: *Rediscovering Psychoanalysis – Thinking and Dreaming – Learning and Forgetting* (2009) he writes:

> The thread that weaves through every page of this book is the idea that it is the analyst's task to engage in a process of rediscovering psychoanalysis in everything that he or she does: in each analytic session, in each supervisory hour, in each meeting of a psychoanalytic seminar, in each reading of an analytic work, and so on.
>
> (Ogden, 2009, p. 1)

The present paper is an extended version of a chapter in his third book: *The Primitive Edge of Experience* from 1989. It was for that time a fresh and innovative way of describing the first meeting, and it marked a change in psychoanalytic understanding of the function of first interviews. The focus shifts from assessment of the patient's analysability to the awareness of the quality of interaction between the two participants, to the specific transference–countertransference dynamics of the meeting between the analyst and prospective analysand. Ogden regards the first interview as no less analytic than any other analytic meeting and demonstrates how he engages in a psychoanalytic dialogue, also when a referral, or no analysis at all could be the result. In an interview (1991), related to the book *The Primitive Edge of Experience*, Ogden describes his conviction that nothing can compare with the powerful experience of creating hope for change than being helped to talk about what is frightening about being in the room with the analyst at that moment. Ogden's experience is:

> that when an analytic approach avoids addressing the patient's anxiety it gives the patient the sense that the analyst is unable or unwilling to grapple with anger and fear the patient experiences at the moment.

and he continues:

> The patient is, of course, correct in his assumption that it will very likely be the limitations of the analyst's capacity to analyse counter-transference that will, to a very large degree, determine the effectiveness of the analytic process that will unfold.
>
> (1991, p. 361)

Ogden does not think that an analyst should be able to work with all patients. To see the limitation of the individual analyst in his or her ability to manage the countertransference as one of the most important indicators of the future of the analytic project, was a new step. It relates to Rothstein's thoughts about reluctance to start analysis (see Part IV, p. 281). What for decades had developed in relation to the understanding and use of countertransference in psychoanalysis, Ogden took and placed right at the beginning of the analytic process, in the first interview.

References

Ogden, T. H. (1982). *Projective Identification & Psychotherapeutic Technique*. London: Jason Aronson.

Ogden, T. (1991). An interview with Thomas Ogden. *Psychoanalytic Diaglogues* 1: 361–376.

Ogden, T. H. (1989). *The Primitive Edge of Experience*. London: Maresfield Library.

Ogden, T. H. (1994). The analytic third: Working with intersubjective clinical facts. *International Journal of Psycho-Analysis* 75: 3–19.

Ogden, T. H. (1997). *Reverie and Interpretation*. London: Jason Aronson.

Ogden, T. H. (2009). *Rediscovering Psychoanalysis – Thinking and Dreaming – Learning and Forgetting*. New Library of Psychoanalysis. Hove: Routledge.

10 COMMENTS ON TRANSFERENCE AND COUNTERTRANSFERENCE IN THE INITIAL ANALYTIC MEETING[1]

Thomas H. Ogden

Psychoanalytic concepts and techniques, in order to retain their vitality, must again and again be discovered by the analyst as if for the first time. The analyst must allow himself to be freshly surprised by the ideas and phenomena that he takes most for granted. For example, he must be able to allow himself to be genuinely caught off guard by the pervasiveness of the influence of the unconscious mind, by the power of the transference, and by the intransigence of resistance, and only retrospectively apply the familiar names to these freshly rediscovered phenomena. If the analyst allows himself perpetually to be the beginner that he is, it is sometimes possible to learn about that which he thought he already knew. The present paper is a collection of thoughts addressed to myself (and other novices) on the subject of the opening of the analytic drama with particular reference to the transference and countertransference. I make no attempt to be exhaustive, since the topic touches upon almost every aspect of psychoanalytic theory and technique. My starting point for a discussion of the first analytic meeting is the idea that there is no difference between the analytic process in the first meeting and the analytic process in any other analytic meeting: the analyst in the initial meeting is no more or less an analyst, the analysand is no more or less an analysand, the analysis is no more or less an analysis than in any other meeting.

Creating analytic significance

Everything the analyst does in the first face-to-face analytic session is intended as an invitation to the patient to consider the meaning of his experience. All that has been most obvious to the patient will no longer be treated as self-evident; rather, the familiar is to be wondered about, to be puzzled over, to

[1] Ogden, T. (1992). Comments on transference and countertransference in the initial analytic meeting. *Psychoanalytic Inquiry* 12: 225–247. Dr. Ogden is a member of the faculty of the San Francisco Psychoanalytic Institute. This article is an expanded version of a paper originally published in Dr. Ogden's book, *The Primitive Edge of Experience* (1989).

be newly created in the analytic setting. The patient's thoughts and feelings, his past and present, have new significance, and therefore the patient himself takes on a form of significance he has never held before. There is a particular form of significance generated in the analytic context that is unique to that setting. For the analysand, the consulting room is a profoundly quiet place as he realizes that he must find a voice with which to tell his story. This voice is the sound of his thoughts, which he may never have heard before. (The analysand may find he does not have a voice that feels like his own. This discovery may then serve as the starting point of the analysis.)

The analyst speaks and refrains from speaking in a way that communicates the fact that he accepts the patient as he is without judgment, and yet it is at the same time understood by both patient and analyst that they are meeting together for the purpose of psychological change. The analyst attempts to understand why the patient is as he is and cannot change and yet implicitly asks the patient to give up his illness sufficiently to make use of the analysis. For example, the schizoid patient must enter into a relationship with the analyst in order to overcome his terror of even the most minimal involvement with other people; the obsessional patient in order to get help with his endless ruminations must give up his ruminations sufficiently to enter into an analytic dialogue; the hysterical patient must interrupt the drama that constitutes (and substitutes for) his life long enough to become an observer in addition to being an actor in it.

The analyst is the object of the patient's transference feelings even before his first meeting. In addition to viewing the analyst as a person trained to understand and (through some as yet unknown process) help the patient find relief from psychic pain, the analyst is also experienced as the healing mother, the childhood transitional object, the wished-for Oedipal mother and father, and so on. With these hopes comes fear of disappointment.

Just as the patient has a (fantasied) analyst before the first session, the analyst also has a patient (more accurately, he has many patients) in his own mind prior to the initial meeting. In other words, prior to meeting the patient, the analyst has drawn upon such particulars as the sound of the patient's voice on the telephone, the source of the referral, the analyst's relationships with his current patients, as sources of conscious and unconscious feelings about the patient that he will bring to the first analytic meeting. In addition, there is regularly a feeling of suspense connected with the anticipation of the initial interview. Both patient and analyst are about to enter into an interpersonal drama for which many scripts are already written (the analyst's and the patient's internal dramas), and yet if the work is to be productive, a drama never before imagined by either will have to be created. Along with the sense of excitement, there is also an edge of anxiety. To a large extent the danger posed by the first meeting arises from the prospect of a fresh encounter with one's own inner world and the internal world of another person. It is always dangerous business to stir up the depths of the unconscious mind. This anxiety is regularly misrecognized by therapists early in practice. It is treated as if it were a fear that the patient will leave treatment; in fact the therapist is afraid that the patient will stay.

A patient recently described with unusual clarity a fragment of her train of thought prior to the first meeting: 'How much should I say in the beginning about the things about which I am most afraid and ashamed? How should I phrase it? I don't want him to think I am so crazy, so deceitful, so selfish, so seductive that working with me will be experienced as so unpleasant that he will soon find some excuse for getting rid of me. Is the humiliation of revealing myself in this way worth it? Did I make a mistake in deciding to see him? He was disappointing to me when I spoke to him on the phone. I wish he were older, more like a grandfather. He sounded a little crazy: he didn't seem to know his own address. His office is in a kind of decrepit neighborhood. I wonder if he's having trouble in his practice?'

When a patient phones inquiring about working with me in therapy or analysis, I suggest to the patient that we find a time to meet for a consultation. I intentionally use the word consultation in order to make it clear that this meeting will not necessarily be the beginning of ongoing work together (despite the fact that I intend it to be an analytic experience regardless of what the outcome of the meeting might be). I do this because I cannot know ahead of time whether, after talking with the patient, I will feel that I can be of help to him and will want to work with him. Among the multiplicity of factors that go into making this determination is the question of whether I feel that I generally like the patient and feel some concern for and interest in him.

It is important that the analyst attempt in part to organize his thinking diagnostically. However, with a few exceptions (e.g., drug- or alcohol-addicted patients, violently acting-out sociopaths, severely organically damaged patients), I am generally open to working analytically with patients suffering from a wide range of psychological disturbances (cf. Boyer & Giovacchini, 1980; Ogden, 1982, 1986). However, it seems to me that one is claiming too much if one claims to be able to work with any patient who is interested in analysis. I believe we do a patient a disservice if we agree to work with someone when we are aware of not liking him. It is sometimes said that the analyst ought to be able to analyze his negative countertransference and therefore should be able to work with any patient who is otherwise suitable for analytic work. In theory this may be true; in practice, however, I believe that the analytic task is difficult enough without attempting to build the analytic edifice upon a foundation of a powerful negative countertransference (or an intense negative transference). In my experience, this is so whether or not the analyst (or the patient) recognizes these transferences to be irrational. This caveat has seemed to me equally applicable to instances in which there are from the beginning very intense erotic transferences or countertransferences.

On the other hand, when speaking with a patient, I do not refer to the initial meetings as an 'evaluation period' or 'assessment phase' since these designations seem to me to convey the idea that the patient is to be relatively passive in this enterprise. Such terms would misrepresent my understanding that the function of the first meeting centrally involves the initiation of the analytic process. The nature of the interaction of the first meeting is not simply that of one person evaluating another or even of two people evaluating one another. Rather, it is in my mind an interaction in which two people attempt to generate analytic significance, including an understanding of the meanings of the decision-making process that is involved in the initial meetings. It is my intention in the initial meeting to facilitate the creation of an interaction that will constitute an analytic experience that will be of some value to the patient in providing him with a sense of what it means to be in analysis.

Despite the fact that transference anxiety is extremely high in the period leading to the initial interview, I do not view it as the analyst's job to put the patient at ease in the first meeting. On the contrary, I believe it is his task to help the patient not miss an important opportunity to recognize and understand something about the transference thoughts, feelings, and sensations with which he has been struggling.

Sustaining psychological strain in the analytic setting

As with all other meetings, the initial analytic hour begins in the waiting room. The patient is addressed as Dr., Mr., or Ms. and the analyst introduces himself in kind. The paradox inherent in this formal introduction is not lost to the patient: the analytic relationship is one of the most formal and at the same time one of the most intimate of human relationships. The formality reflects respect for the analysand and for the analytic process. In addition, it is an expression of the fact that the analyst is not pretending to be, nor does he aspire to be, the analysand's friend. (We do not pay our friends to talk to us.) It is clear from the outset that the intimacy of the analytic relationship will be an intimacy in the context of formality.

Therapists early in their training often feel the impulse to 'put the patient at ease' or 'to act human' as they walk with the patient from the waiting room to the consulting room. For instance, a therapist attempting to ease the tension of the walk to the consulting room said, 'I hope you didn't have trouble finding a parking space. Parking is awful around here.' To make such a comment is not a kind thing to do in terms of the analytic process. In fact, from the perspective being discussed here, this therapist has been rather unkind in several ways. First, he has communicated to the patient his unconscious feeling that the patient is an infant who has trouble making his way in a hostile world and that the therapist feels guiltily responsible for not making the patient's life less difficult. Such a comment immediately puts the patient into the analyst's debt and puts pressure on him to return the 'kindness,' i.e., to help the analyst avoid feelings of discomfort. There is also a hint in the therapist's comment that he is not confident that the therapy he will offer the patient is worth the trouble to which the patient is going.

Further, this sort of comment is an act of theft: it robs the patient of the opportunity to introduce himself to the analyst in a way he consciously and unconsciously chooses. The patient has available to him an infinite number of ways of beginning the analytic discourse. His choice of the way he will go about doing this will be repeated by no other analysand. One must not deprive him of his opportunity to write the opening lines of his own analytic drama by burdening him with the analyst's unconscious contents before he even sets foot in the consulting room. (There will be plenty of time for that later, as the analyst inevitably becomes an unwitting actor in the patient's unconscious fantasies.)

Finally, a comment of the type being discussed misleads the patient about the nature of the analytic experience. As analysts, we do not intend to relieve anxiety (our own or the patient's) through tension-reducing activity, reassurances, gift-giving, or the like. Since maintaining psychological strain is not only something we demand of ourselves but is also part of what we ask of the patient, it makes no sense to begin the analytic relationship with an effort at dissipating psychological strain. Whether the incident is ever spoken of again, the analysand unconsciously registers the fact that the analyst has granted himself license to handle his own anxiety by means of countertransference acting in.

The patient brings to the first interview many questions and worries (usually unspoken) about what it means to be in analysis, what it means to be an analyst, and what it means to be an analysand. The analyst's attempts at answering these questions in the form of explanations of free association, the use of the couch, frequency of meetings, differences between psychotherapy and psychoanalysis, differences between 'schools of psychoanalysis,' and so on, are not only futile, they invariably limit the patient's opportunity to present himself to the analyst in his own terms. As is illustrated by the following clinical vignette, the analyst's most eloquent explanation of what it means to be 'in analysis' is to conduct himself as an analyst.

Mr. H, a 42-year-old television producer, explained in the initial session that he had come to see me because he felt intensely anxious and had 'obsessional ideas' about dying, including fears of suffocating in his sleep and of being trapped and killed during an earthquake. The patient was preoccupied by the thought that his six-year-old daughter, who was mildly hearing-impaired, would 'not be able to make it in the world.' He said that he knew that each of his fears was overblown, but this knowledge did not diminish the intensity of his anxiety.

The patient said that he had been fearful from the time that he was a small child. Mr. H's father, a college professor, was continually dissatisfied with the patient and insisted on 'helping him' with his homework each night. This inevitably ended with the father's shrieking at the patient for his 'incredible stupidity.'

Mr. H told me that his success at work seemed unreal to him. He felt as if he had to be continually preparing for the day when he would no longer be able to function. As a result, he hoarded every penny he earned. He gave several examples of feeling dangerously depleted when he spent money. I then said that it seemed that he was suggesting that the idea of paying for analysis would be frightening because it would mean giving up one of the few sources of protection he felt he had. Mr. H smiled and said he had thought a great deal about this and the prospect of paying for analysis felt to him like a blood-letting in which there would be a race between his 'cure' and his bleeding to death.

When I met Mr. H in the waiting room for our second meeting, he was perspiring and seemed to have been awaiting me like a man anxiously awaiting some terribly important piece of news, perhaps a verdict. Immediately upon entering my consulting room, he walked briskly across the room and reached for the phone, saying, 'I locked my keys in the car and so if it's all right, I'd like to call my wife to ask her to meet me here with a spare set of keys after our meeting.' I said I thought it must seem to him as if his life depended on his making the phone call, but I thought he and I should talk about what it was that was happening between us before attempting to undo it. He sat down and said, 'Actually, what just happened is kind of typical of me. I had my lunch in the back seat of the car, and there was a sign in the parking garage that said, "Leave keys in car." I felt uneasy about leaving my lunch in an unlocked car. I had the thought that somebody might tamper with my lunch, and so I didn't want to leave the car unlocked.'

I said to Mr. H that without realizing it he seemed to have done both things: he had locked his lunch in the car so it would not be tampered with and had left his keys in the car as the sign had directed. He told me he had become very panicky when he realized his keys were locked in his car and immediately thought of calling his wife from my office. He said he felt greatly relieved by this idea. I repeated his realization that he had thought of me as well as his wife at that moment. He said that was so, but he had thought of me earlier when he saw the sign, which somehow seemed to have been put there by me.

Mr. H explained that the request to use my phone was also characteristic of him. He is almost always afraid that people are angry at him and regularly reassures himself that people do like him by asking small favors of them. For example, he frequently borrows change or a pencil from colleagues at work, or he asks directions to a place when he already knows perfectly well how to get there.

He told me he was certain I already thought he was a real jerk. (I assumed there was a wish as well as a fear underlying this feeling, but I did not interrupt the patient at this point since he was in the midst of introducing me to the cast of characters constituting his internal object world.) Mr. H went on to tell me more about his parents. His father had died ten years ago, but had lived his entire life as if he were at death's door. He had suffered from renal disease originating in childhood and was preoccupied with the fear of death. The patient said that he had been frightened that his father would die when he was yelling at the patient. Mr. H told me that his father could at times be very kind and that the patient had loved him despite the fact that he had been frightened of him so much of the time.

I asked if the patient had expected that I would yell at him for locking his keys in the car and for asking to use my phone. He said he thought he had had that feeling in a diffuse sort of way, but had not quite known why he was feeling so frightened while waiting in my waiting room. (It occurred to me that the patient may have been attempting to call his wife in an effort to get her to protect him from me [as his mother had protected him from his father] and to protect me from him.)

In the course of the analytic work that followed, many layers of meaning of this transference enactment (referred to by Mr. H as the 'telephone caper') came to light, including the patient's wish to be treated as a helpless little boy, thus defending himself against his feelings of being a powerfully destructive person who had done great harm to his father and who would do harm to me. A second aspect of this transference enactment involved the wish to provoke me into acting in a manner similar to his father, wherein I would yell at him for his stupidity. In part, he was afraid I would act in that way and was attempting to reassure himself that I would not. Then too, he found sensual pleasure in such intense scoldings. In addition, he felt relief in being punished since this is what he unconsciously felt he deserved for the crime he imagined he had committed in relation to his father (i.e., provoking him to the point that he had made him sick and ultimately had killed him). Further, he felt that his father demonstrated love for him in the father's intense, controlling involvement. The patient unconsciously hoped to elicit from me this form of love in the anticipated scolding. Over the course of the analysis, the 'telephone caper' served again and again as a symbol of the analytic process.

Cautionary tales

In the initial interview I am listening from the outset for the patient's 'cautionary tales,' i.e., the patient's unconscious explanations of why he feels the analysis is a dangerous undertaking and his reasons for feeling the analysis is certain to fail.[2] To say this is to say nothing more than that I am listening

[2] Ella Freeman Sharpe (1943) used the term cautionary tale to refer to fantasies serving the purpose of instinctual impulse control by means of unconscious self-warnings of bodily destruction. In this paper, I have used the term to refer to a more circumscribed and differently conceptualized set of fantasies: the patient's unconscious set of fantasies concerning the dangers of entering into the analytic relationship (McKee, personal communication, 1969).

for (and attempting to put into words for myself and for the patient) the leading edge of transference anxiety in the hour. Whatever the nature of the analysand's disturbances, his anxieties will be given form in terms of the danger of entering into a relationship with the analyst. The patient unconsciously holds a fierce conviction (which he has no way of articulating) that his infantile and early childhood experience has taught him about the specific ways in which each of his object relationships will inevitably become painful, disappointing, over-stimulating, annihilating, unreliable, suffocating, overly sexualized, etc. There is no reason for him to believe that the relationship into which he is about to enter will be any different. In this belief the analysand is of course both correct and incorrect. He is correct in the sense that, transferentially, his internal object world will inevitably become a living intersubjective drama on the analytic stage. He is incorrect to the extent that the analytic context will not be identical to the original psychological-interpersonal context within which his internal object world was created, i.e., the context of infantile and childhood fantasy and object relations.

Everything the analysand says (and does not say) in the first hours can be heard in the light of an unconscious warning to the analyst concerning the reasons why neither the analyst nor the patient should enter into this doomed and dangerous relationship. It must be emphasized that the patient feels that the analysis will endanger the analyst as well as himself and that it is in large part in an effort to protect the analyst that the patient balks at entering the relationship. The analyst, from this perspective, serves as the container for the patient's fears about beginning this relationship as well as for the analysand's hopes that internal change is possible and that pathological attachments to internal objects can be altered without sacrificing the life of the patient. The following account of an initial analytic meeting is an illustration of the way in which the patient often unconsciously attempts to symbolize for himself and for the analyst the dangers he anticipates.

Mr. J began his first meeting by describing his empty relationship with his wife and children, the boredom he felt at work, and the lack of joy he felt in his life in general. He said he had been referred to me by his internist, who thought analysis would be of benefit to him. Despite Mr. J's presentation of his feelings of desolation, I suspected that there were pleasures in his life that he felt he must keep secret both from himself and from me. I had the fantasy that Mr. J was having an affair – perhaps with a woman, perhaps with music, art, or some other 'passionate interest', perhaps with a memory of a childhood romance. This fantasy was not the product of intuition, but a response to something about the patient's presentation of himself. In retrospect, it is easier to see that this had been communicated by his choice of words, by the rhythm of his speech, by his gait, his facial expressions, etc. He behaved like a man with a secret. I surmised (but did not say to Mr. J) that he unconsciously seemed to feel that analysis would contain forms of pleasure that he would have to keep well hidden, and I anticipated that as a result analysis would have a rather arid feeling to it (both for him and for me) for quite a long time.

The patient said he felt convinced that he needed treatment and he knew his wife and children would benefit if he were to get help. Nonetheless, he felt extremely guilty about spending money on analysis which could be spent in buying things his whole family could enjoy. I said, after some time had elapsed in the first hour, that the patient seemed to feel that to begin analysis would be equivalent to having an affair. He told me how devoted he was to his wife and that he had never considered the idea of really having an affair. However, he said, it was strange that I had said what I had because earlier that week for the first time he had heard himself making a comment to his secretary that was sufficiently ambiguous to have been construed as a proposition. She chose not to directly respond to the ambiguously proposed affair. He said that he had felt quite disturbed by this episode and had left work early for the first time in years.

In this instance, I elected to interpret an aspect of what I understood to be the leading transference anxiety (i.e., the most accessible unconscious/preconscious set of transference and resistance meanings). The internal drama the patient seemed to be bringing to the analytic relationship was one in which there was an anticipation of passionate attachment and intense secretiveness. It was within this area of experience (the 'affair') that I suspected Mr. J was afraid that analysis would become extremely painful and perhaps become impossible to continue. In the course of the succeeding several years of analysis the patient was able to make sense of these feelings in terms of a relationship that he had had with a nanny whom he had loved deeply, a love he unconsciously felt he had to keep secret from his mother. His feelings of anger and guilt, as well as fears of becoming involved in similar impossible entanglements, had led to his developing a character defense in which he remained rather detached in all sectors of his life. The idea that he was 'only going through the motions' served important defensive functions in the initial stages of his analysis.

The timing of transference interpretations

As a result of my interest in ideas deriving from the British psychoanalytic dialog, I have often been asked if it is true that Kleinians interpret the transference from the very beginning of the analysis. The question is always a puzzling one to me. It hardly seems surprising that one would attempt to talk with the patient about what it is about this new relationship (the analytic relationship) that is so frightening, exciting, disappointing, futile, etc. Generally, the initial session does not feel complete to me unless the patient's anxiety in the transference has in some way been addressed. One does not have to be a Kleinian to talk with one's patient about one's current (and always tentative) understanding of what it is that is disturbing to the analysand about the initial meeting.[3]

The following is an illustration of a situation in which there was countertransference resistance to discussing transference anxiety in the initial meeting.

A 32-year-old man made a phone call to a therapist for the purpose of setting up a consultation. He told her in the course of asking her for an appointment that he felt in danger of getting into disputes that would end up in his punching someone. Mr. N said that he is a large man, that he speaks in a booming voice, and that people are often frightened by him even when he is not angry. He said that, despite all this, he hoped the therapist would not be afraid of him since he was not a dangerous person and had never attacked anybody.

When Mr. N appeared for his initial meeting, the therapist was surprised to find him a man of average build who spoke in a pressured but not a loud or bullying manner. She learned that Mr. N was a successful owner of a retail business. He was born to a psychotic mother and had been placed in a foster home just before his first birthday. Mr. N had seen neither his mother nor his father since that time. After a succession of five foster home placements in a five-year period, he was finally adopted by a couple with whom he lived until he left at 18 to join the army. In the course of his latency and adolescence, the patient's adoptive parents became alcoholics.

The therapist (who had only recently completed her training) did not discuss with the patient his implicit, ambivalent warning that she would be well advised to have nothing to do with him. There seems to have been an unconscious sense on the part of the therapist that talking to Mr. N about his fear of his destructiveness would make him more dangerous to her. There was also a denial of her own fear of the patient that left her unable to think about his warning. (Other therapists might have refused even to meet with this patient, thus engaging in a countertransference enactment of the patient's experience of himself as a danger to both his internal and external objects. The patient after all had already, from the perspective of his unconscious psychic reality, caused his original mother to become psychotic, leading her to abandon him, had been so unlovable and perhaps dangerous as to have caused five sets of foster parents to refuse to keep him, and had driven his adoptive parents to alcoholism.)

The patient came to his next four weekly meetings in an increasingly agitated state. Several days after the fifth meeting, he phoned the therapist saying that he had felt more and more anxious after each of his meetings with her and that it had become unbearable. He had therefore decided to

3 At the same time, clinical judgment must guide the analyst in every therapeutic situation. There are many instances in which the analyst senses that it is critical he not be too 'clever' (Winnicott, 1969, p. 86) or know too much, and therefore chooses to refrain from offering even the most tentative versions of what he thinks he understands (cf. Balint, 1968; Winnicott, 1969, 1971).

discontinue therapy. The therapist suggested that Mr. N come to his next meeting in order to talk about these feelings.

It was at this point that the therapist sought consultation on the case. I suggested that the patient had indicated from the very outset that he was terrified that his anger (particularly in the maternal transference) would frighten and damage the therapist. The therapist's unconscious fear of the patient had led her to suggest once-weekly meetings with Mr. N despite indirect indications from him that he felt he needed and could afford more intensive therapy. The therapist's unconscious decision to seek a safe distance from the patient had confirmed the patient's belief that she would (with good reason) find him dangerous and would eventually refuse to see him. It seemed to me that Mr. N had telephoned the therapist in order to see whether she had been injured in the previous meeting and that he had been temporarily reassured by her asking him to come to his next meeting. I hypothesized that Mr. N was in a rage at his (internal object) mother for being crazy and unable to love him and for having abandoned him as well as terrified that it was his anger that had driven his mother crazy and had led her to abandon him.

Mr. N began the meeting that followed the telephone call by asking the therapist, 'How are you?' as they walked from the waiting room to the consulting room. Once in the consulting room, he said that his heart was pounding. The therapist suggested that Mr. N was worried that he had scared or perhaps hurt her in the previous meeting and that this had been a concern of his from the very beginning. The patient calmed down considerably after this interpretation. The therapist later in the meeting suggested that since the patient felt such intense anxiety in response to each meeting, it might be useful to meet more frequently in order to discuss what it was that was frightening him. To her surprise, Mr. N seemed receptive to this idea. In a sense, the beginning of the analytic dialogue had been postponed for six or seven meetings largely as a result of unanalyzed anxiety in the countertransference which had led to an inability to think about or interpret the patient's transference anxiety.

Analytic space

Entry into the analytic experience (beginning in the initial interview) involves the enlargement of the psychological space constituting the 'matrix of the mind' (Ogden, 1986) in such a way that this space more or less comes to approximate the analytic space, i.e., the analytic space becomes the space in which the patient thinks, feels, and lives. In a subtle way, the events making up the patient's experience in relation to his internal and external objects, the events making up his daily life, and his responses to these events come to be important to him insofar as they contribute to the analytic experience. Eventually, it is to a large degree the analytic space and not the analysand's individual psychological space in which the unconscious internal drama is experienced. The evolution of this process includes, but is by no means limited to, what is usually referred to as the elaboration of the transference neurosis and the transference psychosis.[4] That which constitutes analytic space is individual to each analytic pair. Just as each mother learns (often to her surprise) that the process of creating a play space differs greatly with each of her children, the analyst must learn that the process of creating analytic space is different with each analysand (Goldberg, 1989). In the same way that each infant's unique character draws upon and brings to life specific aspects of the mother's emotional potential, the analyst must allow himself to be created/molded by his patient in reality as well as in fantasy. Since the infant has a role in creating his mother, no two infants ever have the same mother. Similarly, no two patients ever have the same analyst. The analyst experiences himself and behaves in a subtly different manner in each analysis. Moreover, this is not at all a static phenomenon: in the course of each analysis the analyst undergoes psychological change, which in turn is reflected in the way he conducts the analysis.

More seriously disturbed patients experience the analytic space as a vacuum which threatens to suck out of them their mental contents (which are concretely experienced as bodily parts or contents). One such patient began the first meeting by barraging me with an uninterrupted series of obscenities. Taken aback by the onslaught, I decided to allow the patient to have his say and to observe the impact he was having on me. It was apparent that his barrage was far more anxious than hostile. After about five minutes, I said to him that I thought it was not easy for him to be here with me. He quieted down as I said this. I then told him that I thought he had emptied his garbage into me because he did not mind giving up a part of himself that he did not value. I said that I guessed he had more important things inside of him that he felt he needed to protect. Following this intervention, the patient was able to tell me more about himself, albeit in a psychotic way. I in turn discussed with him the little bit of what I thought I understood of what he was telling me. Almost all of what I said was addressed to the patient's fears about being with me.

Anxious questioning

Analysands often pose direct questions in the initial meeting. A few of these I answer directly. For example, I will in a 'matter-of-course' way (Freud,

4 The termination phase of an analysis is not simply a phase of resolution of conflicted unconscious transference meanings. Equally important, it is a period of the 'contraction' of the analytic space such that the patient comes to experience himself as constituting the space within which he lives and within which the analytic process continues. If this does not occur, the prospect of the end of the analysis is experienced as tantamount to the loss of one's mind or the loss of the space in which one feels alive.

1913, p. 131) answer the patient's questions about my training or my fee. Most questions, however, I do not answer, including questions about whether I have a particular specialty, with which 'school of psychoanalysis' I am associated, whether I see more men than women in my practice, whether I consider homosexuality to be an illness, etc. These sorts of questions I treat as fairly undisguised statements of the patient's fantasies about the specific ways in which I will fail to understand him due to my own psychological difficulties, e.g., my fear of women or men, my fear of homosexuality or heterosexuality, my need to dominate or submit to others, and so forth.

When a patient persistently asks question after question, I often say to him that it must feel too dangerous to wait to see what happens between us; that, instead, the patient hopes he will be able to sample the future through the answers to his questions, thereby short-circuiting the tension connected with waiting.

Very often the analysand uses questions in an attempt to get the analyst to fill the analytic space because the patient feels that his own internal contents are shameful, dangerous, worthless, in need of protection from the analyst, etc., or that there is nothing at all inside of him with which to occupy the analytic space. Other patients may quickly fall silent, thus inviting the analyst to fill the space with his (the analyst's) questions and therefore with the analyst's psychological organization, chain of associations, curiosity, and the like. Under such circumstances, I attempt to talk with the patient about the aspect of the patient's anxiety that I think I understand. In so doing, I make it clear that my understanding is tentative, and in all likelihood, quite inadequate in many ways. I thus invite the patient to tell me which parts of what I have said seem true to him and which parts seem off the mark.

Creating a history

The question often arises of whether one 'takes a history' in the initial meeting. The very form of the question seems to me to have significance. I attempt not to 'take' a history from a patient (by means of a series of questions), and instead make every effort to allow the patient to give me his conscious and unconscious versions of his history in his own way.[5] The patient has come to see the analyst for help with psychological pain, the nature of which

[5] It is essential to keep in mind that a patient's history is not a static entity that is gradually unearthed; rather it is an aspect of the patient's conscious and unconscious conception of himself, which is in a continual state of evolution and flux. In a sense, the patient's history is continually being created and re-created in the course of the analysis. Moreover, it is by no means to be assumed that the patient has a history (i.e., a sense of historicity) at the beginning of analysis. In other words, we cannot take for granted the idea that the patient has achieved a sense of continuity of self over time such that his past feels as if it is connected to his experience of himself in the present.

the patient is often unable to accurately name. He must be afforded all the time and room he needs to tell the analyst, in whatever way he has available to him, what he knows about himself. It is important that the analyst does not interfere with the patient's efforts by introducing an agenda of his own, such as collecting historical data, making a treatment recommendation, or laying out the 'ground rules' of analysis (cf. Freud, 1913; see also Shapiro, 1984).

As the patient tells the analyst, however indirectly, about the nature of his pain (and the ways he consciously and/or unconsciously expects this pain to become exacerbated in the course of analysis), his past experience will be articulated in two ways. First, to the extent that the patient tells the analyst about his understanding of the origins of his difficulties, he will be giving the analyst one form of historical data, i.e., what the patient consciously conceives of as his past. Inevitably, there will be gaps, vaguenesses or complete omissions of large sectors of the patient's life experience. For example, a patient may omit any reference to a given family member, make no mention of his sexual experience, not refer to any event occurring prior to the current crisis or prior to his adolescence. Under such circumstances, when I feel that the patient has told me what he wants to and what he is able to, I may ask him if he has noticed his not mentioning, for example, anything about his father. (This is essentially a process of addressing the patient's relationship to his external and internal objects in terms of resistance, i.e., in terms of the patient's conscious and unconscious object-related anxiety.)

As with any comment addressing resistance, it is not the information 'behind' the resistance that is of central concern; the focus is on what it is that the patient is afraid will happen if he tells the analyst about a given aspect of his internal life and the ways the patient has of protecting himself against this danger. Hence the act of 'taking a history' (by means of direct inquiry) is a form of overriding resistances and thereby losing a good deal of what is most important to the analysis, for example, an understanding of who in the patient's internal object world would be betrayed, injured, killed, lost, made jealous, and so on, if the patient were to talk about his feelings about 'the past'; or what sort of loss of control over the patient's relationships to his internal objects would be experienced in his giving up exclusive access to them.

The second form of personal history provided by the patient is data conveyed in the form of the transference–countertransference experience. This is the patient's 'living past,' i.e., the set of object relations established in infancy and early childhood which has come to constitute the structure of the patient's mind, both as content and context of his psychological life. It is therefore this past that is of central analytic interest.

Of course, the two forms of history under discussion, the consciously symbolized past and the unconscious living past, are intimately intertwined. As the patient's internal object world is given intersubjective life in the transference–countertransference, both patient and analyst have an opportunity to experience directly the forms of attachment, hostility, jealousy, envy, etc., constituting the patient's internal object world. In the transference–countertransference, the past and present converge as 'old' contents are brought to life in a new context, i.e., the context of the analytic relationship.

It has been my experience that in the period surrounding (and including) the initial analytic meeting, the patient is in a 'de-integrated' (as opposed to 'dis-integrated') state that involves unusual potential for psychological change. It is regularly the case that the external circumstances of the patient's life are not significantly different from what they had been six months, a year, or even several years earlier. (Of course, there are many exceptions to this observation.) What is different at the time the patient finally seeks analysis is the state of the patient's internal world. The defensive structure that the individual has been relying on is temporarily in a state of flux sufficient to allow him to unconsciously experience himself as having the potential to live differently, i.e., to make changes in his internal world so that he might come to experience himself and conduct himself in the world differently.[6] It seems to me a shame to squander the unusual 'ripeness' for psychological change associated with the patient's state of de-integration in the initial analytic meeting by conducting the meeting as a 'history taking' session.

Concluding comments

The ideas I have discussed in this paper are simply that – ideas. They are not intended to be used as rules or guidelines, nor are they intended as a statement of how the initial analytic meeting should be conducted. At the same time, the thoughts discussed here are thoughts of a specific nature – they are psychoanalytic thoughts. This represents one of the dialectics constituting psychoanalytic technique: analytic technique is guided by a set of ideas that are roughly recognizable as forming a method or group of methods, with a set of principles that gives coherence to this group of methods. From the first meeting, analytic practice occurs between the poles of the predictable and the unpredictable, the disciplined and the spontaneous, the methodical and the intuitive.

The initial face-to-face analytic meeting is viewed as the beginning of the analytic process and not merely as a preparation for it. In the first meeting all

[6] This state of 'de-integration' (Fordham, 1977) associated with the initial analytic meeting might be compared with the experiential state of a married couple during the last trimester of the woman's pregnancy. Not only is each of the individuals comprising the couple in a period of de-integration of his/her personal identity (as a man/woman, an adult/child, a son/daughter, father/mother, husband/wife), but also the couple is in a state of de-integration in preparation for the creation of a new set of relationships (internal and external) that is larger and more complex than that which had constituted the marriage to that point. In other words, they are consciously and unconsciously attempting to make room in their internal and external object worlds to become a family (cf. Brazelton, 1981).

that was familiar to the patient is no longer treated as self-evident. The analysand takes on a form of significance for himself that he has never held before. The analyst attempts to convey to the patient something of what it means to be in analysis, not by means of explanations of the analytic process, but by conducting himself as an analyst. To this end, psychological strain is not dissipated through reassurance, forms of acting in, suggestion, and so on. All that the patient says (and does not say) in the initial meeting is understood as an unconscious warning to the analyst (and to the patient) concerning the reasons why the patient unconsciously feels that each of them would be well advised not to enter into this doomed and dangerous relationship. The analyst attempts to understand the patient's warnings in terms of transference anxiety and resistance.

References

Balint, M. (1968). *The Basic Fault.* London: Tavistock.

Boyer, L. B., Giovacchini, P. (1980). *Psychoanalytic Treatment of Schizophrenic, Borderline and Characterological Disorders.* New York: Jason Aronson.

Brazelton, T. B. (1981). *On Becoming a Family: The Growth of Attachment.* New York: Delacorte/Seymour Lawrence.

Fordham, M. (1977). *Autism and the Self.* London: Heinemann.

Freud, S. (1913). On Beginning the Treatment. *SE* 12.

Goldberg, P. (1989). Actively seeking the holding environment. *Contemporary Psychoanalysis* 25: 448–476.

Ogden, T. (1982). *Projective Identification and Psychotherapeutic Technique.* New York: Jason Aronson.

Ogden, T. (1986). *The Matrix of the Mind: Object Relations and the Psychoanalytic Dialogue.* Northvale, NJ: Jason Aronson.

Ogden, T. (1988). Misrecognitions and the fear of not knowing. *Psychoanalytic Quarterly* 57: 643–666.

Ogden, T. (1989). *The Primitive Edge of Experience.* Northvale, NJ/London: Jason Aronson.

Shapiro, S. (1984). The initial assessment of the patient: A psychoanalytic approach. *International Review of Psychoanalysis* 11: 11–25.

Sharpe, E. (1943). Cautionary tales. In: *Collected Papers on Psycho-Analysis* (pp. 170–180). London: Hogarth Press, 1950.

Winnicott, D. W. (1969). The use of an object and relating through cross identifications. In: *Playing and Reality* (pp. 86–94). New York: Basic Books, 1971.

Winnicott, D. W. (1971). Playing: Creative activity and the search for the self. In: *Playing and Reality* (pp. 53–64). New York: Basic Books.

11 OBSERVATIONS ON THE SUBJECTIVE INDICATION FOR PSYCHOANALYSIS

by Josef Dantlgraber

Commentary

Peter Wegner

Freud himself had no specifically formulated interview technique. But he knew that the psychoanalytical process quickly leads to inextricable entanglements and that, especially at the beginning of treatment, an examination is still available: 'Anyone who hopes to learn the noble game of chess from books will soon discover that only the openings and end-games admit of an exhaustive systematic presentation and that the infinite variety of moves which develop after the opening defy any such description' (Freud, 1913, p. 123).

The first German systematic and sustained examinations on interview technique are by Hermann Argelander (and colleagues) in Frankfurt. In numerous studies Argelander defined helpful differentiations amongst various 'data sources' of the interview situation: objective information, subjective information, as well as scenic and situational information. In this regard: 'The reliability of the picture gained of the personality and its psychic disturbances grows with the integration of the information from all three sources . . .' established through the situational or scenic evidence, 'which is practically never capable of being checked by repetition, and it is therefore discarded or not mentioned by most interviewers even though it is richest in what it discloses regarding the prognosis of the therapeutic process' (Argelander, 1970/1976, p. 28).

Argelander further found that Freud first documented his abandonment of suggestive techniques in his case study 'Katharina', which brought with it the new insight that resistance against the communication of relevant data cannot be overcome through questions and pressure[1]. It bears mentioning that, following Argelander's work, regular so-called initial interview seminars for candidates in training were established at almost all local German training institutes beginning in the seventies of the last century. These seminars, which are offered in the first stage of psychoanalytical training, usually take place weekly, provide the first clinical experience for candidates, and have made a lasting contribution to the improvement of analytical skills.

The controversy about the diagnostic and/or therapeutic function of interviews was heightened by the acceptance of 'psychotherapy rooted in

[1] See also in Part I of this volume.

depth psychology' and 'psychoanalytical psychotherapy' by the public health care system in 1967, as well as by attempts to shorten classical psychoanalysis (focal therapy, brief psychotherapy, flash-technique, counselling, and group therapy). Such outside influences, which led to an increase in training of psychoanalysts (due to greater financial security in the field of psychoanalysis) and restrictions of indication through corresponding control systems (for example by limiting the indication to special diagnoses and limiting the number of sessions), were accompanied by attempts to acquire objective or measurable information about the indication for psychoanalyses (systematic surveys of biographical data, questionnaires, psychological tests, creation of suitable personality profiles, etc.). Every treatment has to be applied for (health insurance) by the patient, with a special written report of the psychoanalyst to an expert adjudicator. Formally, the term 'psychoanalysis' does not exist in this system, which recognizes only the term 'psychoanalytic psychotherapy'.

It is owing to the work of Josef Dantlgraber (1982) at the first Department for Psychoanalysis, chaired by Wolfgang Loch, at the University of Tübingen that an essential psychoanalytical position effectively established itself in this controversy. Josef Dantlgraber's 'Observations on the Subjective Indications for Psychoanalysis' marks a central change in direction for psychoanalytical interview technique from the so-called 'analysability of the analysand' to the examination of the events in the relationship between patient and analyst that lead to a positive subjective indication for fundamental psychoanalytical work. Analysability is not understood as a quantity that is measurable with objective criteria applied to the patient; rather, it is measured according to the subjective capacities of the analyst. This change in direction meant that, in addition to 'objective' or 'measurable' criteria for analysability, the psychoanalyst's reactions, or rather his countertransference, and his subjective possibilities were incorporated as the basis for indication. This shift of emphasis also established a close connection to the implicit interview technique of Freud, who turned against systematically ascertaining data from patients early on. In Freud's opinion, '. . . the most lengthy discussions and questionings in ordinary consultations . . .' (Freud, 1913, p. 124) do not lead to information that can adequately predict the therapeutic possibilities. Thus, Dantlgraber argues that the psychoanalytical method of free association, of free-floating attentiveness and of the interpretation of transference and countertransference, can be understood as a therapeutic position from the initial contact onward. As a result of this change in direction, the range of indications for psychoanalysis could be significantly expanded and was thus no longer dependent upon the existence of the so-called transference neuroses alone. In fact, the so-called therapeutic diagnosis becomes the basis for the productive development of a psychoanalytic pair. It takes into account not only the potential for change through insight or reason, but also the emotional experiences that accompany it, which lead to a sustainable relationship between analyst and analysand.

The following article closely examines the underlying factors and illustrates them with clinical examples. The initial unconscious communication is affectively perceptible and is a shared experience of a drive. The patient's entire potential of transference, which can be examined on various levels of transference and countertransference, moves into the foreground. It is therefore of interest for the subjective indication how much the analyst can maintain the agency of his imagination in the presence of a patient who is momentarily unable to communicate. Thereby benign and malign unconscious forms of communication can be differentiated, as well as predominating types of encounters either in concrete or symbolic areas. The analyst makes certain adjustments in reaction to the patient and provides maximal mobilization and help to integrate certain ego-capacities. In the process the patient can take on various roles and the sustainability of the setting can become an indicator for the formation of the future psychoanalytical process. Trial interventions in initial encounters have the character of affective trial experiences; they can lead to a stronger cathexis of the analyst and have a strong influence on the formation of the therapeutic alliance – understood as the therapeutic bond between analyst and patient – a further criterion for subjective indication. In favourable cases such trial interpretations respect the affirmative character of the patient's defence, that is, if the insight that they convey does not endanger the relationship to the patient's primary object.

Based on Racker's (1957, p. 311) differentiation between concordant and complementary identification[2], Dantlgraber finally describes another favourable condition for subjective indication, namely the analyst's ability to produce an empathic triadic relation. In the analyst a triangular object relationship is formed, which represents the patient's 'current self' in concordant identification and the analyst as object of transference in complementary identification, provided that the patient possesses sufficient ability for a therapeutic dissociation of the ego (Sterba, 1934, p. 120)[3]. Empathic triadic

[2] 'Direct countertransference referred to the analyst's emotional response to the patient. Indirect countertransference referred to the analyst's emotional response to someone important to the patient. Direct countertransference had two subcategories called "concordant" and "complimentary" countertransferences. The former included the analyst's empathic resonance with the patient's felt conflicts: this was, of course, more marked if the analyst also had similar conflicts himself. The latter referred to the analyst's unconscious identification with some unfelt and projected part of the patient's psychic structure; the analyst's emotional experience in this case was "opposed" to that patient.' (See Akhtar, 2009, p. 61.)

[3] 'Concept first proposed by Richard Sterba (1934) to highlight that, during the course of his work, the analyst "endeavours to oppose those elements in the ego which are focused on reality to those which have a cathexis of instinctual or defensive energy" (p. 118). Sterba declared that states where the ego is permanently fused with the id (e.g. severe narcissism, psychosis) are not amenable to psychoanalysis since the co-operation of ego is required to overcome its own neurotic entanglements. "The therapeutic dissociation of the ego is a necessity if the analyst is to have the chance of winning over part of it to his side, conquering it, strengthening it by means of identification with himself, and opposing it in the transference to those parts which have a cathexis of instinctual and defensive energy" (p. 119). Sterba noted that calling on the analysands to co-operate with the analyst against something in himself sets the ground for such ego dissociation.' (See Akhtar, 2009, pp. 285–286.)

relation also means that the interpretation or intervention as 'third element' transcends a 'drive-dyad' activated by the transference–countertransference, turns it into an experience, names it, and thereby at least for the present suspends it. In this case we say that the analyst is able to take an ex-centric position bound to the truth, which in turn presupposes that the analyst is not permitted 'to need the patient'.

The concentration of psychoanalytical interview technique on the microanalysis of unconscious communication, or rather on the interaction between transference and countertransference, facilitated increased experience and security in the contact with patients in the psychoanalytical initial interview, which Freud had incidentally already anticipated (see above), as well as the eventual 'therapeutic diagnosis' with 'subjective indication'.

A few years later, the Department for Psychoanalysis in Tübingen once again initiated research based on the work of Argelander and Dantlgraber by using the 'initial scene' of the psychoanalytical initial interview systematically as a further data source; another aspect of the first interview which was previously seriously neglected in most interviews but had been recognized – and later forgotten – as an important diagnostic source by Freud (Wegner, 1988; Wegner & Henseler, 1991). The empirical work on which this study was based not only illustrated the diagnostic-therapeutic relevance of the initial scene, but also demonstrated that a successful methodological interview technique is learnable and teachable within a group of psychoanalysts.

One additional study had special significance because its approach made it possible to successfully defend high-frequency psychoanalysis (at least four sessions a week) in the framework of the public health care system. It justified observing the progress not only in the initial interview, but also in the course of all conversations preliminary to treatment. It was thereby possible to draw conclusions about, for example, whether a necessary indication for psychoanalysis exists (e.g. about manifestations of repetition compulsion, Danckwardt and Gattig, 1998).

References

Akhtar, S. (2009). *Comprehensive Dictionary of Psychoanalysis*. London: Karnac Books.

Argelander, H. (1976). *The Initial Interview in Psychotherapy*. Translated by Hella Freud Bernays. New York: Human Sciences Press. (Originally published 1970.)

Danckwardt, J. F., Gattig, E. (1998). *The Indication for High Frequency in Analytical Psychotherapy in the Contractual Medical Health Service. A Manual*. Stuttgart: Frommann-Holzboog.

Dantlgraber, J. (1982). Bemerkungen zur subjektiven Indikation für Psychoanalyse. *Psyche – Zeitschrift für Psychoanalyse und ihre Anwendungen* 36: 193–225.

Freud, S. (1913). On Beginning the Treatment. Further Recommendations on the Technique of Psychoanalysis. *SE* 12: 121–144.

Racker, H. (1957). The meanings and uses of countertransference. *Psychoanalytic Quarterly* 26: 303–357.
Sterba, R. (1934). The fate of the ego in psychoanalytic therapy. *International Journal of Psychoanalysis* 15: 117–126.
Wegner, P. (1988). *Die Bedeutung der Anfangsszene im Psychoanalytischen Erstinterview.* Dissertation an der Eberhard-Karls-Universität Tübingen.
Wegner, P., Henseler, H. (1991) Die Anfangsszene im Prisma einer Analytikergruppe *Forum der Psychoanalyse* 7(3): 214–224.

11 OBSERVATIONS ON THE SUBJECTIVE INDICATION FOR PSYCHOANALYSIS*†a

Josef Dantlgraber

Summary

In evaluating the analysability of a prospective analytic patient at the initial interview, the concept of subjective indication puts the focus on the therapist's reaction, the countertransference. Thus, analysability is not regarded as a dimension to be measured solely by applying objective criteria to the analysand but must also be assessed in regard to the subjective capacities of the analyst.

1

As is generally known, Freud defined the field of indications for psychoanalytical treatment as made up of the transference neuroses: hysteria, obsessive-compulsive neurosis, depression, sexual disorders and character neuroses. He considered other mental disorders to be understandable with the aid of psychoanalytic theory, but not treatable by psychoanalysis. Exceptional pessimism in regard to the therapeutic possibilities of psychoanalysis is expressed in Freud's essay 'Analysis Terminable and Interminable' (1937). Indisputably, the scope of indications has since grown considerably (Cremerius, 1979, p. 593). This development is due to a fundamental change in attitude towards the relationship between analyst and patient, as conceptualized in terms of the concepts of transference and countertransference. Today, particular attention is bestowed on countertransference, seen by many as preliminary to transference (Loch, 1965/66, p. 173; Béjarano, 1977, p. 8), because it structures the entire

* Dedicated to Wolfgang Loch.

† The author's original notes to this paper are numbered 1 to 55. Some editors' notes have been added for this translation and they are labelled in lower-case letters, a to f.

a Originally published as: Dantlgraber, J. (1982). Bemerkungen zur subjektiven Indikation für Psychoanalyse. *Psyche* 36: 193–225.

analytical situation in relation to the transference and so becomes the motor of the cure (Béjarano, 1977, p. 8). Opening new fields of indications brought problems to the practice of psychoanalysis and left some looking back wistfully to Freud's limited indications. In order to come to grips with these problems, personality 'types' or 'structures' supposedly by nature inaccessible to analysis have been researched in ever more sophisticated ways (Pontalis, 1980, p. 5).[1]

In contrast, centring on the transference–countertransference relationship emphasizes the indicatory function of the analyst's subjectivity by shifting the limits of analysability from the limitations of the patient's psychopathology onto the limitations of the analyst's personality (Cremerius, 1979, p. 587). To my mind, the fruitless attempt to objectively detect non-analysable patients is avoided, and the so-called 'therapeutic diagnosis' (Flarsheim, 1972) within the psychoanalytical diagnostic which must precede every indication, is accorded special significance.[2]

This article is limited to the therapeutic diagnosis and accordingly to the question of analysability, and therefore disregards questions of nosological diagnosis as well as discussions on research into indication processes (cf. Blaser, 1977, e.g. p.218 et seq.).[3] In the following text and in order to circumvent a debate on terminology (which among other things would require us to go into the relationships and differences between the terms indication, applicability and analysability [cf. Blaser, 1977, p. 133]), I will call the described group in the field of therapeutic diagnosis the subjective indications.[4]

In choosing this term I express my conviction that the crucial question for an indication – i.e. if, on the basis of his relationship to the analyst, a patient will be able to identify and internalize something, meaning that he will achieve in analysis 'a better object relationship than was possible during a crucial period of development' (Zetzel, 1970, p. 103) – will be answered through the analyst's subjectivity.

This implies a concept of healing – according to object relations theory – in which the 'changing power of rationality' (Cremerius, 1979, p. 581) by means of interpretation becomes therapeutically effective only when

1 Pontalis (1980, p. 6) mentions the 'anti-analysand' described by Joyce McDougall, as well as Nathalie Zaltzman's 'untreatable' and Micheline Enriquez's 'parasitic' analysands, and complains polemically about increasing tendencies in this direction.

2 Despite the great significance attributed to the 'therapeutic diagnosis', the necessity of an extensive psychoanalytic diagnosis may not be overlooked. According to Loch (1979b, p. 188 et seq.) a psychoanalytical diagnosis should contain statements covering the following areas: (1) the psychiatric classification; (2) the relationship dynamics; (3) the patient's characteristic anxiety and danger situations; as well as (4) the patient's conflict structure.

3 Leuzinger (1980) gives a very extensive overview of the stand of empirical research on the indication process and within her own research she presents, among other things, a very interesting approach based on a theory-driven computer-assisted content analysis.

4 Cf. also the terms 'therapy-centered indication' (Blaser, 1977, p. 219) and 'subjective therapist variable in the indication' (op. cit., p. 135), which are used synonymously for 'subjective indication'.

accompanied by an emotional experience. Consequently, the questions of whether and to what extent both partners in the analytic dialogue will be capable of having an emotional experience together is of central importance to me in a 'subjective indication'. Moreover, I will trace only one central aspect of analysability and do not propose to give a comprehensive and systematic overview of this topic.[5]

The following considerations are in principle valid for all forms of individual psychoanalytic treatment *sensu stricto* (psychoanalysis, psychoanalytic psychotherapy, and focal therapy), but not for psychoanalytical couple or group therapies and the like. The given time period in which a decision for a positive or negative subjective indication is made extends over the entire 'first screening', which begins with the initial interview and includes follow-up interviews, and in individual cases, a trial treatment (Freud, 1913; Parin, 1958; Tyson & Sandler, 1971). It goes without saying that the following deliberations are only pointers or suggestions and not meant to describe a norm for the individually creative process of subjective indication.

2

The central focus of this article is to examine which events in the relationship between the patient and the analyst favour a positive subjective indication for essential[6] psychoanalytical work and a positive outlook regarding therapeutic efficiency.

In my opinion, the occurrence of a mutual emotional experience during the initial interview – I shall call this an 'encounter' – is an essential requirement for the patient and analyst to be able to develop a sustainable relationship as the basis for psychoanalytic work. It is a very general term, but at the same time rather overloaded philosophically and pedagogically.[7] I will therefore examine the question of what I mean by 'encounter' in an analytical context.[8] An encounter is a 'normal process of unconscious interaction' (Klauber, 1975, p. 835) between analyst and patient where there

[5] I would especially like to point out Limentani (1972), as well as Bachrach and Leaff (1978). I will not deal any further with the very important positive (outer) criteria for subjective indication (according to Loch, 1979b, p. 190): The patient's capability to keep set appointments, to come to terms to a large degree with the demands of the real world, and the presence of at least one person in his surroundings who is close to the patient.

[6] 'Essential' psychoanalytic procedure, very briefly formulated, is characterized by the work done on transference and resistance with the essential instruments used in the areas of reconstruction and construction such as free association, interpretation and use of the object relationship as such (cf. Loch & Pohlmann, 1977, p. 30 et seq.).

[7] Cf. e.g. Martin Buber.

[8] Here I would like to draw attention to Klauber's book (1980) on the 'analytical encounter', which was published in a German edition after the completion of this article.

is communication of the one's unconscious with the other's unconscious. This unconscious communication is affectively perceptible.

An example from a psychoanalytic treatment may illustrate this: At the beginning of a psychoanalytic session the patient remains silent while at the same time she appears restless. During this lengthy interval the analyst experiences painful feelings which in his fantasy[b] are connected to a parting he experienced the previous day. At the same time he experiences the intensity of these feelings as inappropriate for the remembered event because in reality the parting was only a temporary one, which the analyst registered with a touch of melancholy but in which he sees no cause for this noticeably anxious reaction more akin to an abandonment experience. Experienced at the moment of pain, he explains this discrepancy – or better still, this ego-dystonic experience – to himself in a provisional hypothesis as a reaction to the patient's affective communication. After a time he interprets that she feels abandoned. In fact, in the material which followed this, the patient was able to express her fears concerning the continuance of the therapeutic relationship.[9]

Without going into the implications of the transference, I would like to examine this more closely as an example of the affective communication mentioned above. At the beginning of the session the 'associative exchange' (Cosnier, 1976, p. 43) was interrupted because the patient was defending herself against the unbearable notion of losing the analyst. Because the fear of loss was so intense the repression of this image did not suffice and this led to an additional splitting of the instinctual representatives into ideational and affect representatives. The affects were now no longer bound to their ideas and lost their signal anxiety function; instead, they flooded the patient to such an extent that she no longer had space for different ideas and consequently her associations flagged. In this phase the affects transmitted to the analyst assume the 'communicative function' (Green, 1977, p. 140).

But how can it be explained that the analyst was not only able to intuitively apprehend the affects conveyed but could also understand them? I join Green in his conjecture, following Lacan, that the unconscious is structured in a way that is analogous to a language,[10] whereby affects are granted a signifier function when they are integrated in the rest of the significant material of the

[b] Editors' note: The author uses the German word 'Phantasie' to refer to a wide range of phenomena ranging from conscious daydream-like phenomena in the analyst, to his inferences about unconscious phantasies that may be operative in the patient's mind. In order to respect the author's own usage, we have decided to translate this as 'fantasy' throughout, except where he specifically refers to the Kleinian concept of unconscious 'phantasy'.

[9] Not until this point is the provisional hypothesis confirmed, and the counter-hypothesis that the actual experience of pain stems from unresolved conflicts in the analyst can be discarded.

[10] I refer to Lacan's theory only insofar as it signifies that, in agreement with Freud – who speaks of the possibility of the most complicated 'mental performance without participation of the conscious' – thinking activity can be carried out in the unconscious in a way that is analogous to language in the conscious system.

unconscious chain (Green, 1977, p. 149). In the described vignette with this patient, the affect, 'by its intensity and its meaning (signification)', was not integrated in the unconscious chain (ibid.). For the analyst to be able to understand the patient's affective signal it was necessary that his affect – analogously evoked by the patient's affect – be in intra-psychic associative connection with ideas, thus integrating the affect into his unconscious chain. After the analyst had named the affect in terms of the fantasies he associated with it, he became aware of the meaning of the affect in the communication between himself and the patient (Cosnier, 1976, p. 34). In this way he helped her so that she was able to integrate the split-off affect into a meaningful context.

An 'encounter' like the one described consists in the analyst's ability to allow the patient's affects to evoke similar and/or complementary affects in himself and to transpose these into emotional images, or fantasies.[11] These fantasies can show different structural levels, they originate in the analyst's unconscious and preconscious, and they usually excel in equal measure in the rediscovery and 're-formulation' of emotional images of memories. They are felt with all the personal implications they hold for the analyst. As analysts we are affectively 'approachable' – and here lies the source of our intuition – when what the other brings forth is 'similar to our own background' (Sandler, 1976a), when it somehow correlates with 'our personal idiosyncrasies' (Thomä, 1974, p. 391).

As a result, the analyst's subjectivity has a very important impact on the analytical relationship. The analyst must avail himself of his subjectivity and employ it (Racker, 1957) in order to cathect the patient narcissistically and as an object. The advance libidinal input required here from the analyst is a consequence of the realization that transference is always preceded by countertransference. 'Translated back into the early period of its origins, it is the child's answer to the transference from its most important early objects' (Loch & Pohlmann, 1977, p. 33).[12]

The successful affective rapport of an encounter (Freud, 1925, p. 42) opens up an opportunity for a 'communal transitional activity' to develop in the interaction between the analyst and the patient (Cosnier, 1976, p. 43). Independent of the conflictualization of the transference relationship, this activity ensures 'the opportunity for a continuous connection . . ., which will be free of the opposites, ego-non ego' (ibid.).[13] Insofar as psychoanalytical treatment aims to release the attachment to the infantile object (Loch &

[11] Contrary to a representation, with which affect is merely associated, a phantasy, according to M. Klein, is an 'elementary unity of fantasied affect' (Green, 1977, p. 145).

[12] For Giovacchini (1973), it follows that it is actually the analyst who construes the patient's psychopathology.

[13] Caruso (1980) probably means this activity, which in certain areas reconciles the narcissistic with the object relationship, when he speaks of the 'symbiotic channel'.

Pohlmann, 1977, p. 36) and so to enable bearing its loss, this 'transitional activity' is of special importance. It makes it possible[14] that the ideas which were earlier defended against on different levels in order to avoid the fear of separation need not to be banned from the relationship between the analyst and the patient 'because they are now no longer dangerous for the object relationship' (Cosnier, 1976, p. 43).

If a communal transitional activity has been established an analytic climate will prevail in which, for example, the sudden appearance of tension will effect 'progress or a delay in understanding' (ibid.). The analyst is not allowed to understand everything because it would overwhelm him traumatically (Sandler, 1976a). The delay in understanding protects the patient from a sudden break-down of his defences. The 'equilibrium of force and meaning necessary to the pursuit of the process' (Cosnier, 1976, p. 43) is established only when the analyst sympathizes with the stabilizing effects of the patient's early solutions to his problems (Klauber, 1975) and thus is – analogous to the 'regression in the service of the ego' (Kris, 1952) – ready and willing for 'regression in the service of the relationship'. This is a guarantee that as analysts we are able to accompany the patient in his efforts to find new solutions and will not hasten away in premature understanding.[15]

As an emotional-affective relationship between analyst and patient, the encounter is localized within the transference–countertransference events, insofar as one subscribes to a broad understanding of the term transference (Loch, 1974, p. 432 et seq.). The core of the encounter pertains to the 'real character' (Loch, 1978, p. 105) of the analyst–patient relationship and relates – expressed in transference and countertransference dimensions – to the layer of 'primal transference' (Stone, 1961, pp. 71, 77, 86; Loch, 1967, p. 262) and the 'mild and unpronounced positive' transference (Freud, 1914, p. 151; Loch, 1974, p. 436ff.). Of course, components that are part of 'transference and countertransference, *stricto sensu*' (Loch, 1967, p. 262)[16] also flow in during an encounter. But in my opinion, the encounter obtains the prognostic significance necessary for indication primarily through the real relationship[17]

[14] The constitution of this transitional activity opens the possibility that in the course of the therapy the analyst takes on the characteristics of a 'transitional object' (Winnicott, 1953) for the patient.

[15] Take note of the affirmative character of defence (Schafer, 1973; Loch, 1979b, p. 190; Loch, 1977, p. 226).

[16] I name this – the neurotic and psychotic forms together – the 'pathological transference and countertransference dimension' because, contrary to forms which relate to the real relationship, it requires psychoanalytic interpretation on principle.

[17] The treatment alliance (which is composed of the working alliance constituted in the relationship between the patient's 'fiction of a normal ego' and that of the analyst [Freud, 1937, p. 239], together with the 'therapeutic alliance' that is part of the real relationship) belongs, in my opinion, to the area of 'objective indication' and will therefore not be discussed here. [Editors' note: for this distinction between 'treatment alliance', 'working alliance' and 'therapeutic alliance', see also section 4.1 below.]

because only this concrete[c] connection – in terms of the experienced 'fusion of primary object and analyst' (Loch, 1978, p. 105) – lends 'vital meaning' (Loch, 1976, p. 886) to the therapeutic interaction. I can not here go into the profound questions touched on in the interrelationship between meaning and existence or finding meaning through object relationship (cf. Loch, 1976, 1980). Instead, a real, concrete, emotional-affective relationship as the basis for the analyst–patient relationship should again be emphasized – together with a reference to Winnicott, who sees that the first goal of the analyst is to keep the patient 'alive' (Winnicott, 1962, p. 166). Seen in light of libido theory, an encounter is characterized by the analyst's reaction to a patient's spontaneous drive impulse, with a synchronous and isomorphic countertransference (Loch, 1977, p. 224).[18] Thus the encounter is also always a mutual drive experience (Winnicott, 1954/55) in the sense of a conjoint, concrete and real experience. It must be:

> because the mutual objects reactivated in the transference (to the analyst; J. D.) are those which were constituted through direct, concrete, executed actions determined by the activating instinctual modalities at the time when the sensomotoric and pre-operational stadiums of intelligence were dominant (J. Piaget).
>
> (Loch, 1978, p. 101)

Only the restoration of this cathected object relationship in the psychoanalytic situation opens up the possibility of resolving the neurotic (or psychotic) transference during the psychoanalytic process (ibid., p. 100).

3

During the initial interview the analyst pays close attention to see if he can enter into an emotional relationship with the patient. The patient's 'transference ability' (his ability to develop a 'neurotic transference') is no longer an issue as it was in Freud's day. Instead, the analyst observes the

[c] Editors' note: The author uses the German adjective 'konkret' to refer to two closely related but also distinguishable clinical phenomena. The first usage, which appears here, refers to his understanding of the 'real' relationship, in which the interaction between patient and analyst takes place partly at the level of un-symbolized experiences. He considers this phenomenon, which we have translated as 'concrete', to be primitive, but necessary for the encounter and not pathological, so long as the analyst simultaneously remains able to use his capacities for symbolization. The second usage, which first appears in section 4.1 below, concerns situations in which the analyst's capacities for symbolization are temporarily so overwhelmed that it hampers his ability to work analytically with that patient. If it is not overcome, this second phenomenon can argue against a subjective indication. Because of this difference in accent, we have decided to translate this second use of 'konkret' as 'concretized'.

[18] Reik (1948) describes how the analyst can grasp the nature and direction of the patient's drive tendencies.

entire 'transference potential' (Glover, 1955)[19] as it organizes itself on different transference–countertransference levels[20] in the interview situation. We also encounter patients who cannot – as expected in terms of 'transference ability' – experience the past in the transference, but who instead have the tendency to want 'to transform the analyst into a past object' (Aarons, 1962). These patients do not recognize the 'as if' character of transference as it is typical for 'neurotic transference' (these patients do not treat the analyst as if he were, for example, their father – instead they treat him as their father). Processes of this sort indicate a defect in the patient's 'development of the representational world of instinctual objects' (Loch & Pohlmann, 1977, p. 35). Nevertheless the patient 'transfers', if not in the sense of a neurotic transference, and a relationship exists between the analyst and the patient which can be sustainable enough for therapy.[21]

However, a defect in the construction of the representational world can be so severe that formation of the 'mild and unpronounced positive' transference fundamental to therapy can not be counted on, since this form of transference is tied to a preliminary reconciliation between the ego and the id. Under such circumstances, the analyst will be cathected by drive elements which are *quasi in statu nascendi*, i.e. have not yet found their psychic representation, their transformation into wishes . . .' (Loch, 1965/66, p. 178). In this case the affective communication between the analyst and the patient is interrupted,[22] the affective-emotional relationship (on which the analytical therapy 'pivots') is threatened by drive impulses such as feelings of envy and hate (Heimann, 1962). If such a disturbance hinders the development of an emotional relationship between the patient and analyst, it is not necessarily an indicator for a negative subjective indication. Instead, it is the analyst's countertransference fantasies which now especially matter. Decisive is whether fantasies develop in the analyst directly in the setting when affective communication is blocked and what these fantasies contain.

The following considerations can only serve as guidelines: the analyst feels the patient's inability to establish affective communication. How does he react to this? Does this make him feel rejected or less able to maintain the boundaries he needs to protect himself from the patient's 'affective block'? Or is he successful in identifying with the patient's affective state (Loch, 1967, p. 246) and taking him into his own inner self, in his 'own privacy' (Stephanos, 1980,

[19] In addition to the depth of symptom formation and the strength of secondary gain from illness, Glover (1955) sees the 'measure of transference potential' as the decisive criteria for an indication based on nosology.

[20] Cf. Loch, 1967, p. 261–265; 1974, p. 432.

[21] In a broad understanding of the term 'transference', the proposed differentiation between transference capability and relationship capability (Blaser, 1977, p. 131) is unnecessary.

[22] In Green's words (1977, p. 149) the affect is not integrated in the rest of the significant material of the unconscious (or preconscious) chain.

p. 192), so that at that moment patient and analyst are transitorily identical in their sense of self?[23] The analyst must cope with this situation – which is usually marked by a state of decreased mental clarity – so that he can replace the disturbed affective communication with identification. When the analyst is in this mental state, which is primarily dominated by affect, memory traces that are coherent with his emotions come up into his consciousness – at first vague and hazy, then more structured. From these memory traces, concrete fantasies are formed, which can remain in different stages of differentiation. But the objective is always that the emotional states the patient is not yet able to communicate are integrated into the analyst's experience, take form in the analyst's fantasies and are brought into – at least for the analyst – a more understandable and communicable form closer to the level of verbalization than they have been up to now.[24] It cannot be expected – and indeed it happens in only the rarest cases – that a verbal formulation, representing and transcending this situation (Loch, 1980), will already be found in this initial phase.[25] It is only the extent to which the analyst is able to develop fantasy activity in the presence of a patient momentarily incapable of communicating, as discussed above, which is of interest and relevant for the subjective indication. In my opinion, these fantasies stand in close relationship to 'reverie' as Bion (1970) describes it: the child's early anxieties are contained by the mother, given shape through her 'reverie', and then returned to him in this reworked form.

The fact that these fantasies arise indicates a sufficient measure of security and wellbeing[26] in the analytical relationship – a circumstance which can be considered to offer a certain guarantee that the relationship will not be too threatened by libidinal irruptions in the future.

It is important to me to differentiate and separate these sorts of fantasies in the analyst from those that do not develop during a direct encounter with the patient. The latter are concepts[27] which prematurely try to

23 Racker (1988, p. 143) calls the state where a union of both unconsciousnesses occurs a 'psychological symbiosis'.

24 In my opinion, understanding does not occur in a sudden act of insight, but instead runs through a continuum from a very vague, emotionally determined inkling to clearly articulated knowledge. But only when this inkling originates from the same continuum as the knowledge (thus springing from the same unconsciously, or consciously dominant 'chain' [Green, 1977, p. 149]), can it be regarded as its precursor. However, this is 'only' subjectively determinable as affective coherence, or better still, as an associative entity of the affective contents. This is perhaps more easily understood using an analogy to music, which as a communication system can convey emotional content linked and reshaped – quasi associatively – from different structural levels.

25 'Access to the imaginable sometimes demands a long stay in painful confrontation with something that has neither name nor face' (Pontalis, 1980, p. 12).

26 Security and wellbeing are factors that are prerequisite for fantasy activity. In the circumstances postulated here, where projective identification is the decisive factor in the relationship, it is indifferent whether a psychic phenomenon – here fantasy activity – happens in the patient or in the analyst.

27 The necessity of such concepts for the psychoanalytic process – however in a different context – remains indubitable.

make sense of an event not experienced, but instead observed from a distance.[28]

4

Before a positive subjective indication for psychoanalysis (or for psychoanalytical psychotherapy) can be given, it is vital to assess the prospective capacity for the entire psychoanalytical process. The initial interview should yield clues as to how far the relationship between a particular analyst and a particular patient appears to be suitable in order to successfully come to terms with (1) the opening and consolidation phases, (2) the phase of the appearance and analysis of the transference neurosis, and (3) the phase of treatment termination.[29]

4.1

The opening phase demands a special effort in adaptation on the part of the analyst. For our concerns, the question arises as to what extent he can muster this effort with a particular patient. The analyst's efforts in adjusting are reactions comparable to 'the mother's adjustment to her child's inherent potential . . . during the period preceding the differentiation between the self and the object' (Zetzel, 1970, p. 266). Each analytical situation demands a maximum of mobilization and assisted integration for those ego capacities 'which also earlier were already successful in areas outside the area of the neurotic conflict' (ibid.). But the analyst's adapting capacities are of particular importance with patients suffering from a 'structural disorder of the ego' (Fürstenau, 1977, p. 201) with whom the early phases of the analysis should not be concentrated primarily on analysis of defence mechanisms, as with structural neuroses, but should instead work on the formation of the ego-self (Loch & Pohlmann, 1977, p. 30).[30] 'The capacity for constant object

[28] They are often referred to as 'unconscious fantasy', based on a misunderstanding of M. Klein (who 'substituted for the classical Freudian opposition of representation and affect, *the elementary unity of fantasied affect*' [Green, 1977, p.145]) but are in fact nothing more than the analyst's ' "ready made" representations', which – when they are conveyed too early – only hinder the patient in his own psychic work (ibid., p. 151).

[29] Oriented on Zetzel's (1970, p. 163 et seq.) three-phase division of the psychoanalytical process.

[30] A difference in meaning between the terms 'structural disorder of the ego' and 'structural neuroses' (Fürstenau, 1977, p. 197 et seq.) has largely prevailed, not least owing to their reference to Freud's structural theory. However, it should be pointed out that structures resulting from earlier object relationships with significant others are 'solidified completed acts' and must be seen as the result of a conflict. A differentiation between conflict and structure appears very problematic to me.

relationships' is so diminished in these patients (Zetzel, 1970, p. 268) that they have great difficulties in entering into a stable 'treatment alliance';[31] their capacity for a 'working alliance', on the level of a relationship between the patient's 'fictive normal ego' and that of the analyst, seems to be particularly impaired. In such cases, the analyst's objective in his adaptive efforts is to establish a temporary treatment alliance by forming and strengthening the 'therapeutic alliance'. 'Therapeutic alliance' means the unconscious anaclitic factor within the therapeutic relationship and refers to a level where primitive wishes and impulses, especially those stemming from childhood, play a great role. At this level the patient unconsciously attempts to achieve and experience a particular object relationship 'as a vehicle of instinctual gratification' (Sandler, 1976a, p. 45).[32] In doing so he allocates to the analyst a 'role' that is complementary to the momentary orientation of his ego state. This is an attempt to 'actualize' an intra-psychic role relationship 'in a disguised way' (Sandler, 1976a, p. 44),[33] by externalizing certain parts of the self (ibid.) in order to resist awareness of the relationship. Recognition of this must be prevented because it threatens the relationship adhered to for the sake of its connection to the primary object (Loch, 1978, p. 106ff.; Loch & Dantlgraber, 1980, p. 520). In psychoanalytical practice this form of transference commonly appears as resistance and when it occurs during the initial interview it becomes relevant to our topic, through the analyst's possible reactions. If the analyst merely 'registers' its defensive character, no encounter in the sense of communication between both unconscious systems – substantiating a positive subjective indication – will follow.[34] If the analyst takes on the role the patient assigns to him, a role acceptance occurs (see: 'Role Responsiveness', Sandler, 1976a, p. 45), which can take various different courses.

In any case, affective signals from the patient meet up with the analyst's affectivity in such a way that he allows them to 'touch' him or to 'push' him to behave in a particular way unconsciously intended by the patient.[35] The extent to which the analyst experiences the intensity and the quality of the affective signals reaching him does, however, seem relevant to me. As a rule

[31] I follow Loch (1967, p. 262; 1974, p. 432) in differentiating the treatment alliance into the components working alliance and therapeutic alliance.

[32] 'However, what I have to say here applies not only to unconscious instinctual wishes, but *to the whole gamut of unconscious (including preconscious) wishes related to all sorts of needs, gratifications and defences*' (cf. Sandler, 1976a, p. 44).

[33] Expressed in more familiar language, this is the patient's unconscious attempt to draw the analyst into complementary countertransference (Racker, 1988, p. 136).

[34] I am convinced that unconscious communication of the latent content of thoughts, wishes and fantasies goes on continually, and that this communication can occur because of the normal capacity to make an unconscious 'good guess' in translating the meaning of the behaviour and communications of others of similar cultural background (Sandler, 1976b, p. 41).

[35] It is highly probable that there are links from this to the term 'acting out countertransference' (Fürstenau, 1977, p. 204).

he will have the internal 'space' that he needs in order to receive the affects streaming in on him in such a way that he can transform them into fantasies – fed from his own memory material – and so have the opportunity to gradually integrate the role-accepting process into his unconscious or preconscious area. From time to time it happens that the analyst is directly hit by an affective signal. There is something unrelenting and merciless in the primitiveness of these types of affects and they can only be answered with either self-involvement or a strong affective defence. It seems as if they directly affect the analyst's unconscious and there trigger impulses to act according to the allocated role, leaving no decision-making space open for reaction.

In my opinion, the differentiation between these two forms of role acceptance is an indicator as to whether a psychic conflict expressed in a particular interaction became unconscious through repression or never was conscious (Freud, 1939, p. 97), on the basis of the knowledge 'that the psychic apparatus registers the traces of affective experiences before it is ready to establish mnemic traces of perceptions' (Green, 1977, p. 152). Early affective experiences do not, therefore, correspond with memory traces of perception. If the psychic apparatus is not able to lend these affects content (i.e. meaning), thus to transform them into an idea (a psychic representation), they will diffuse into other areas of the psychic apparatus.

The affects that have not yet acquired psychic representation are those which affect the analyst directly (as long as he doesn't close himself off from them). Because these affects without 'symbolic messages' communicate themselves quite concretely to the analyst, I call an interaction proceeding in this fashion a concretized encounter. In contrast, more highly organized unconscious affective signals leave the analyst with enough space to transform them into 'private' fantasies. There are messages hiding behind these which had already once been symbolized before the repression process took place and which can now be re-symbolized. When I refer to affective interactions of this latter pattern, I speak of an encounter in a symbolic space.

The difference between an 'encounter in a symbolic space' and a 'concretized encounter' can be illustrated by means of a comparison. I would like to point out the parallels between perceptions arising from unconscious signals and those arising from listening to music: just as the analyst experiences unconscious affective messages as his own, the music listener, after overcoming the original threat and playfully repeating this successful coping accomplishment, also experiences the feelings expressed in the music as his own (Kohut & Levarie, 1950, p. 85). In both cases a state of fusion is reached which requires the ability to regress to an earlier ego-state by the analyst and music listener alike. But for our concerns it is decisive whether or not the analyst simultaneously has access to the complicated ego functions necessary for organizing the affective material streaming into him at that very moment.[36] When this simultaneous presence of different levels of ego functioning does not develop, I interpret this as an indicator for the occurrence of a 'concretized encounter'. It is probably not necessary to especially emphasize that the analyst must examine himself (in self-analysis or through supervision) to see to how far a 'concretized encounter' has actually occurred and to what extent he was not capable of simultaneously maintaining these different ego functions due to difficulties of his own. It likewise goes without saying that the occurrence of an encounter can only be positively assessed for subjective indication when the process becomes analytically clear to the analyst, either simultaneously or after self-reflective work.[37] When a 'concretized encounter' occurs, areas of the patient's psychic disturbance connected to his non-mastery of the 'depressive position' (Klein, 1935; Winnicott, 1954/1958) enter into the relationship with the analyst. As is generally known, from an evolutionary point of view, the depressive position resides 'in the transitional area between the pre-symbolic and the symbolic world' (Loch, 1979a, p. 161). With patients suffering from disturbances on this structural level, the subjective indication is above all a question of whether a projected analysis will be able to penetrate into this area. In this context it is worth taking into consideration Winnicott's suggestion that the analyst must take on the characteristics of a 'transitional object' (Winnicott, 1953) for the patient, so that 'the experience, like the separation and the consolidation of self and object representations . . . is accomplished in a not too intensively pathogenic manner' (Loch & Pohlmann, 1977, p. 32). The patient must have the chance in the psychoanalytic dialogue to experience the analyst as 'the actual object . . . which faces him, in his or her "as is" state, quasi as his own creation' (ibid.). Such a step on the patient's part can of course only be the result of an analysis that has already run for a lengthy period of time and may not be expected in the beginning, at the time of the indication. And still – because in making the decision to undertake a psychoanalytic treatment it is ultimately a matter of exactly this inner step the patient must take – it seems important to me if during the indication signs can already be found which suggest that it will be possible to achieve this step later on in the psychoanalytical dialogue. The analyst's role acceptance, triggered by a 'concretized encounter', for example, already at the commencement of the analytical relationship gives the patient the feeling that he can 'move' the object (the analyst) with his affective impulses and that by triggering affective reactions in the analyst he can 'create' something of his liking. Processes like these have a stabilizing effect on the 'therapeutic alliance', mobilize the patient's unconscious motivation and consequently have a very favourable influence

36 According to Kohut and Levarie (1950, p. 85), an analogue, simultaneous process is a prerequisite for the enjoyment of music.

37 'It is useful to grasp in another only what the analyst has accepted within himself as his own, and what therefore can be *recognized* in the other person *without anxiety or rejection* . . .' (Racker, 1988, p. 17).

on the treatment alliance. This effects the basis for an inner (therefore still non-verbal, affective) dialogue which, in creating 'psychic space' (Green, 1975), first enables the evolution of the analysis.

What is ultimately at stake is whether the 'setting' can become a good enough 'facilitating environment' (Winnicott, 1965, p. 239) in a given psychoanalytic situation. Should such an encounter occur during the initial interview, it can, in my opinion, be considered a decisive sign that a sustainable analyst–patient relationship will develop.

4.2

Whether a patient can develop a 'transference neurosis' in a particular psychoanalytical situation is not, in a narrow sense, a question which affects the subjective indication. In fact here it is a matter of examining those inner conditions of the patient which are prerequisite for the formation of a transference neurosis (cf. for example, Zetzel, 1970, p. 163). On the other hand, it is known that specific contributions are also needed from the analyst for a transference neurosis to appear (Loewald, 1971, p. 61). Thus the appearance of a transference neurosis should be looked upon as a phenomenon of a particular analyst–patient relationship. Consequently, it seems to me that any statements relating to the question of whether the evolution of a transference neurosis can be anticipated are highly relevant. Without going into the still controversial problem of how far an efficiently conducted, 'good enough' psychoanalytic treatment is tied to the formation of a 'real' transference neurosis, I would like to pursue the following considerations. I will begin with the basic question: what transference constellation presents itself at the initial interview and to what extent can it be diagnosed by the analyst? For the subjective indication, it is not a matter of whether 'the transference dynamic which is decisively causing the symptoms' (Kutter, 1977, p. 967) appears, but rather of whether the transference actualized in the initial interview is a conflict dynamic contained in the overall 'psychodynamic syndrome',[38] which the analyst recognizes as such and formulates (at least internally) in a trial interpretation. The trial interpretation focuses on the transference dynamic constituted in the initial interview and not on the patient's 'central conflict' (ibid., p. 961).[39]

It is crucial how the analyst constructs this trial interpretation, and therefore how it develops in the analyst. It is well known that the pathological

[38] According to more recent findings in psychoanalysis, the psychodynamics behind the symptomatic picture are to be seen as a syndrome of interrelated conflicts each belonging to different psychogenetic developmental stages.

[39] In certain cases both can coincide. In such cases, the analyst is encouraged to give thought to implementing focal therapy.

relationship patterns primarily transferred are those which are rooted in traumatic relationships with persons of the early socialization phase (Loch, 1978, p. 100). Certain pathological interaction patterns presented in the initial interview are the basis of the trial interpretation(s). The constructive use of a trial interpretation that we expect for a positive subjective indication is only possible for the patient when the insights it conveys do not endanger his relationship to the primary object. This kind of trial interpretation takes into consideration that any defensive steps 'ultimately aim to preserve the connection to the primary love object or its representation' (Loch, 1978, p. 106). This means that defences in the service of a transference may not become the content of a trial interpretation if the patient has not yet cathected[40] the analyst far enough for the analyst to be fused with the primary object on the level of the real analyst–patient relationship (ibid., p. 105).

The analyst, when 'feeling held at distance, outside the (affective; J.D.) communication' (Cosnier, 1976, p. 42), senses the patient's lack of sufficient cathexis and along with this the lack of a sufficiently sustainable relationship. This situation can be significant for subjective indication, because it provides a test of the analyst's ability to develop his 'holding' function (Winnicott, 1960) with a given patient. It is important that the analyst be successful in formulating the patient's possible mental state as it is presented in the interaction, through his own 'identification with the actual ego in its process of forming'[41] (Loch, 1977, p. 223).[42]

In this way the patient senses that the analyst respects the affirmative character of his defences and understands 'the tendencies of the ego to preserve its safety' (Loch, 1977, p. 223). Proceeding in this way will specifically take into consideration the 'safety principle' (Sandler, 1961/62) that is crucial for the constitution of the ego-self. Expressed technically and schematically, we are dealing here with trial interpretations in which the dimension of the causal 'whence' is omitted (Loch, 1979b, p. 190), and the dimension of 'whither' or 'what for' (Loch, 1978, p. 106)[d] is subsumed under the 'use' of the object relationship (Balint, 1968, p. 173). This presupposes that the analyst must be able to actively cathect the patient in order to induce the transference relationship.[43] In intervening from a concordant identification position, the

[40] When there is not sufficient cathexis of the analyst, fixation on an inner object can not be relinquished. This leads to a powerful inner gain from illness, which generally speaks against a positive indication (Loch, 1979b, p. 190).

[41] Cf. 'concordant' and 'homologous' identification (Racker, 1988, p. 133ff.).

[42] The trial interpretations meant here aim 'for an understanding of his (the patient's; J.D.) situational mental state in the sense of a semantic, definitional designation of their mood as well as their intentionality' (Loch, 1979b, p. 190).

[d] Editors' note: These passages from Loch refer to Freud's differentiation of the 'sense' of a symptom into its two 'directions' of 'whence' and 'whither' or 'what for' (Freud, 1916–1917, Introductory Lectures on Psychoanalysis, *SE* 15, pp. 277, 284); see also Loch, 2006, pp. 2–3.

[43] 'For only Eros can originate Eros' (Racker, 1988, p. 30).

analyst opens a 'symbiotic channel' (Caruso, 1980, p. 31) from the patient to the analyst, so that on this basis the patient will be able to give up his fixation on an inner object sufficiently to allow a gradual cathexis of the analyst. At times an indirect route is needed for this cathexis to be accomplished. When it exactly matches the pathogenic behavioural pattern of the inner object that the patient is fixated on, the analyst's spontaneous affective reaction based on a complementary identification (Racker, 1988, p. 124), can result in the completion of a 'libidinal circuit'. Later on the analyst would have to transcend this situation so that it does not result in a possible collusion (Dicks, 1967, p. 76). In making these suggestions it is especially important for me to show that the trial interpretations described here include the aspect of affective 'trial experiences', which open up a chance for, or are the start of, a corrective emotional experience. In my experience, such trial experiences lead to a stronger cathexis of the analyst which in turn has a great influence on the development of the treatment alliance. They are, therefore, valid positive criteria for a subjective indication.

4.3

Another part of making a subjective indication is to assess to what extent the patient will be able to complete the treatment successfully in this particular psychoanalytic situation. Psychoanalysis, as a 'technique of human evolution and transformation' (Racker, 1988, p. 24), reaches its goal only when a new concept of the future opens up in the patient's life. The analyst accompanies the patient only part of the way on his journey through life – and usually he does this at a difficult point where no continuation of the way opens up to the patient, or where there are so confusingly many ways that he cannot decide, and here, too, he remains at a standstill (repetition compulsion). Should a new move into the future open up to the patient at a particular point in the analysis, and if he has been able to overcome the developmental disorder in his personality, a phenomenon occurs which has been described since Balint (1932/1952) by the term 'new beginning' (Loch, 1978, pp. 97, 109f., 113). The close connection between the completion phase and the phenomenon of the new beginning is evident. It may appear far-fetched to expect a statement about the patient's capabilities for completion as early on as in the indication phase. But when one understands the term 'new beginning' in its broadest sense, as a giving up of old pathological object relationships made possible by the reality of the actual therapeutic situation (Loch, 1978, p. 109, footnote), it can be relevant to our topic. Independently of the necessary assessment of fixation strength, which is part of the objective indication criteria, it is also necessary to examine the extent to which the patient can be expected to bear the pain of object loss, as one aspect of the diagnosis of the relationship. Of course it cannot be emphasized enough that it is the first and foremost task of analysis, in particular with disorders primarily in the constitution of the ego-self, to help the patient to develop the skills needed to cope with the psychic pain of the loss of a drive cathected object (Freud, 1926, p. 171; cf. 1920, p. 30).[44] In view of these considerations, I find it useful when the analyst attempts to evaluate the patient's 'pain capability' in the course of a trial experience in the actual moment to moment relationship. We said earlier that an encounter with reciprocal cathexis between patient and analyst constitutes a positive subjective indication. When this happens, a 'symbiotic channel' (Caruso, 1980, p. 31) is produced on a level of experience characterized by the internal fusion of the primary object and the analyst. If the analyst frustrates this connection in the 'symbiotic channel', be it through a trial interpretation or in a partial withdrawal from the object relationship, he can learn something about the patient's 'pain capability' from the latter's reaction. Of course this estimation can only be approximate and 'subjective' (i.e. only concerning that particular analyst–patient interaction). Ultimately, the experience of isolation or splitting of feeling and intellect, which is frequently experienced in interviews and occurs in accordance with the 'pain principle' (Loch & Pohlmann, 1977, p. 34f.), suggesting that the loss of the libidinal object will not yet be risked, is not a reason for making a negative subjective indication.[45]

For this reason I would like to illustrate with a brief example how it became evident during a first interview that, owing to a total incapacity to bear even slight frustrations in the symbiotic channel connection, a positive indication could not be made even though a reciprocal cathexis occurred.

A 24-year-old woman came to the interview because of a break-up with her boyfriend. At first the patient was not able to initiate contact with the analyst and as he later gradually realized, the unutterable helplessness radiating from her brought him into a role in which he was concerned to an unusual extent, spoke a lot and tended to pre-formulate for her what she might mean. In this way a 'symbiotic' relationship was established on the basis of which the patient increasingly grew at ease, and in due course was able to speak quite articulately about her difficulties. She reported that she often ran around for hours in panicky fear of losing her boyfriend when he didn't immediately arrive home at the given time. But when she was alone with him she felt as if she went numb and became 'fixed'. In situations like this she either completely abandoned herself or she very aggressively picked a quarrel, ranted

[44] Dependency on the infantile drive object can be given up only by bearing the pain associated with the loss of the object, and only then can the transformation of 'experiences with the object and their correlating "sensual" interactions into symbolic representations' (Loch & Pohlmann, 1977, p. 35) succeed, that step necessary for the constitution of the ego-self.

[45] When the atmosphere of the feelings in the first interview has a completely different quality than the contents that are reported by the patient, it can be an indicator that the patient's 'sensual' experiences are bound to the libidinal object.

and raged and indiscriminately threw things around. As the analyst scaled back his marked 'verbal concern' somewhat during the interview – indeed because he had become aware of the split between her wish for fusion, which was actualized in the momentary transference, and the anxiety of total self-abandonment connected to this which forced her into aggressive attempts to defend her boundaries – the patient reacted with an appalling ego regression. She again became incapable of making verbal contact. Even when this situation could be held it was no longer possible to communicate on a rational basis about any further therapeutic procedure. The unusually strong concern felt by the analyst can by all means be interpreted as a symbolic 'giving the breast', which in her helplessness she had unconsciously encouraged. (As it later turned out, the patient suffered from drug addiction.) The analyst's attempt to transcend the symbiotic relationship in the interview, which resulted in a certain withdrawal from complementary role behaviour (quasi 'thinning out' the connection in the symbiotic channel), triggered such intense oral destruction in the patient that she defended herself from her fear of object loss by breaking off communication. Now this does not mean that analytical therapy is categorically not indicated for this patient, but it does signify that this particular analyst–patient relationship did not enable the patient to even partially risk experiencing pain and transform this into a constructive ego experience.

All in all, throughout my examination of the subjective indication for psychoanalysis in the perspective of the sustainability of the patient–analyst relationship throughout Zetzel's three treatment phases, the central question has always been: can we assess the extent to which the goals of psychoanalysis will be achieved in a given analyst–patient relationship?

5

It would be beyond the scope of this discussion if I were to go here into the goals of psychoanalytic treatment. But whatever definition of goals one follows, whether we speak of 'emotional maturity' (Racker, 1988, p. 24) or of a 'new beginning', they all have in common a central focus on the potential psychoanalysis has to bring about change. In short, the objective is to dismantle the repetition compulsion. The essential psychoanalytical moment, above and beyond other forms of psychotherapy, is leading the patient out of an unfruitful vicious circle of symbiosis and not binding him through symbiotic satisfaction to the illusionary character of a false reality where dependency on the libidinal object is shifted onto a different object, thus hindering any development towards emancipation.

We must therefore ask what position (and inner attitude, as the case may be) is necessary on the part of the analyst to achieve this dimension of emancipation. In my opinion, this dimension has much to do with Freud's

(1912, p. 115) remark that the analyst should take an inner stance like the surgeon's towards his patient (cf. also Racker, 1988, pp. 24, 30f.). It appears important to me whether and how the analyst's inner attitude can be engaged in the object relationship. (Primarily relevant for subjective indication is not the analyst's stance in itself, but whether it can be engaged in a particular analyst–patient relationship.) Racker's (1988, p. 134) considerations on this are of special importance to me. As already noted several times, Racker differentiates between two forms of identification which also play a role as trial identifications in the initial interview: concordant identification and complementary identification. Insofar as concordant identification is based on introjection and projection and on 'the recognition of what belongs to another as one's own' (ibid.), it leads to a complementary identification 'in that the analysand treats the analyst like an inner object' (ibid.). The analyst senses this and consequently identifies with this object. Racker emphasizes the dynamic relationship between these forms of identification. If the analyst in a psychoanalytic first interview takes on concordant identification with the patient in the same measure as complementary identification, and is at the same time able to transcend from both positions, a phenomenon appears which I would like to call empathic triadic relation[46] (after an expression used by Fürstenau [1979]). By this I mean that in a way that is analogous to the psychoanalytic situation,[47] a triangular object relationship is represented in the analyst's mind which consists of the following factors: in the concordant identification the patient is represented by the patient's 'actual ego',[48] while in the complementary identification the analyst is represented as the transference object. But prerequisite for the differentiation of these two identifications is a process analogous to 'therapeutic ego splitting' whereby, owing to his ability to take on an ex-centric[e] position, the analyst can theoretically name the dyads represented in his mind.

I would like to explain in greater detail the key importance I attach to implementing the 'empathic triadic relation' for subjective indication. I am referring here to the role of the 'third' (the third element; in socialization it is usually the father) for the individuation of the individual, which Loch

[46] 'Empathic' because the ability for concordant identification is comparable to empathy.

[47] Which encompasses virtually three persons: 'the patient and the two relationship figures the analyst is split into, namely in that of the transference object, duplicating an infantile drive object, and in that of the object making this transference explicit and thus taking an ex-centric position to the drive dyad' (Loch & Pohlmann, 1977, p. 40).

[48] The term 'actual ego' implies among other things, a reference to the psychosexual stage of development' (Loch, 1974, p. 451, footnote).

[e] Editors' note: The German adjective is 'exzentrisch', referring to the ability to step away from the centre and look at the situation from outside as in a third-person position, as explained in the next paragraph. Technically speaking, the correct translation would be 'eccentric', but this has negative connotations in English, which render it quite unsuitable to convey the author's meaning. (Another alternative is 'decentered', but this might suggest being passively thrown off-centre, whereas the author is referring to an active function in the analyst.)

(Loch & Jappe, 1974; Loch, 1979a, 1980) convincingly demonstrated and which is increasingly emphasized by other authors (for example, Rotmann, 1978; and by Fürstenau, 1979, who includes the sociological dimension). Similarly, the emergence of the third element is indispensable for the development of emotional autonomy in the psychoanalytical situation. The third element is always present in essential psychoanalytic work and can be constituted in different ways.[49] It is central to our interests to view the psychoanalytical intervention as the third element because it transcends the reactivated drive dyad in the transference. Or, in Stone's words, it replaces 'the primordial fantasy of a single original object as alternative to the rest of the world' (1961, p. 92), with a relationship that includes the world (reality).[f]

This would make reality the third element – but only insofar as it is bound to the truth (Loch, 1974, p. 441, 1976). For if it were only a matter of the analyst's reality in the form of a 'super-ego intropression' (Ferenczi, 1932) forced on the patient, to which he can respond only with positive or negative identification, no third element of an emancipatory character could develop. 'Passion for investigation' ('investigative zeal', Giovacchini, 1973, p. 155), which is seen by Loch (1974, p. 440f.) as a search for truth not bound to the person of the analyst but instead to the moment of investigation, if it is authentically exemplified by the analyst, allows the patient a margin of freedom in which the inner dialogue occurring in the analyst between his ego-self and his analytic function[50] (and thus between the analyst's privacy and his function as investigator) becomes transparent. The transparency of these two aspects of the analyst, if they are brought together and integrated in the analyst's person (Thomä, 1974, p. 391), offers a model with which the patient can gradually identify, enabling him to use the analytic method to take up a similar inner dialogue. Only in this way can the patient subject himself to the method and subsequently make use of it.[51] Thus the method becomes an instrument, shared by the patient and the analyst, which helps to 'interpret' the truth and so create a piece of 'new reality shared by both' (Loch, 1974, p. 439).

Of course in our considerations on subjective indication, the central focus is on countertransference and, in particular, on concordant identification, or empathy (which, following Racker [1988, p. 136], is incorporated in the term countertransference). The focus on empathy could easily be construed

[49] I have not overlooked the fact that the third element can also have a potentially destructive character (cf. Loch & Pohlmann, 1977, p. 40), but can not elaborate on this here.

[f] Editors' note: These last words probably refer to Stone's description of the patient's 'potentiality for a genuine distribution of libido and aggression from a single object to the remainder of the world, and a mode of communication with an appropriate object *about* the world, or indeed (and importantly) about himself' (Stone, 1961, p. 94).

[50] The analyst's function is to act in an organizing and structuring way according to 'a reality principle in the broad sense of the term' (Loch, 1974, p. 440).

[51] Cf. Grunberger (1958/59, p. 270): 'transference onto the method'.

as a magical-mystical approach. But I see nothing more in empathy than the capability to perceive 'infinitely small signs' (Waelder, 1962), whereby it must be considered that even minimal messages from the patient's speech or facial expression can lead to fleeting countertransference reactions, stemming from preconscious judgements (Kris, 1952).

If we admit that the patient's transference is primarily a response to the psychoanalyst's transference (Loch, 1965, p. 173–175), and thus that what the analyst experiences as countertransference is a response to his previous transference to the patient, then empirical studies that seek to eliminate the subjective therapist variable from the countertransference (cf. Blaser, 1977, p. 195; Heising & Beckmann, 1971) seem irrelevant to my question. Namely, it is not decisive if transference originally stems from the patient or the analyst, but rather if a transference–countertransference relationship – therefore an encounter and unconscious communication – can come about at all.

There are, of course, intentions and attitudes on the part of the analyst which make an encounter impossible or have a malignant influence on it. Both mind-sets lead to a negative subjective indication, but it should be taken into consideration that a malignant unconscious communication can be transformed into a benign one through effective supervision. However, when there is an absence of unconscious communication,[52] absolutely no basis for analytical work exists. Malignant forms of unconscious communication arise when the relationship to the patient and reflection on it from the ex-centric position do not have priority for the analyst and the relationship instead serves some other purpose. For example, in contrast to the above mentioned 'passion for investigation', the 'detective-like' approach already criticized by Balint would be a malignant form because here the analyst unconsciously uses the patient to satisfy his sadistic impulses. Freud already warned about '*furor sanandi*' (1915, p. 171), where the analyst enters the relationship to the patient for the sake of narcissistic satisfaction. In both of these examples of the analyst's attitudes towards the patient, a malign unconscious communication came about because the relationship became 'perverted'[53] by the analyst. Loch's thesis that the analyst may not 'be in need of' the patient, may not

[52] Loch (1965, p. 45) speaks of the 'iatrogenic border of the 2nd dimension', which rests on the absence of countertransference: 'Where no countertransference develops, one can not analyse.'

[53] This is the kind of relationship in which only one partner, namely the analyst, can have wishes and interests, while the other – here, the patient – can only be in harmony with the wishes and interests of the first (cf. Balint, 1956, p. 179). I see an interesting aspect of a relationship to a patient perverted by the analyst in a relationship constellation I call in a different context the 'Tannhäuser phenomenon'.

I base this on the following events from the plot of the Tannhäuser saga. Tannhäuser wanted to renounce his ruinous relationship to Venus and went to the Pope to obtain forgiveness, but was refused with the pronouncement that he was as likely to obtain deliverance from his sins as the Pope's walking stick was liable to sprout and grow green leaves.

Transferred to our context, Tannhäuser is the patient and his relationship to Venus represents the (longed for, versus feared) dyadic relationship; the Pope plays the role of the analyst.

'use' him, whereby here the accent lies on the psychic dimension of dependency, becomes understandable in this context.

The efforts of different authors (especially Beck, 1974; Riemann, 1968; cf. also Blaser, 1977) to examine certain patterns of therapist–patient interaction that depend on the therapist's personality structure (for example, therapists of schizophrenic, depressive, obsessive or hysterical personality structure) are interesting and deserve mention. But in my opinion, the definition of particular structural types contradicts the transference–countertransference dynamic which, in favourable cases, can have the effect of promoting a creative potential for change in both partners in the analytical dialogue. I therefore limit myself here to pointing out these and similar research approaches.[54]

6

At this point, in the following case study, I will attempt to point out several relevant factors for subjective indication.

I still remember very well a first interview that I had years ago with a woman who at that time had recently moved here from a rural area in southern Germany. The patient had severe symptoms of depression, which had been triggered by the birth of her daughter (the psychiatric diagnosis was post-partum psychosis). I would like to say in advance that the interview resulted in a positive subjective indication. For external reasons – I had no vacancies at that time – no psychoanalytical therapy was undertaken. I was able to refer the patient and later heard about the favourable course of her psychoanalytical treatment, after its completion.

Something difficult to define, something antagonistic, dominated the atmosphere at the outset. This was expressed in her appearance and in her affected behaviour as she entered my working room. Superficially, the casually groomed, slim young woman made a markedly intellectual and emancipated impression; she signalled sexual promiscuity. In crass contrast to this was her facial expression: depressively depleted, pale eyes, very pallid.

He cannot help the patient to free himself from the dyad because he refuses the patient's participation in the method: in other terminology, the mental phallus, symbolized in the walking stick. The refusal ensues because he is not able to identify concordantly with the patient's passive position. This occurs because he denies his own passive position in his acquisition of the method. He does not convey an inner dialogue between his ego-self and the method, which could serve the patient as a model for identifying with the method. Instead, the analyst and the method appear as one, leaving no relationship open to the patient. In the saga this condition is expressed symbolically in the Pope, who – in the language of psychoanalysis – is narcissistically tied to the primary object symbolized by the church. But it would take us too far afield here to pursue further analytical implications of this.

[54] Cf. Masterson's (1976, p. 105f.) description of unfavourable therapist variables, in particular with borderline patients.

When she sat down she made a stiff and rigid impression. She said nothing and I, too, felt as though I were paralysed: there was a complete standstill in the interaction. Suddenly, quite unexpectedly, she asked me if she could smoke. I was surprised to hear myself consent just as promptly, knowing that I do not appreciate cigarette smoke in my consultation room. I gave in to an inner feeling that I might on no account refuse her anything and I also felt that any attempt to explore her wish would be highly inappropriate. Only then did she begin to speak about her symptoms. This resulted in a contradiction for me: while the patient explained how badly she needed help, how much she was depending on therapy – thus intellectually signalling the highest degree of dependency – she provoked quite different feelings in me. Although I was 'objectively' convinced of the severity of her suffering, emotionally I lacked conviction. Her hefty torrent of words and her harsh and 'sharp' diction triggered defensive feelings in me which made me feel aggressive.

In this situation I avoided intervening in any way. Instead, I used the defences provoked by her torrent of words to busy myself with the feelings I had while listening to her. In addition to the aggressive feelings, others pushed themselves to the fore, condensed into fantasies and finally into thoughts. It was not just the patient's self-interpretations that heightened my impression that there was nothing I could do for this patient – again contradicting my 'objective' stance, where from the beginning I saw the patient as very much in need of therapy. This feeling spread, I would say in a regressive way, so that I felt myself quite empty, exhausted and incapable of giving anything. At this point I felt a need to reflect on these two conflicting feelings I was having, in short, on the aggressiveness and the emptiness. In her aggressive diction – which first provoked my counter-aggressiveness but then the emptiness – I began to recognize her unconscious impulse to empty me, the analyst, whom she envied for being 'rich in objects' (for example, I have many patients, she doesn't even have a therapist, and so on). But she had to split off her aggressive affect because it would threaten her primary relationship. And at this point, it seems to me, the course of the interview was decided. The interaction at that moment was undoubtedly about the aggression stemming from her envy. Had my defensive counter-aggression prevailed, it may have resulted in an interpretation of her envy. But in this situation I succeeded in imagining myself back into the feeling of emptiness, which I recognized as her own feeling hiding behind her aggression, and I interpreted her emptiness and helplessness in the face of her fantasized 'full' and 'rich' surroundings. Thereupon the patient reported bitterly that she and her siblings had never experienced a mother's love. For this reason she had early on taken her 2½-year-younger brother under her wing so that she could at least make up for his loss of a mother's care and devotion. Some pride slipped in as she described how she was able to protect him from their mother's attacks . . . After my intervention I no longer experienced a contradiction between the contents and accompanying affects, as I had at the beginning.

In the further course of the interview – I will not go into its content here – the relationship intensified. I learned much more about her life and it became a lively interview; enough 'space' remained for me while I was listening to follow the traces of my own fantasies developing on the periphery. For example, fantasies of my own experiences in the countryside emerged as she talked about her childhood, which she had spent in the country, and so on . . . In the course of this I could increasingly cathect the patient and bring greater personal interest to her. A primarily 'mild' transference–countertransference relationship carried the interview to its end.

What had happened? I will summarize briefly. The initial standstill in the relationship I see as an 'aggressive block': the destructiveness induced by her envy, from which she had to defend herself, flooded and blocked the relationship at the beginning. By lighting a cigarette the patient protected me from her oral greed. I would term my spontaneous agreement to her smoking as a 'concretized encounter'. (Her smoking represents an oral attack on the breast and the phallus alike, in the sense of a contamination of the mother and father imago. Later deliberation on these psychodynamics brought me to see her smoking as an oral incorporation – according to the dominant drive modality – of the father's phallus to replace, in a concrete fantasy, the insufficient introjection of the father as the good third object needed to overcome the depressive position.) It was my participation in this part of the defence which first enabled the dialogue to unfold. A further relevant factor is that I did not enter into a sadomasochistic relationship in accordance with my feelings, but instead let myself be 'robbed', be 'emptied' by her, and yet not 'destroyed'. But now it was a matter of reflecting on the interactions occurring in the concrete situation from my ex-centric position and in terms of the 'empathic triadic relation'. Only this enabled me to understand my contradictory feelings as expressing concordant and complementary identifications. On top of this, one had to keep in mind that, under such circumstances in which projective identification predominated, a shift from concordant to complementary identification took place. These identifications corresponded to the patient's shifting defensive positions. Finally the trial interpretation, which was fashioned from the concordant identification and took the form of a description of her affective state in the interview situation, enabled the patient to avoid a particular layer (the sadomasochistic layer) in her defences. It wasn't until this point that the 'actual' encounter, on which the positive subjective indication was eventually based, occurred between the patient and myself.

In closing, I would also like to mention that during this initial interview only one facet of the patient's 'central conflict' was presented. The interview (as far as it has been depicted here) revolved primarily around the patient's problem with envy, in connection with which she soon also mentioned her younger brother, the cause of her original attack on her mother and whom she protected by projecting her destructive parts onto the mother. During the initial interview the hysterical parts of her personality, possibly more crucial for her pathology, remained in the background. I should like to note here that the trigger for the patient's pathology lay in the relationship to her father, who was an alcoholic. Due to her deficient identification with her father, orally fixated himself, she didn't dare maintain positive oedipal feelings towards him because of her fear of the mother's envy (which represented the projection of her envy of the brother). Later the birth of her daughter triggered her breakdown because she feared a reactivation of the envy problem in her relationship to her mother.

7

I will summarize. The occurrence of unconscious communication (an 'encounter') between patient and analyst during the initial interview is a prerequisite for a subjective indication. This communication, which requires 'regression in the service of the relationship' and expresses itself in the analyst's immediate emotional responses to the kind and direction of the patient's drive and safety tendencies, has been examined in different ways and conceptualized. Under a broad understanding of the term 'transference', the encounter belongs in the field of transference–countertransference relationships. When neurotic (or psychotic) components of the transference enter the encounter, i.e. the real relationship – as is almost always to be expected – then this involves the analyst in one of the patient's pathogenic conflict patterns. The analyst then needs to be able to make use of his emotional reactions in the specific scene[55] of the initial interview, and of his successive concordant and complementary identifications (Racker, 1957). This allows him to experience within himself the conflict between the patient and the patient's significant other that is causing his pathology and is being actualized in the here and now. He also needs to be able to take on an ex-centric position in order to transcend and/or to recognize this. By both experiencing and recognizing the conflict presented in the here and now scene, the analyst produces an 'empathic triadic relation'. This process involves a synchronous drive and ego experience in the analyst. What is decisive here is whether the analyst manages to find a formulation for this interaction that 'makes a meaningful reference to the patient's ego functions' and that is 'synchronous to a spontaneous instinctual impulse of the patient's . . . and isomorphic with the modality of this instinctual impulse' (Loch, 1977, p. 224). Depending on the nature of the relationship

[55] 'The scenic function of the ego enables the presentation of an unconscious, infantile configuration suitable to the situation – a relatively stable drive scene bound to the personality which has the status of the latent dream thoughts' (Argelander, 1970, p. 325).

dynamics and of the actualized conflict, this formulation is either given in a full trial interpretation, or it leads the analyst to verbal interventions in which the dimension of the causal 'whence' is omitted and is subsumed under the use of the object relationship. It is a positive criterion for a subjective indication if the patient can deal constructively with trial interpretations, at least with those of the second type.

The fact that a conflict in the sense of a 'unified issue' (Malan, 1976, p. 68) is experienced to some extent by both partners in the dialogue of the initial interview is significant for the subjective indication, but this is not so for the relative importance of the actualized conflict with respect to the 'central conflict' (Kutter, 1977, p. 961). Thus no confusion with focal therapy can arise, since in examining the criteria for subjective indication for psychoanalysis as a 'non-focused individual treatment' (Fürstenau, 1977, p. 199), it is not necessary to find a central focus. Of course the conflict presented in the actual scene will be connected to the conflict constellation responsible for the patient's pathology. But the conflict dynamics experienced in the analytic encounter are only one part, albeit an important one, of the patient's relationship dynamics. Thus it can happen, for example, that only one aspect of the triangular relationship comes to the forefront, while another perhaps more crucial Oedipal situation does not immediately enter the transference. Diagnosing the interrelationships of these experienced conflicts in the structure of the global conflict constellation is a necessary task, but not one that is indispensable for the subjective indication.

References

Aarons, Z. A. (1962). Indications for analyses and problems of analysability. *Psychoanalytic Quarterly* 31: 514–531.

Argelander, H. (1970). Die szenische Funktion des Ichs und ihr Anteil an der Symptom- und Charakterbildung. *Psyche* 24: 325–345.

Bachrach, H. M., Leaff, L. A. (1978). Analysability: A systematic review of the clinical and quantitative literature. *Journal of the American Psychoanalytic Association* 26: 881–920.

Balint, M. (1932). Character analysis and new beginning. In: *Primary Love and Psycho-analytic Technique*. London: Hogarth Press; London: International Psychoanalytic Library, 1952.

Balint, M. (1956). Perversions and genitality. In: *Perversions, Psychodynamics and Psychotherapy*. New York: Random House.

Balint, M. (1968). *The Basic Fault: Therapeutic Aspects of Regression*. London: Tavistock.

Beck, D. (1974). *Die Kurzpsychotherapie*. Bern: Huber.

Béjarano, A. (1977). Countertransference and narcissism. *Bulletin of the European Psychoanalytic Federation* 12: 5–10.

Bion, W. R. (1970). *Attention and Interpretation*. London: Tavistock.

Blaser, A. (1977). *Der Urteilsprozeß bei der Indikationsstellung zur Psychotherapie*. Bern: Huber.

Caruso, I. A. (1980). Bemerkungen zum idealisierten Ich oder Die Falle des Idealichs. *Psychoanalyse* 1(1): 24–39.

Cosnier, J. (1976). Interpretation and countertransference. *Bulletin of the European Psychoanalytic Federation* 9: 34–44.
Cremerius, J. (1979). Gibt es zwei psychoanalytische Techniken? *Psyche* 33: 577–599.
Dicks, H. V. (1967). *Martial Tensions. Clinical Studies towards a Psychological Theory of Interaction.* New York: Basic Books.
Ferenczi, S. (1932). Cit. from Balint, M. (1968). *The Basic Fault: Therapeutic Aspects of Regression.* London: Tavistock.
Flarsheim, A. (1972). Treatability. In: Giovacchini, P. L. (ed.), *Tactics and Techniques in Psychoanalytic Therapy* (pp. 113–131). London: Hogarth Press.
Freud, S. (1900). The Interpretation of Dreams (1955). *SE* IV–V.
Freud, S. (1912). Recommendations to Physicians Practising Psycho-Analysis. *SE* XII: 109–120.
Freud, S. (1913). On Beginning the Treatment (Further Recommendations on the Technique of Psycho-Analysis I). *SE* XII: 121–144.
Freud, S. (1914). Remembering, Repeating and Working-Through (Further Recommendations on the Technique of Psycho-Analysis: II). *SE* XII: 145–156.
Freud, S. (1915). Observations on Transference-Love (Further Recommendations on the Technique of Psycho-Analysis III). *SE* XII: 157–171.
Freud, S. (1920). Beyond the Pleasure Principle. *SE* XVIII: 1–64.
Freud, S. (1925). An Autobiographical Study. *SE* XX: 1–74.
Freud, S. (1926). Inhibitions, Symptoms and Anxiety. *SE* XX: 75–176.
Freud, S. (1937). Analysis Terminable and Interminable. *SE* XXIII: 209–254.
Freud, S. (1939). Moses and Monotheism. *SE* XXIII: 1–138.
Fürstenau, P. (1977). Die beiden Dimensionen des psychoanalytischen Umgangs mit strukturell ich-gestörten Patienten. *Psyche* 31: 197–207.
Fürstenau, P. (1979). *Analysieren als Beruf.* Vortrag, gehalten auf der Herbsttagung der Deutschen Psychoanalytischen Vereinigung (DPV) am 23.11.79, Stuttgart.
Giovacchini, P. L. (1973). Charakter disorders: Form and structure. *International Journal of Psychoanalysis* 54: 153–160.
Glover, E. (1955). The indication for psychoanalysis. *Journal of Mental Science* 100: 393–401.
Green, A. (1975). The analyst, symbolization and absence in the analytic setting. *International Journal of Psychoanalysis* 56: 1–22.
Green, A. (1977). Conceptions of affect. *International Journal of Psychoanalysis* 58: 129–156.
Grunberger, B. (1958/59). Über-Ich und Narzißmus in der psychoanalytischen Situation. *Psyche* 12: 270–290.
Heimann, P. (1962). Curative factors in psychoanalysis. *International Journal of Psychoanalysis* 43: 228.
Heising, G., Beckmann, D. (1971). Gegenübertragungsreaktion bei Diagnose- und Indikationsstellung. *Zeitschrift für Psychotherapie und Medizinische Psychologie* 21(1): 2–8.
Klauber, J. (1975). Über einige Schwierigkeiten, Psychoanalytiker zu sein. *Psyche* 29: 835–839.
Klauber, J. (1980). *Schwierigkeiten in der analytischen Begegnung.* Frankfurt/M.: Suhrkamp.
Klein, M. (1935). A Contribution to the psychogenesis of manic-depressive states. *International Journal of Psychoanalysis* 16: 145–174.
Kohut, H., Levarie, S. (1950). On the enjoyment of listening to music. *Psychoanalytic Quarterly* 19: 64–87.
Kris, E. (1952). *Psychoanalytic Explorations in Art.* New York: International Universities Press.
Kutter, P. (1977). Konzentrierte Psychotherapie auf psychoanalytischer Grundlage. *Psyche* 31: 957–974.

Leuzinger, M. (1980). *Kognitive Prozesse bei der Indikation psychotherapeutischer Verfahren.* Dissertation, Universität Zürich.

Limentani, A. (1972). The assessment of analysability: A major hazard in selection for psychoanalyses. *International Journal of Psychoanalysis* 53: 351–362.

Loch, W. (1965). *Voraussetzungen, Mechanismen und Grenzen des psychoanalytischen Prozesses.* Bern: Huber.

Loch, W. (1965/66). Übertragung – Gegenübertragung. In: *Zur Theorie, Technik und Therapie der Psychoanalyse* (pp. 156–181). Frankfurt/M.: S. Fischer, 1972.

Loch, W. (1967). Über theoretische Voraussetzungen einer psychoanalytischen Kurztherapie. (Anmerkungen zur Begründung der Fokaltherapie nach Michael Balint.) In: *Zur Theorie, Technik und Therapie der Psychoanalyse* (pp. 253–268). Frankfurt/M.: S. Fischer, 1972.

Loch, W. (1974). Der Analytiker als Gesetzgeber und Lehrer. *Psyche* 28: 431–460.

Loch, W. (1976). Psychoanalyse und Wahrheit. *Psyche* 30: 865–898.

Loch, W. (1977). Anmerkungen zum Thema Ich-Veränderungen, Ich-Defekte und psychoanalytische Technik. *Psyche* 31: 216–227.

Loch, W. (1978). (unter Mitarbeit von J. Dantlgraber). Anmerkungen zu wissenschafts-theoretischen Problemen der psychoanalytischen Praxis. In: Drews, S., u. a. (ed.), *Provokation und Toleranz.* Festschrift für Alexander Mitscherlich zum siebzigsten Geburtstag (pp. 93–118). Frankfurt/M.: Suhrkamp.

Loch, W. (1979a). Depression und Melancholie – oder depressive Position und Vatermord. In: Englert, E. H. (ed.), *Die Verarmung der Psyche. Igor A. Caruso zum 65. Geburtstag* (pp. 157–171). Frankfurt/M.: Campus.

Loch, W. (1979b). Tiefenpsychologisch fundierte Psychotherapie – Analytische Psychotherapie. *Wege zum Menschen* 32: 177–193.

Loch, W. (1980). Triebe und Objekte. Bemerkungen zu den Ursprüngen der emotionalen Objektwelt. In: *Jahrbuch der Psychoanalyse* XII: 54–81. Bern: Huber.

Loch, W. (2006). *The Art of Interpretation. Deconstruction and New Beginning in the Psychoanalytical Process.* Edited and introduced by Peter Wegner. London: Publication committee of the International Psychoanalytical Association.

Loch, W., Dantlgraber, J. (1980). Wissenschaftstheoretische Probleme der psychoanalytischen Praxis. In: Speck, J. (ed.), *Handbuch wissenschaftstheoretischer Begriffe* 2: 517–523. Göttingen: Vandenhoeck & Ruprecht.

Loch, W., Jappe, G. (1974). Die Konstruktion der Wirklichkeit und die Phantasien. *Psyche* 28: 1–31.

Loch, W., Pohlmann, U. (1977). Psychoanalyse – Heilmittel oder Forschungsmethode? In: Kutter, P. (ed.), *Psychoanalyse im Wandel* (pp. 27–41). Frankfurt/M.: Suhrkamp.

Loewald, H. W. (1971). The transference neurosis: Comments on the concept and the phenomena. *Journal of the American Psychoanalytic Association* 19: 54–66.

Malan, D. H. (1976). *The Frontier of Brief Psychotherapy.* New York: Plenum Press.

Masterson, J. F. (1976). *Psychotherapy of the Borderline Adult. A Developmental Approach.* New York: Brunner & Mazel.

Parin, P. (1958). Die Indikation zur Analyse. *Psyche* 12: 376–387.

Pontalis, J.-B. (1980). The negative therapeutic reaction: An attempt at definition. In: *Bulletin 15, European Psycho-Analytical Federation* (pp.1–13). London: Goodwin Press.

Racker, H. (1957). The meanings and the uses of the countertransference. *Psychoanalytic Quarterly* 26: 303–357.

Racker, H. (1988). Transference and countertransference. *International Psycho-Analytical Library* 73: 1–193.

Reik, T. (1948). The surprised psychoanalyst. In: *Listening with the Third Ear: The Inner Experience of a Psychoanalyst* (pp. 258–271). New York: Grove.

Riemann, F. (1968). The structure of the analyst and its influence on the course of treatment. *American Journal of Psychoanalysis* 28(1): 69–79.

Rotmann, M. (1978). Über die Bedeutung des Vaters in der Wiederannäherungs-Phase. *Psyche* 32: 1105–1147.
Sandler, J. (1961/62). Sicherheitsgefühl und Wahrnehmung. *Psyche* 15: 124–131.
Sandler, J. (1976a). Countertransference and Role-responsiveness. *International Review of Psychoanalysis* 3: 43–47.
Sandler, J. (1976b). Dreams, unconscious fantasies and 'identity of perception'. *International Review of Psychoanalysis* 3: 33–42.
Schafer, R. (1973). The idea of resistance. *International Journal of Psychoanalysis* 54: 259–286.
Stephanos, S. (1980). The contribution of psychoanalytic object theory to psychosomatic medicine. *The Annual of Psychoanalysis* 10: 187–204.
Sterba, R. (1934). The fate of the ego in analytic therapy. *International Journal of Psychoanalysis* 15: 117–126.
Stone, L. (1961). *The Psychoanalytic Situation: An Examination of its Development and Essential Nature.* New York: International Universities Press.
Thomä, H. (1974). Zur Rolle des Psychoanalytikers in psychotherapeutischen Interaktionen. *Psyche* 28: 381–394.
Tyson, R. L., Sandler, J. (1971). Problems in the selection of patients for psychoanalysis: Comments on the application of the concepts of indications, suitability and analysability. *British Journal of Medical Psychology* 44(3): 211–228.
Waelder, R. (1962). Selection criteria for the training of psychoanalytic students. *International Journal of Psychoanalysis* 43: 4–5.
Winnicott, D. W. (1953). Transitional objects and transitional phenomena – A study of the first not-me possession. *International Journal of Psychoanalysis* 34: 89–97.
Winnicott, D. W. (1954). The depressive position in normal development. In: *Through Paediatrics to Psychoanalysis* (pp. 262–277). London: Hogarth Press, 1958.
Winnicott, D. W. (1960). The theory of the parent–infant relationship. In: *The Maturational Processes and the Facilitating Environment: Studies in the Theory of Emotional Development.* London: Hogarth Press.
Winnicott, D. W. (1962). The aims of psycho-analytical treatment. In: *The Maturational Processes and the Facilitating Environment: Studies in the Theory of Emotional Development.* London: Hogarth Press.
Winnicott, D. W. (1965). *The Maturational Processes and the Facilitating Environment: Studies in the Theory of Emotional Development.* London: Hogarth Press.
Zetzel, E. R. (1970). *The Capacity for Emotional Growth.* London: Hogarth Press.

12 THE OPENING SCENE AND THE IMPORTANCE OF THE COUNTERTRANSFERENCE IN THE INITIAL PSYCHOANALYTIC INTERVIEW *by Peter Wegner*

Commentary

Elisabeth Skale

Peter Wegner is a training and supervising analyst of the German Psychoanalytic Society (DPV); he works in private practice in Tübingen and has published several papers on the psychodynamics of psychoanalytic first interviews based on his psychoanalytic research at the University of Tübingen.

Under the directors Wolfgang Loch and Heinz Henseler at the Department for Psychoanalysis at the University of Tübingen from 1971 to 1998, the 'opening scene' of psychoanalytic interviews and so-called 'preliminary phenomena' were important issues of research (Wegner & Henseler, 1991).

Based on the observation that the decision to look for analytic treatment and to seek out and make contact with a particular psychoanalyst is 'often an outcome of a lengthy internal process', the author states that patients nevertheless 'come to the initial interview with reservations and critical objections' (p. 225). He describes that at 'the beginning of the initial interview, patient and analyst move from a protected situation into an unprotected one'. The analyst also is 'unprotected' as everything new that reaches him 'has not yet been understood or it remains unclear whether it can be understood'. This 'labilisation of the intrapsychic equilibrium' (cf. Kind, 1986) in patient and analyst is associated with intense affects – Bion (1987) refers to an 'emotional storm' (p. 247).

Peter Wegner defines the *opening scene* as the 'entirety of the interaction' from the personal greeting up to the opening of the interview by the first sentence of the patient. This includes verbal and nonverbal interaction, every direct and indirect communication, and all concomitant 'conscious, preconscious and unconscious psychic processes (cognitive and affective; intra- and interpersonal) of the analyst and the patient'.

There are two different elements to the characteristics of the 'opening scene': '(1) the inevitable scenic interaction in what is the only encounter between analyst and patient that begins without any prior knowledge of the other and his reactions; (2) the associated actualization of preverbal realms of the personality and pre-oedipal conflicts or states, which Stone

(1973) considered especially likely to be actualized by the analytic situation'. In an empirical study Peter Wegner (1988) was able to establish that the opening scene has significant diagnostic importance and could confirm that it has – like the initial dream – a significant prognostic relevance. Moreover he found that in particular the awareness and report of the analyst's countertransference reactions connected with the opening scene is of central importance. Based on these findings he points out in the following paper that, besides Freud's 'evenly suspended attention' towards the patient, a process of 'free floating introspectiveness' concerning countertransference reactions has to be present in the analyst from the very beginning and especially concerning the opening scene, in order to maintain an analytic attitude throughout the first interview. More than interpretation, he states, the analytic attitude seems to be particularly important in first interviews with severely disturbed patients, when the analyst is confronted with patterns of object-relations to the primal object and catastrophic anxieties of dependence and object-loss from the very beginning, in the opening scene and sometimes even in preliminary phenomena.

To illustrate his theoretical considerations, the author gives a vivid clinical example of an intricate beginning and demonstrates how the analyst's countertransference served as an important diagnostic tool. He shows that the systematic analysis of the initial countertransference is indispensable and has to be central in the technique of first interviews.

References

Bion, W. (1987). Making the best of a bad job. In: *Clinical Seminars and Four Papers* (pp. 247–257). Abingdon: Fleetwood.

Kind, J. (1986). Der Stundenanfang in der analytischen Psychotherapie. *Zeitschrift für Psychosomatische Medizin und Psychoanalyse* 32: 216–230.

Stone, L. (1973). *Die psychoanalytische Situation.* Frankfurt/M.: Fischer. (Originally published as: Stone, L. (1961). *The Psychoanalytic Situation, an Examination of Its Development and Essential Nature.* New York: International Universities Press.)

Wegner, P. (1988). *Die Bedeutung der Anfangsszene im Psychoanalytischen Erst-interview.* Dissertation, Universität Tübingen.

Wegner, P., Henseler, H. (1991). Die Anfangsszene im Prisma einer Analytikergruppe. *Forum der Psychoanalyse* 7(3): 214–224.

12 THE OPENING SCENE AND THE IMPORTANCE OF THE COUNTERTRANSFERENCE IN THE INITIAL PSYCHOANALYTIC INTERVIEW[1]

Peter Wegner

1. Introduction

A patient does not find his way to the analyst entirely as a matter of course. The decision to seek out a particular psychoanalyst at a certain point in time is structured, among other things, by a combination of many previous experiences, reactions to life history and its sufferings and specific forms of contact with treatment institutions (e.g. Junker & Waßner, 1984). Making contact with an analyst is often the outcome of a lengthy internal process and there are very few patients nowadays who have not heard or read anything about the psychoanalytic method in one way or another. Many patients, nevertheless, also come to the initial interview with reservations and critical objections. Actually making the initial contact presents many problems: which analyst can I trust, who is actually an analyst and how can I tell which analyst really understands me?

However, chance factors probably play a much smaller role in an interview taking place than appearances would suggest. For example, it would seem that the choice of a psychoanalyst in private practice or of an analyst in a public institution is definitely significant. Making contact in an out-patient department or an advice centre is more anonymous than in a private practice. Accordingly, the 'preliminary phenomena' prove to be different (Argelander, 1970). In a private practice, a preliminary explanation is often given on the phone; in some cases an initial interview is not actually arranged because the psychoanalyst has no vacancy for a patient in the foreseeable future and for good reasons does not choose to have a waiting list. If, however, an appointment is made, then such an action will create for both the patient and the psychoanalyst a connection through a particular expectation with the anticipated meeting before the initial interview takes place.

If the initial interviews are arranged by the secretarial office of an institution, patients are generally given an appointment automatically. This

[1] Published originally as: Wegner, P. (1992). Zur Bedeutung der Gegenübertragung im psychoanalytischen Erstinterview. Psychoanalyse, Klinik und Kulturkritik. *Psyche* 46: 286–307.

gives rise to other problems. In particular, patients who have been sent by others, without their own personal motivation, often have false expectations and encounter an interviewer who has a different understanding of his function. It is clear from psychoanalytic practice that the analyst is often not the first port of call when a patient has diagnosed an insoluble psychic problem or symptom himself.

The initial psychoanalytic interview helps to answer the questions brought by the patient. The analyst further has to ask himself some questions and answer them for himself:

- What is the patient's problem and what psychic conflict is hidden behind his symptoms?
- What problem does this generate for the analyst?
- Is the specific analyst–patient relationship going to allow a therapeutic alliance to be introduced and maintained in the purpose of bringing out the patient's unconscious conflicts under the stated conditions of the setting, so that a healing process can be instigated for the psychic, psychosomatic and somatic disease that has been diagnosed?

The analyst has three different sources of data at his disposal: (1) objective information; (2) subjective information; and (3) scenic or situational information. It is therefore accepted that: 'the reliability of the acquired image of the personality and its psychic disorder increases with the integration of information from all three sources . . . ' (Argelander, 1970, p. 28). With the scenic information, the experience of the situation with all its emotions and representational sequences predominates, even when the patient remains silent. The connection with other data is the secondary act. The criterion for the reliability of the information is the situational evidence that could also be described as scenic evidence with regard to shifts in emphasis. 'Information of this kind can hardly ever be verified by repetition and is therefore rejected or goes unremarked by most interviewers, although it is the most conclusive for the prognosis of the therapeutic process' (ibid., p. 27; also Danckwardt, 1978).

A crucial precondition for starting and maintaining a therapeutic relationship is the analyst's skill in gaining some understanding of the patient and the emerging relationship. Conversely, the patient, unless his helplessness has assumed extreme proportions, will generally only then maintain such a relationship if he feels sufficiently understood by the analyst's attitude and interventions. The patient himself hardly has a systematic means of deciding whether or not the analyst is doing justice to his questions and to him. Whether or not a patient can tolerate inadequate understanding is often a gauge of a patient's ego capacities. If the analyst succeeds, or if the patient allows him to listen precisely, he will ascertain that the patient has already arrived, at least implicitly, with a diagnosis of his own. It remains the analyst's task to organize this diagnosis cognitively and affectively, as well as the history of the patient's sufferings and relevant life circumstances, taking into account the patient's potential, which can then possibly be verified with therapeutic interventions. In this a role is played by recourse to theoretical knowledge, clinical experiences and situation-specific skill in therapeutic action, as well as specific subjective factors belonging to the analyst and the patient, such as personal abilities, interests and so on, which we can summarize under the term 'subjective indication' (Dantlgraber, 1982). In addition to this, the analyst's engagement in the investigative process entails for him the opening of a space in which abductive thinking can also be established, as a specific form of knowledge that seems to belong to the psychoanalytic method (Hinz, 1991).

In addition to this, the analyst's diagnosing standpoint constitutes one of his foremost tasks – this standpoint is characterized by the endeavour to achieve an attitude that should facilitate an optimum of unguarded communications by the patient in an atmosphere that receives to the greatest possible extent the patient's non-neurotic or non-psychotic structures and wishes, without this leading to drive-satisfying interactions or gratifications; it is therefore an attitude that conforms to the principle of abstinence. Freud described this task as follows in *An Outline of Psycho-Analysis*: 'The analytic physician and the patient's weakened ego, basing themselves on the real external world, have to band themselves together into a party against the enemies, the instinctual demands of the id and the conscientious demands of the super-ego' (1940, p. 173).

It is precisely the diagnosing aspect of the interview process that received attention and was studied in the first few decades after Freud (for a summary of the development of the initial interview see Gill *et al.*, 1954; Thomä & Kächele, 1985).

Freud himself had no specially formulated interview technique (Kerz-Rühling, 1984). But he knew that the psychoanalytic process very quickly leads to complications that seem impossible to disentangle and that the very beginning of a treatment could still be accessible to systematic examination. He wrote:

> Anyone who hopes to learn the noble game of chess from books will soon discover that only the openings and end-games admit of an exhaustive systematic presentation and that the infinite variety of moves which develop after the opening defy any such description.
>
> (Freud, 1913, p. 123)

This gave rise to the suggestion of examining the initial interview in various ways, and so-called trial analysis also emerged – which was supposed to provide information as to whether and with what purpose a psychoanalysis with a particular patient might be possible – as a procedure that did not seem to be tenable in most cases for economic, ethical and therapeutic reasons. Furthermore, evolving modifications in the classical psychoanalytic treatment (depth-psychology-based psychotherapy, focal therapy, brief psychotherapy, counselling, group therapy, couples and family therapy), as well as other advances in treatment technique, generated an increased interest in the therapeutic function of the initial interview. This therapeutic function of the initial interview was also reinforced by the requirements of ever increasing tasks in psychotherapeutic treatment for many psychoanalysts (Nedelmann, 1990a, 1990b).

Making a diagnosis and therapeutic interventions and establishing indications and a prognosis are therefore elements of the psychoanalytic work in the initial interview. For the patient, the initial interview often represents a first psychoanalytic self-experience (Schubart, 1989) that has a decisive significance for his later life that should not be underestimated. A precondition for the success of this self-experience is an analyst who is able to understand and interpret his patient's unconscious conflicts; this is precisely where a fundamental difference lies between psychoanalytic and non-psychoanalytic interviewers. No small demands are therefore made on the psychoanalyst, but 'if we miss the ideal by a hair's breadth, we gain our analytic counterpart as a human being and thus enable the partner to be a human being, for absolute omnipotence excludes the other person's autonomy' (Loch, 1965a, p. 22).

Furthermore, Bolognini has rightly indicated the clinical-technical and ethical implications in psychoanalytic consultations when the interviewer himself has no vacancy available for a patient, as is often the case in treatment or advice centres, but of course as can also occur in private practice. For this then means 'an interview with a patient who will be not taken in treatment by the consultant analyst, who will be sent to another, perhaps specifically chosen, colleague after one or more assessment sessions' (2006, p. 25). Bolognini's thoughts about the necessary inner work and attitude of the interviewer in such consultations correspond entirely to the basic considerations that I am also putting forward and they further point to basic factors such as curiosity, responsibility, empathy and identification and to the fact that psychoanalytic interviews should also be considered and conducted with strict regard to the possibilities of the setting on the interviewer's part.

2. The opening scene in the initial interview

The actual beginning of the initial interview has been studied systematically by some authors (Hartmann, 1978; Künzler & Zimmermann, 1965; Gill *et al.*, 1954; Friedrich, 1984; Bastiaans, 1971, 1981, 1982; Argelander, 1981, 1982; Lai, 1976; Kind, 1986). I have described the existing literature in more detail elsewhere (Wegner, 1988).

In summary, it should suffice here to point out that a special meaning always attaches to the beginning of the interview, as with initial dreams, symptomatic actions or the end of an analytic session. It seems obvious to suppose that every moment of an analyst–patient relationship, where it is possible to examine it more closely, expresses an unconscious, ever-specific communication that can be perceived, understood and interpreted. The beginning of the interview is specifically defined by one element, namely by the fact that both participants in the process have still not had any experience together, apart from the preliminary phenomena already mentioned.

We might say that at the beginning of the initial interview, patient and analyst move from a protected situation into an unprotected one. The analyst is also unprotected insofar as everything new that reaches him has not yet been understood or it remains unclear whether it can be understood. In the light of the consideration that this 'labilisation of the intrapsychic equilibrium' (Kind, 1986) in both the patient and the analyst is associated with intense affects – Bion (1987) refers to an 'emotional storm' – we have described the beginning of the initial interview as the *opening scene* (Wegner, 1988; Wegner & Henseler, 1991) and have thereby emphasized two different elements: (1) the inevitable scenic interaction in what is the only encounter between analyst and patient that begins without any prior knowledge of the other and his reactions; and (2) the associated actualization of preverbal realms of the personality and pre-Oedipal conflicts or states, which Stone (1973) considered especially likely to be actualized by the analytic situation. It is precisely the state of ignorance of the other person that already leads before the interview to an accumulation of projections, expectations, wishes and anxieties on the patient's part, which can find their expression in an intensified actualization of the preverbal parts of the personality and states.

In an empirical study, I was able to establish that the opening scene has significant diagnostic importance and that it is advisable not to overlook this, as actually often happens in practice. There I defined the opening scene as the entirety of the interaction that occurs between analyst and patient (in content terms), from the personal greeting up to the outset of the interview, including the first spoken sentence (in temporal terms) under the basic conditions of psychoanalytic advice and treatment that is offered (in spatial and setting terms). The 'entirety of the interaction' denotes all the verbal and non-verbal actions, all the direct and indirect communications, as well as all the same accompanying conscious, preconscious and unconscious psychic processes (cognitive and affective; intra- and interpersonal) of the analyst and the patient. Here it is not always possible to set a precise limit on the temporal range of the content-related aspects of the opening scene, if for example we think of chance interactions that have already taken place beforehand or other advance information provided by the analyst or the patient (Wegner, 1988).

In relation to the above-mentioned study, it should be emphasized that the communication and detailed investigation of the analyst's initial countertransference reactions were of central importance, which is why I shall now consider more closely the question of the importance of the countertransference in the initial interview.

3. The importance of the countertransference in the initial interview

3.1. The analyst as an investigative tool

The analyst is required not only to diagnose and to intervene; he must observe himself as a part of the interaction that occurs. From the psychoanalytic perspective, this is a task that needs to be connected with the analysis of the transference and countertransference. Here I will emphasize that the analyst does not merely react, but is influenced by a multiplicity of assumptions and is subjected to very different psychic processes in the interaction that takes place in the interview.

The analyst brings a great deal to the opening scene: quite apart from the verbal and non-verbal communications, there is also his foundational attitude, which results from his individual life history (including his educational history), his early transference and countertransference thoughts and feelings, and his models and strategies of enquiry and problem solving, all of which will reduce and organize the flow and processing of available information.

Here I am following, on the one hand, Heimann (1950, 1960, 1964), who has accorded major importance to countertransference analysis as a diagnostic tool and, on the other, Rosenfeld's noteworthy formulation that: 'The most common blockages in the patient–analyst interaction relate to the analyst's unconscious, infantile anxieties' (1987, p. 40).

In the literature, there are two main trends of thought concerning the countertransference, which is understood, on the one hand, solely as the analyst's unconscious reaction to the patient, thus as a disturbance in his working capacity ('classical approach'; Kernberg, 1965) and, on the other hand, as the totality of the analyst's cognitive and emotional responses to the patient ('totalistic approach'; ibid.).

The latter viewpoint is put forward by works by Balint and Balint (1939), Winnicott (1949), Heimann (1950, 1960, 1964), Sandler (1976), Sandler *et al.* (1973), Little (1951, 1957) and Racker (1957, 1988). Loch states 'that we are dealing with a relational system [transference and countertransference, P. W.] in which one factor is also the function of the other' (Loch, 1965b, p. 15) and he thereby underlines the object-relations-analytical aspect of the mutuality in the psychoanalytic relationship. Formulations such as Heimann's that the countertransference is 'the patient's *creation*' (1950, p. 83) or Bion's that 'analytic interpretations can be seen to be theories held *by* the analyst about the models and theories the patient has *of* the analyst' (1963, p. 17) certainly emphasize the mutuality of the influence, but they ultimately assume that the analyst only reacts to the patient, which is an ideal-typical assumption that has been avoided in Loch's formulation.

We might also say that the field has hitherto been dominated by works that regard the analyst as a dependent variable (in relation to the patient as an independent variable) in the investigative field, in which it is he alone who reacts to the patient as he diagnoses or intervenes (on the history of the countertransference, see for example Thomä & Kächele, 1985; Minauf, 1986). In contrast to this, there are only a few attempts to examine the analyst as an independent variable, in other words, as a factor that exists independently of or before the patient's transference. Fliess writes, 'The interpretation of transference behaviour reactive to countertransference is one of these problems' (1953, p. 273) and Loch himself incisively states: 'The analyst needs the countertransference in order to be able to understand the patient, although he must simultaneously overcome it in order to be able to give the patient an interpretation' (cf. Loch 1965a). This leads to the assumption 'that the dialectic of double negation is an operational principle of our technique' (ibid., p. 20f.).

In reality, an intricate network of interacting, reciprocally influencing processes will thus arise between patient and analyst that can only be described and conceptually grasped with a language (representational model) that always has to be sought anew; this also means that we cannot work theoretically from the premise of a one-dimensional causality.

The investigative tool is the analyst alone, unaided by equipment, instruments, tests and so on, and confronted with the difficulty that 'the object of investigation and the instrument of research . . . belong in the same category' (Loch, 1965a, p. 21). He thereby registers and processes signals in two directions, two vectors as it were in the psychodynamic field of the investigative situation:

- One vector is directed at the conscious communications and their possible unconscious correlate, in which recognizable distortions of the patient's communications in the context of the here-and-now (such as countertransference aspects) are especially important.
- A second vector is directed at the processing activities (we might also say, the effects triggered by the signals) as they occur in the analyst – a dimension that I shall term 'introspective' and that relates to conscious internal processes and to some extent also to unconscious processes.

Even in the first few moments of an interview, the amount of data processed by the analyst increases towards an infinite level, especially since along with the patient's information that is communicated and becomes perceptible many processes of reaction and verification are added each time that are to some extent highly subjective. In other words, the psychoanalyst is dealing with a problem-solving situation that can be described as a complex system and in which he can only maintain skilful therapeutic action by means of an artificial reduction or hierarchization. Otherwise the analyst system would collapse, which in any case often actually happens to some extent and is of great diagnostic relevance on his part. If the situation of the initial interview is considered from this perspective, the psychoanalyst as an independent variable moves into the foreground of the investigation.

In general, a certain period of time is required before an interviewer has actually adapted to a new patient. Not only the patient but also the analyst must overcome a threshold before he can truly listen to the patient's complaint. This threshold also involves the interviewer's right to freedom of decision, for instance as to whether he is prepared to take over responsibility for a particular patient. There is much to suggest that such decisions are reached very quickly, albeit unconsciously. Above all, however, this threshold is directed at the onrushing force of the patient's uncontrolled wishes, which the analyst can then only really be ready to work on if he has gained an idea that he will be given access to unconscious intrapersonal and interpersonal conflicts (Dantlgraber, 1982). It actually proves to be a special requirement of the work to keep newly confronting a long-running battle with a patient's repetition compulsions. Most patients actually know this very specifically, for they are not only victims of their symptoms but also the directors of the history of their sufferings, even when they prefer other explanatory concepts for their conflicts at a conscious level. Furthermore, this threshold protects the analyst from the fact that every patient in a specific way is in a position to make contact with the analyst's unconscious personality and conflict-structure and so to touch on areas of narcissistic vulnerability.

All these processes are further accompanied by specific affects that must themselves be considered and can only be used for understanding the patient following an inner psychic work and translation activity on the analyst's part that has yet to be explained – an aspect that specifically relates to the analyst's anxiety about his own feelings.

3.2. The analyst in the action dialogue

One of Freud's important indications concerning treatment technique is his recommendation to the analyst of an attitude that enables him to listen to the patient while suspending control and directedness, as well as conscious influence. So-called free-floating attention is a representational model that forms a cornerstone of the foundations for the construction of analytic work.

Using various additional constructions, Sandler (1976) and Klüwer (1983) attempted to shed light on the interplay of transference and countertransference in analytic work. For free-floating attention is certainly not a permanent condition that it would be possible for the analyst to sustain over a long period, even if it is indispensably to be striven for, and indeed in alternation with reflective inner processes.

In his work on acting out and joint acting out, Klüwer (1983) addresses phenomena that are related to the analyst's actions in the dual psychoanalytic situation, actions that are induced in the analyst through 'a . . . treatment that the patient carries out with the analyst' (ibid., p. 837) but which, if tolerated in the sense of an action dialogue, as a part of the countertransference, in the context of the analytic relationship are 'not detrimental to the development of the therapeutic process, but a common transitional stage on the path to attaining insight' (ibid., p. 839).

In a similar endeavour, Sandler (1976) used concepts from role-theory to differentiate the verbal and non-verbal interactions between analyst and patient, which he then saw as 'the link between certain countertransference responses and transference' (p. 44). He stated that the analyst's 'role-responsiveness', as a 'complementary role' to that which the patient assigns himself, structures the interaction between the two, starting from the patient's 'intrapsychic role-relationship' (ibid., p. 44), which in one sense contains the preliminary model of the desired interactions with the objects (which would correspond to the transference). In this sense, these are also phenomena that can be interpreted in terms of object-relations theory, with the accompanying drive wishes, which press for satisfaction in the analytic situation as well. With the concept of 'free-floating responsiveness' – in addition to the hitherto familiar 'free-floating attention' – Sandler offers the analyst a possible way of conceptualizing the necessary 'compromise-formation between his own tendencies and *his reflexive acceptance of the role which the patient is forcing on him*' (ibid., p. 46). There undoubtedly exist in the analyst continual primary-process influences that can be said to be unconscious – including in relation to a specific patient. The opposition between the 'classical' and the 'totalistic' approaches to the countertransference leads to the constantly recurring question: what hinders the analyst from perceiving and investigating his countertransference without anxiety?

3.3. Free-floating introspectiveness

This form of analysis of the countertransference is an important part of the analyst's task, which contributes to enabling the patient to experience his ego (or self). This experience is in fact constituted through the slowly evolving recognition of the separateness of the 'You' (object), and is therefore a product of lively interaction that comes about through libidinal and aggressive drive-demands and their restriction (this ontogenetic developmental aspect is repeated in parts during the psychoanalytic process and can, if everything goes well, correct specific fixations, that is evoke new experiences through the analyst's interpretations of their meaning).

The dimension of the therapeutic alliance in the patient (or the capacity for 'therapeutic ego-splitting'; Sterba, 1934, quoted in Leupold-Loewenthal, 1986, p. 267) is here just as much a condition for the functioning of the psychoanalytic interaction as the analyst's own identification with the method. The capacity to take an ex-centric position represents in one sense an operationalization of the analyst's introspective activity, which alone brings to consciousness the countertransference in the sense of therapeutic action. Until we are in a position to perceive the countertransference, we cannot understand it or even define it, regardless of whether and how it does or does not exist. Acquiring the capacity to assume an ex-centric position, however, is based according to Britton (1988) on an inner mental structure that develops through the internalization of the Oedipal constellation, which 'makes possible objective self-observation in subjective participation. That means that "insight" and "feeling" can come together internally, which gives the understanding a feeling of inner reality' (1989, p. 24).

Neyraut (1974, p. 15ff.) has contributed an important work on the countertransference, although his formulation of the 'procession of the countertransference' (1974, p. 13)[2] has generated some confusion. It may be that the formulation 'procession of the countertransference' is not an absolutely precise rendition of what is intended. What I think Neyraut meant by this is that the analyst in the analytic process, especially when he is protecting the basic conditions, makes a specific advance concession from the very outset to the patient and the analytic situation or, in other terms, he pays a specific tribute,[3] which is 'namely, to be directly, even personally involved and possibly to shed light on this involvement [in the analytic situation with each particular patient, P. W.]' (ibid., p. 15f.) This specific advance concession in reality assumes the specific transference of the patient, who may not in fact yet know that in opening up to the psychoanalytic process he is transferring specific object-relations models on to the analyst. It is critical to note, however, that the concept of the countertransference, especially when it is further differentiated from the analyst's transference on to the patient, is diluted and loses its selectivity.

Neyraut uses an 'expanded theory of the countertransference, the concept of which is now so far extended as to encompass all the analyst's comments, ideas, feelings, interpretations, actions or reactions' (ibid., p. 18) and then strives to 'grasp a paradox of the countertransference: that on the one hand it precedes the actual analytic situation (training analysis, education, misrepresentations or orthodoxies of every kind) and on the other hand it gains its true dimension only when it is confronted with the inner demands that arise from the analytic situation itself' (ibid.).

2 In the original, 'procession du contretransfert', translated into German as 'Vorgängigkeit der Gegenübertragung'.

3 In the original, 'cession' [Abtretung], meaning 'transfer' or 'assignment'.

This paradox could be more precisely stated analytically by clarifying that 'both transference and countertransference [are (P.W.)] . . . generally known to be motivated forms of behaviour in that they represent object-relations that are directed or induced by drive needs' (Loch, 1965a, p. 41). Drive needs are, however, to be described as an independent variable in the psychoanalytic perspective (e.g. while the analyst is certain and is prepared for his part to [counter-]transfer his object-relations models on to the patient and, wherever possible, to analyse this). The paradox of the countertransference would then be resolved by referring to parts of the analyst that we describe as independent variables and that in this respect precede the patient's transference or already exist independently of a particular transference.

Perhaps though this conceptualization would also become less ambiguous if, for example, like Köhler-Weisker (1986) we draw a conceptual distinction between the 'psychoanalyst's attitude towards the patient' (ibid., p. 143), the stance, the action and the basic conditions of the therapeutic process. Her definition of attitude contains those elements that Neyraut subsumed under the 'procession of the countertransference':

> The attitude is the part of the psychoanalytic technique that constantly accompanies the process of insight and interpretation. It constitutes both the security-giving containment that the analyst as a person offers the patient and the limiting context that he presents to the patient. It serves the analyst's boundary and self-assertion towards the patient and thus contributes to preserving the reality principle in the analytic situation. It forms the static, firm element in contrast to the patient's flow of associations and the interaction that develops during the transference and countertransference. The attitude must be internalized by the analyst during the training and be consciously adopted by him. It is in a special way to be differentiated from the countertransference that develops along with the patient's transference, which is unconscious by definition and is only made conscious to the analyst through the analytic work.
>
> (Köhler-Weisker, 1986, p. 145)

Another author (Béjarano, 1976) had previously distinguished a 'general countertransference' from a 'specific countertransference' (p. 10), in which the latter only applies to a particular individual patient, while the former would correspond to the analyst's professional introductory attitude. These distinctions are also particularly relevant to the treatment technique: we can then distinguish between the psychoanalyst's attitude, which enables him to adopt a particular functioning towards the patient, and the interpretation. But the analyst's attitude incorporates aspects of the interest that belong to the analyst's perspective as an independent variable in the investigative field.

In this precise sense, in addition to 'free-floating attention' and 'free-floating responsiveness' on the analyst's part, it is necessary to conceptualize a further dimension or vector in the field of the investigative and treatment situation, namely a 'free-floating introspectiveness', which differs from free-floating attention precisely through a specific directedness and, moreover, is connected with the identification with the psychoanalytic method.

All these considerations of the countertransference are also highly significant in that they are closely connected with a second domain of further development in psychoanalytic treatment technique, namely the expansion of the indication for psychoanalysis and its scope of application in relation to more disturbed patients or patients with a more primitive psychic structure.

As Béjarano (1976) revealed in the summary of all the papers at the first Congress of the European Psychoanalytical Federation ('Countertransference and Narcissism', Aix-en-Provence, August, 1976), what applies for these patients in particular is that interpretations, at least stage-by-stage ones 'in the sense of the classically interpreting attitude are ineffective, indeed even dangerous' (ibid., p. 5) and what takes their place is the 'analyst's attitude, that is what he experiences and learns in the analytic situation' (ibid.), which is constantly being corrected among other things by the analysis of the countertransference (see also Dantlgraber, 1989; Treurniet, 1991).

However, in my view precisely this highly effective therapeutic factor is largely invariant in relation to the patient's transference, and thus belongs to the analyst as an aspect of the independent variables. However, the attitude concerns the analyst's special capacity to relinquish his internal objects (cf. Loch, 1965b, p. 44). Transcending his own involvement in drive-motivated object relations, and thus being able to carry out a separation, is here to Loch simultaneously the

> inner reason for the abstinence of which the analyst must be made capable, which is possible only if he can be alone without becoming lonely; for solitude experienced as abandonment and isolation is itself a psychopathological phenomenon that complicates and hinders understanding, let alone freeing and opening up the patient [from the very outset – P.W.].
>
> (Loch, 1965b)

This particularly applies to patients with a more primitive psychic structure, where the analyst's attitude has particular therapeutic relevance, and it should be added that such patients can trigger effects with full force in the analyst even in the initial meeting. If the analyst is dealing with object-relations models from the relationship to the primary object, the securing of existence (manifested as catastrophic fear of dependency and object loss) moves into the foreground of the therapeutic work, in contrast to the interpretation of the conditions of a specific anxiety (manifested, for example, as Oedipal fear of libidinal drive excitations).

The systematic analysis of the countertransference is therefore a key component of modern psychoanalytic interview technique. It is generally clear that it is becoming increasingly important for research endeavours to enable the analyst to gain freer access to an anxiety-inducing and complicated initial meeting with the patient in order to be able to understand him better. This development also brings us full circle and back to Freud's extremely noteworthy formulation: 'Psycho-analytic therapy was created through and for the treatment of patients permanently unfit for existence, and its triumph has been that it has made a satisfactorily large number of these permanently fit for existence' (1905, p. 263). This observation is also valid today in that we must recognize that the psychoanalytic method is always sought precisely when other methods of psychotherapy have already failed.

4. Conflict, repetition compulsion and countertransference in an initial interview

The patient I was waiting to see for an initial interview in the out-patient section of the Department for Psychoanalysis, Psychotherapy and Psychosomatics at the University Clinic in Tübingen (Head doctor: Prof. Dr H. Henseler), had been announced to me by the secretary with the comment that she was 'a remarkably beautiful woman'. From this I could gather that the patient had made an appointment in person, so presumably in some way had connections with the department. The majority of our patients make contact by telephone otherwise.

Only just before the interview, I remembered the inapposite comment about the patient's outward appearance and, in addition to the ordinary excitement that I usually experience before interviews, I felt a particular curiosity that I found not merely pleasant. I felt pushed in a particular direction, less free than otherwise, biased. When I went to fetch the patient from the waiting-room in the usual way, I did not find her there. Instead I saw her standing on the other side of the hall smiling mischievously, as if she had witnessed my failed attempt to find her with a degree of pleasure. I felt I had been made a fool of, but was unsure whether this feeling was justified. After we had greeted each other, she immediately took her seat in the designated place. But she barricaded herself behind a handbag and a raincoat, which lay between us on her knees. I was able to confirm my secretary's judgement, but was surprised to observe a slight touchiness in connection with the question of what the patient wanted from me. Before I had been able to formulate this question, the patient opened the conversation: 'unfortunately I was unable to reach you on the phone. The waiting time was too long. I have only come now to cancel the appointment; I have since begun a gestalt therapy treatment.'

I felt 'made a fool of' a second time; I was annoyed, offended, and felt the wish to say a dry farewell in order at least to dispel my annoyance. The patient was robbing me of an appointment time. In addition, I could clearly discern a second feeling, namely the wish to rival the patient's therapist.

Without realizing this at the time, I assumed, naturally, that this must be a woman. These thoughts were scattering in various directions and I silently tried to gain some time, for it seemed obvious to me that the patient and I would urgently need some time after this opening. I was also trying to make clear to myself that by communicating that the interview was over, the patient had opened the interview. I was helped here by the consideration that there must have been reasons why the patient had found it necessary to seek me out. In any case, I could not credit that she had been unable to reach me on the phone. The patient must therefore have an interest in seeing me and it seemed that the condition for the fulfilment of her wish to be understood in some way culminated in getting me to accept that she certainly would not be needing me: my help came too late, had long since been disappointing, was based on the wrong method, and also I was not a woman.

All things considered, I should with all ambition have proved to the patient, counter-acting-out, that I was indeed the right person. However, this was contradicted by the fact that the patient was sitting 'as if on packed suitcases' behind the protective wall of her bag and her coat. I said to the patient something like: 'I am grateful to you for seeking a way of cancelling the appointment.'

After that came a longer pause, during which I began to feel certain that the interview had indeed begun. Neither I nor the patient made a move to get up. The patient also seemed reassured that we had gained some breathing space. But my above-mentioned annoyance returned. Almost as if the patient had guessed what was preoccupying me, she began the interview for the second time, as if it were the most normal thing: 'I don't think I'm well enough informed about the different types of therapy. I've heard that psychoanalysis takes too much time. I tend to make decisions on an economic basis and to want to see quick results. Is my prejudice right, that psychoanalysis goes on and on?'

My annoyance quickly returned at this direct answer from the patient, and I also now felt pressurized. However, I also did not want to be diverted from the path that had been taken until now by the further attack on the analytic attitude. Through the tone of my answer, I indicated my view that these kinds of questions would not get us any further. I said: 'It is correct that a psychoanalysis takes a lot of time.'

There was a brief silence, during which the patient was clearly preoccupied with wondering what had actually happened between us. She continued: 'My problem is that for far too long I've made quick decisions in my life that only appeared to have a clear, rational basis. I have begun to be mistrustful towards myself!' Now I felt the necessity to arrange an appointment with the patient beyond the immediate setting. I also had the impression that it would benefit the patient if she herself had the possibility to reflect further on a decision that she had just reached, and then possibly to correct it. In other words, the patient seemed to me to be repeating the problem that she had just identified, and I wanted to open up for her the possibility of making this discovery herself. I said: 'If we had the conversation as we had arranged, then I might ask you now what specific experiences led you to be so mistrustful towards yourself.' The patient acknowledged my intervention with an understanding smile, which also seemed to express some gratitude that I was able to free her from the impossible situation in which she had placed us. Then she began her actual, fluently presented account, which revealed a very introspectively gifted woman who was suffering from an intense conflict between dependency wishes and panic-type fears of dependency. At this point, I had internally come to the decision that I would be prepared to treat this patient if it should prove to be appropriate and necessary.

Here I must break off the detailed chronological account. A part of the patient's psychodynamics had been illustrated, it had been possible to produce an initial therapeutic alliance, and the patient had an impression of my identification with the psychoanalytic method and got to know an aspect of psychoanalytic self-experience for herself. In order to demonstrate this better, I will summarize the main contents of the further course of the interview. The patient was experiencing acute distress. She had recently begun an extramarital love relationship that her husband did not accept. The marital relationship offered her great security without really fulfilling her sexual needs. Her boyfriend was also unable to tolerate the continuation of her relationship with the husband. Under this pressure, she had hastily decided to move into a new flat and to get divorced. The hectic pace of her decisions had frightened her and made her mistrustful. In fact, she did not want to lose her relationship with either of the two men. Later she came to talk about her mother, whom she blamed for never having allowed any criticism and for never having really loved her daughter. Under the impetus of the first few gestalt therapy sessions, she had made all her rage and disappointment felt to her parents for the first time.

The interpretation of the repetition of the triangular relationship on the level of the therapeutic relationship opened the way to a domain of 'cold hatred' and 'cool distance' that the patient already knew about herself and that I tried to understand as a way of protecting herself from intense and seemingly intolerable feelings in dependency. It became clear that the husband had survived her destructive attacks until now with consideration and great stability, albeit at the cost of reducing the relationship to a quasi-sibling level. The fear of dependency and the associated irrational fears of destruction were impeding a development in the marriage. The intense sexual relationship with the lover was aggravating the conflict and simultaneously leading down a blind alley.

Only then did I learn about a further triangular relationship, in that just a few months after her birth the patient had been placed in the care of a sister of the mother's. The mother had suffered from long-term illnesses and periods in hospital. Well into her schooldays, the patient had lived with her mother's sister, whom she still idealized. The relationship with the father was described by the patient as more indifferent. The relationship to the mother was still marred by mistrust and hatred. It also emerged that the patient's mother had herself been taken into care for years as a child.

At this point in the interview, we both became aware of the connection between the patient's life history and her present suffering, as well as our shared experience. The patient was very pensive and calmly accepted my thought: 'It is as if you are persistently seeking the "right one" but you have failed to realise that something inside you has been preventing you from keeping it. Instead, you have to persistently test whether the right one would really survive your wishes.'

In the countertransference, a first dimension was actualized that held the danger of a failure from the very outset: the initial communication to the analyst that he was not 'the right one', combined with the previously induced expectation that a 'remarkably beautiful woman' wanted to talk with him, had to have a wounding impact. After the analyst had survived the opening scene, a second dimension of the transference and countertransference events came to the fore. The analyst found himself in the role of the idealized foster mother (or the lover) and therefore in danger of joining in the patient's denigrating tendencies towards the mother/father (or husband). The patient had communicated that she had already started a gestalt therapy treatment. Was the analyst able to confirm this indication after the interview? What would it mean to place this in question? On the other hand, would he have been able to conceal from the patient that a low-frequency, non-investigative psychotherapy would be unlikely to resolve her central conflicts, as well as her many symptoms not mentioned at all here? It was necessary to encounter the patient's experience that other people had for so long been deciding for her and about her by interpreting, as well as to remind her of the appointments with her therapist and simultaneously in an unobtrusive way not to exclude the possibility of a future psychoanalytic work.

References

Argelander, H. (1970). *Das Erstinterview in der Psychotherapie.* Darmstadt: Wissenschaftliche Buchgesellschaft.

Argelander, H. (1981). Der Beginn des ärztlichen Gesprächs als Erkenntnisquelle. *Jahrbuch der Psychoanalyse* 6: 112–122.

Argelander, H. (1982). *Der psychoanalytische Beratungsdialog. Studien zur Textstruktur und Deutung an formalisierten Protokolltexten.* Göttingen: Med. Psychol. bei Vandenhoeck & Ruprecht.

Balint, M., Balint, A. (1939). On transference and countertransference. *International Journal of Psychoanalysis* 20: 223–230.

Bastiaans, J. (1971). Die Übersetzung der Klage. *Zeitschrift für Psychotherapie und medizinische Psychologie* 21: 167–181.

Bastiaans, J. (1981). Das erste Gespräch mit psychosomatischen Patienten. In: Jores, A. (Ed.), *Praktische Psychosomatik* (pp. 69–83). Bern: Huber.
Bastiaans, J. (1982). On freedom and induction. *Psychotherapy and Psychosomatics* 28: 24–31.
Béjarano, A. (1976). Counter-transference and narcissism (in the patient . . . and the analyst). *Bulletin of EPFs* 12: 5–10.
Bion, W. R. (1963). *Elements of Psycho-Analysis*. London: Heinemann.
Bion, W. R. (1987). Making the best of a bad job. In: *Clinical Seminars and Four Papers* (pp. 247–257). Abingdon: Fleetwood.
Bolognini, S. (2006). The profession of the ferryman: Considerations on the analyst's internal attitude in consulting and in referral. *International Journal of Psychoanalysis* 87: 25–42.
Britton, R. (1988). The missing link: Parental sexuality in the Oedipus complex. In: Steiner, J. (Ed.), *The Oedipus Complex Today. Clinical Implications*. London: Karnac.
Britton, R. (1989). Zwischen innerer und äußerer Realität: die Borderline-Position. In: Luft, H., Maus, G. (Eds), *Die Abwehr unbewußter Phantasien* (pp. 17–36). Wiesbaden: Tagungsband.
Danckwardt, J. F. (1978). Zur Interaktion von Psychotherapie und Psychopharmakotherapie. *Psyche* 32: 11–154.
Dantlgraber, J. (1982). Bemerkungen zur subjektive Indikation für Psychoanalyse. *Psyche* 36: 193–225.
Dantlgraber, J. (1989). Die psychoanalytische Haltung als Stufe in der Übertragungs-Gegenübertragungsbeziehung. *Psyche* 43: 973–1006.
Fliess, R. (1953). Countertransference and counteridentification. *Journal of American Psychoanalytic Association* 1: 268–284.
Freud, S. (1905). On Psychotherapy. *SE* 7.
Freud, S. (1913). On Beginning the Treatment. Further Recommendations on the Technique of Psychoanalysis, I. *SE* 13.
Freud, S. (1940). An Outline of Psycho-Analysis. *SE* 23.
Friedrich, H. (1984). Anamnese als Drama – die ersten Sätze. *Zeitschrift für Psychosomatische Medizin und Psychoanalyse* 30: 314–322.
Gill, M. M., Newman, R., Redlich, F. C. (1954). *The Initial Interview in Psychiatric Practice*. New York: International Universities Press.
Hartmann, E. (1978). Der erste Satz des Kranken im Gespräch mit dem Arzt. *Therapiewoche*, 28: 8056–8062.
Heimann, P. (1950). On counter-transference. *International Journal of Psychoanalysis* 31: 81–84.
Heimann, P. (1960). Counter-transference. *British Journal of Medical Psychology* 33: 9–17.
Heimann, P. (1964). Bemerkungen zur Gegenübertragung. *Psyche* 18: 483–493.
Hinz, H. (1991). Gleichschwebende Aufmerksamkeit und die Logik der Abduktion. *Jahrbuch der Psychoanalyse* 27: 146–175.
Junker, H., Waßner, T. (1984). *Psychotherapeutisch denken. Patient und Therapeut in der analytischen Arbeit*. Berlin: Springer.
Kernberg, O. F. (1965). Notes on counter-transference. *Journal of American Psychoanalytic Association* 13: 38–56.
Kerz-Rühling, J. (1984). Einführung in das Interviewverfahren. In: *Curriculumsenrwurf: Einführung in die Psychoanalyse Sigmund Freuds*. Materialien aus dem Sigmund-Freud-Institut, Frankfurt, 1: 67–70.
Kind, J. (1986). Der Stundenanfang in der analytischen Psychotherapie. *Zeitschrift für Psychosomatische Medizin und Psychoanalyse* 32: 216–230.
Klüwer, R. (1983). Agieren und Mitagieren. *Psyche* 37: 828–840.

Köhler-Weisker, A. (1986). Zum Begriff der Haltung des Psychoanalytikers am Beispiel einer Fokaltherapie. *Jahrbuch der Psychoanalyse* 18: 143–173.
Künzler, E., Zimmermann, I. (1965). Zur Eröffnung des Erstinterviews. *Psyche* 19: 68–79.
Lai, G. (1976). *Die Worte des ersten Gesprächs*. Bern: Huber.
Leupold-Löwenthal, H. (1986). *Handbuch der Psychoanalyse*. Wien: Orac.
Little, M. (1951). Countertransference and the patient's response to it. *International Journal of Psychoanalysis* 32: 240–254.
Little, M. (1957). The analyst's total response to the patient's needs. *International Journal of Psychoanalysis* 28: 240–254.
Loch, W. (1965a). Übertragung und Gegenübertragung. *Psyche* 19: 1–23.
Loch, W. (1965b). *Voraussetzungen, Mechanismen und Grenzen des psychoanalytischen Prozesses*. Bern: Huber.
Minauf, M. (1986). Zur Entwicklung und Bedeutung des Begriffes der 'Gegenübertragung'. *Sigmund Freud House Bulletin* 11 Special Issue (Festschrift zum 60. Geburtstag von Dr. Harald Leupold-Löwenthal): 224–236.
Nedelmann, C. (1990a). Die Psychoanalyse als Krankenbehandlung in der kassenärztlichen Versorgung. 1. Teil: Ein Kommentar zu den Psychotherapie-Richtlinien. *Forum der Psychoanalyse* 6: 1–14.
Nedelmann, C. (1990b). Die Psychoanalyse als Krankenbehandlung in der kassenärztlichen Versorgung. 2. Teil: Ein Leitfaden zur Antragsstellung. *Forum der Psychoanalyse* 6: 147–162.
Neyraut, M. (1974). *Die Übertragung*. Frankfurt/M.: Suhrkamp, 1976.
Racker, H. (1957). The meanings and uses of countertransference. *Psychoanalytic Quarterly* 26: 303–357.
Racker, H. (1988). Transference and countertransference. *International Psycho-Analytic Library* 73: 1–196.
Rosenfeld, H. (1987). Impasse and interpretation: Therapeutic and anti-therapeutic factors in the psychoanalytic treatment of psychotic, borderline, and neurotic patients. *New Library of Psychoanalysis* 1: 1–318.
Sandler, J. (1976). Countertransference and role-responsiveness. *International Review of Psycho-Analysis* 3: 43–47.
Sandler, J., Dare, C., Holder, A. (1973). *The Patient and the Analyst. The Basis of the Psychoanalytic Process*. London: George Allen & Unwin.
Schubart, W. (1989). The patient in the psychoanalyst's consulting room – the first consultation as a psychoanalytic encounter. *International Journal of Psychoanalysis* 70: 423–432.
Stone, L. (1973). *Die psychoanalytische Situation*. Frankfurt/M.: Fischer. (originally published as: Stone, L. (1961). *The Psychoanalytic Situation, an Examination of Its Development and Essential Nature*. New York: International Universities Press.)
Thomä, H., Kächele, H. (1985). *Lehrbuch der psychoanalytischen Therapie (1)*. Berlin: Springer.
Treurniet, N. (1991). *Support of the analytic process and structural change*. Privatdruck.
Wegner, R. (1988). *Die Bedeutung der Anfangsszene im psychoanalytischen Erstinterview*. Dissertation, Universität Tübingen.
Wegner, P., Henseler, H. (1991). Die Anfangsszene im Prisma einer Analytikergruppe. *Forum der Psychoanalyse* 7(3): 214–224.
Winnicott, D. W. (1949). Hate in the countertransference. *International Journal of Psychoanalysis* 30: 69–79.

13 THE CONSULTATION IN PSYCHOANALYSIS AND ITS 'LOCATION'

Working on the frontier *by Agostino Racalbuto*

Commentary

Ronny Jaffè

As mentioned in the introduction to the paper by Bolognini (p. 146), there has been a long tradition of practice in and thinking about psychoanalytic consultations in Italy; and during four decades an important development in how they are understood has taken place. In 1972 Piero Bellanova wrote a paper on the difference between a psychiatric and a psychoanalytic interview with special focus on the analyst's capacity to listen. In 1981 the same author, together with other analysts, published a paper on the dynamics of the analytic couple in the first interview. 'This means that concepts such as diagnosis, prognosis, indications and counter-indications for a possible analysis – "analizzabilità" – and treatment lose their usual meaning . . . and are considered as professional defences of the analyst' (Bellanova *et al*., 1981). One way of phrasing a fundamental turning point in the understanding of the process in an analytic consultation was given by the Italian analyst Morpurgo (1998): the analyst must 'make a place for the other inside himself.' Besides considering the analysability (Italian: analizzabilità) of the patient it has to be considered whether the analyst is inclined to measure up to or match that specific patient in that specific treatment (Ferro: the 'cimetabilità' of the analyst).

In the present paper by Agostino Racalbuto the focus turns primarily to the analyst, to the pressure the first interview puts on him and the consequent demands on his functioning. In this text an important meta-psychological area is revisited from a modern viewpoint. The author pays particular attention to the analyst and to his psychic functioning during the consultation. He defines the analyst's psychic function as 'a psychic functioning on the frontier': a sort of dissociation of the analyst's Ego, which takes place in a border area – the consultation – between two subjects who have just begun a relationship, and whose destiny and potential future are yet to be created.

It is a psychic functioning at the limits of representation, which can be activated by new experiences, such as the consultation; it is a functioning that needs a new elaboration along the border between the internal and the external world, between subject and object, and, on a meta-psychological level, between the conscious–pre-conscious and the unconscious system. On an operational level the analyst needs to move between the use of the psychoanalytical setting and the necessary modulations and changes required by a new situation, since the work is taking place on a borderline between the two modes of operation.

On this border the analyst must work with his/her pre-conscious – the internal borderline between conscious and unconscious: in this way he/she can discover and re-discover her/his reverie function, integrating her/his empathy towards the patient with the capacity to create new forms of communication and forms of living. In this sense Racalbuto pays tribute to and uses Winnicott's concept of 'found-created', embodied in Bion's theory of reverie.

The analyst must be able to move into a regressive state of functioning and at the same time maintain a position of asymmetry and differentiation, in order to better understand the regressive level of a potential patient. But the analyst's capacity to regress often implies getting in touch with un-representable zones not only within the patient but also within him/herself, meeting his/her own 'psychic functioning on the border', going beyond the frontier of his/her Ego to explore the most archaic, primitive and un-representable level with the patient with whom he/she is working.

As Racalbuto underlines at the end of his paper, the analyst will often, during the consultation, find him/herself in a clinical and theoretical 'identity crisis', wondering: 'What am I doing with this patient? Why do neither analytical theory nor clinical experience give me an answer now?' These central questions in an analyst's mind can cause 'a depressive state consequent to a (transitory) loss of the Self and of the object', which obliges an analyst to continually revisit his/her theoretical and clinical paradigms, but especially to revisit him/herself, his/her history, his/her transference and countertransference.

Agostino Racalbuto (1948–2005) was a training and supervising analyst of the Italian Psychoanalytic Society and IPA; From 2003 until his death in 2005 he was the editor of the *Italian Psychoanalytic Review*. He was professor in the Faculty of Psychology at the University of Padua, where he taught psycho-dynamic psychology, and he was a prolific writer.

References

Bellanova, P., Amati Mehler, J., Argentieri, S., Batini, M., Calvesi, A., Cargnelutti, E., De Lauro, L., Giannitelli, S., Merendino, R., Paulin, P., Tappa, G., Vergine, A., Zerbino, E. (1981). Formazione della coppia analitica e identita' dello psicoanalysta. *Rivista di Psicoanalisi Anno* XXVII No. 1.

Morpurgo, E. (1998). *Chi racconta a chi?* Milano: Angeli.

13 THE CONSULTATION IN PSYCHOANALYSIS AND ITS 'LOCATION'

Working on the frontier[1]

Agostino Racalbuto

I am flattered to have been asked to make a contribution on consultation, since I have less direct experience and practice in consultation than many of my colleagues. I have had the opportunity, however, in my role as scientific secretary, and later as President of the Centro Veneto di Psicanalisi, to engage with colleagues who are more involved than myself in conducting consultations, exchanging my own views with theirs.

I was told that one of my papers in particular, a paper about the 'border line', which appeared in the *Rivista di Psicanalisi*, had been well received. In this paper I posited the existence of a 'borderline psychic functioning', by which I mean a mental functioning engaged in search for meaning and affectively meaningful and appropriate representation; this mental functioning is activated by new experiences, and needs to develop along the borderline between the internal and external dimensions, between subject and object, and on an intra-psychic level between the consciousness/perception apparatus and the unconscious.

These ideas, enriched by my colleagues' contributions, and supported by my being a psychoanalyst who is faced, one way or the other, with the task of consultation, have emboldened me to discuss the 'location' of this particular experience. I am of course referring to *psychic location*, in other words to a mental environment, to modes of psychic functioning, which are proper to a psychoanalyst/person and are based on a psychoanalytic background and 'style', but which need, during the process of consultation, to move away from the classic *setting* required by psychoanalysis. In fact there is a self-evident distance between a proper analysis, or even between a psychoanalytically oriented psychotherapy and a consultation that takes place over one, two or three meetings.

However, it is this very distance which constitutes the boundary between a psychoanalyst's ownership of his role and his wealth of experience on the one hand, and the realization, on the other hand, that he is doing something else, which is not an analysis, even while it draws from a libidinal-emotional

[1] Paper presented at: *L'assetto mentale dello psicoanalista nella consultazione* [*The analyst's mental attitude in consultation*], Milan, 8–10 October 2004.

psychoanalytic knowledge; in this way, a 'specific' psychoanalytic aspect is retained in the absence of a real analysis.

I think this can happen not only during consultations, but also in borderline situations (such as with 'difficult' patients, or in the treatment of non-neurotic patients), and during particular moments in the so-called classic analyses. Indeed, as Semi points out, the assessment interview came into practice after the birth of psychoanalysis, and makes use, at least in part, of psychoanalytic theories and 'constructs'; however, from the 'phenomenological viewpoint', it takes its place before psychoanalysis, in other words before an analysis can begin.

What comes into play on the boundary line between the classic psychoanalytic management of the *setting* and any variations appropriate to the specific requirements of the assessment, is the actual psychic functioning of the person offering the assessment.

I am referring to a mode of psychic functioning operating on the 'frontier' between what is already acquired knowledge, for instance an introjected, conscious *setting* and well-tested technical procedures, and what is 'on the other side', pertaining to the pre-conscious – in direct contact with the unconscious – since this 'frontier' is, I believe, the location of invention, of creativity, of authentic *reverie*, the breeding ground of emotional response to new psychic forms of knowledge.

When we speak of 'frontier' we must remember that we are referring to Freud (1915). In 'The Unconscious' Freud used a metaphor to show that, according to his topical model, there are two 'frontiers': one between the pre-conscious and consciousness and the other between the pre-conscious and the unconscious. To Freud's argument we can add that the pre-conscious itself, being situated between consciousness and the unconscious, is a (virtual) borderline, principally engaged in negotiations between one 'territory' and the other; a line along which particular psychic (pre-conscious) elaboration must take place in order that the experience of reality, both external and internal, can be faced in the most appropriate manner, away both from the 'desert' of absolute rationality and from the soggy 'swamps' of instinctual life. To this borderline La Scala (2001) attributes the function of a 'frontier'; I call it an area of psychic elaboration (Racalbuto, 1996, 2001), which is capable of providing adequate responses to the experiences of life.

This adequate functioning of the pre-conscious, with its appropriate capacity for elaboration, is what guarantees, for instance, both the isolation of past memories from the immediate awareness of contingent experience, preventing an exposure of consciousness to overcrowding and chaos, and the selection, out of the archive of memory, of those elements from the past which can give shape and intelligibility to present experience.

Yet another function of the pre-conscious, in my view, is to preside over any communication qualifying as 'psychoanalytical', in other words to be a reliable mouthpiece for the (more or less repressed) unconscious, with which it is in contact and from which it takes its cue in bringing rhythms, images, perceptions, emotions and verbal representations to conscious awareness. What this means is that the transferential regression brought by each patient into the assessment interview (a transference which cannot be analysed outside of an analytic situation) comes into contact with the analyst's own resonant regression, and can be adequately understood only if such regressive drives in the analyst cause a creative wavering of any fixed theoretical representations present in his consciousness; through this process new images and new verbal forms appear, evidencing the dynamism of previously unused psychic forms.

Such forms, in my view, are impelled exclusively by the unconscious instinctual drives, when new opportunities for contact arise; they provide reliable 'evidence' of a germination with no previous history and bring such evidence to life.

The purpose of this process is to enable us to move towards a 'primary' psychic environment, a sort of primary nebula, promoter of a fresh opening to a renewed path of civilization, where 'nature' (Id) and 'culture' (Ego and Superego) can find integration so as to enable the expression, precisely through new psychic forms (such as verbal forms, perceptions, relational moods, emotional atmospheres and vital rhythms) of the innovative and transforming passage made possible by regression in the service of the Ego. This passage is well described, in my view, by Ogden (2001), who translates the Freudian '*Wo Es war, soll Ich werden*' (rendered in the official Italian translation as 'Where Id was, Ego shall be') as 'Where It was, there I shall come into being'. I believe that the preconscious is akin to Charon, mediating and negotiating the passage from consciousness to the unconscious and back, through the regressive event occurring asymmetrically in the patient and in the analyst. In the analyst who successfully recovers his capacity for *reverie*, integrating his empathic qualities with his ability to coin new forms of experience and communication, this coming back from the unconscious is enriched by vital representative and affective forces which can produce in him a positive 'novelty effect' (Semi, 2000) in relation to his own self, but which can be communicated also *in equal measure* (Giaconia & Racalbuto, 1997) as having the potential to renew and restructure the history and life of his patient. In this way consciousness, or one might say the conscious Ego, is enriched and integrated by the psychic process just described; in other words, the 'I' comes into being on the basis of what 'is', along both intra-psychic and relational coordinates, following a route which I believe to be possible only if both these coordinates can be used. In 'borderline' situations (with seriously ill, non-neurotic patients, in situations not clearly ruled by the classic psychoanalytic *setting*, such as assessments), such work 'on the frontier' is more stimulated, and in a sense more necessary and unavoidable, than in the orthodox psychoanalytic scenario.

The psychic work which takes place at the frontier between the unconscious and the pre-conscious makes up the core, as Ogden (2001) says, of 'what it means to be alive' for a person. This 'frontier' is therefore the 'location' where primary psychic energy manifests itself, it is the birthplace of dream experience and creativity, the germination bed for the liveliness and libidinal vitality, the emotional intelligence (in the vital sense of the word) which flow into a rich affective experience, a happy intuition, a brilliant idea, a precious, deep and fruitful conversation between persons, an inspired psychoanalytic interpretation; all this happens without an apparent source or origin that is open to discovery. Something similar is described in Freud's famous metaphor about the grain of sand which, later becoming invisible, allows the formation of the pearl, and the pearl is all we can see. If the metaphor about the grain of sand and the pearl can be properly used to describe the development of a psychic unit, of an intra-psychic functioning, as a mythology of personal origins, I believe we must also recognize how a 'primary something' is formed at every new meeting, every new experience, every new successful and fruitful conjunction between separate minds; in fact I think that a 'primary something' in the analytical consulting room does not apply only to the unconscious–pre-conscious of the two persons involved, but also describes the new products – what Ogden (1994) would perhaps call the 'analytic third' – which are generated and constructed, together and in different ways, jointly and distinctly, by the analyst and the patient. This is in line with the assumption that it makes little sense to talk about the Origin except in mythical terms, and it makes more sense to imagine a complex network of psychic new births, a matrix representing these 'places of origin' of psychic life, which, while varying across time, occur along the entire psychic lifetime of an individual; this network is related to the axis of maternal, paternal and interpersonal relationships, which are woven between persons in the course of a lifetime and which make up the history of each individual.

If we agree with Steiner that the crisis of post-modernity, all projected into a fast-moving future, which has lost its bonds with the past, consists in the statement 'we have no more beginnings', here I wish to state that the 'primary something' I speak of is related to a recovery of the history of beginnings: by which I mean the recovery of an innovative productive function, which can begin in a familiar psychic 'place', where we have already lived and stayed, but where 'repetition' had denied the possibility of a beginning, and therefore of an end.

Therefore work 'on the frontier' finds its definitive 'primary location' in the consultation, since the consultation makes possible a beginning of a (more or less analytical) process only on the basis that it gives birth to an initial transformation which – among other things – tests and eventually strengthens, or sustains any existing motivation to change in the patient.

For the consultation to work properly it should, in my view, make the *setting* a safe place guaranteed by set rules understood by the patient, but above all it should provide a guaranteed meeting place between the patient's desire and motivation and the analyst's receptivity and capacity to embody the enactment of transformative events: events which the patient must relate to in order to perceive them as credible and effective, so that he or she gains an initial new self-awareness, different from what he or she had before the consultation.

In this sense the 'primary something' is connected with the primary elaboration of experience, with the source of *co-participation* as the foundation of being alive, of the experiential – and pre-representative formation of a basic sense of I-ness and otherness in relation with each other, perceived and lived in the psyche-soma dimension before finding clear verbal representation. Of course what is implied in 'participation' is an attitude of humanity, sensitivity, tolerance and receptive listening, not a waiving of analytic neutrality, which is seen here as the capacity to step aside in a timely way and to leave the stage to the patient.

In this connection I would like to highlight the *borderline psychic functioning* I mentioned at the beginning, a functioning characterized by continuous experience, by repeated perceptions which cannot be ignored, by having to go back and forth along those boundaries which – especially in particular situations, such as consultations – are activated by the work of getting to know someone new, an experience which both participants have to undergo during the first meetings, when faced with a new case, a new form of meeting. I think that what is at play here, in psychoanalytic terms, is the 'borderline concept' of drive, of an instinctual drive caught between the biological and psychological dimensions, between soma and psyche, between sensory–affective perceptions and verbal representation, as well as the borderline of psychic capacity wavering between self-awareness and a cognitive contact with and experience of a new object/other. Which makes it inevitable that, when we wish to 'talk rationally' (Semi, 1985) in a conversation about any patient, 'our' image can only be a subjective reading of the object. This result points us towards both an intra-psychic and a relational perspective.

From an intra-psychic perspective, the two foundational categories in Freud's psychoanalytic metapsychology make it necessary to envisage, in addition to the concept of 'frontier' mentioned earlier, the existence of boundaries, or 'demarcation lines' (Freud, 1923) between the different states of being, which can be imagined as distinct, but not separate. We can imagine these borderlines, which are typical of the psychic structure as a whole, as *areas of psychic elaboration* (from the instinctual drive of the id to the instinctual 'derivatives' of the ego, or from the unconscious or the pre-conscious to the conscious), which facilitate the passage from one state of being to another, and which can link or disconnect the various psychic structures or levels; these are areas which can generate new instances of psychic birth.

From the relational perspective, the boundaries and borderline areas involved are those between the ego and the object, the drive and its object, which point to the problem of experience, formation, individuation and differentiation between 'in' and 'out', between 'me' and 'not-me'; however, these boundaries also indicate the *frontier*, the 'limen' or threshold, the point of confluence, the 'free zone' between the two persons, the subjects and objects of the relationship. Masciangelo (2003), whose metapsychological thinking was strictly Freudian, has talked about 'frontier metaphors' not only in the intra-psychic field, but also in the transferential–countertransferential relational field, as did La Scala with a different meaning. Frontiers can lose their power of defining the boundary between body and mind, between narcissistic cathexis and object cathexis, between traumatic experience (loss of self) and mourning experience (object loss). So one can say that the whole psychic apparatus implies the existence of boundaries, which can lose their structure-giving aspect: could this risk of loss of boundaries, with the loss of structure it entails, be the real explanation for the so-called 'borderline cases'?

If these frontiers are truly 'areas of psychic elaboration', we can visualize them both as boundaries within the intra-psychic dimension and as intermediate 'spaces' in the relational dimension between a certain subject and its object, as well as between the sense of belonging to one generation as well as to another. The genetic element, intertwined with the internalization of relationships with parents, as well as the exposure to the social network with its new models of identification, combine to alter a person's sense of identity: in this process the boundaries between self and other, the modes of interaction, are reconfigured through the encounters and clashes between what is ours and what is alien, between tradition and change, past and present, thought and experience. Here too we have to imagine areas of psychic elaboration, generating the birth of new psychic forms. The failure of such work on the 'frontier' leads to psychopathology.

What I mean here is that every new psychic beginning, in order to exist, needs a functioning identification model, just as every subjective consciousness, in order to take shape, needs the presence of otherness. Every psychoanalytic work, especially the work we can do during a consultation, can only be based on the specific dynamics of the encounter between two persons, rather like the primary encounters which first generate life, and then give birth to it: these are dynamic encounters which open up a space for identification, a space where time after time one of Freud's brilliant intuitions takes on new life: the self is constructed through the other and the existence of the self is reached through the assimilation of the other.

In 'Civilization and its Discontents' Freud argues that there are 'pathological states' in which

> the boundary lines between the ego and the external world become uncertain . . . there are cases when parts of a person's own body, even portions of his own mental life – his perceptions, thoughts, feelings – appear alien to him and not belonging to his ego . . . Thus even the feeling

of our own ego is subject to disturbances and *the boundaries of the ego are not constant* . . . .

(Freud, 1930, p. 65)[2]

In fact, some years later, Freud (1933) in the *New Introductory Lectures*, warned that, in respect to psychic normality, we should not picture 'sharp frontiers like the artificial ones drawn in political geography', but instead it is better to think of 'areas of colour melting into one another as they are presented by modern artists. After making the separation we must allow what we have separated to merge together once more'.

The bleeding of colours into each other which appears in 'modern painting' and the indistinct boundaries between separate 'colour blocks' illustrate aptly, in the terms used by Freud, the borderline quality of the relationship between so-called 'normality' and 'pathology', as well as between id, ego and superego in the intra-psychic dimension, between the unconscious, the preconscious and the conscious; this imagery also helps to describe, in my view, the 'work on the frontier' and interpersonal relationships, which Freud pays less attention to in his metapsychology. The concept of a 'contact barrier' (Bion, 1962/1984), or 'point of contact and separation between the conscious and unconscious elements' (p. 45), which I believe to be the preconscious, can do much to explain interpersonal relationships, beginning with the mother–child dyad, if we equate the term 'barrier' with the idea of a frontier or boundary. Freud therefore uses the idea of a frontier to suggest the contiguity of 'pathological states' with 'psychic normality'.

On the basis of these arguments, we can broadly maintain that pathology implies a failure of work on the frontier, where the ego has not assimilated the object, and has therefore been unable to enrich and define itself sufficiently (ego deficit, inability of the ego to sustain conflict effectively); whereas the capacity to elaborate this work on the frontier helps the ego to activate subtle but noticeable identification processes: the 'making' of the bodily ego, the physical sense of existing, the 'making' of the ego as mind inhabiting the soma, and growing able to handle conflict and, finally, the 'creation' of a life project: these could be described as the main goals of any psychoanalytic treatment, including a consultation. In regard to the latter, I believe it requires from the patient some new form of self-awareness, which might be simply a physical and psychic perception of the real state of his/her self, which has prompted him/her to seek help.

It seems to me that in the task of consultation, a psychotherapeutic task like that of any treatment or any truly receptive attitude, it is crucial – as shown by the examples quoted – that the patient should be 'seen' in an effective way; above all, he/she should be seen in such a way as to avoid a symmetrical and exact 'mirroring' of what is actually there. To be a human

[2] Author's italics.

'mirror', as McDougall says, means to be able to reflect back the image of the other 'enhanced' by one's own 'gaze'; which means that the presence of the subject inevitably shapes the object, and that the frontier functions if aspects of the neighbouring 'country' are marked out through a process of comprehension and assimilation, while at the same time proof is given that a part of the other is always present in one's self, just as the other is understood to contain in some way a representation of the self. Of course the so-called neutrality of the analyst is not under discussion here: what matters is for the analyst not to introduce his own 'things' unexpectedly in what could be called, by extending the metaphor, a smuggling operation; it is quite a different thing to promote an exchange which enhances and defines the potential development of both bordering territories. We might say that the very qualities which Semi (1985) described as fundamental for anyone offering a consultation, such as 'a careful and respectful receptiveness, a non-intrusive curiosity, an ability to be actively neutral, a sufficient awareness of one's own style of communication . . . a sufficient clarity about the goals of the specific interview', are only accessible if we work on the 'frontier' between our self and the other, between the internal and the external, between the unconscious/pre-conscious system and the perception/consciousness mode.

From this perspective, a consultation should help the patient to recover, even if slightly, a sense of intimacy with his/her self, in the face of the fear of *loss of boundaries* and the sense of disorientation which can affect him when he comes for a consultation; such an intimacy implies an acknowledgement of the other, which is required if one dares to be oneself. It is a matter of acquiring a form of initial self-awareness, which can be described metaphorically as the recovery of an initial familiarity with one's own 'country', a sort of recovery of the right to citizenship within one's own 'places', and therefore the definition of a 'frontier' which can tolerate contact with the 'borderline' of psychic life.

But the 'borderline' of psychic life, the area where the differences between me and not-me may be uncertain, the boundary area between consciousness and the unconscious, between what is represented and what cannot be, even between life and death, does not spare, even temporarily, any human being of any age; it also affects what we call 'normality', however uncertain this state may be. The formation of such a 'borderline', a space 'empty' of concepts and codified thoughts, belongs to everyone's experience, as a *borderline psychic functioning* present in every human being. 'Being out of one's depth' with its sense of experiencing something uncanny, incomprehensible, unspeakable, unrecognizable, even when it is an 'aesthetic' experience, which can render one speechless, strikes us in all those human experiences which cannot be classified with ready-made thoughts. On the other hand, as analysts we know that to be struck by such 'borderline' moments is an inevitable part of our work, especially where – as in a consultation – we are working on the outer limits of our well-established working methods. We also know that our art consists in finding solutions, or better still ways of evolution, by disengaging from what is incidental, recovering an optimum 'distance' or a greater empathy matched with creativity, with the possibility of generating new psychic forms, both affective and representational, by crossing the 'void' *or crossing the frontier* – as long as we experience living on the 'borderline' (in the sense of borderline space, place and time) for as long as necessary with the patient. Such a disengagement from 'empirical' reality is in fact often a necessary condition – as long as one doesn't get lost, of course – for a moment of creative thought, for a fruitful meeting of minds; it is absolutely vital to any profound innovation and, at the same time, to the recovery of the most intimate part of the self. In the work of analysis the transference/countertransference area is the 'place', this too situated on the frontier, where such psychic conditions are most present.

In connection with what has been described, we know that in 'borderline' psychic functioning the only remedy to disorientation may be a *dissociative response*, on the borderline between the dissociation involved in *borderline disorder* and hysterical disorder.

We can therefore hypothesize, as we did for the patient, a 'dissociation' of the analyst's ego or of his/her 'person', also functioning on the 'borderline'. The point has been made that, in order to be effective, the analyst's regression, while resonating with the patient's regression, must be somehow asymmetrical and distinct from the patient's. We might argue that the regression of narcissistic pathology represents a strenuous defence in the face of an irreconcilable conflict, or an unbearable anxiety; whereas the analyst's regression, induced through empathic attunement or identification with the patient's affective state, can be seen – in light of Terence's dictum '*nihil humani mihi alienum puto*' – as a readiness or openness to venturing along the frontiers of psychic life.

In other words, in pathological states what we have described as the 'borderline area' fails to work as a place of psychic elaboration, whereas the analyst is able to activate his/her own 'areas' in order to carry through this work for the patient, and in the place of the patient. Along the lines of this different regression, the analyst's 'dissociation' would not therefore mirror the patient's dissociation. In the analyst's case this would be *a dissociation linked to a libidinal-emotional aptitude for comprehension* (a kind of transient and fruitful hysterical dissociation), which operates psychically on the frontiers of psychic life. In these cases we must not fear the 'void' associated with separation or castration anxiety, nor the 'void' resulting from the inevitable absence of images – a sort of necessary blank screen – which must precede any new affective or representational insight. Perhaps in this instance we should consider that the analytic 'couple' may not be functioning all the time. At times the analyst is alone in these circumstances, on a playing field without a partner; in this case he/she will need to persevere alone for as long as it takes, without retaliating against the patient, so as to re-create a couple as soon as possible, or if need be, to choose when not to do so.

This decision may become particularly important when doing a consultation may involve a referral to a colleague, or to another professional. Why establish a couple, if the couple is to be dissolved immediately? A referral leads one onto rather dangerous ground, in which interventions made to stimulate a new form of self-awareness can also foster the development of a transference and of an attachment which may prove difficult or even harmful for the patient to let go of; such developments can have a negative impact on a referral to another analyst. Just as the pre-conscious takes Charon's role, as a mediator between the conscious and the unconscious, so the analyst undertaking a consultation must remember at such times – perhaps through the message of his pre-conscious – that he is only a ferryman between the experience of consultation and the new place symbolized by the colleague to whom the patient will be sent and by the relationship which will spring up between them; he must be especially careful not to trigger the transference in the patient and not to create a bond which will then make treatment with another therapist more difficult.

In order to be able to take care of the person who seeks help, by identifying the patient's problem and providing the necessary information, while maintaining a sufficiently enigmatic attitude, it is probably vital not to establish too clearly a working alliance with a given patient. I have sometimes heard from colleagues to whom I had referred a patient that either the patient had not contacted them or that it had been difficult, a couple of times impossible, to establish a therapeutic relationship because of a 'strong' bond those patients had formed with me; probably in such cases I either did not manage to be enigmatic enough, or I may have forced the 'creation' of a couple through my own narcissism. I personally think that the ability to remain enigmatic, especially if the patient needs to be referred to another analyst, may be linked to the analyst's capacity or disposition to 'be alone in company', to experience a constructive separation, to embody a 'pathos of distance' (Lopez, 1987).

To sum up, it is clear that we need to make distinctions between different situations and different patients, and we should remember that – in my view – the consultation is the main opportunity and the setting par excellence for the 'ensemble' created by the analyst's analytic function and the particular features of a given patient; this ensemble of two persons is both a borderline area of separation and a boundary line, since it provides a borderline 'area' of psychic elaboration. For instance, if the patient who comes for a consultation is unable to allow, due to his dual narcissistic structure, for the analyst to act as an analytic 'third', connecting between the two, between the here-and-now and the there-and-then, it will be more difficult to suggest that he sees another analyst; how can we suggest 'another place', if his need is to be received, if it is all too possible that the statement implied in such a suggestion

('I will not treat you') will be experienced as an unacceptable rejection (Semi, 1985). How can we avoid the risk of an excessive closeness or an excessive distance, which would annihilate the patient, and would then make a referral impossible? Besides, we must bear in mind that the patient is always free not to follow our recommendations, since these are the result of an encounter between two entities.

While being aware that I too am theorizing, by making the following arguments, my emphasis on 'borderline functioning' is intended to leave the different theories in the background. It is important to be able to function – and consultation requires a special psychic 'work area' – in a dimension where the psyche, and its 'labour' to produce representations, is obliged to reckon from the start with the impossibility of representing the enigma of an unconscious, both instinctual and non-instinctual, which cannot be tamed or understood in the slightest. As a consequence, the consultation may force the analyst to deal with elements which at first cannot be represented both in the patient and in him/herself. The area in common which develops between the two may indeed induce states of intense *merging*, sometimes furious, sometimes erotically seductive (not to be confused with shared experience!), or instead, the experience of infinite distance, devoid of any feeling, or of reciprocal *confusion*, which can over time prevent the gaining of analytical insight. When making a formulation in the consultation it is therefore important to have access to psychoanalytic models, and to choose what use to put them to, and to express our gratitude to those who have elaborated these models and made them comprehensible. What I feel is much more important, though, is the analyst's complementary openness to experiencing the consultation as an enterprise which draws fully and specifically on his or her psychoanalytic identity, while operating on the borderline of his/her being a psychoanalyst, on the margins of his/her theory and knowledge; the intention of this enterprise being to grasp the 'borderline psychic functioning' within the analyst's own self, to cross the boundary of his/her ego in the authentic exploration of the case at issue and to bring back into his/her territory the meaning of the experience gained.

The ego, 'a borderline being' according to Freud, especially the pre-conscious ego in my view, and the borderline situation have a necessary task in common, achieved by pushing the boundaries: they need to delimit spaces which are crying out to be encountered, defined and determined, so that subjectivity can be recovered. What this really turns on is the narcissistic problems of borderline functioning, which need to be managed in such a way as to demonstrate a constructive approach in response to the patient's communication which bears signs of destruction within it.

What is needed, therefore, is to work on the initial countertransference: such work always involves staying on the borderline or frontier. The actual *analytic function* of the therapist, which is activated by these experiences, cannot often draw on the interpretative model of the transference, conflict and defences, which it might be premature to use, but *responds better to the need of building a pre-conscious bridge* between psychic life and death, between what is represented and what cannot be represented, between consciousness and the unconscious, between subject and object.

What is essential, in my view, is that this pattern/framework is not something 'given', something 'established' in which the patient should place himself in a predetermined way. The functional coherence of the analytic consultation would therefore stem from a process of identification and assimilation/appropriation; its structure, changing as the encounter develops, depends on the subtle interplay in the patient's mind between the preconscious–conscious use he/she makes of the 'place' of treatment, the way he/she feels received, and the (unconscious) transferential cathexis which associates the analyst with the analytical context as a whole.

In such cases providing a rigid *setting* is less important than re-establishing a *continuity of being*, to build up (or restore) a good *primary narcissism*. By primary narcissism I mean not a development stage, but a primary condition of human psychic life, beyond time, where the internal/external split and the self/object split are healed. To go back to Freud's painting metaphor, in the merging of individual 'shades of colour', in the blurring of the various 'areas of colour', in the intersecting of their respective boundaries: in short, in their coming together, the separation and distinction of the individual is preserved rather than prevented. At the beginning of psychic life this type of narcissism is the 'oceanic experience' referred to by Freud (1937), in his reflections on the early stages of the mother–child union. Those who live *on the edge of psychic life*, a narrow and dangerous space or, better still, a non-space, suffer from a lack of nourishment and support from this 'ocean', a 'place' of origin which is neither experienced in full nor trusted: in its place what is sensed is a boundless territory where no creative illusion, linked to a 'personal' mother or father in a real sense, has taken ground; all that is there is an apprehension which is devoid of clues about an uncharted space, the boundaries between life and death, good and evil, on an archaic level.

To sum up, every consultation meeting is a first meeting between strangers, each bearing their own story and each with their own pattern of transference. In this meeting, while respecting the unchangeable aspects and discipline of the analytic setting, the actual analytic situation of the consultation requires a different 'analysing' ambience, which might be directed towards the discovery of something new, along the lines of Winnicott's 'in-between' space, where room is made for discovery/creation. This paradoxical style of 'making a place' for the patient in the consultation is highlighted in the importance Freud assigned to the emergence and self-renewal of a spontaneous transference, which has crucial value in treatment; while he showed a much lesser interest in familiar explanations and the use of the analytic context. The first meeting thus brings together the patient's need for treatment, and his/her competence in communicating this need, with the analyst's aptitude and capacity to shape an effective response. I consider this *coming together, if successful and worked out, to be the place where the previously forbidden areas of psychic elaboration are first reached*; the place of merging of two minds working together, *the opening of a real intermediate space for relationship and at the same time the materialization of new subjective psychic places.* A new entity (the true dawn of the 'analytic third') is reconstituted in the in-between space connecting the patient and the analyst.

While thinking of the consultation as a frontier experience in psychoanalysis, as psychoanalysts we can also argue that no effective analysis, meaning an analysis which takes into account the analyst's unconscious, can take place unless the analytic experience leads us right up to the edge. As a matter of fact, the cases which give us material for thought, argument and writing are the 'difficult cases', the unknown situations, such as those occurring in consultations. The borderline status of a 'difficult case' or of a situation which cannot be approached in a straightforward analytic process, such as a consultation, can bring about an *impasse*, or an impediment to thought; to be more exact, what cannot at first glance slot into our thinking and our theoretical framework – even though, by becoming manifest, it belongs to our analytic body of work – forces us to question ourselves, to discover new ways or paths for reverting to thinking. Going through a stage of narcissistic deprivation, often through an identity 'crisis' ('What on earth am I doing with this patient?', 'Where is the analysis?', 'What is this patient trying to tell me in this consultation?', 'How can I lay the ground for referral to a colleague?'), *which I compare to a depressive state after a (temporary) loss of self and of the object which guarantees its acknowledgement and validation*, means experiencing the emotional and cognitive condition which re-establishes the boundaries of our being analysts and restores our feeling and working as subjects/objects, as persons in the course of analytic treatment, even during a consultation.

References

Bion, W. R. (1962). *Learning from Experience.* London: Karnac, 1984.

Freud, S. (1915). The Unconscious. *SE* 14.

Freud, S. (1923). The Ego and Id. *SE* 19.

Freud, S. (1930). Civilisation and its Discontents. *SE* 21.

Freud, S. (1933). New Introductory Lectures on Psycho-Analysis. *SE* 22: 1–182.

Freud, S. (1937). Analysis Terminable and Interminable. *SE* 23.

Giaconia, G., Racalbuto, A. (1997). Il circolo vizioso trauma-fantasma-trauma, *Rivista di Psicoanalisi* 4.

La Scala, M. (2001). Rappresentazione e limite. In: Racalbuto, A., La Scala, M., *Costantini M.V. (a cura di) La nascita della rappresentazione fra lutto e nostalgia.* Roma: Borla.

Lopez, D. (1987). Memoria e oblio. *Gli Argonauti* 68.

Masciangelo, P. M. (2003). *Scritti Psicoanalitici* (1956–1998). Seminario Psicoanalitico di Lugano.

Odgen, T. H. (1994). The analytical third: Working with inter-subjective clinical facts. *International Journal of Psychoanalysis* 75.

Odgen, T. H. (2001). *Conversation at the Frontier of the Dreaming.* Northvale, NJ: Jason Aronson.
Racalbuto, A. (1996). L'area del non-verbale: il territorio degli oggetti come negativo (da sviluppare) del (in) pensiero. *Gli Argonauti* 70: 185–199.
Racalbuto, A. (2001). Vivendo lungo il border. *Rivista di Psicolanalisi* XLVII(1): 29–49.
Semi, A. (1985). *Tecnica del colloquio.* Milano: Rafaello Cortina Milano.
Semi, A. (2000). Per una metapsicologia della coscienza. *Rivista di Psicoanalisi* XLVI(1): 45–67.

14 CONSULTATION, REVERIE AND STORY-TELLING *by Antonino Ferro*

Commentary

Ronny Jaffè

In the following paper Antonino Ferro compares the consultation to a detective story in which the role of the analyst is to find the clues in a field immediately constituted by emotional tensions between the consultant and the potential patient. This idea refers to Baranger's theory of the field (Baranger, 1993) where the meeting is seen as at once generating powerful interaction.

Of course the consultation is just the beginning of a potential and future analytical process. According to Ferro, we can only give the patient a small taste of what is happening within him/herself and in the relationship during a consultation, a taste based on what the analyst is able to and chooses to formulate about his/her own experience. The analyst must also keep in mind that what can be communicated to the patient depends on whether the latter can be taken into treatment directly by the consultant or not.

This idea of the analyst discovering traces like in a detective novel is linked to Ferro's other powerful metaphor of the analyst as a chef who is able to taste continuously what is happening in the analytical field in order to correct 'the baking, the salting, the sweetening and the introduction of new ingredients'. He shows his way of working through the presentation of vast clinical material regarding children, adolescents, adults and supervisions. These metaphors are embodied in Ferro's very personal and original theoretical and clinical viewpoint, based mostly on the work of Bion and on Baranger's theory of the field. Regarding Bion, Ferro refers especially to the concept of 'negative capability', to the theory of transformation in dreams and to the narrative transformation theory. Bion's concepts are, in turn, inserted in Baranger's theory of the analytical field.

For Ferro, the theory of the analytical field involves many aspects, only one of which is the relationship between theory and technique. The field has a spatial dimension containing split-off elements, and a temporal dimension that includes all the periods and ages of life. Moreover, in line with Bion's ideas about mental functioning, the field is in continuous spatial and temporal expansion.

Ferro's very specific and original position is shown in his proposal that the field model, when applied to the consultation, implies the possibility of a continuous generation of characters in the field. The generated characters become figures in a kind of narrative of the mental functioning of both analyst and patient. The originality of Ferro's contribution is that the analytical field is seen as a living space with a history with inhabitants derived from the patient's inner world, but which is constantly being enriched through the appearance of new inhabitants in continuous movement.

The clinical vignettes illustrate and illuminate the author's rich and original thinking, immersing the reader in a strong emotional contact with a way of practising psychoanalysis in which clinical experience and theory are embodied one within the other.

Antonino Ferro is a training and supervising analyst of the Italian Psychoanalytic Society and the IPA. He has supervised and lectured at the psychoanalytic societies of several countries in Europe, North America, South America and Australia, and has published several widely translated books. In 2007 he was selected to be a recipient of the Mary S. Sigourney Award.

Reference

Baranger, M. (1993). The mind of the analyst: From listening to interpretation. *International Journal of Psycho-Analysis* 74: 15–24.

14 CONSULTATION, REVERIE AND STORY-TELLING[1]

Antonino Ferro

I see the first interview rather like a novel containing an enigma, to which I have to find a clue; or perhaps, as portrayed on television, a situation requiring a detective like Lieutenant Columbo or Inspector Derrick. Somebody comes to me with a problem, and I am expected to find a clue, to follow a track towards a possible solution.

Sometimes the person who comes for a first interview has no idea what the problem is exactly, or can only describe symptoms, as manifestations of a yet unknown problem. But it is the patient (or would-be patient) who will, without knowing it, show me what clue to pick, what path to take, what assumptions to make.

So, this is a situation comparable to a detective story, where I need to find out who or what is responsible for the patient's suffering, and what is the story, what is the plot that needs to be developed into a narrative. In this work I have two precious resources: my *negative capacity* (Bion, 1963/1984), i.e. my ability to wait and not let my mind be saturated too early by the clues I have to follow, and my capacity for *transformation into a dream* and for *narrative transformation*.

Having a negative capacity also means emptying my mind of all ready-made psychoanalytic theories and waiting for a fact to emerge as significative, until it establishes itself as a 'selected fact' (Bion, 1963/1984); therefore it is important to gather the data brought by the patient, especially the data he is not aware of bringing, without polluting the evidence with remnants of theories, which would entail a transformation into hallucinosis (Bion, 1965/1984; Ferro, 1996), i.e. a functioning through which I project something of my own and read it as belonging to the patient. This would produce a kind of 'over-exposure' of the evidence, which actually needs a 'dark-room' in order to be gradually developed.

The transformation into a dream has two aspects: the first consists in reverie, a mental activity occurring during wakeful states, and consisting of images (Bion, 1962/1984; Ferro, 1999; Grotstein, 2007) which build up a

[1] This paper was written for this book at the invitation of the editors.

visual representation of the material: a pictorial language of symbols that help to cast light on the investigation. Reverie can be described as a process of capturing and organizing meaningful elements in an image, which functions like a snapshot.

The second aspect consists in a dreamy listening to the patient's communication; I need to pay attention to the facts the patient recounts as clues to the way his/her mind functions. The dreamy listening to the patient is not only an 'openness' towards all that is coming from the patient, but also a deconstructive way of listening to the patient's communications, as if his/her narratives were introduced as dreams. This enables us to let go of the realities outside the consulting room, in order to get a better feeling of the phantasies manifesting within it, which are far more important to us.

Narrative transformations refer to the way we as analysts select certain facts in the patient's story and build up our own narrative. At this stage I would refrain from offering interpretations as decoders of the patient's communications: I prefer open, exploratory interventions, which may help to unlock doors, windows, drawers and strong-boxes in the patient's mind, as well as letting in facts of which the patient himself is (apparently) unaware. Narrative transformations depend on my ability to link individual reveries I may have had (or their absence) with the narrative text I have deconstructed, dreamed and dreamed again, i.e. reconstructed in a different way (Ogden, 1997).

I shall illustrate these points with the following examples.

So, where is . . . the tail?

Luciano is a seven-year-old boy, who has been suffering from an allergic disease which is both debilitating and disabling. At our first interview, since he appears relaxed, I ask him to tell me a story. He says: 'I'll tell you about my Lucky.' He picks up a sheet of paper and tells me he has had this little pet for some time. While he is drawing, he tells me that he keeps his pet in his father's study, because, if he gets close to Lucky and picks him up, his skin suddenly turns red, from the place of contact with Lucky outward, and then . . . he goes on to describe the particular type of disabling allergy he suffers from. While he goes on drawing I realize with astonishment that these names have special meanings.

Luciano tells me that his pet lives underground, and digs deep burrows, where he hides. I find myself liking Luciano's easy-going manner. While he draws, I ask him a few generic questions, to which he repeatedly answers, 'What did you say?' I am struck by his description of Lucky as a breed with no tail: Luciano tells me there is another very unruly and aggressive breed which does have a tail.

At this point I have a unifying vision: I see Lucky Luciano as unable to hear me because he is hidden in his burrow, above which there are two long

Figure 14.1 Luciano's pet.

tails; in my mind this picture is transformed through reverie into a drawing, featuring two large animals, where Lucky occupies the upper part, and Luciano the lower part. Thus the field becomes re-defined by my hypothesis about the meaning of Luciano's drawing: I am able to phantasize that Luciano is allergic to unknown parts of himself, which will have to be metabolized and transformed in order to prevent the formation of the antibodies which his 'non-self' parts keep on producing.

While refraining from communicating this insight to the child, I store it to help me organize my thoughts and hypotheses about what is going on here.

Maria Pia and the microwave oven

On our first meeting Maria Pia, a 17-year-old girl, turns up with her parents, who had phoned me to ask for a consultation.

They ask to speak first with me in private, while Maria Pia waits in the waiting-room.

The problem, they say, is that their daughter has lost too much weight, 10 kg in fact, within a short time; her periods have stopped and they fear that these are signs of anorexia.

Maria Pia is attending a language school, with fairly good results, after having left the grammar school where her mother is a teacher.

Her father is genuinely worried about his daughter's 'superficiality,' which he cannot stomach. A leftist democrat, he cannot understand how his daughter can 'want to vote for the Lega' (the Northern League, a right-wing populist party), why she has no particular cultural interests, how she could say, 'I feel ashamed for having two university-educated parents' and aspire to a 'boorish' boyfriend.

Furthermore, he cannot understand how, up to two years ago, she seemed extremely 'bound' to him, waiting for him every evening to play with her, and now she hardly speaks to him.

He concludes by saying: 'I'd give anything for her to be a child again.'

Immediately afterwards I let the parents out and let Maria Pia in.

After a short silence, I break the ice by asking her, 'Will you tell me something about yourself?'

She answers: 'I want to go to university and become a PR person; I don't want to be a dancer in a disco, but a PR person attending the Bicocca University.' She tells me about her school and says she has an easier relationship with her mother than with her father. She is a very beautiful girl, who could pass for a model, but her features still look child-like at times.

I tell her that her father has told me about her playing a lot with him as a child; she brightens up and describes the many games she played until two years ago, games with Barbie dolls. I am struck by how moments of real connection (as in her smile when I voice my impression that 'there is a secret Maria Pia whom few people get to know') alternate with moments of superficial, commonplace communication, bordering on emotional dullness.

At last she mentions a dream: she is at home, when a goose suddenly appears, giving her a fright. She chases it, catches it and puts it into the microwave oven, hoping to cook it, but the goose jumps out 'uncooked' and frightens her even more.

I ask her whether she would like someone to help her 'cook this goose' and, cheering up, she tells me quite easily that this is the reason she has come.

We make arrangements for therapy.

In Maria Pia's case one interview has produced enough material for the following hypothesis:

The sudden change into an attractive adolescent has confused her; on the one hand she doesn't know how to untie the familiar bonds, and so she stills 'votes for them' (a play on the words 'lega' = league and 'lega' = binds) by causing her periods to stop. She also shares with her father, and partly with her mother, the project of remaining a child (a bi-cocca, which means a pet twice over, both her mother's and her father's pet). However, her real task is to grow up, to differentiate herself, to acquire a 'different' way of being, distinguishing and separating herself from her parents.

But there is a mourning which has yet to be experienced, therefore her adult identity is a kind of false identity: hence the image of the superficial girl, the 'goose' actually, which feels persecutory to her; she doesn't as yet have the right tools to 'cook the goose' or to vote for 'unbinding' ('s-lega') instead of for 'binding' ('lega'), and so to experience, together with her parents, the mourning for her childhood which is irretrievably over.

Stefania and the sacristan

My first sight of the patient is stunning. I open the door in a dismal mood, of the kind that often comes over me at nine o'clock on a foggy Saturday morning, and am confronted with a gorgeous young woman with a dizzily plunging neckline and an enormous suitcase. I need not dwell on the fantasies inspired by this vision, which lights up the gloom of that April morning.

She sits down and tells me that she has come after reading an interview I gave on 'infantile seductions and the memories associated with them' which she read in *L'Unita'* (*L'Unita'* is an Italian communist newspaper, whose name means 'unity'). She has a tormenting memory of a childhood episode, when, aged ten, she went for a catechism lesson in preparation for her First Communion, and the sacristan tried to slip his hand inside her blouse.

I am struck by the coincidence with my own instant fantasies, and try to direct the conversation to her suitcase and to all the things she must be carrying around with her.

She tells me a long story about a difficult adolescence, and a remote mother and father, who were separated and locked in mutual conflict . . . and goes on to say that she yearns for a 'deep spiritual communion' in her relationship with her boyfriend, whereas all he can think of is sex.

Stefania's 'childhood memory' is in fact an image portraying her current problem: how to reconcile her need for tenderness and intense emotional closeness (communion) with an explosive sensuality which she has been unable to integrate. She has come to me with a view to unifying these aspects of herself (*L'Unita'* = unity). Here we have a particularly apt dream-like vignette (alpha-elements) featured on the front page (of a suitably named newspaper) as a representation of the unresolved subject-matter – the undigested fact – that calls for a narrative transformation in order to facilitate new developments (Ferro, 2002).

So far I have offered only a partial vision of the detective work involving the analyst on one side and, on the other, the patient who is 'under investigation', as we say in Italy about a potentially suspect witness. The real work is much more complex, since the meeting between analyst and (potential) patient immediately generates emotional tensions in the psychic field resulting from their interaction (Renik, 1993). This interaction involves not only the two persons, but also the various functions taking place within the field thus generated. As an analyst I would only give the patient a vague 'taste' of what emerges, what I suspect or sense from our interaction: we are still, after all, in a preliminary phase of the consultation, where I am testing the conditions for a potential journey together. The provisional formulation I may come up with helps to trace a route on a hypothetical map for this journey; a route that will need to be continually adjusted according to what is learned from the patient at every successive encounter (Grotstein, 2007).

I wish to stress that I behave differently depending on whether I know I can take the patient on for therapy or whether I am sure that I cannot do so. In the latter case, I try to have a minimum number of meetings, to avoid the building up of an emotional relationship between myself and the patient, which might prove difficult to unravel and may create problems with the patient's next analyst. In the first case, I am more inclined to arrange more than one, in fact usually three, meetings.

Sometimes the first interview may, unintentionally on my part, turn into a *therapeutic consultation* (this happens especially with the parents of difficult children or adolescents), which may be of support until the symptom possibly disappears or the therapeutic project is tolerated.

Carlotta's pain

I receive a very alarming phone call from a colleague, who tells me about the distressing situation affecting this couple, who are friends of his: their nine-year-old daughter has been affected by a total paralysis of the legs, which set in over a few days. The child has been treated in hospital, to no effect. Carlotta's father is a diplomat, working in a country which borders with Italy, while her mother is a successful journalist.

It appears that Carlotta first had chicken-pox, then a pain in one of the trigeminal nerves, after which the paralysis of her legs set in. She has been hospitalized twice in hospitals with excellent neurological departments: no organic cause was diagnosed, however the paralysis was undeniable and unexplainable.

Knowing this did not relieve the parents, since their child had been lying motionless in bed for four months, suffering from a flaccid paralysis in both legs.

Carlotta's mother tells me that for a while she had contemplated giving up her job, which she found stressful after receiving threats, so she had thought of stopping work for a while and giving herself time to think; but this new situation at home has actually forced her to stop working in order to care for Carlotta full time, as she did for Carlotta's elder brother Luigi, at the time of whose birth she only worked on an occasional basis.

I find her story alarming and feel a great responsibility to respond to these parents' expectations: they are travelling hundreds of kilometres to see me. I decide to see them a few more times and then to work out what can be done.

I see two clues here: the first clue is that the mother's work problems have been 'solved' by Carlotta's illness, so I start working on this theme with her parents. Carlotta's mother says she would prefer not to work, but feels obliged to by her husband's expectations; the husband is taken aback and says he has no objection to his wife staying at home and looking after the children; he adds that, once she no longer feels obliged to work, she may wish to return to work at the newspaper . . . and so this problem, which risked ratifying an unconscious alliance between mother and daughter, starts to unravel.

The other clue concerns the *pain*, which I try to focus on as a metaphorical communication: what kind of pain might Carlotta have or have had during this period, what suffering of hers has not been acknowledged and how much anger might this have generated?

Carlotta's parents are both intelligent and sensitive people, so they have no difficulty in following this line of thinking.

We arrange some meetings every fortnight, working through the themes they bring to me about pain and the mother's professional choices. They also invent a new game, a kind of pain chart which shows how Carlotta's pain is progressively decreasing as her parents start owning the various problems that were causing her to suffer.

I use metaphors to try and make sense of what is happening; I say, for instance: it is as if water had flooded a control panel and, while the water is subsiding, the controls start drying out and functioning again. Carlotta goes through a process resembling a toddler learning to walk: she starts by crawling, then goes on to walk on all fours, until at our fifth meeting the astonished parents tell me that, after drawing a chart showing the decrease of both pain and anger towards point zero, Carlotta has started walking again and has even performed a dance with her friends to celebrate.

Carlotta is now set to begin therapy to help her express her yet unresolved suffering and problems, and her mother has opted for a part-time job.

I wish to clarify a technical aspect. Since I am often asked to provide consultations, when I need to book an appointment while knowing I have no room for therapy, I prefer to say that I am happy to offer a consultation; however, should I find that therapy is advisable, I will suggest the name of a reliable colleague. This on the one hand prevents the 'natural' formation of a field, and on the other avoids for the patient the disappointment of being told this after the consultation, which would add a fear of not having proved interesting enough.

Another situation which may arise is when I am asked for a *consultation for a single supervision*, often by colleagues who live far away, with whom a weekly supervision is impossible to arrange. In such cases too, which happen frequently, my mental attitude and functioning is the same one I adopt in the preliminary interviews with potential patients: it is based on the three pillars of negative capacity, transformation into dream and narrative transformation. From this perspective, it is most useful to listen to the patient's history as told by the analyst, because it can be listened to as a dream by the analyst about his patient and, as such, it is loaded with potential communications.

I recall a case, related by a Canadian colleague, about a patient of his, a judge by profession, who was severely inhibited and devoid of social relationships. When the patient's history was recounted, I was struck by the fact that he allowed his cleaning lady to tidy up the whole house, except for a room which remained secret and inaccessible.

This immediately triggered a reverie: Bluebeard! (the famous fairy tale by Perrault), and the thought came up that the analyst had access to the whole of the patient's house, except for a room in the patient's mind: the room containing his crimes. This opened up a new course in the analysis.

The following cases present vivid clues which provide a key to the patient's internal world:

Carla's antidote

The 'case' is introduced as follows: Carla, a 45-year-old woman, is in therapy following a court order.

She says she has always been 'rejected' by her parents, while her brother was their darling. She has two children: she rejects the older child because his birth 'wasn't planned'; the younger child suffers from esophageal reflux and can hold nothing down; he 'spits poison'. Carla's prevalent symptom is bulimia, with episodes of uncontrollable vomiting.

After missing a session with her therapist, she informs her that she has been constantly vomiting, that her house feels narrow, that in spite of that she only wants to wear short, tight-fitting clothes; she would like to set fire to her house and she doesn't give a damn about her husband. She likes to go to the pub, play cards and stuff herself with food.

Then she adds that she can only show two per cent of herself . . . and that she would like to vomit on her husband's head.

The meanings we could find in these communications could lead us in all kinds of directions; however, in my view, a first gestalt seems to be the incontinence theme. What is most apparent, though – and here is the key – is the use of bulimia as an antidote.

In Carla, her sense of being 'rejected' (by life, by her internal objects, by the Other) triggers an increasing amount of anger, rage, fury and jealousy, which are 'plugged' by food, before the whole amount is vomited as in a gastric washout after poisoning.

She is poisoned by the emotions rising within her, which she is unable to name, acknowledge or work through; she can only purge herself of them through bulimia and violent evacuation.

The same process takes place on a different scale when, having 'rejected' the therapist by missing a session, she then feels there is less room for her: 'the house feels narrow,' 'she wants short and tight-fitting clothes,' she is in an incendiary rage, she denies every need. She avoids depression by eating and vomiting. . . .

A courtroom for Marina

Marina's therapist tells me that, at their first meeting, Marina wore the traditional costume of the Val d'Aosta, her native region.

She immediately described the tragedy of her life; twenty-five years previously, while they were skiing together, her sister Nadia – their mother's favorite – died in tragic circumstances. Ever since then life has changed for everyone and 'what could not be mentioned disrupted everyone's life.'

Marina works all week, and then goes back to the Valley for the weekend. She talks about this accident, dating back a quarter of a century, as if it had just happened: she conveys the idea that the Valley (not quite a Vale of Tears yet) is an enclave outside time, outside history, where time has stopped on that fateful day.

She then talks about her mother's depression, about her own worry that she may be drifting into alcoholism, about the fear of losing control which sometimes grips her.

At her first session she describes a dream she had after reading a book about the deaths of the anti-mafia judges Falcone and Borsellino: 'The mother kills the two sons of a mafia boss; she is an accomplice herself, because she let her sons go out, so she is guilty as well.'

There seems to be a plot with unknown ramifications here; what appears evident is violence, guilt, murder, implicit fear of retaliation, possibly repentance. Are the mafia bosses Riina and Buscetta also hinted at in this dream?

What may be assumed is that [in the patient's mind] the analysis takes the form of a trial which could not take place at the time [of the accident]; while there were no explicit charges against the patient, she was forced nevertheless to be on parole, to atone, to have nothing of her own for fear of retaliation. Guilt, jealousy, rivalry, fantasies, aggressive desires (acted out?) provide the elements for this trial, in a courtroom where a ritual indictment and conviction, followed perhaps by acquittal and repentance, will need to be played out.

Rosanna's stammer

In a similar way, the presentation of Rosanna's case by her analyst instantly highlights the key aspects of her suffering: hers is a situation in which incontinence and suppression alternate, exactly as in her speech patterns in childhood, when she stammered.

Rosanna suffers from uncontainable anxieties, including many phobias and depressive features; as an adolescent, she was also anorexic. Phobias can be described as no-go areas: perhaps the same areas where, during adolescence, Rosanna deposited the most primitive aspects of her mind, through a splitting and 'starvation' process, in the hope of diminishing their power and making them easier to manage.

I am also told that the patient describes her father as a 'hot-tempered man' and her elder sister as very rebellious. These descriptions must refer to the 'uncontainable' aspects [in Rosanna herself]. What I am using here is a narrative deconstruction approach, through which I identify every person and event in the story as playing a major role in the patient's present emotional state and casting light on it. I see the narrative subunits as forms of transport of emotional states from one place in the [patient's mind's] field to another. The theme of incontinence is illustrated by the story of the nightmares which frighten Rosanna at night and wake her up (when the dream is not able to contain in itself certain primitive aspects of her mind), by the bed-wetting which plagued her in childhood, and lastly by the convulsive crises through which she managed to evacuate the contents which could not be dealt with by splitting or suppression.

From the field viewpoint (Baranger & Baranger, 1961–1962; Baranger, 1993), even after the consultation and once analysis has started, it is not necessary nor often useful to relate what the patient says to the 'here and now' of the session or of the relationship. What in a relational approach might be a 'collateral transference', which should be brought back into the relationship itself through an interpretation, in a field-based approach can be 'played out' in the field, without necessarily referring it to the 'here and now' of the relationship. The field includes many routes: one of these is the 'relational route', but there are many more besides. Furthermore the field extends out both in terms of space, i.e. it includes all the split elements, and in terms of time; hence it includes all times and ages of life, besides expanding forever in both time and space.

If from the field viewpoint – for instance – one needs to interpret a negative transference on the spot, almost stifling any budding rebellion, in the field it is useful to understand how, where and when the negative transference has arisen and what mental operations the analyst can perform in order to transform it.

After a detailed interpretation, which a patient was not prepared to listen to, since he wanted first to be listened to (welcomed) by an analyst who appeared unreceptive in that moment, the patient mentioned an attempt towards homosexual seduction by a homosexual acquaintance, who tried to get him to experience this type of lovemaking. From the field viewpoint it would not be difficult to relate this to the image of the homosexual couple formed by the patient and the analyst, emerging during the session as a graphic representation of two non-receptive mental states, between which either abuse or subjugation might occur. Other models would have prompted other thoughts. In the field model we are aware of the continuous generativity of the characters in the field itself as an almost live narrative of the functioning of the patient's and the analyst's minds in the consulting room.

Of course it is vitally important to see the field as continuously provided with material from history and from the inhabitants of the internal world, who keep on enriching the field itself. The field becomes the great receiver of what cannot be remembered, of what is projected from the internal world, with the advantage of a continuous monitoring of the transformations occurring in the field, made possible [by analysis]. This monitoring allows the analyst, in a role which could be compared to that of a master chef, to keep 'tasting' the contents, and his tasting enables him to adjust the cooking temperature, the degree of saltiness or sweetness, and the adding of new ingredients.

References

Baranger, M. (1993). The mind of the analyst: From listening to interpretation. *International Journal of Psycho-Analysis* 74: 15–24.

Baranger, M., Baranger, W. (1961–1962). La situacion analitica como campo dinamico. *Revista Uruguaya de Psicoanalisis* 4: 3–54.

Bion, W. R. (1962). *Learning from Experience*. London: William Heinemann [Reprinted London: Karnac Books, 1984].

Bion, W. R. (1963). *Elements of Psycho-Analysis*. London: William Heinemann [Reprinted London: Karnac Books, 1984].

Bion, W. R. (1965). *Transformations*. London: William Heinemann [Reprinted London: Karnac Books, 1984].

Ferro, A. (1996). *In the Analyst's Consulting Room*. English translation, London and New York: Psychology Press – Routledge Brunner, 2002.

Ferro, A. (1999). *Psycho-Analysis as Therapy and Story-telling*. English translation, London: New Library/Routledge, 2006.

Ferro, A. (2002). *Seeds of Illness, Seeds of Recovery*. English translation, London: New Library/Routledge, 2004.

Grotstein, J. (2007). *A Beam of Intense Darkness*. London: Karnac Books.

Ogden, T. (1997). Reverie and interpretation. *Psychoanalytic Quarterly* 66: 567–595.

Renik, O. (1993). Analytic interaction: Conceptualizing technique in the light of the analyst's irreducible subjectivity. *Psychoanalytic Quarterly* 62: 553–571.

Part IV

DARING OR RELUCTANCE TO START ANALYSIS?

IV DARING OR RELUCTANCE TO START ANALYSIS?

Introduction

Bernard Reith

Lena Ehrlich writes in the conclusion to her paper reproduced at the end of this section (Ehrlich, 2004, this volume p. 330) that 'one of the many paradoxes that characterize our "impossible profession" is that we are reluctant to practice it'.

Freud described psychoanalysis as an 'impossible' profession in part VII of his *Analysis Terminable and Interminable* (1937), where he discussed the role of the analyst's personality in the limits of the psychoanalytic process, as well as the need for personal analysis and re-analysis. When he lumped psychoanalysis together with 'education and government' as the three impossible professions, this was ostensibly because of their frustrating nature, but we may safely assume that he also had in mind other demanding and paradoxical characteristics of work at the service of others: work involving intense and conflicted relationships and requiring strong personal commitment, but whose results depend on the abilities and collaboration of others, thus constantly challenging the meaning and purpose of the professional's activity as well as his or her personal capacities and sense of identity.

Of course, what sets psychoanalysis apart even amongst such professions is the fact that unconscious drives, phantasies, conflicts and identifications not only intrude with their unexpected and disturbing effects as they do in all walks of life, but that they are at the very core of the analyst's work and so of his/her conscious and unconscious experience while at work. The psychoanalyst's receptiveness to the strange and unsettling impact of unconscious life in others and in him/herself is so fundamental to the profession that no amount of personal analysis and professional training could, nor should, be expected to shelter him or her from it. If the analyst were to remain unaffected and never taken by surprise, he/she would no longer be an analyst. No wonder, then, that we can be reluctant every time we are called upon to do our job!

It is our contention that these effects can be particularly strong in initial encounters with potential analysands, not just because the analyst senses that he or she may once again become involved in such a doubly impossible relationship, but also because the unconscious dynamics and their impact are exceptionally powerful whenever an analyst and a patient meet for the first time. In contrast to what may happen later on in an established analytic setting, they are both unprepared for what may ensue between them. As a result, defensive reactions are equally strong on both sides. A potent and enigmatic transference and countertransference scene of wishes, expectations, fears and defences is thus immediately set up, which can be very disturbing, sometimes so much so that the analyst can be impelled to repudiate it through denial, repression or rationalization.

Many of the papers reproduced in the preceding sections have highlighted aspects of this forceful initial scene. For example, Argelander (1978, this volume, p. 26) shows how, when Freud met Katharina, he was not only finding out about her story, but was also immediately involved in a transference and countertransference scene that affected what he could learn and how he learned it. Dantlgraber (1982, this volume p. 26) describes how the analyst's subjective perspective on the dynamics of that scene and on his own reactions to it can be used as a source of information, while Wegner (1992, this volume p. 194) puts more emphasis on the inevitably disturbing effects of these dynamics on the analyst, requiring careful self-monitoring and self-reflection. Racalbuto (2006, this volume p. 225) adds that, when he first enters this novel scene, the analyst is so confronted with the unknown in the other, as well as in himself in reaction to the other, that he can undergo a transient loss of his sense of identity. Ogden (1992, this volume p. 245) opens his paper by underscoring that the analyst is perpetually a 'beginner' and concludes it with the dire observation that 'all that the patient says (and does not say) in the initial meeting is understood as an unconscious warning to the analyst (and to the patient) concerning the reasons why the patient unconsciously feels that each of them would be well advised not to enter into this doomed and dangerous relationship'.

Under such circumstances, it doesn't seem excessive to say that the analyst must not only overcome his own 'reluctance' to begin new analyses, but that he must even show some 'audacity' (Quinodoz *et al.*, 2006) to even consider such an undertaking.

The papers chosen for this section have in common that, each in their own way, they address these issues of reluctance and daring. They are presented in order of publication, but this chronological order also shows some degree of logical development in terms of content.

Arnold Rothstein's 1994 article (this volume p. 173) is one of his earlier papers on the subject. It contains many short case vignettes and provides a general overview of themes that he has expanded in later work. His main thesis is that analysts can be reluctant to take on some potential analysands because they find them disturbing, and that they express this reluctance in their tendencies to assess and diagnose, which he thinks are often countertransference enactments. But as his case material shows, considerable daring is required to accept the countertransference and to engage psychoanalytically with some patients as he does.

As compared to Rothstein's optimistic and matter-of-fact clinical writing, Christian David's 1998 essay (this volume p. 281) is more meta-psychological. Although he doesn't refer to Rothstein, one could say that he extends that author's argument about the risks of using evaluation and diagnosis to the more general hazard of a defensive recourse to psychoanalytic theory and the psychoanalytic setting as a way of avoiding the disturbance created by the first analytic encounter. He emphasizes the profound modifications that the analytic encounter produces in both protagonists, and he shows how any definitive dissociation between the analysing function and the analyst's person is not only illusory, but also unauthorized by psychoanalytic theory. The analyst, therefore, cannot be anything but personally involved, although in reaction to this he may be tempted to structure the preliminary interview in such a way as to prevent the encounter from evolving in directions that would disturb him.

With Danielle Quinodoz (2001, this volume p. 310) we are back to a very clinical paper. It is also an inspiring one, in which she pursues the above mentioned arguments about the analyst's involvement as a person and her sense of disturbance in theoretically innovative ways. She shows how the analyst can engage positively with her sense of inner disturbance and how she can use it to understand the more primitive aspects of the patient's personality. She also describes how this work can require a willingness on the part of the analyst to experience within herself some of the madness that the patient is consciously or unconsciously experiencing. She suggests that this willingness to engage with madness is an integral and necessary aspect of analytic work and that this is where daring is above all required.

Next, Lena Ehrlich's fine 2004 paper (this volume p. 330) squarely addresses the analyst's reluctance to begin new analyses, the impact of her reluctance on her ability to help her patients understand and overcome their own resistances to analysis, and the self-analytic work that is required to deal with the resulting impasse. After a useful overview of some of the literature on the subject, she offers two detailed case reports in which she analyses her own internal conflicts that were responsible for her temporary collusion with her patients to avoid analysis. Her courageous and thoughtful discussion of these inner resistances, and of how the analyst can overcome them to offer her patients better analytic treatment (and so increase her analytic case load), is a fitting and heartening contribution to the literature. Her paper is also notable for her willingness to address the analyst's retrospective response to her training analysis and her phantasy relationship with her training analyst, issues that the other papers do not really take up.

There are some other interesting currents running through these four papers. These authors share the conviction, grounded in their practice, that psychoanalysis is the best possible treatment for many of their patients. They are interested in how the analyst's reluctance to engage in analysis can enter into collusion with the prevailing sociocultural factors opposing full analysis. Psychoanalysts may be more involved than they realize in these public resistances to psychoanalysis, which can provide rationalizations for their own fears. But all authors are optimistic about the analyst's ability, not just to overcome his or her inevitable reluctances but, more importantly, to use them positively to improve the analyst's understanding of the patient and to offer an optimal treatment relationship. While they all insist in one way or another on the central role of the self-analytic effort that is required to achieve this, they convincingly show the rewards of such work.

We end this section and the book with a chapter by our WPIP colleague Rudi Vermote, inspired by the original 1979 paper, *Making the Best of a Bad Job*, in which Bion described the unconscious 'storm' that we have found to be such a useful metaphor for the unconscious dynamics of first interviews. Bion's paper is too complex and covers too wide a range of issues to be included in this collection, but Rudi Vermote pursues the ideas developed there and in Bion's other work to remind us why, no matter how much we may come to understand about initiating psychoanalysis, it is also so important to be able to bear *not* understanding.

This takes the issues brought up in the other papers in Parts III and IV (in particular those by Racalbuto and David) a step further with a description of how the confrontation with the inevitable, disturbing unknown in any new encounter can draw the psychoanalyst into yet another pitfall, that of a 'pseudo-understanding that may block an eventual transformation'. Although he doesn't say so in so many words, between the lines Vermote is suggesting that striving too hard to understand can be another expression of the analyst's reluctance to engage in the deep experience of psychoanalysis. Being aware of the risks of pseudo-understanding may also be our best bet to keep our minds open and available for as yet unforeseeable future developments in our field.

References

Bion, W. R. (1979). Making the Best of a Bad Job. In: Bion, W. R., Bion, F. (Eds) (1987), *Clinical Seminars and Four Papers*. Abingdon: UK: Fleetwood Press.

Freud, S. (1937). Analysis Terminable and Interminable. *SE* 23.

Quinodoz, D., Aubry, C., Bonard, O., Dejussel, G., Reith, B. (2006). Being a psychoanalyst: An everyday audacity. *International Journal of Psychoanalysis* 87: 329–347.

15 A PERSPECTIVE ON DOING A CONSULTATION AND MAKING THE RECOMMENDATION OF ANALYSIS TO A PROSPECTIVE ANALYSAND

by Arnold Rothstein

Commentary

Bernard Reith

Arnold Rothstein practices psychoanalysis in New York, where he is a training and supervising analyst with the New York Psychoanalytic Society and Institute. He has held prominent institutional and teaching functions in psychoanalysis, as well as numerous academic posts in psychiatry. His publications cover important aspects of psychoanalytic theory and technique, including psychic conflict and structure, understanding narcissism and beginning psychoanalyses.

This paper, which was first published in 1994, is one of his earlier papers on initiating psychoanalysis and summarizes many of his ideas on the subject. Although very optimistic, the paper also contains a stern admonition to us psychoanalysts that if we don't have enough analytic patients, this may be because we avoid doing our work as analysts and so would have mostly ourselves to blame.

Arnold Rothstein's basic starting-point is that, with rare exceptions, psychoanalysis is the optimal treatment for the patients he sees, unless proven otherwise in a (sometimes long) trial analysis. He affirms that it is impossible in a consultation to predict accurately the outcome of an analysis and that the analyst's tendency to diagnose and predict is best understood as a countertransference enactment that will have negative consequences on the analytic relationship, which he sees basically as a collaboration that must develop between analyst and patient. As he says in a later paper, 'an analyst whose mind is focused on the task of evaluating a prospective analysand contributes to creating an environment in which certain patients are experienced as sicker than they might otherwise be' (Rothstein, 2000). This can be the result of an unconscious co-construction in the interaction between analyst and patient, designed to evade the disturbing impact of the analytic experience on both participants (Rothstein, 2002).

Instead of trying to evaluate the patient, the analyst should work analytically. This means that he must be able to understand the patient's hesitations about analysis as a compromise formation and as an 'enactment resistance'

(Rothstein, 1990, 1995) that may need to be tolerated for a while and to which the analyst must be able to adapt, for example by accepting having to begin with face-to-face psychotherapy before the resistance can be meaningfully interpreted. But more fundamentally, Rothstein believes that the analyst should address his own resistances and be prepared to take on board, and strive to understand, extremely powerful and disturbing countertransference experiences. Indeed, his main criterion for deciding that a patient will not benefit from analysis with him is when 'the countertransference trends they evoke in me interfere significantly with my ability to maintain an analytic attitude suitable for successful analytic collaboration'.

Lest the reader be deceived by the apparent simplicity of the clinical illustrations, it might be worthwhile to point out that Rothstein's clinical work is grounded in his longstanding interest in the complex unconscious dynamics of narcissism, sadomasochism and 'sadonarcissism', which, following Brenner's (1982, 1994) work on compromise formation, he understands as defensive organizations against the 'calamities of childhood' (Brenner, 1982; Rothstein, 1991a, 1991b, 2002). For example, in his most detailed – and moving – vignette about Mr X, it can be seen how his deceptively simple interpretation ('That sounds like great fun') is based on his internal elaboration of both the patient's disturbing communications and his own countertransference responses to them. As a result, his interpretation expresses a sophisticated and humane understanding of the patient's sadistic homosexual fantasies as an eroticized defence against his feelings of rejection and his longing for closeness to a protective father. Although he does not describe it in such terms, this internal process seems similar to what Dantlgraber describes as an 'empathic triadic relation' (this volume, p. 194) leading to an 'encounter in symbolic space' (p. 169). Rothstein finds a way to use his countertransference to interpret the patient's longing in a playful, non-defensive and non-reproachful way. In doing so, he demonstrates his ability to listen analytically to his patient's violent provocations as symbolic communications in the analytical play-space. One can identify with Mr X and with how this may have given him a sense of profound contact and a taste of the unique quality of the psychoanalytic experience.

Much of Rothstein's work on initiating psychoanalysis, including some of the papers referred to here, is collected in his book *Psychoanalytic Technique and the Creation of Analytic Patients* (Rothstein, 1998). Together with Theodore Jacobs, he has also co-edited a collection of papers on the subject (Jacobs & Rothstein, 1990). His work has set off considerable debate (Rothstein, 2000, 2010b) and it has inspired authors like Lena Ehrlich (2004, 2010), whose 2004 paper is reproduced in this volume (p. 330). His latest book, *Making Freud More Freudian* (Rothstein, 2010a), returns to many of his ideas mentioned in this introduction and pursues them in interesting ways.

Rothstein's work is included in this section on the analyst's daring or reluctance to begin analyses because it stimulates us to think about our unconscious resistances to doing psychoanalytic work and their origins in the countertransference. His work shows how such resistances can reappear under the guise of seemingly professional attitudes like diagnosing patients or questioning the efficacy of psychoanalysis, which may actually amount to rationalizations for our rejection of our patients.

References

Brenner, C. (1982). *The Mind in Conflict*. New York: International Universities Press.

Brenner, C. (1994). The mind as conflict and compromise. *Journal of Clinical Psychoanalysis* 3: 473–488.

Ehrlich, L. T. (2004). The analyst's reluctance to begin a new analysis. *Journal of the American Psychoanalytic Association* 52: 1075–1093.

Ehrlich, L. T. (2010). The analyst's ambivalence about continuing and deepening an analysis. *Journal of the American Psychoanalytic Association* 58: 515–532.

Jacobs, T. J., Rothstein, A. (Eds) (1990). *On Beginning An Analysis*. Madison, CT: International Universities Press.

Rothstein, A. (1990). On beginning with a reluctant patient. In: Jacobs, T. J., Rothstein, A. (Eds), *On Beginning An Analysis*. Madison, CT: International Universities Press.

Rothstein, A. (1991a). On some relationships of fantasies of perfection to the calamities of childhood. *International Journal of Psychoanalysis* 72: 313–323.

Rothstein, A. (1991b). Sadomasochism in the neuroses conceived as a pathological compromise formation. *Journal of the American Psychoanalytic Association* 39: 363–375.

Rothstein, A. (1994). A perspective on doing a consultation and making the recommendation of analysis to a prospective analysand. *Psychoanalytic Quarterly* 63: 680–695.

Rothstein, A. (1995). Psychoanalytic technique and the creation of analysands: On beginning analysis with patients who are reluctant to pay the analyst's fee. *Psychoanalytic Quarterly* 64: 306–325.

Rothstein, A. (1998). *Psychoanalytic Technique and the Creation of Analytic Patients*. Madison, CT: International Universities Press.

Rothstein, A. (2000). A response to the contributors. In: Bornstein, M., with Escoll, P. J., & Levine, H. B. (Eds), Where have all the psychoanalytic patients gone? Commentaries inspired by Arnold Rothstein's Psychoanalytic Technique and the Creation of Analytic Patients. *Psychoanalytic Inquiry* 20(4): 611–627.

Rothstein, A. (2002). Reflections on creative aspects of psychoanalytic diagnosing. *Psychoanalytic Quarterly* 71: 301–326.

Rothstein, A. (2010a). *Making Freud More Freudian*. London: Karnac Books.

Rothstein, A. (2010b). Psychoanalytic technique and the creation of analytic patients: An addendum. *Psychoanalytic Quarterly* 79: 785–794.

15 A PERSPECTIVE ON DOING A CONSULTATION AND MAKING THE RECOMMENDATION OF ANALYSIS TO A PROSPECTIVE ANALYSAND[1]

Arnold Rothstein

In psychoanalytic training we have all been taught to do a consultation in which a diagnosis is made and a judgment is rendered about a patient's suitability for analysis. We were taught from a perspective that asked, 'Is this patient analyzable?' Following Stone (1954), we have learned to ask, 'Is this patient analyzable with "modifications"?' Another question that analysts are trained to consider in making assessments of analyzability is, 'Is this prospective analysand analyzable only by an experienced graduate analyst rather than by a candidate analyst?' Finally, analytic candidates are trained to ask, 'Might this prospective analysand be suitable for analysis after a preparatory psychotherapy?' Forty years ago, when Stone published his seminal paper, the collective wisdom was that such preparatory psychotherapy 'contaminated' and interfered with the prospects of the therapy evolving into an analysis with the preparing psychotherapist.

These questions and the conjectures, hypotheses, and ideals from which they derive equip the neophyte analyst with a number of premises and shape his/her attitudes as he/she enters the consultation experience. First is the idea that a judgment about suitability for analysis can be made in a consultation of one to six sessions with a patient in an interview type of engagement. This premise has persisted in spite of the fact that significant research has been reported to suggest it is fallacious. Bachrach's (1990) review of the research on analyzability clearly demonstrates that a judgment of analyzability and a related assessment of prognosis cannot be made with accuracy *until an analysis is completed.* Second is the notion that a prospective analysand should have certain aspects of character, thought of as capacities or ego strengths, manifest at the time of the consultation, in order to be suitable for a trial of analysis. This second premise derives, to a significant degree, from a deficit model of the development of psychopathology. This deficit model conceives of people as 'defective' and 'lacking' in the required aspects of character. Another

[1] Originally published in 1994 as: A perspective on doing a consultation and making the recommendation of analysis to a prospective analysand. *Psychoanalytic Quarterly* 63: 680–695.

analytic conception of character suggests that all aspects of an adult analysand's personality be understood as manifestations of a mind in conflict. Abrams's (1992) comments on what is required of a prospective analysand reflect what remains a majority point of view. He stated:

> The patient brings – among other things – psychological mindedness, a capacity for controlled regression, competent integrating and organizing functions, the potential to observe at a distance and experience with immediacy often at the same time, and a reasonably intact psychological foundation arising from a more or less successful Oedipal-age organization. This grouping of aptitudes helps define the sources of problematic analyses . . . due to faulty ego equipment or limited developmental progression. . . .
> (pp. 76–77)

Third, the majority of analysts are taught from a perspective that conceives of analysis as indicated for a select suitable minority of those who seek analysts' help.

The decline in the number of such ideal potential analysands, even in the consultation rooms of respected established analysts, has contributed to the interest in questioning some of these pedagogic assumptions concerning assessment of prospective analysands.

My experience has led to different conclusions about doing a consultation and making the recommendation of analysis. It is important to emphasize that, given the current state of research methodology, my conclusions and the premises that underlie them are, like all such clinical dictums, no more than *opinions*.

I approach a consultation with an *optimistic attitude* that influences my capacity and success in helping prospective analysands begin and experience a fruitful analytic collaboration. This attitude is associated with three related hypotheses about the prospective analysand and our anticipated analytic collaboration. First, in my opinion, psychoanalysis is the *optimal* treatment, the best form of psychotherapy for most adults. Second, my *attitude* about patients, whom I see for the first time in a consultation, is that they are all potential analysands. I work to maintain that attitude throughout the consultation. I assume that their analyses will be successful. Third, I will accept another conclusion only after a prospective analysand proves to me that he/she is unanalyzable in a *trial analysis*, a trial that may last months to years. It is important to emphasize that it is difficult to answer with certainty the question, 'How long should a trial of analysis continue before the analyst considers it a failure?' I suggest that the trial continue as long as the analyst believes there is progress. The fifth case reported in this paper did not demonstrate the kind of self-observing capacity reflective of genuine analytic work until the fourth year of our collaboration. In a related vein, it is noteworthy that failed analyses are not infrequently associated with therapeutic gains that are, in part, derived from unanalyzed transference gratifications. In a previous communication on the subject of analyzability (Rothstein, 1982) I noted:

> Analysts are left with the awareness that among a large group of subjects considered 'typical' narcissistic personality disorders, some will have optimal analytic experiences while others will accomplish much less. Paradoxically, it is worth emphasizing that an unanalysable narcissistic personality disorder may experience significant therapeutic gain from an incomplete analytic endeavour.
>
> (Rothstein, 1982, p. 178)

In this paper I wish to emphasize that if any particularly positive, hopeful, negative, or pessimistic ideas about the patient, the diagnosis, or the prognosis occur to me during a consultation, I view it as possibly reflective of an emerging countertransference–transference engagement. Because I assume the patient is analyzable, I am more interested in understanding the patient's responses to me, to the consultation, and to the recommendation of analysis than I am in manifest aspects of his/her personality or presenting complaints. My attitude toward prospective analysands is quite different from the one described by Abrams. I do not expect the patients to bring much other than themselves to a *trial* of analysis, and I regard the trial as beginning with my first contact with the patient. In my experience many analysands who have successful analyses do not begin their analyses with the manifest capacities that Abrams believes are required of prospective analysands. Many successful analysands do not begin to experience the world in such an integrated fashion until they are well into the mid-phases of their analyses. The attainment of these capabilities and their relative stabilization is one of the goals of many analyses. Thinking of a patient as lacking in aptitudes, or as possessing faulty ego equipment, or as defective or arrested in development may represent a countertransference intellectualization in response to unpleasure evoked by the patient's personality, symptoms, or intense affects. Such a conceptualization about a prospective analysand can be productively thought of as an evoked or induced fantasy and responded to as data reflective of the beginning of the analysis.

It follows from the foregoing that if I find myself thinking about differential diagnoses rather than considering a patient's sensitivity, I assume that I am responding to some transference trend that evokes unpleasure in me. Countertransference unpleasure associated with feelings of revulsion for a patient may be defended against by distancing oneself in the process of considering the prospective analysand's diagnosis. Conjectures about diagnoses that carry a negative valence, such as borderline, narcissistic, psychopathic or perverse, may signal such a countertransference trend.

It is worth remembering that most of the diagnoses that one might consider derive from the descriptive *psychiatric* perspective of DSM-III-R. It is clear that there are psychiatric diagnoses that are contraindications to a trial of analysis. The fifth case presented in this paper represents such a clinical exigency. However, from a *psychoanalytic* perspective, one of the important functions of diagnosis is to facilitate the analyst's task of helping a prospective analysand begin a trial of analysis. This point of view emphasizes that psychoanalytic diagnoses are no more than descriptive indicators of the data to be analyzed in both the transference and countertransference. From this pragmatic vantage point I employ three descriptive 'diagnoses': I suggest that prospective analysands can be grouped descriptively as (1) *inhibited*,[2] (2) *enactment prone*, and (3) too disturbed and disturbing for me. The so-called 'good cases' are more usually found among the first group of patients.

Before presenting clinical material shaped by my optimistic attitude, two cautionary notes are indicated. They are related to the subjective nature of the analytic enterprise: every analyst has his/her individual contraindications to beginning a trial of analysis, and every analyst will find patients who are too disturbed and disturbing to work with.

In agreement with Gedo (1981) I would not begin analysis with patients suffering with 'the continuing influence of unalterable, but disavowed, delusional convictions' (p. 78). In addition, I would not begin a trial of analysis with an addict, with a patient suffering from a serious psychosomatic illness such as chronic ulcerative colitis, or with a patient who has made serious attempts at suicide. *I prefer not to work with such patients because my experience with them has taught me that the countertransference trends they evoke in me interfere significantly in my ability to maintain an analytic attitude suitable for successful analytic collaboration.*

During an extended consultation with a successful businessman who was addicted to cocaine, I was impressed with the serious impairment of judgment that accompanied the patient's intoxicated states. I could not be reasonably certain that he would not murder someone or get himself killed during the outbursts of anger that often accompanied his altered states of mind.

However, it is important to remember that other colleagues have worked successfully with such patients. Karush *et al.* (1977) and Wilson (1990) have reported successful work with patients suffering from serious psychosomatic illnesses. I am emphasizing that uniquely personal factors can influence the prognosis of a trial of analysis. Stone (1954) stressed the same point when he stated that 'the therapist's personal tendencies may profoundly influence the indications and prognosis' (p. 593).

In an earlier paper (Rothstein, 1990), I described the process of making the recommendation of analysis to two reluctant patients. In that

[2] Renik (1990) has implicitly approached this question of psychoanalytic 'diagnoses' in his description of 'two complementary affect–defense configurations: inhibition in response to anxiety and enactment of wishful fantasy in response to depressive affect' (p. 226).

communication I emphasized that 'particularly in the introductory phase, it is the analyst's attitude toward the patient and his behavior and verbal associations rather than the frequency and/or the use of the couch that is the essential characteristic of the analytic method' (p. 153). In a related communication (Rothstein, 1992), I noted that

> success is facilitated by a *flexible* attitude toward the structure of the analytic situation as well as toward the parameters of its technique. What is *essential* in analytic technique is the analyst's attitude . . . Other features of the analytic situation, such as frequency of sessions and use of the couch, though important, are not always and absolutely essential.
>
> (Rothstein, 1992, pp. 521–522)

At this point I will describe six experiences of recommending analysis. Three have worked out well. Of the remaining three, with one it is too early to tell if the trial will be successful, another seems to be working out well after three years of 'preparatory' psychotherapy, while another patient is involved with reacting negatively to the recommendation for analysis while maintaining a tenuous, less intense involvement with me.

Case No. 1

This is an example of an 'easy' case. In the first session, during the process of hearing the patient's story, and without forethought, we engaged the question of beginning a formal analysis.

Prof. A, a forty-eight-year-old successful college professor, sought help because of chronic dissatisfaction with his significant professional achievements, longstanding anxiety (fear of humiliation) associated with experiences of speaking in public, as well as stage fright associated with his hobby of singing in a chorus. Prof. A had five previous experiences of once- or twice-a-week psychotherapy over a thirty-year period. In our first session, after listening to this sophisticated New Yorker describe his life's journey, I spontaneously and incredulously asked, 'How have you avoided having an analysis?'

It is important to emphasize that the optimism I am stressing in this paper shaped the content of my spontaneous utterance. Inevitably, my attitude about the efficacy of analysis exerted a shaping influence upon the prospective analysand's fantasies about analysis. These evolving fantasies undoubtedly influenced his motivation. The productive analysis of these fantasies is a characteristic of mid- and terminal-phase process. My confrontation concerning Prof. A's avoidance elicited a laugh and heralded the beginning of our understanding of the specific influences that had motivated him to avoid analysis. We agreed to begin an analysis. In the process of arranging hours, I mentioned that I did not think one could expect to get the job done working at a frequency of less than four times per week. We worked productively at a frequency of four times per week for fifteen months and have worked five times per week since that time.

Case No. 2

This case represents the somewhat more complicated problem of a patient seeking a consultation while engaged in a psychotherapy with which he was dissatisfied. Because his therapist was an analyst, I recommended that the patient attempt an analysis with that analyst. That did not work out, and he subsequently began an analysis with me.

Mr. D, a successful forty-nine-year-old banker, sought a consultation while in the midst of his second twice weekly psychotherapy. Six years ago he had entered psychotherapy with a man in another part of the country during the break-up of his first marriage. He remarried during the second year of that therapy and was transferred to New York by his bank four and a half years ago. He subsequently began psychotherapy in New York with a woman whom his therapist recommended. He sought my opinion about his dissatisfaction with his current therapy. He presented in significant distress, visibly upset at the prospect that his second marriage would fail. He felt there were personal issues that were intruding on his happiness and was pessimistic about the possibility of his therapist's providing sufficient help.

In our second session I pointed out that despite his concerns about his therapist, he had never had an experience with analysis, *the optimal method* of treatment for his problems. I noted that his therapist had a couch in her office, he was involved with her, and I suggested that his therapy might evolve into an analysis. Four months later Mr. D called to tell me he had interrupted his therapy and requested that we begin an analysis. We began a trial of analysis, at a frequency of four times per week, which has worked well. Mr. D is currently in the second year of a very productive analysis.

Case No. 3

This was a situation similar to that in Case No. 2. Mr. X, a lawyer, sought a consultation four months after the termination of a seven-year analysis. After hearing Mr. X's story, my impression was that his analysis was prematurely interrupted, an interruption which I conjectured was in part evoked as a countertransference response to Mr. X's depressive affect and intransigent hostility. I felt it would be optimal if Mr. X could work these issues out with his first analyst.

With Mr. X's permission, I called his first analyst and shared my impression. The analyst responded that Mr. X was a 'severe borderline.' It seemed clear to me that the analyst had had enough of Mr. X's depressed, enraged longings and was glad to be rid of him. I am emphasizing that from my point of view on analyzability, it was not the patient's symptoms per se but the analyst's reaction to them that was determinative.

Some time later, Mr. X related to me that he had attempted unsuccessfully to resume his analysis and again requested he begin a second analysis with me. In spite of his wish to begin an analysis with me, I felt he was still too disturbingly involved with his first analyst for that to be a wise undertaking. I told Mr. X that because of his disturbed state it would be better that he wait a year before making the decision to begin a second analysis.

Mr. X began a second trial of analysis with me fifteen months later. He began the first session of his re-analysis stating, 'For the last two years I felt I was slapped in the face by Dr. N [his first analyst] and angry. For the past two weeks I have been joyful and thought of kneeling next to you and stroking your chin to supplicate you. I had a dream: I was lying with a man and stroking his penis until he ejaculated and then fucking a man in the ass. In the dream I had the sense, "Now I'm going to get mine," as if I had been stroking Dr. N and now it's my turn.' Somewhat later in the hour Mr. X remarked, 'It's clear to me that I destroyed the analysis with Dr. N by establishing rigid stable patterns with him that put control on what I was feeling toward him.' Later in the hour I suggested to him that he was worried that I would reject him as Dr. N had by thinking he was too sick for an analysis and that he was worried that I would be frightened by his anger and by his sexual longings for me. He began the second session by stating, 'I have a profound sense that you are really disgusted with me 'cause I can't be analyzed.' He began the fourth session with ten minutes of silence and then said, 'I wish you'd say something.' He paused and said, 'I have a sense of being blocked.' I suggested that he was afraid his anger would really hurt me. He responded, 'Just your saying that is such a relief. I thought I'd like to spit on your floor.' To my response, 'Only on my floor?' Mr. X stated, 'In your face; I'd like to knock you down and kick dirt all over you. I'd like to take a shotgun and point it in your face and pull the trigger and blow your brains all over the wall.' I sighed and thought to myself, 'And this is the first week of the analysis.' Then I recalled earlier work with a latency boy who had shot me in the head with a rubber dart, and I said aloud to Mr. X about his wish to shoot me, 'That sounds like great fun.' Mr. X roared with laughter and remarked that he could not remember laughing with Dr. N. Later in the hour Mr. X[3] recalled his mother slapping him in the face in response to his complaining that neither of his parents did much for or with him. He remarked, 'My anger seems so vitriolic and bottomless. I get a real sense of pleasure in being angry.'

Cases No. 2 and No. 3 suggest that in spite of the difficulties involved, whenever possible, I try to help analysands attempt to complete the work

[3] I have reported aspects of mid-phase process of Mr. X's second analysis (Rothstein, 1991a, 1991b).

they are in the midst of before beginning a new trial of analysis with the consulting analyst. This recommendation helps emphasize to the patient that it is his/her analysis, rather than the consulting analyst's acquisition of analytic cases, that is important.

Case No. 4

This is an example of the common exigency experienced by the analyst when a prospective analysand confronts him/her with his/her 'realistic' inability to schedule regular hours. The manner in which Dr. M presented his difficulties required some flexibility in devising a way to begin the necessary work, a flexibility that patients like Dr. M require and demand at the beginning of their analytic collaborations.

Dr. M, a chief resident in surgery, sought a consultation with me after being referred by a senior colleague to a contemporary of mine. My contemporary 'diagnosed' Dr. M as 'too disturbed and disturbing for him.'

Dr. M had been informed by the senior consultant that, because of his self-destructive and self-defeating tendencies, analysis was indicated as a 'life saving procedure.' In spite of his past experiences of a failed analysis and of multiple failed psychotherapies, all with analysts we both knew were truly competent, Dr. M expressed his desire to begin an analysis with me. The only problem was that, because he was a surgical resident, he could not agree to regularly scheduled appointments. I agreed to schedule his four appointments weekly in response to the exigencies of our, but mostly his, schedule. After six months, a new job, and interpretations concerning his fantasy of being special to me by virtue of the nature of our scheduling procedure, he was able to schedule regular appointments.

Subsequent changes of schedule initiated by me have triggered anxiety, rage, depressive affect, and self-destructive enactments. These experiences have revolved around his sense of the loss of the narcissistically invented fantasy of being special to me.

In spite of a guarded prognosis, Dr. M and I continue to work productively in a disturbing analysis.

Case No. 5

This case illustrates the kind of patient for whom analysis is *not* the treatment of choice at the time of consultation. Her presenting complaints and the associated *psychiatric* diagnosis suggested that a more reality focused psychotherapy soon to be combined with medication was the indicated beginning treatment for her agitated depression. *However, I maintained an attitude that communicated that analysis was the optimal treatment to initiate at some future time in order to help protect the patient from a recurrence of her acute state.*

Dr. O, a twenty-eight-year-old pediatrician, sought help in an agitated state after being abruptly rejected by the first man she had been seriously involved with since college. This shy, self-effacing young woman was seriously depressed in our first session. Her appetite was poor, she was crying spontaneously, and was having trouble sleeping. She expressed profound pessimism about her ability to ever be truly successful in her work or in a relationship with a man.

Because of her acute state and the diagnostic consideration of a depression that might require medication, I suggested that she see me (sitting up) at a frequency of three times per week. During the first month of our work I mentioned to Dr. O that after she got over her acute (depressive) response, analysis was the optimal treatment to help her with her shyness, fear of humiliation, pessimism, and self-esteem problems.

However, after a month of psychotherapy her depression was getting worse. Referral to a psycho-pharmacologist and subsequent treatment with tricyclic antidepressants were effective in alleviating her depression. Dr. O was treated with antidepressants for eight months, and we worked productively in a three-times-per-week psychotherapy for almost three years. During that time Dr. O attempted analysis. She found the experience of being a patient in psychotherapy embarrassing and the prospect of being an analysand even more humiliating. She lay on the couch rigidly, arms crossed with one foot on the floor. Because the experience of the couch was excruciatingly painful and because the prospect of being an analysand was so humiliating, we resumed the psychotherapy with its here and now extratransferential emphasis. Throughout this work she maintained a respectfully idealized view of me as the doctor who should have answers that would help her with her problems.

As we approached the end of the third year of her psychotherapy, Dr. O expressed her sense that she did not need any more treatment. Her wish to stop represented, in part, her response to her fantasy that being in analysis meant that she was a failure as a person, failure she experienced as a profound humiliation. Her wish to stop was associated with a narcissistically invested fantasy that she could manage her own affairs. Such fantasies are commonly employed by young, ambitious, professionally successful prospective analysands, in resistance to the recommendation of a trial of analysis. Such patients need time to test the recommendation against their own capacities and the exigencies of their lives.

We agreed to stop meeting with the understanding that she could return if she felt it was necessary. Six months later, in response to a rejection by a man, Dr. O began an analysis at a frequency of four times per week. During this second trial of analysis, which is now approaching the end of its first year,

Dr. O is more comfortable with the use of the couch. She misses an occasional session for work-related 'realistic' reasons. She is aware that these 'realistic' reasons are occasionally employed as enactment resistances. Although her prognosis is still in doubt, her trial of analysis is ongoing.

Case No. 6

This represents the type of patient for whom analysis is clearly the treatment of choice but who is unable to accept the recommendation at the time of the initial consultation. Nevertheless, it is important for the analyst to indicate and explain clearly, to such reluctant patients, that analysis is the optimal treatment for their current and lifelong difficulties. This patient and many other reluctant patients require time to assimilate the narcissistic injuries they experience in hearing the recommendation of a trial of analysis and in the prospect of relinquishing the gratifications they long for in anticipated enactments. Even though the recommendation is not immediately accepted, it can be employed as a referent in working with subsequent resistances.

Prof. R is a forty-year-old scholar of English literature and an aspiring playwright. He was referred by his best friend, an analyst, who described him as a talented narcissistic personality who has never allowed himself to have treatment.

In the first session he presented agitated and distraught at the prospect of divorce. Although he had not had sex with his wife in twelve years, he was burdened by the intense guilt he felt at the prospect of abandoning her. This prospect was more imminent because his daughter was about to leave for college and because he was involved in a passionate love affair with a much admired married writer. In addition Prof. R was preoccupied with the exciting fantasy of pursuing many love affairs with all the young women he felt his wife and marriage deprived him of.

Because Prof. R conceived of his difficulties as deriving from external circumstances and because he believed he could solve his problems by himself, it was clear that he would not accept the recommendation of analysis. Yet I felt analysis was the treatment of choice for his lifelong difficulties. I believed that Prof. R would have to fail repetitively before he could accept my recommendation and begin a trial of analysis. I am emphasizing that despite an anticipated negative response from a prospective analysand, the analyst should nevertheless make the recommendation of analysis as the optimal treatment. After making the recommendation, the analyst should work with the prospective analysand on the patient's terms. Because Prof. R had difficulty with the ideas of scheduled appointments and with paying for missed appointments, I agreed to see him on a catch-as-catch-can basis.

I have seen him once or twice a week, in response to the exigencies of his day-to-day pursuits of conquests and humiliations. It is my judgment that he will begin an analysis in two to three years.

In conclusion I reiterate the basic premise of this paper. The analyst's *belief* that analysis is the optimal treatment for most patients she/he sees in consultation is an important factor in her/his ability to help a prospective analysand collaborate in a trial of analysis. This belief is bolstered by an *attitude* toward the prospective collaborator that communicates optimism about the outcome of the trial. Prospective analysands are analyzable until they prove they are unanalyzable in a trial of analysis.

References

Abrams, S. (1992). Ambiguity in excess: An obstacle to common ground. In: Wallerstein, R. S. (Ed.), *The Common Ground of Psychoanalysis* (pp. 67–79). Northvale, NJ/London: Aronson.

Bachrach, H. M. (1990). The analyst's thinking and attitude at the beginning of an analysis: The influence of research data at the beginning of an analysis. In: Jacobs, T. J., Rothstein, A. (Eds), *On Beginning an Analysis* (pp. 3–26). New York: International Universities Press.

Gedo, J. E. (1981). *Advances in Psychoanalysis*. New York: International Universities Press.

Karush, A., Daniels, G. E., Flood, C., O'Connor, J. F. (1977). *Psychotherapy in Chronic Ulcerative Colitis*. Philadelphia: Saunders.

Renik, O. (1990). Comments on the clinical analysis of anxiety and depressive affect. *Psychoanalytic Quarterly* 59: 226–248.

Rothstein, A. (1982). The implications of early psychopathology for the analysability of narcissistic personality disorders. *International Journal of Psychoanalysis* 63: 177–188.

Rothstein, A. (1990). On beginning with a reluctant patient. In: Jacobs, T. J., Rothstein, A. (Eds), *On Beginning an Analysis* (pp. 153–162). New York: International Universities Press.

Rothstein, A. (1991a). Sadomasochism in the neuroses conceived of as a pathological compromise formation. *Journal of the American Psychoanalytic Association* 39: 363–375.

Rothstein, A. (1991b). On some relationships of fantasies of perfection to the calamities of childhood. *International Journal of Psychoanalysis* 72: 313–323.

Rothstein, A. (1992). Observations on the utility of couples therapy conducted by a psychoanalyst – Transference and countertransference in resistance to analysis. *Psychoanalytic Quarterly* 61: 519–541.

Stone, L. (1954). The widening scope of indications for psychoanalysis. *Journal of the American Psychoanalytic Association* 2: 567–594.

Wilson, P. C. (1990). On beginning with patients with eating disorders. In: Jacobs, T. J., Rothstein, A. (Eds), *On Beginning an Analysis* (pp. 243–260). New York: International Universities Press.

16 IN WHAT FRAME OF MIND SHOULD THE FIRST INTERVIEW BE APPROACHED? *by Christian David*

Commentary

Alain Gibeault

Christian David is a French medical practitioner and psychoanalyst who became a full Member of the Paris Psychoanalytical Society in 1965 and was one of the co-founders of the Paris Psychosomatic School with Pierre Marty, Michel de M'Uzan and Michel Fain; his early interest in the 1960s in psychosomatic patients has certainly influenced his way of conceptualizing the issue of the setting and process in psychoanalysis and naturally his approach to the first interview. Since psychosomatic patients present a psychic deficiency with regard to fantasizing and symbolizing, it was necessary to take into account the *therapeutic* aim of psychoanalysis.

This is a major issue in Christian David's paper on the first interview, in which *cure* in psychoanalysis is opposed to *knowledge*. This is a part of a major debate in France where Lacan was strongly opposed to the therapeutic aspect of psychoanalysis and fostered an approach in terms of knowledge and, as David says in his paper, 'of understanding a flow of signifiers' to the detriment of listening to the analysand's affects of distress and suffering. This debate can be seen in Freud's warning not to attempt an immediate 'cure' of the patient's symptoms and thus to encourage a *flight into cure* through their swift resolution. This was an invitation to examine the psychoanalytic treatment not only in terms of *outcome goals* demanded either by the external environment (family, the law or analytic institutions) or by the inner world (relief of suffering), but also of *process goals*, which would take into account unconscious issues.

While it is important to take the suffering expressed by the patient seriously, the analyst must be suspicious of the patient's conscious goals. After all, the Ego is an agency of ignorance whose autonomy is an illusion; while it can be regarded as an ally in the forthcoming process, it is also a representation of social and external goals, albeit internalized, and thus both judge and part of the conflict. The analyst's conscious goals must also be questioned in terms of the wish to cure; this is a point which was underlying Bion's recommendation to the analyst of being 'without memory or desire'. From this point of view, the wish to recover could be seen as a symptom to be analysed and recovery considered as an 'added-benefit' outcome.

This is why the differences in goals between analyst and analysand are in fact mutative and a factor of psychic change. It is essential to see the analyst–analysand relationship as '*dissymmetrical*'; by this term, Christian David is conveying the distinction between the analytic function and the real person of the analyst. This distinction is essential if one is to avoid falling into the trap of the intersubjectivist approach, which emphasizes the symmetry between analyst and analysand. Technical neutrality and its expression, the rule of abstinence, are the conditions for a possible distinction between identification with the analyst and investment of the analyst as a person. In the space between lies the possibility of symbolization and working through in analysis, which depends on the possibility of displacement and differentiation of the parental imagos. This is what Christian David calls the *radical heterogeneity* of psychoanalysis.

However, the major statement of his paper concerns the necessity of not isolating and dissociating cure and knowledge in psychoanalysis, but of taking into account the *psychic continuities*. He is critical of a purely conceptual and dehumanized approach to psychoanalysis. From this point of view he is opposed to Lacan and much closer to two other pioneers of French psychoanalysis after World War II (Gibeault, 2010). Sacha Nacht criticized Lacan's insistence on language to the detriment of non-verbal communication (Nacht, 1963b) and 'The Psychoanalyst's Presence' (Nacht, 1963a). Maurice Bouvet (1958) took into account the patient's capacity to move between distance from and closeness to the object as a criterion in selecting the appropriate setting. This is the reason why, at the beginning of his paper, David quotes John Klauber who speaks of the importance of 'the personality of the psychoanalyst'. Along the same line Klauber (1972) had criticized James Strachey's (1934) famous paper on mutative interpretation as not taking the analyst's countertransference into account.

David's approach to the first interview is concerned with the importance of valuing both the analyst and the analysand as 'human beings'. This is especially so in the first analytic encounter, which is different from an analytic session as well as from an ordinary encounter: hence the idea that the first interview becomes an *ambiguous space*, which can be understood as a 'transitional space' according to Winnicott, in which a continuity is maintained between psychic reality and external reality, yet forming the basis for an acceptance of their differentiation. David compares this experience to the creation of the *chimera*, as conceptualized by Michel de M'Uzan (1994), as the co-creation of a psychic space emerging from the encounter between the analyst's and the analysand's unconscious. This approach recognizes *unconscious* transference and countertransference as the condition for a fruitful first encounter and the basis for 'a greater degree of inner freedom', a space for creativity and surprise. Thus, Christian David insists on the importance of the analyst's *presence*, but in order not to over-evaluate the importance of *knowledge* to the detriment of the *cure*. The first encounter would then be a unique opportunity to experience a process that would not oppose but link essentially the issues of cure and knowledge, of the analytic function and the analyst as a person, of transference and countertransference. This dialectic between different factors in the theory and practice of the first interview is an example of the importance of 'thirdness' in French psychoanalytic thought (see the introduction to the paper by Baldacci and Bouchard, p. 108 this volume).

References

Bouvet, M. (1958). Technical variations and the concept of distance. [Contribution to the Panel Discussion on Variations of Classical Psycho-Analytic Technique, read before the 20th Congress of the International Psychoanalytical Association, Paris (July–August, 1957)]. *International Journal of Psycho-Analysis* 39: 211–221.

Gibeault, A. (2010). Introduction to 'The pioneers and their legacy'. In: Birksted-Breen, D., Flanders, S., Gibeault, A. (Eds), *Reading French Psychoanalysis* (pp. 88–96). London and New York: Routledge.

Klauber, J. (1972). On the relationship of transference and interpretation in psychoanalytic therapy. *International Journal of Psycho-Analysis* 53: 385–391.

M'Uzan, M. de (1994). *La bouche de l'inconscient* [The Mouth of the Unconscious]. Paris: Gallimard, 205 pp.

Nacht, S. (1963a). *La présence du psychanalyste* [The Psychoanalyst's Presence]. Paris: Presses Universitaires de France, 204 pp.

Nacht, S. (1963b). The non-verbal relationship in psycho-analytic treatment. *International Journal of Psycho-Analysis* 44: 334–339.

Strachey, J. (1934). The nature of the therapeutic action of psycho-analysis. *International Journal of Psycho-Analysis* 15: 127–159.

16 IN WHAT FRAME OF MIND SHOULD THE FIRST INTERVIEW BE APPROACHED?[1]

Christian David

> The psychoanalytic function cannot be conceptualized in isolation from the personality of the psychoanalyst who exercises it. . . . to ignore the influence of his personality results in denials of the realities of the psychoanalytic process.
>
> (John Klauber, 1986, p. 138)

The purpose of an analyst's first encounter with someone who comes to see him can only be conceived of in close relation with the purpose he attributes to analysis and analytic therapies. Of course, the immediate aim of the meeting is to assess the analysability of the individual who is seeking treatment and to appreciate the exact nature of their request. From the outset, however, there arises the fundamental question of therapeutic accessibility, and thus of the meaning of the process which may be entered into. So the analyst can say to himself: in my beginning is my end just as in my end is my beginning.[2] If by any chance he rejects ideas of cure and improvement as being too marked by a medical, or medico-social conception from which the experience of analysis has to keep its distance, he must remember that the therapeutic aim, for Freud and those who follow him, is an integral part of the definition and thus the essence of psychoanalysis. To allege that a judgement of analysability implies nothing more than a positive evaluation concerning the possibility of a transference being established and of a process developing with the indefinite richness of its fluctuations, nothing more than a possible change in the patient's mental functioning linked to the efficacy of interpretation within the setting established, cannot fail to have repercussions on the way that the first encounter (or non-encounter) will be experienced and evaluated on both sides.

[1] First published as: David, C. (1998). Dans quel esprit aborder le premier entretien? *Revue Francaise de Psychanalyse* 62(1): 87–99.

[2] Editors' note: This beautiful English translation refers to T. S. Eliot's poem, *East Coker* (*Four Quartets*, Part 2), but there is also wordplay here, perhaps more obvious in the original French, between two meanings of 'end', as 'outcome' and as 'aim', so that the sentence also means: 'the beginning contains the outcome just as the aim determines the beginning'.

The person who comes to 'consult', assuming of course that they do this entirely on their own initiative, is not aware of everything that the request involves and signifies. The analyst himself is not aware of all the eventual ramifications of his own response. But on both sides a relational virtuality is now in play, and exists from the moment the encounter is anticipated. Admittedly, the person consulting generally only has a very confused idea of the singularity of this encounter; they will even tend too readily to liken it to an 'ordinary' meeting, while nonetheless being aware of the peculiar situation in which they are going to find themselves. For his part, the analyst knows in advance that the structural dissymmetry that will necessarily orientate the meeting will always, to a greater or lesser degree, be disconcerting for his interlocutor who will feel caught in a precarious situation between presence and absence, between exchange and evasion. The analyst's methodical attitude of reserve and neutrality, however veiled it may be on occasions or in some analysts, creates a certain nascent sense of malaise. This malaise will be treated differently in each case, but nonetheless requires of the analyst an attitude of benevolent attention – a formula which would be completely hackneyed if it was not indispensable – that is, as far as the first interview(s) is/are concerned, the presence of someone who is genuinely concerned to understand the person in front of him and, as we say familiarly, to bring him something whatever is decided and whatever happens. Now a poorly tempered analytic attitude can easily give the patient the feeling that he is in front of a pure technician, entrenched behind a shield of silence and impassiveness, in front of an investigator who is much more interested by the dysfunctioning of the human machine than by the anxiety, suffering and disturbances of all kinds which constitute the reason for the encounter. Even if the first interview does not result in the patient being taken into treatment directly, what is important for him or her is to be heard – even, and especially if he/she understands nothing of what is happening – enlightened, oriented, and even supported, and, in any case, to see a way forward, whatever it may be, simply as a result of the 'open' character of the welcome he receives. As J.-B. Pontalis (1997) writes: 'What happens in what we call the analytic process' – and this begins potentially from the very first contact – 'eludes both subjects. Neither of them are masters of it; which does not mean that they are absent, since it is because of their strange encounter, one between two strangers who are open to what is unknown in themselves, that it happens as it happens . . .'. J.-B. Pontalis, an enemy, as I am, of analytic arrogance, is thus squarely in favour of an attitude of modesty, both professional and metapsychological, which places the protagonists of the analytic encounter (already during the preliminary interviews) in a common dependence on the unconscious. With, of course, the difference that the analyst recognizes it and has had an experience of it in his own analysis(es) and pursues it daily in his clinical and intellectual elaboration. One can of course contest the assertion of a total absence of mastery on the part of the therapist or investigator; it remains true, however, that sharp awareness of the specificity as well as the strangeness of what is at stake in every analytic encounter can and should always be associated with a true participation with others as 'fellow beings'.

If the analyst, in the first interview or after a few meetings, considers that neither an analysis nor even an analytic therapy can be proposed, he renders a service to the person consulting by not encouraging him or her to continue along this path, because in general their state would be likely to get worse, and, in any case, it would involve them in a situation of pure loss. Of course, there is a risk of error in a dissuasive conclusion, but it is minimal; and if the dissuasion is formulated with tact it will be much less traumatic and the subject will generally feel led to turn towards another form of treatment that is more in accordance with his situation and structure.

I am not in favour of conducting an initial interview along the lines – even if approximately – of an analytic session. Even if the person consulting already behaves like an analysand – in which case it is someone who is familiar with the analytic situation – it counts among the indications of analysability, but no more. Owing to the fact that the encounter must culminate in a decision, the analyst is not in an analytic situation either (even less so I would say), and it is important that he makes this clear if necessary. The first, and often the only preliminary interview will in fact be the only direct reference for the eventual future analysand to his analyst's way of being in the face-to-face position. This situation is different both from common encounters and from the analytic situation proper, where each of the participants has one foot in external reality (and sometimes both in the case of the patient who has gone down the wrong path!).

Caught in the sometimes laborious, multiform, and variable process of the investigative interview, the analyst will scarcely have the leisure of formulating to himself in an abstract and precise manner the problematic which is gradually taking shape. He will not elaborate for himself some sort of metapsychological or even technical counterpoint, but will devote all his energy to remaining continually available, whatever efforts he makes to understand and whatever his affective reactions are. It is only retrospectively, and out of a need to put things in perspective for himself or for the purpose of giving a report, a didactic exposition, or for subsequent elaboration, that he will perhaps translate into theoretical terms the trace of the immediate experience. In effect, the Witch Metapsychology, from which all theory of technique proceeds, and which has done so much for the diffusion of psychoanalysis in the world, was very opportunely posed at the outset by Freud as an ensemble of 'auxiliary constructions' designed to help the analyst map out his clinical experience and render it communicable. They are in fact 'the tailor's threads'; but one sometimes has the feeling that the consistency and weight of the cloth are in danger of being sacrificed to the *sciendi*, or even *dominandi* libido of metapsychology while technique becomes an end in itself, or at the very least an object of secret narcissistic *jouissance*. The psychoanalyst is then in danger of seeing himself as a highly specialized engineer. The same is true in the quite different domain of art, where the public is often called upon today to form an aesthetic appreciation of works which are the exclusive products of ingenuity.

It is hardly surprising, then, that many laymen, when reading contemporary analytic writings – without any ill-will *a priori* – get the impression that a vast theoretical and technical apparatus is being developed in isolation along the lines of a new scholasticism. And correlatively, that there is a feeling, shared by many members of the 'establishment', that psychoanalytic corporations are becoming too cerebral in their elites and, for the great majority, too pragmatic.

The unconscious does not change – which, incidentally, is only a partial truth – but our societies change and we, as individuals, change, too. Although psychoanalysis changes with us and with them, it remains what it was at the beginning and faithful to its generative principle: the recognition and effort of exploring the unconscious.

Over the course of the last century, its theory and practice evolved and diversified, was deepened and refined, but it was also sometimes rendered insipid. Sometimes it was even modified to the point of dissidence or corruption. Consequently, by way of reaction, there were many calls to order, but also many reflective and even frankly speculative efforts aimed at linking up more satisfactorily the diverse acquisitions with the invariants of the foundational work. A whole body of studies, particularly in France, were produced with the intention of preserving the broad outlines of the Freudian inspiration while justifying sometimes very sweeping technical variations, the need for which the analytic community had in fact always recognized since the very beginning.

The purpose of the present volume,[3] as it has been subtly defined, thus forms part of a long-standing preoccupation and tenacious determination to maintain the course of psychoanalytic navigation, whatever the obstacles. Today these obstacles are commensurate with the evolution of psycho-pathological forms, the crises within the analytic world, and the crisis of civilization, which all a result from the decline of the West and the process of globalization.

The impressive upheavals of our *fin de siècle* are translated in the professional and intellectual sphere in which we as analysts find ourselves by a state of polymorphous anxiety. This leads to a questioning of the future of psychoanalysis, and, more particularly, the future of the classical treatment, and even, in the longer term, of the various treatments which are inspired by it. It is as if, obscurely, we imagine we can intuit ways of living and thinking

[3] Editors' note: this refers to the special 1998 issue of the *Revue française de psychanalyse* devoted to 'La rencontre analytique [The analytic encounter]' in which this paper was first published: see David (1998).

that are at complete odds with those that permit us to speak of analysability and to hope for essential intrapsychic modifications. We should nonetheless have confidence in the most solid and reliable acquisitions of the Freudian and post-Freudian edifice in order to be able to envisage gradual therapeutic and technical adjustments in accordance with the demands of sociocultural evolution. And furthermore, we must not overestimate the scientist tidal wave triggered by certain personalities in the neurosciences and cognitivism. As for behavioural therapies, when they are obviously successful, which is still rare it seems, should we not rejoice and think about the specific fields of action and thought which still remain open and, until we are more fully informed, exclusively our own?

At any rate, there seems to be a correlation between the rising concern about the rapid extension of unanalysability, as many colleagues see it, and the equally rapid growth of the discredit into which psychoanalysis, and, especially at the present time, the classical treatment would fall.

Neither the sun . . . nor the unconscious can stare at themselves. This is true for everyone, starting with analysts themselves; and the point, first of all, is not to lose sight of the internal temptation that each of us has to collude – often in a very roundabout way – with a massive repression of the most distinctive and assured aspects of the Freudian discovery. It would be naïve, moreover, to believe that analysts might one day cease to wage war, even if only to preserve what has been acquired and to demonstrate it in a sufficiently convincing way.

The first analytic encounter, historically, was one of a man with himself, of Freud with his dreams, with his daily psychopathology and the incompatibilities of his emotional life. This encounter was more or less contemporaneous with his first tentative therapies with hysterical patients and with his friendship with Fliess. One could consider Freud's relationship with his hysterics – and with J. Breuer – as having prepared his mind for the discovery in himself of hitherto unknown modes of functioning. From this perspective, Fliess, Breuer, and the hysterical patients were the virtual and prehistoric protoanalysts of Freud . . . The very complex relations that he maintained with each of them contributed at the same time to the gradual process of refining and establishing the analytic situation and frame. It is clear that the intuition of the Unconscious – in the dynamic sense which specifies it as psychoanalytic – had to occur before the first elements of the method and the technique could be defined. This truism is not, however, without interest, for it follows that it is not thanks to the analytic situation and frame that the emergence of the Unconscious occurred. The notion that there is an immanent dynamic, both quantitative and qualitative, in psychic life, a trend of latent meaning which eludes consciousness and resists efforts of self-perception, is the fruit of a non-reproducible creative moment.

It can no doubt be seen what I am driving at: the concrete history of the Freudian discovery excludes any possibility of hypostasizing and idealizing the analytic situation and relationship, the setting, the frame, the associative method, free-floating attention, etc., in short the classical and necessary conditions for an analytic encounter worthy of the name to occur. This implies, in particular, not trying to follow an ideal model which would impose the idea of a standard or typical first encounter between analyst and patient. In other words, the conditions involved are only the result of empirical and progressive adjustments which were designed to enable Freud to continue with others what he had inaugurated blindly, if I may say so, with himself.

The conscious desire for knowledge and intelligibility, of curing in order to become rich and famous, governed the courageous efforts of the first psychoanalyst. The wish to succeed in overcoming the vicissitudes of his mourning of his father and to counter the anxieties linked to the sense of therapeutic and intellectual helplessness in the face of unknown mental or psychosomatic affections provided a powerful motivation to do psychic work on himself, the likes of which had never been done before.

So we may consider, analogically, that strong and deeply personal motives are necessary for seeking analysis and no doubt for any genuine request to work with a psychotherapist. Every analysand is thus (if one pushes things to the limit) led to make once again, in his own way and in accordance with his own means, and, of course, in quite different and more conducive conditions, the inaugural Freudian journey. In the same deliberately excessive and paradigmatic vein of thought, one could say that the first analytic encounter (if indeed it takes place, that is, if it is a true encounter, and at least potentially an analytic encounter) supposes an event which is reminiscent, even if very remotely and following a slow and hesitant process, of the discovery of the unconscious.

Two people must be present for an encounter to occur. This is equally true for the analytic encounter, placed under the sign of a certain community. But it often seems that this fundamental duality is forgotten in favour of confidence as a matter of principle in the epiphany of the unconscious as soon as the conditions are favourable. Now, as I have already pointed out, I tend to think that there is something toxic in concentrating almost exclusively on this expected emergence without according the central importance that it involves to the singular and even unique nature of the encounter between the analysand and the analyst. It is true that the analytic encounter is unquestionably different from an ordinary encounter. And furthermore it is true that what makes the analytic encounter analytic is the conjunction of the presence of two human beings functionally defined and 'framed' in such a way that the irrational powers of the psyche can emerge and be deciphered within the transference and countertransference. But the technical arrangements and the strategical and tactical application of the method do not mean that the encounter dissolves in the analytic process; it retains, as it were, a common core with the ordinary encounter. 'One is no less a man for being an analyst', Maurice Bouvet used to say to me very profoundly, while stripping – with characteristic humour – the citation of any possible pejorative connotation. It is equally true that one is no less human for being a potential analysand or patient or even someone seeking blindly to be taken into some form of care. Am I once again simply stating the obvious? I don't think so at all; for the simple reason that the fact of feeling one possesses knowledge, experience, and thus power linked to the position, to the role of psychoanalyst, and to the image that is attached to it, can lead – and in fact too often leads – to dehumanizing the analytic relationship and, even before that, the preliminary interview or simply a consultation, which is absurd because during the first encounter, as I have already stressed, both protagonists find that they keep one foot on the ground of so-called objective reality. To undermine, on the pretext of preserving from the outset the purity of an eventual subsequent analysis, what inevitably exists in the way of communication and conscious and preconscious exchanges, verbal and nonverbal, in the analytic relationship or in its preliminaries, in short, to empty the analytic encounter of its fundamental value of encounter, out of a so-called concern for rigour and professionalism, is to subvert the psychoanalytic approach and to amputate one of its essential elements.

There is no doubt in fact that the experience the person consulting has during the first contact with the analyst depends closely on the latter's disposition, which will obviously govern his manner of conducting the preliminary interview (or interviews). The style – for there is one – of this interview will 'emblematize', in many ways of which he is unaware, the psychoanalyst's craft, the knowledge to which he refers, and the profile of the eventual treatment.

Two decisive elements distinguish this first encounter from any other. First, the fact that the analyst imposes a non-reciprocity and a basic dissymmetry on the dialogue (however reduced it may be, there is inevitably one). The patient is encouraged to speak and to express himself as faithfully as possible, whereas the analyst not only will say nothing about himself but will filter out – it has become second nature for him – any form of personal emanation. And secondly, the fact – which follows from the first – that the purpose of the interview consists first and foremost in triggering and observing eventual transference reactions (reactions, and not obviously organized transference) which are related in a significant way to the patient's structure and mental mode of functioning.

It is understandable that, on these grounds, some analysts are tempted – already at the stage of the initial investigation – to push the specificity of the relationship to the point of treating it as if it were focused for them on the emerging field of the diverse manifestations of the patient's unconscious and on the first noticeable elements of his countertransference as an indispensable source of clinical information, notably for determining the therapeutic indication at the end of the interview. Thus, even before an eventual setting is established, the encounter with the patient may seem to them totally heterogeneous in comparison with any other encounter. The analytic encounter will be reduced for them to understanding a flow of signifiers which escape to a very large extent the analysand's spontaneous apprehension and which will have to be gradually and opportunely brought to his notice by means of interpretation, punctual interventions, as well as by silence inasmuch as it occasionally leads to moments of new awareness. According to such a conception, whether it is openly advocated or latent, the encounter is limited in fact to the temporally unsynchronized and more or less precisely programmed reception of a series of specific messages which cannot be dissociated from the interaction of the transference and the countertransference in the analytic couple. Thus the encounter could ultimately be exclusively dependent on the application of the method, strictly synchronous with its application during the duration of the treatment (or of the single interview) and in the setting – unlike any other – in which it takes place. Once the analysis is finished and supposing it has been successful – that is, that it has led to tangible intrapsychic modifications allowing for a better circulation between the agencies of the subject – the partners once again become for each other the strangers they were before the analytic encounter.

It is true that the analyst has at his disposal a mass of information about the patient, recorded for the most part in his unconscious memory; and it is also true that he has experienced for himself a largely enigmatic interaction which has followed its course, but he cannot consider – still from the same perspective – that he has at his disposition anything other than a certain processual 'working model' that allows him to form a picture of the ordinary life of the patient who was on his couch. This explains why, when the analyst happens to run into a former analysand, the analyst will very often have the impression of not really recognizing the person who he has now come across in external reality. He may even have the paradoxical feeling of apparently sensing or discovering certain unsuspected personal traits. Reciprocally, for the patient, his former analyst – whom, at certain times during the treatment, he thought he had met outside the setting, whereas in fact it had been other people – will seem more or less different from the person he thought he was, based on the only indications he had at his disposal (vocal inflections, clothing, style of intervention, etc.), and so will also be disconcerted.

With these remarks, arising from everyday observation, I am making myself, as it were, the devil's advocate. By that I mean that I am providing arguments for the thesis of what I shall call analytic purism. I would support the idea that the analytic encounter as such has nothing much (if anything) in common with the so-called ordinary encounter. After all, the question is one of knowing if a 'true' encounter can exist between an analyst and an analysand – and before that, a 'postulant': that is to say, an encounter from subject to subject, from person to person, from human being to human being in the global nature of the interpersonal exchange. Does not the very structure of the situation and of the analytic relationship necessarily lead to profound modifications – different in each partner – in ego functioning and in intra- and intersubjective relations? By entering the analytic field, one is penetrating a psychological dimension all of its own.

According to such a characterization, the analyst is a bit like an astrophysician of the internal world, dependent on the object of observation and treatment – though, it goes without saying, in quite another way – but confined within the intrinsic limits of his research and action. One might even say confined within an epistemic solitude if he were not, owing to the transference, dependent on his human object; and if, moreover, the ordinary references of identity were not also turned upside-down.

The epistemological justification for such confinement is generally linked to the exclusive focalization of the conscious interest of quite a large number of analysts on mental functioning alone. This frame of mind seems to imply a state of dissociation between the analysing function and the analyst's person. This is the crucial point. It is on the basis of this implication that the absolute specificity of the analytic encounter is posed, whether explicitly or not. But what I am contending here is that this scission is illusory in character, however important is the interplay that exists, owing to the discovery of the unconscious and of the analytic situation, between person and function, between ordinary encounter and analytic encounter. I think that the 'purism' which I referred to earlier proceeds from a defensive reaction that is sometimes more phobic and sometimes more schizoid, and linked to clinical reality insofar as it is sometimes very anxiety provoking. So one then sees a fundamental epistemological choice emerging secretly from a poorly managed state of anxiety. In fact the choice we are concerned with belongs – notwithstanding its strictly intellectual and gnosological aspect – to a whole system of values in which affectivity is involved. Every scientific position, incidentally, has an implicit system of values, and the diverse positions held by psychoanalysts are no exception. So once again, I entirely agree with John Klauber when he affirms forcefully that 'a theory of technique which ignores the immense influence on the psychoanalytic transaction [and I would like to insert here: on the transaction of the first interview] of the value systems of patient and analyst alike ignores a basic psychic reality behind any psychoanalytic partnership' (Klauber, 1986, p. 128).[4]

Analytic theory, method, and treatment are singular and incomparable owing to the very fact of the novelty of the field that was opened up by their founder: of this every analyst is certain. But recognizing this undeniable specificity does not at all imply any sort of structural transcendence which would authorize or impose dissociation between the analysing function and the person – the personality itself – of the analyst. When one has had personal

[4] Editors' note: The insertion in square brackets is by C. David.

experience of analytic treatment both on the couch and in the armchair, as well as the very instructive experience of supervised treatments, and when, as a practitioner and 'researcher', one has observed a large number of colleagues within their various groups and groupings over quite a long period of time, how can one doubt that the role of the analyst is indissociable from the human being who fills it? At the same time, how can we believe that the analytic encounter is, so to speak, soluble in the process that it presupposes?

The methodical self-effacement which the analyst imposes on himself, by trying to make himself the 'mirror', and above all the living resonator of his patient, undoubtedly implies a certain degree of asceticism, but this cannot go as far as excluding the personal coefficient. Even if we consider the patient–analyst couple as the connection of two 'psychic apparatuses', one of which lends itself to the deployment of the functioning of the other by 'renting out', as it were, his own – within the limits of the spatio-temporal frame of the treatment or of the interview – according, for example, to the felicitous metaphor of the 'chimera' proposed by Michel de M'Uzan, these 'apparatuses' do not function independently of the person and of the intrinsically personal movements of the analyst and of the patient.

And I firmly believe that it is right that this is the way things are, that it is in harmony with the genius of psychoanalysis, even beyond Freud's own genius. If the specificity of the unconscious is to be unconscious and, consequently, it remains unknowable as such – because the understanding that we attempt to have of it is always based on its 'derivatives', and, as Pontalis says in the article that I cited earlier, 'in the intertwining of associative networks' – it follows that the radical heterogeneity that characterizes it must not, and can not, ever be considered in isolation. As Freud stresses in the *Outline* (1940), it goes hand in hand with 'psychic continuities'. Without these continuities, psychic life would be impossible and psychoanalysis itself would be unthinkable. This coexistence of two concepts which, at first sight, are incompatible, implies in fact that they are linked up within a common theoretical – ontological perhaps? – interplay. The capacity of the psychoanalyst to maintain them simultaneously in his mind seems to me to be the key to an open mentality and practice. It is in terms of this line of thinking that we can consider the analysing function and the person of the analyst as cooperating in one and the same movement, and in association with the person of the analysand placed in the analytic situation. The sole fact, which is unanimously recognized, of the unconsciousness of the major part of the therapist's countertransference in relation to the patient's often totally unconscious transference – which, as we know, goes well beyond a counter reaction – constitutes in itself a demonstration of the indissociability which I have perhaps emphasized somewhat excessively. This fact alone (and there are others) would be sufficient reason, in my view, to reject the psychoanalysm which marks every exclusive emphasis placed on psychic functioning taken in isolation, every mummification of the technique, whether it be Freudian,

Kleinian, Lacanian, Bionian . . . culminating in an eviction of the personal living core of the protagonists of the analytic relationship.

The conception and the mode of conducting the first interview with a patient, whoever he/she is, and in whatever setting it is, depend – directly – on everything that I have just discussed. The epistemic mentality of each analyst, even if it is very far removed from exclusively speculative considerations, or seems to be as much at first sight, governs his technique, and his style, which is unique to each analyst.

The difficulties and the new questions with which the practising analyst is faced today sometimes only embarrass him so much because, without clearly realizing it, he is confined within a certain professional superego-like straightjacket that is both technical and theoretical. The obsession with analysability in the light of fixed norms and in conformity with such and such received teaching, in cases where the process of transmission through personal analysis has not allowed a real freedom to think, to evaluate and to decide, can lead to impasses or to a sense of helplessness which will not necessarily be shared by another consultant or another analyst. Where no existing concept can be found which allows us to think about the opacity of a disconcerting, and even frightening reality, a new concept has to be invented to conceptualize it (not everyone is a Hegel, Freud or Winnicott . . .); at the very least, we need to allow ourselves a greater degree of psychic freedom and to require more flexibility of ourselves, thanks to which we will be able to let ourselves be carried along by what presents itself to us, including that which we are expecting but which does not appear. And we will have the surprise – not always, certainly, but more often than we would tend to think – of gradually finding a path of intellection and efficacy through an apparently insurmountable chaos. And if, by any chance, a patient seems not to know why he is in the situation of interview or investigation, seems to reject it or to remain in a discouraging state of inertia, while nonetheless presenting a pathology and state of suffering which in themselves constitute a demand for the analyst's ear, it is sometimes enough to show that one perceives and senses in the patient, the human being, the fellow other, a core of suffering that for the moment is unqualified and which he neither sees nor feels himself, for an echo to be heard, for the outlines of a response to emerge, the beginnings of a potential initiation of the process.

Freud and the most creative of his successors since the beginning of the century have shown us in diverse ways how to proceed. In his continual journeying back and forth between practice and theory, Freud recommends subordinating metapsychological working hypotheses to the observed clinical realities, and he himself was an example for this throughout his working life. Analysis has never ceased to be defined as a fundamentally dynamic praxis. This means that it constitutes a living approach to a psychic reality in perpetual movement. The conflicts, contradictions, and antagonisms which essentially characterize it are themselves caught in an incessant dialectic of repetition and change. There is thus no question of ever resolving entirely, with the analytic instrument, instinctual and defensive tensions and vicissitudes. Analytic treatment proposes only – but resolutely – to awaken or to permit the favourable pursuit of a work of subjectivization. The Id will not cease to manifest itself noisily even when the work of acquiring fresh insight and new levels of integration has allowed the ego to gain ground. The work of psychic 'draining', in the nature of things – of psychic things – is an infinite task, and even a work of Sisyphus since nothing is ever acquired once and for all. The only consolation is that the complete resolution of tensions would be equivalent to death. But the psychoanalyst himself – independently of his theoretical and technical options – finds himself, in his practice as well as in his own life, caught in this constant stir. His countertransference makes him feel this constantly, as soon as he has contact with patients. Already at the stage of investigation – whether or not it culminates in an indication of analysis or psychotherapy – he listens both receptively and selectively. The whole difficulty of the psychic work during a first interview is to remain as available as possible throughout it, and, simultaneously, to allow the outlines of an understanding of the case to form in one's mind. This does not happen in the same way as in the analytic situation, where an 'appropriate' space is constructed. The space of the preliminary interview is necessarily an ambiguous space, a space whose topography is all the more confused when the therapeutic accessibility of the patient seems limited. But notwithstanding his eventual obtrusion or his defensive prejudices, or alternatively his deep negativism, one could argue that even in such problematic situations as those where the forces of unbinding make themselves felt heavily, the elements of analytic non-encounter and transferential inertia do not necessarily determine the investigator's attitude. The precession of the countertransference in relation to the transference, to which M. Neyraut has forcefully drawn our attention, can be operative in such conditions, for the worse, moreover, as well as for the best. What I mean is that the mentality of the analyst who 'conducts' the interview structures in advance a major part of what will or will not happen during the interview. As the space in which it takes place is ambiguous by nature and is also characterized as non-isomorphic, as structurally dissymmetrical, it is crucial in many difficult cases that the investigator is able, thanks to innate personal resources which have been developed in his analysis(es), to compensate partly for the negative effects of the dissymmetry and the heteromorphism of the thorny clinical situation. The 'spirit' in which an analyst approaches a patient who will never do analysis, or even a therapy, plays a particularly important role with regard to the effects and consequences of the interview, whether it is repeated or not.

To my mind, discussions of details – which can, moreover, involve highly significant elements – concerning the theory of technique and the technique of the preliminary interview, are directly linked to the global conception of psychoanalysis formed by the practitioners who take part in them. Hence my remarks in these pages, which sometimes get lost in generalities as if to avoid the heart of the subject. In fact, even if I have not always avoided 'going round in circles', it is because I have not turned away from the powerful attraction of what precisely are the most decisive and acute aspects of the problematic of the analytic encounter.

References

David, C. (1998). Dans quel esprit aborder le premier entretien? *Revue Francaise de Psychanalyse* 62(1): 87–99.

Freud, S. (1940). An Outline of Psycho-Analysis. *SE* 23: 141–207.

Klauber, J. (1986). *Difficulties in the Analytic Encounter.* London: Free Association Books and Karnac [First published in 1981, New York: Jason Aronson].

Pontalis, J.-B. (1997). *Ce temps qui ne passe pas.* Paris: Gallimard.

17 THE PSYCHOANALYST OF THE FUTURE

Wise enough to dare to be mad at times
by Danielle Quinodoz

Commentary

Bernard Reith

Danielle Quinodoz is a training and supervising analyst with the Swiss Psychoanalytical Society, working in private practice in Geneva. Her work, written from a Kleinian perspective, is innovative, theoretically rigorous and enlightening. One of her interests, which is already manifest in her work on emotional vertigo (Quinodoz, 1997), is the impact of projective identifications on the analyst and how this can be used as a source of information about the patient. She is also very involved in helping analysts in training to develop their own capacities for beginning psychoanalyses (Quinodoz, 2002; Quinodoz *et al.*, 2006). She has a talent for describing the complexity of her patients' inner worlds and the challenges of the transference and countertransference relationship in ways that are lively, straightforward and experience-near. These strengths and interests are combined in this paper in which she explains why, in her opinion, if 'we are ready to take on those patients for whom analysis can be an invaluable source of help . . . there will be no danger of analysts' couches remaining empty.'

The patients she has in mind are those she describes as 'heterogeneous' because they have simultaneous and contrasting developed and archaic modes of functioning. They may be afraid of analysis, or unaware of their wish for the integration that full analysis can bring, because they are 'afraid of discovering archaic aspects of themselves that feel mad to them'. In order to relate to these more archaic aspects of their lives in meaningful ways, the analyst must be willing to 'take the plunge' with them and so she must be prepared to feel 'mad' herself at times, in a professional way, 'without making a drama out of it'.

When she writes about the analyst's 'madness', what she means is a readiness to be in contact at all times with the psychical world, however unsettling it may be. That is where freedom and unexpected solutions are to be found, as opposed to the 'real' world in which patients feel that they have shut themselves up. This general disposition puts specific technical demands on the analyst. In particular, Danielle Quinodoz describes the ability to tolerate uncertainty, which is needed to let a representation of the patient's phantasy world emerge; willingness to experience oneself as the bad object that the patient cannot represent or would like to repudiate, as a first essential step to helping the patient move towards representation and integration; and receptiveness to projective identifications, involving especially one's own physical sensations and phantasies about one's body, which may offer clues to projective counter-identifications (Grinberg, 1962, 1979).

Such work involves bearing to think and talk in ways that seem strange to conscious experience, in 'words that touch' (Quinodoz, 2003) because they are very close to the patient's intimate experience, akin to symbolic equations (Segal, 1957) but sufficiently ambiguous to open up possibilities for symbolism and development. As the case vignettes demonstrate, such interventions are the result of the analyst's perceptiveness and thoughtfulness, but also of her attention to her own reactions, as evinced in her (unspoken) comments like 'I felt pervaded by a great feeling of sadness and disappointment' or 'I was then submerged by a sensation of collapsing'.

Although Danielle Quinodoz makes no bones about the disturbing quality of psychoanalytic work, she shows how it can be easier than we expect if we open up to it, and how gratifying it can be to offer our patients the living experience of a relationship that can help them to come into contact with aspects of their inner world that they had not seen or imagined before. The work described in this paper is expanded on in her book *Words That Touch: A Psychoanalyst Learns to Speak* (Quinodoz, 2003).

References

Grinberg, L. (1962). On a specific aspect of countertransference due to the patient's projective identification. *International Journal of Psychoanalysis*, 43: 436–440.

Grinberg, L. (1979). Countertransference and projective counteridentification. *Contemporary Psychoanalysis* 15(2): 226–247.

Quinodoz, D. (1997). *Emotional Vertigo: Between Anxiety and Pleasure.* London and New York: Routledge, The New Library of Psychoanalysis. Originally published in French: (1994). *Le vertige entre angoisse et plaisir.* Paris: Presses Universitaires de France.

Quinodoz, D. (2002). Are analysands extinct? Recognising a patient's latent request for psychoanalysis. *European Psychoanalytic Federation Bulletin* 56.

Quinodoz, D. (2003). *Words That Touch: A Psychoanalyst Learns to Speak.* London and New York: Karnac. Originally published in French: (2002). *Les mots qui touchent: une psychanalyste apprend à parler.* Paris: Presses Universitaires de France.

Quinodoz, D., Aubry, C., Bonard, O., Dejussel, G., Reith, B. (2006). Being a psychoanalyst: An everyday audacity. *International Journal of Psychoanalysis* 87: 329–347.

Segal, H. (1957). Notes on symbol formation. *International Journal of Psychoanalysis* 38: 391–397.

17 THE PSYCHOANALYST OF THE FUTURE

Wise enough to dare to be mad at times[1]

Danielle Quinodoz

Wisdom often consists in following one's madness rather than one's reason.

(E.-E. Schmitt, *Le visiteur*, 1994, p. 26)

At the beginning of the third millennium I have been reflecting on my clinical experience as a psychoanalyst. Two questions I have been asking myself are: first, in my daily practice with patients in analysis today, what path is the unconscious using to manifest itself; and second, how can we recognise it?

'You're mad!' I then found myself thinking, 'Today, you have to be mad to be a psychoanalyst!' Then I recalled the moment when a transsexual patient, a man who had undergone a sex-change operation (vaginoplasty) several years before and who was suffering from a serious sense of a 'lack of being', asked me if I could take him into analysis (Quinodoz, 1998). By having this operation, this patient had done something mad that put 'her' in a situation that was irreversibly mad; yet, in many respects she seemed well adapted, particularly in her professional and social life. On the one hand, this patient was disavowing reality; and, on the other, she was able to take reality into account: she presented a splitting of the ego. I had serious reservations about accepting her into analysis, which was why I discussed the matter with colleagues.

For once, my colleagues' opinions were unanimous: 'You're mad!', they said to me. The mere fact that I had even considered taking on this analysis already seemed to be a sign of madness. Could the 'mad' part of the patient evolve in analysis? Would it not be dangerous for this patient to develop psychically, since in reality her castration was irreversible? But it was precisely the latter question that troubled me. This patient wanted to develop; should she be refused the help she was asking for on the pretext that the consequences of her madness, in reality, could not be undone? Would she find herself ensnared in concrete reality? This was what seemed mad to me; for I was

1 Originally published as: Quinodoz, D. (2001). The psychoanalyst of the future: Wise enough to dare to be mad at times. *International Journal of Psychoanalysis* 82: 235–248.

convinced that if it was possible for a patient to develop, he or she would be able to find a solution.

The unanimity of the comments made me realise that the condition for my taking this patient into analysis was, perhaps, that I myself would have to accept being mad . . . not mad in a general way, of course; that is, it was not a question of believing that I was omnipotent and that I was capable of achieving anything. It was a matter of becoming aware of the mad aspects of myself, without making a drama out of it, and while keeping my feet on the ground. If, as psychoanalysts, we are to be able to work with the patients of the third millennium who turn to us for help, we will undoubtedly need to be aware of the archaic side of ourselves, our own splits, our psychotic mechanisms; in short, the mad aspects of ourselves. If we hope to understand our most disturbed patients, we have to be prepared to expose ourselves to troubling and uncomfortable countertransference experiences.

I had this patient in analysis for several years. Now the analysis is over, and the quality of life obtained by my patient has convinced me that psychoanalysis can be an invaluable resource for patients such as these, who suffer from a lack of ego unity.

Heterogeneous patients

This patient may seem to be a rather extreme case, owing to her transsexualism. Yet I feel she is representative of many of the patients I have in analysis, as well as of many of the patients that training candidates whom I supervise have in analysis. With her and with them, we can observe the coexistence of contrasting aspects: a more developed aspect and an archaic aspect. These patients, whom I would call heterogeneous, suffer from experiencing incompatible attitudes within themselves; on the one hand, they are capable of symbolising and of using secondary psychical mechanisms, and on the other, they resort to primitive psychical mechanisms such as disavowal, projection, massive projective identification and different forms of splitting. The extent to which these mechanisms are employed may hinder the functioning of their symbolic capacity, which they could otherwise make use of. I have chosen the term 'heterogeneous patients' in order to avoid using psychiatric diagnostic labels; and I have tried to find a term that simply refers to the patient's drive and defensive organisation as it can be observed by a psychoanalyst in the relationship that develops between himself and these patients. This is why I do not use the term *borderline patient* in the sense in which it is used by Kernberg (1984). Nor do I speak of borderline states, a notion introduced by Green who, from a different perspective, proposes that 'the borderline be considered as a concept' (1999, p. 33) and is interested in this frontier, which is not just a frontier line but rather a frontier zone between two territories with its own characteristics (1986). I am purposely using a general descriptive term that is not part of a particular conceptual framework, but with which clinicians with different personal references may be able to identify.

This heterogeneity can be found in each one of us in proportions that vary from person to person and can evolve over time: 'there is a psychotic personality concealed by neurosis as the neurotic personality is screened by psychosis in the psychotic, that has to be laid bare and dealt with' (Bion, 1967, p. 63).

Personally, I tend to speak of different parts of the patient when splitting predominates, whereas I speak of his different aspects when unity prevails. But the patients whom I call heterogeneous all have the particular feature of suffering from their heterogeneity; not that they are aware of the heterogeneity itself, since it originates in unconscious splitting, but they suffer from its consequences – that is, from the discomfort, which is often difficult for them to define, of having attitudes and forms of behaviour that are in conflict with each other, as well as discordant feelings. These patients are therefore the victims of an unconscious struggle between, on the one hand, the force driving them to split off, and keep frozen, certain parts of themselves and, on the other, a force driving them towards reunification.

What can we offer these patients who, without being psychotic, nonetheless sometimes use psychotic mental mechanisms? Psychoanalysts have different answers here. Some psychoanalysts prefer to take them into psychotherapy. They think that the patient will be in less danger of disorganisation, or 'malignant regression, in a non-analytic sense' (Gibeault, 2000) if he can relate to the reality of his therapist in the face-to-face sessions. Why not? Many fascinating things happen in psychotherapy. But a note of warning: if by preferring psychotherapy we think we are leaving madness undisturbed, it should not be forgotten that even if we let it sleep, it still does not go away.

This is why I think that, as psychoanalysts, we find we are being led to take heterogeneous patients into psychoanalysis and that this will increasingly be the case in the future. But this being said, it is a matter of evaluating not just the patient's analysability but also what the analyst feels he or she is capable of offering the patient in a psychoanalysis. If we are ready to take on these patients for whom analysis can be an invaluable source of help, I think there will be no danger of analysts' couches remaining empty.

Freud had already foreseen these patients of the third millennium

In 1940 Freud described the splitting of the ego as follows:

> Two psychical attitudes have been formed instead of a single one – one, the normal one, which takes account of reality, and another one which under the influence of the instincts detaches the ego from reality. The two exist

> alongside of each other. The issue depends on their relative strength. If the second is, or becomes the stronger, the necessary precondition for a psychosis is present . . . The view that postulates that in all psychoses there is a splitting of the ego could not call for so much notice if it did not turn out to apply to other states more like the neuroses, and finally, to the neuroses themselves.
>
> (p. 202)

The more I practise psychoanalysis, the more I notice both in my analysands and in myself the perspicacity of Freud's remarks describing the presence in each of us of these two attitudes in varying and fluctuating proportions. Moreover, in addition to the splitting of the ego discussed by Freud, we can also observe multiple forms of splitting, and I think an analysand may feel extremely ill at ease, without knowing why, if he (or she) finishes his personal analysis without having taken into account his own most important splits. Even if everyone, however well-analysed they may be, always retains some shadow zones, we cannot minimise the importance of the return of what is disavowed: 'Probably in a psychosis the rejected piece of reality constantly forces itself upon the mind, just as the repressed instinct does in a neurosis' (Freud, 1924, p. 186).

The 'non-request' in psychoanalysis

Should we only take into analysis neurotic patients and, specifically, neurotic patients who explicitly ask us for psychoanalysis, or patients who have been referred to us by a colleague who has already suggested that psychoanalytic treatment is indicated? Such situations are exceptional nowadays. We rarely meet a purely neurotic patient, especially as a neurotic person is sometimes a borderline case without knowing it. Furthermore, if a patient is already familiar with psychoanalysis, he will choose to have his analysis with a psychoanalyst of long experience. If these were the only patients who were accepted into analysis, psychoanalysts would psychoanalyse amongst themselves and we would then only be dealing with '*des psy de psy*'[2] as Mauger and Monette (2000, p. 28) call them, which would really be a pity. I think that as a result of extending the heritage left by Freud, the current state of our of psychoanalytic knowledge allows us to undertake analyses with patients who are not purely neurotic, if they exist at all. Freud was the first to take the risk. Personally, I have always made sure that at least half of my patients in analysis belong to a professional world other than that of psychiatry or psychology and have no prior knowledge of psychoanalysis.

[2] Translator's note: A common abbreviation in French for a psychoanalyst, as well as a psychiatrist or a psychologist.

If heterogeneous patients do not ask us directly for psychoanalysis, in most cases it is because they do not even know what it is. Yet they turn to us, as psychoanalysts, for help, and their decision to do an analysis or not will generally depend on the attitude of the psychoanalyst whom they see. It is for us to recognise their unconscious or preconscious request, to know how to welcome them and to propose this adventure to them. They make me think of Brassens's song entitled 'La non-demande en mariage' (The non-proposal of marriage): 'I have the honour of not requesting your hand'. When, during preliminary interviews, I am thinking of proposing psychoanalysis to a patient, my first concern is not to know whether I am dealing with a neurosis, psychosis or borderline state, or even to rely on an evaluation – which often proves to be mistaken – of their capacity or incapacity to symbolise, but to discern whether the patient has an unconscious or preconscious desire for the unification of himself, and whether he shows at least the beginnings of a capacity to use a transference object constructively. In my experience, more patients could benefit from a psychoanalysis than we think. It would be a pity to respond to the manifest request for psychotherapy without noticing that behind it there may be a latent request for the kind of work that can only be done in psychoanalysis. Further, with the aim of helping new candidates to find analytic cases, I ran a clinical seminar for several years on the theme: how to enable a patient to become aware of his eventual wish to have psychoanalysis. I shall now try to mention a few points that may facilitate such awareness.

How can a patient decide to undertake an analysis when he does not know what it is?

During preliminary interviews, when we want to propose psychoanalysis to a patient who knows little or nothing about it, even if he (or she) sometimes thinks he does, we can of course explain to him rationally what the unconscious is, or make a fine comparative description of the scope and limits of psychotherapy and psychoanalysis; and the patient will listen to this as if we were telling him a nice story, but without being ready to embark on the journey we are proposing. What matters is not to explain rationally, or to awaken an intellectual interest, but to arouse conviction. To discover what psychoanalysis is, the patient needs to experience it for himself from within. This insight may then bring with it the adherence of the whole person, allowing him to make a vital decision. This is also true for patients who have an intellectual knowledge of psychoanalysis through their profession.

What sort of interview is likely to allow a patient to gain such insight? If the psychoanalyst shows the same reserve towards his heterogeneous patients as he adopts with neurotic patients who, with full knowledge of the facts, have asked him for an analysis, nothing will happen. A patient cannot embark on an adventure about which he has not the slightest idea, with the aim of discovering a world whose existence is unknown to him, or of which he only has rational knowledge. This patient needs the analyst to interpret what happens between them at the level of the transference relationship emerging during the preliminary interviews, in a sufficiently suggestive way and in a language that speaks to him, so that he is then free to make a choice.

The patient who cannot imagine what the unconscious world or phantasies are will have considerable difficulty in understanding what the analyst is offering him, for he cannot perceive the world that the analyst is speaking to him about. For his part, the analyst sometimes has great difficulty in realising that his patient cannot perceive this world of phantasies or the world of the unconscious that he is speaking to him about, but with which he himself is familiar. The analyst sometimes infers too quickly that the patient is not interested in it or cannot get in touch with it. Yet I have often been surprised to observe that when a patient gets a glimpse of this world of which he previously had no inkling, he can show great interest in it. Indeed the patient often finds himself in a situation that is all the more anxiety-producing because he is enclosed within a real world, every aspect of which he has gone over in his mind in vain, without being able to see a solution. When, during the preliminary interview, the patient has even a fleeting revelation of the reality of this psychical world, of whose existence he was unaware, he may hope that his internal and external situation will perhaps become clearer and take on meaning, and that an unexpected solution, previously invisible to him, may exist for his problems. He will want to explore this space that is new for him and perhaps to accept the means that the analyst is offering him to try and get there. At times, he will also be afraid of going there. But, even in this case, the patient will know from then on that he has had a glimpse of a space of which he was previously unaware.

The period of uncertainty for the analyst

Of course, if a patient is to be able to get a glimpse of his own world of phantasy, of whose existence he has hitherto been unaware, the psychoanalyst must already have discerned it himself; but, the latter will only have been able to do so if he has adopted an inner attitude of floating attention. If the analyst adopts any other attitude – for instance that of a psychiatric interview – he will be able to notice interesting things, make an excellent anamnesis, but he will not be in a position to help his patient get an inkling of his unconscious phantasy world. There is a period of uncertainty for the analyst, since the representation of the patient's phantasy world does not emerge immediately, and it requires patience, confidence and serenity. In any case, for the heterogeneous patient, to be listened to actively and with the utmost attention, over and beyond the manifest discourse, is a precious experience, for it enables him to feel that he exists as a whole person for the analyst.

Sometimes, it is true, the patient's world of phantasy does not take on any meaning for the analyst; nothing emerges, the way in cannot be found, and the analyst in this case cannot offer psychoanalysis. Perhaps psychoanalysis is not suitable for this patient. Moreover, it is also possible to imagine that a different psychoanalyst would be able to conduct an analysis with this patient.

A clinical example: The emergence of insight during a preliminary interview

Let us look more closely now at how Albert found the conviction to do an analysis. Albert did not ask for an analysis; he did not even know what it was. He simply came to see me because things were not going well. He wanted to resign from an important job because he was feeling so anxious. In particular, when his wife was away for a few days, his anxiety reached dramatic levels. His psychiatrist, who felt at a loss as to what to do, told him to come and see me: medication had had no effect; in the face-to-face sessions Albert had been unable to speak about himself and in the sessions lying down he had been completely blocked. Albert obeyed, very sceptically, for he could see no other option but to go into a psychiatric clinic.

In the initial interviews, Albert spoke very little and only through third parties, as if he only existed by procuration. Instead of speaking about himself, he spoke to me a bit about his children and his animals, and, noticing that this interested me deeply, he became more lively and talked more. But then he stopped suddenly, 'You see, I'm blocked, I'm not speaking about myself . . .'. Yet, for me, as an analyst, Albert's psychical world was beginning to take shape: Albert felt he existed not where he was but elsewhere, through others, even animals. I could well imagine that he might feel empty when a partner went away, since he projected his ego so much into the other. With conviction, I said something quite simple but which had a very powerful meaning for Albert: 'When you were telling me that your son was "a bit of a savage", don't you think you were also telling me about yourself?' I felt that for Albert a door had half-opened: he had found himself again, projected into his son. My question, which touched upon his projection and his identification, gave him a glimpse of a world that he wanted to know; Albert was beginning to show interest but was still a long way from psychoanalysis.

Albert then told me, without attaching any importance to it, that he had had a happy childhood. From the age of 18 months he had lived with a couple who loved him a lot, his aunt and uncle, as his parents were divorced and his mother was too involved in her profession abroad to have time to take care of him, even if she said that she would have liked to. Then after talking about the unhappy childhood that many delinquent adults have had, followed by a long silence, he said to me, 'I would be very interested in doing an analysis with you, but I'm so tied up professionally and have so little time that I would never find the time to come and see you several times a week. It's impossible'. At this point I felt pervaded by a great feeling of sadness and disappointment. I then wondered: this sadness, could it be due to projective counteridentification? Could this be the sadness that Albert, as a child, had disavowed and split off, and consequently could not speak to me about? Was he sharing it with me unconsciously by projecting it into me? After a period of silence, I said to him in a tone that probably reflected the sadness I had felt, 'Your mother was very interested in looking after you when you were a child, but she was so involved with her profession and had so little time that it was impossible for her to find the time to come and look after you.' A heavy silence, charged with emotion, set in. Albert recognised his mother's discourse in what he had said to me and he also recognised in the tone of my response what he had never been able to admit to himself. He had just had the experience of what could happen during an analysis in the transference relationship between us. We had both just experienced an exchange that reminded him of the exchange that had once occurred between him and his mother and that now acquired new meaning. A door had begun to open for Albert on to the world of the unconscious; he was now convinced that with this new dimension there was still perhaps a way forward. He agreed to undertake the work that I felt I could offer him, i.e. an analysis.

The analyst's confidence in the patient's own capacity to find a solution

It is my experience that in order to 'take the plunge' with a heterogeneous patient, the presence of this confidence can prove to be an important factor both for the patient and for the analyst. To return now to the example of my transsexual patient: initially, I really could not see what solution this patient would be able to find at the end of her analysis. Reality seemed to block the situation: if at the end of the analysis the patient remained convinced of her identity as a woman, it would be the sign that the delusion had been reinforced; if, on the contrary, the patient rediscovered her identity as a man, she would be in despair, as she would not be able to find again either a male body or a male role in society.

However, at the end of her analysis, the patient, who no longer disavowed reality, adopted an attitude I had not imagined; she said to me, 'I have accepted now, as far as is possible, to live with the paradox; I know that I am not a woman and that I will never be able to be one. Neither will I ever be able to be a man like other men. What I can say is that I am a transsexual, who has a woman's position'. By recuperating the part of herself that had been split off she had allowed her phantasies to evolve: 'I've definitely changed since the time when I detested my masculine aspects; I wanted to be a woman out of my loathing for men; now, for me, being a woman means being a woman who likes men'. The patient had found a realistic and integrative solution that, by escaping the dilemma that we had seemed to be caught in, appeared to me to be the best possible solution in a situation that nonetheless remained difficult. It was now possible to end the analysis.

Initially I had made a seemingly mad gamble, because I was convinced that if the archaic phantasies and the psychic functioning of a patient could develop, the patient could find an answer that the psychoanalyst could not have imagined at the outset.

Certain specific aspects concerning the analysis of heterogeneous patients

The analyst who accepts a heterogeneous patient into analysis is led to analyse aspects that he would not have to analyse in a patient who was merely neurotic. Equally, he finds he is led to use language that does not merely speak to these patients but which touches them. These patients have difficulties in having access to the symbolic meaning of language, and they need the analyst's discourse to awaken or reawaken bodily phantasies in them so as to be able to find emotional meaning in forgotten sensory experiences. They will then become a point of departure for mental representation.

The analyst as the guarantor of the patient's desire for integration

It is sometimes the case that a psychoanalyst's training has been based primarily on knowledge of neurotic patients and that, as a result, he has a great deal of experience of neurotic defences and can easily detect them in his patients. A special effort of attention may then be required for him to be able to detect the eventual presence of primitive defences in a patient and to understand the link (or absence of link) that exists between the two aspects of the patient.

Freud presented the world of phantasy as a 'storehouse' that the patient can draw on to feed both his neurosis and his psychosis. I quote:

> It is from this world of phantasy that the neurosis draws the material for its new wishful constructions . . . the world of phantasy plays the same part in psychosis and there, too, it is the storehouse from which the materials or the pattern for building the new reality are derived.
>
> (1924, p. 187)

Thus, by putting the patient in contact with his phantasy world, psychoanalysis offers a special setting for a patient who is oscillating between the psychotic and the neurotic aspects of himself.

Generally speaking, depending on the analyst's listening, the patient will put more emphasis on one aspect or the other. But for a heterogeneous patient to agree to undertake an analysis and for a process to be established, he needs to feel that the psychoanalyst is aware of the presence of these two aspects and that he is listening to both. To illustrate this I will make use of an old example (Quinodoz, 1996): Laure had begun the first preliminary interview by saying to me, 'I was born when I was 6 months old'. This first statement could be understood in different ways: it could simply be a tribute to her adoptive parents who adopted her when she was 6 months old; but it could also be a disavowal of the existence of the first months of her life – the one did not exclude the other. I want to emphasise, then, that an analyst can consider the same statement of the patient from either the angle of neurosis or that of psychosis, or again he can take both into account at the same time. Generally speaking, heterogeneous patients need to hear that, even if he has chosen to interpret at the more developed, neurotic level, of the patient, the analyst has not forgotten the existence of the primitive side, and vice versa. Similarly, if the patient leaves an aspect of himself outside the session, the analyst can draw his attention to it. The analyst is, so to speak, the guardian of the patient's desire for integrity and the guarantor of the possibility of achieving it.

Verbalising the shame of a patient upon discovering an aspect of himself that seems to him to be mad

While expressing in a latent way the wish for the reunification of their ego (self), heterogeneous patients are afraid of discovering archaic aspects of themselves that feel mad to them. In particular, they fear that this mad side may contaminate the rest, as was described by Klein. But the patient's anxiety begins to lessen if the analyst can verbalise the shame that the patient feels – even though the latter cannot admit it to himself – when he begins to become aware of his mad attitudes, even though in other respects he rightly sees himself as being a responsible adult. The analyst de-dramatises what the patient is experiencing by verbalising the anxiety that the patient experiences at the idea of getting more in touch with aspects of himself that he has hitherto unconsciously and carefully kept separate from each other. The simple fact of making this anxiety explicit implies that, for the analyst, it is obvious that in each of us the presence of one aspect does not exclude that of another. The heterogeneous patient needs to identify himself with a psychoanalyst who dares to verbalise mad thoughts and who is able to look not only at the patient's madness but also at his own without being scandalised.

I shall now return to the example of Albert. When we began to make connections between his current anxieties concerning separation and the apparent insensibility which, according to him, he had experienced when his mother had left when he was 18 months old, I said to him: 'It might be very disconcerting for you to feel like a small child who suffers so much if his mummy goes away, while at the same time you have to take such important decisions for an entire population'. Albert then exclaimed, 'I want to kick this child in me out!' His reaction consisted, then, in wanting to evacuate the disturbing part of himself. In reality, he had always fulfilled this wish unconsciously. On hearing himself say this, Albert had become aware of his tendency to expel and abandon the side of himself of which he disapproved. But to be able to adopt and reintegrate in oneself a split-off part, one first has to realise that one has expelled or abandoned it. I said to him, 'You would like to kick this child in you out? Just as you reproach your mother for doing so when she left you to go and work abroad?' Albert then had the surprise of finding himself identified with a mother whom he consciously believed he detested. So he began swinging back and forth between an abandoning ego and an abandoning object; persecution anxiety then diminished thanks to a better knowledge of the object through phantasy and an increased capacity to put himself in her place in phantasy. His mother could begin to be an internal object with more nuances for him internally, just as in the transference the analyst could appear as a more tolerant object and be regarded more tolerantly. With heterogeneous patients, I think that it is important for the analyst to draw attention to the difficulty that the adult side of the patient may have in accepting the child in him. These interpretations show implicitly that although the patient has a tendency to reject an aspect of himself, the analyst will be able to remember its presence.

Heterogeneous patients harbour a desire to get better and a dread of doing so at the same time; particularly because it would bring them nearer to the end of their analysis and therefore separation from the analyst. In order to be able to get better the patient is led to trick the part of himself that unconsciously wants to sabotage the progress that has been made, sweeping it away as soon as it is noticed. The analyst's task is a delicate one; for, on the one hand, these patients are led to hide their progress from themselves in order to preserve it, and yet they need the positive points to be pointed out by the analyst so that they can gain confidence in their capacity for reparation and identify with an analyst who treats his objects well. The patient needs to understand that if the analyst mentions a positive point, he has nonetheless not forgotten the negative points, and vice versa; it is as though the patient had an unconscious wish to encounter in his analyst a concern to bind the forces of destruction and construction in order to put them at the service of vital life processes. In any case, it is when the destructive force of the patient is silent – that is, inaudible for him – that his destructivity has the greatest effect; and, by verbalising it, the analyst tries to prevent it from acting in silence.

What kind of language 'touches' patients? A clinical example from Elise's analysis

Elise, who was single and rather charming, but had never been able to make the most of herself in her professional plans or in her love life (her relationships had led to impasses), had made a very vague request for help; I will summarise it by saying that she wanted to feel she was alive: it was as if, for her, life was going to end without ever having begun. From the first preliminary interviews, Elise had appeared to me two-sided. On the one hand, there was a lively and generous side to her, which was perfectly visible to those around her; and, on the other, a dead and greedy side, well-hidden, harbouring suicidal ideas. Elise spoke in a factual way and she cut the links I tried to suggest. In the analysis, Elise talked to me as if I was a useless object, unable to understand her despair, but she had no awareness of the transference meaning of my role. On the other hand, the sessions were filled, in accounts impregnated with unconscious phantasies, with the presence of a man (who, in reality, was far away) who had dropped her.

At the beginning of a session, Elise recounted a dream: 'In a covered pool, there was a big dog, with a broken leg, being dragged round and round in the current. It had a dull look in its eyes and was going to die. I left feeling helpless; then I came back because I couldn't let this dog drown like that, but I didn't know what to do'. Elise associated: 'Once, when I was travelling, I saw an injured dog dying under the indifferent gaze of passers-by. I would have liked to ask for help but I couldn't speak as I didn't know the language of the country'. The look in the dog's eyes in the dream made Elise think about the look in her mother's eyes, an old lady who was dying slowly. Elise had further associations: 'This makes me think of a drama which occurred near the place where I used to go on holiday as a small girl. There were holes in the torrent, hollowed out by the current; this made whirlpools which pulled you towards the bottom; we called them "pots". A couple was out walking with a dog. The dog fell into one of these holes; the man dived in to save it and he drowned with the dog'.

As I listened to the account of the dream and the associations, I heard Elise's plea for help as well as her fear and unconscious wish to drag me into the deadly whirlpool. I then felt a moment of intense relief: at last Elise had brought a dream and associations; she seemed to be elaborating her conflicts. The lively side of Elise was definitely present. But suddenly the other side of Elise reappeared: in a flash Elise had adopted her distant and cold tone again: 'Analysis, it's just words; analysis is useless'. I was then submerged by a sensation of collapsing; I felt myself falling into one of the pots in the torrent. In my countertransference I thought that perhaps my sensation of collapsing was linked with the massive projective identification used by Elise and that it thus corresponded to a projective counteridentification. Elise had certainly had an unconscious need to communicate an early pre-verbal experience to me so that I could help her to find meaning in it: 'I couldn't speak . . .'.

If Elise unconsciously projected into me her feeling of falling into the whirlpool, just as in the analysis she had been going round and round for months, it was no doubt so that I could help her make sense of it. I had already noticed that Elise had the tendency to act out instead of representing her conflicts mentally. Accordingly, during the preliminary interviews she had broken her leg like the dog in the dream and had said to me: 'I forgot about the step in the middle of the living-room, even though I knew it well; the ground went from under me and I fell'. At the time, I did not make an interpretation. Now I thought that Elise was projecting the emptiness outside so as to avoid feeling it in herself, and that she unconsciously wanted someone to drop her to confirm the presence of this external emptiness. By making a displacement on to a man who would drop her, she had unconsciously protected the analyst.

How could Elise be helped to feel that she had unconsciously projected a deadly emptiness outside of herself in order to avoid feeling it within herself? I imagined that, even though she had always denied it, as she had no direct memory of it, she must have already experienced this emptiness when she was eight months old; that is, when she had to spend several weeks in a clinic because her mother, who was ill and contagious, was unable to take care of her. According to family accounts, when they met up again, Elise had turned her head away, refusing to look at her mother. I had sensed all this myself when I had the bodily impression that everything was collapsing. How could I use my projective counteridentification to interpret Elise's excessive projective identification? I refrained from interpreting the projection directly to Elise by saying, for instance, that she may have unconsciously put into me what was causing her anxiety. I feel that this kind of interpretation can be experienced as being extremely intrusive, rather as if I had said to Elise that I knew what she was feeling better than she did. I reserve this type of interpretation for analysands who will be future analysts, when they are particularly interested in gaining insight into their psychic functioning. It seemed to me that what Elise needed was for me to help her to picture the bad internal object that was present in the depressed side of her. Not the missing good object, the absent good mother, but the presence in her of the bad object; i.e. the absence of the good object that had become the presence of the bad object. How was I to get her to feel that in the transference? I thought that I could make interpretations about myself, in the transference, as a representation of the unrepresentable internal part-object.

This is why when I heard Elise say, 'I'm really wondering whether you have any use for me in the analysis!' I replied with deep conviction: 'Perhaps I am the pot'. Elise gave a start, and said incredulously, 'What?' I added: 'Yes, the pot which could contain good things to eat but instead of which is a hole sucking you to the bottom of the torrent in which you go round and round and drown . . .'. Elise remained silent, concentrating hard, and calm. And as it seemed obvious to me that if I offered myself to Elise as an object, she would be able to experience the corresponding affect, I added: 'And you turn your head away in order to tell me about all your feelings of sadness and anger and how much I disappoint you'. To help Elise discover what was happening inside her at this early level, I tried to start with her gesture so that, through rediscovering sensation, she could then discover its emotional significance. She asked: 'I turn my head away?' I replied: 'When you tell me that I can't help you, it's a bit like turning your head away from me, rather like when your mother came to collect you after your stay in the clinic'. There was a silence and then Elise said emotionally: 'No one has sensed before that I really have a hole at the bottom of myself . . . (silence) . . . I think that's why I cannot take care of my mother properly; I do it out of a sense of duty. My brother, he really takes care of her . . . (silence). Before the analysis, no one ever knew that there was this sadness within me. My mother has always been the presence of an absence'.

I had offered myself as the 'negative' of a part-object. In the transference I was the breast that was lacking, the 'hollow form' of the breast, as it were. The next time I saw her, Elise told me that after this session she had felt like vomiting and had dreamt of a caged panther (her cannibalistic aspect). She had also thought again about a separation that occurred when she was older, involving her brother. She then associated by talking about sexual differences and conflicts of rivalry with her brother situated at a secondary level: if one point in the network of associations is affected, it has repercussions throughout the network. After this session the phantasy construction of Elise's love life was no longer so invasive.

What was it, in this session, that 'touched' the patient? Certain characteristics of a language that has the capacity to touch

The analyst as the representative of the bad object

Often for heterogeneous patients the bad object is either unrepresentable or it has to be repudiated. This is why, by daring to offer them a representation of the bad object, the analyst is able to touch them. As there is a correspondence between the ego and the object, de-dramatising the bad character of the object results in de-dramatising the bad character of the ego; consequently, the patient is better able to tolerate aspects of himself that he considers bad and so can re-own them. Moreover, once the patient is able to imagine the bad object, he will also, by way of contrast, have a better idea of the good object, even if it is simply to deplore its absence; and, owing to the correspondence between the ego and the object, he will also acquire a better idea of what is good in himself. The patient can then begin to realise that once a non-idealised (ambivalent) good object has been established in himself, the ego will prove capable of sharing its richness without feeling impoverished and can thus begin to feel gratitude towards the object. On the other hand, when he unconsciously sets up a bad internal object within himself, he feels dispossessed by other people of his own richness.

Listening to the bodily manifestations that accompany countertransference affects

Heterogeneous patients often make use of projective identification; the analyst is thus led to interpret it, and, in order to do this, he needs to make use of his projective counteridentification. I have noticed that in order to become aware of his projective counteridentification, and to be able to use it, the psychoanalyst needs to listen not only to his countertransference affects but also to the bodily manifestations and bodily phantasies that accompany them. Indeed, in the case of early affective experiences, it is through bodily experience that the patient can rediscover his affects and bodily phantasies. In order to gather the patient's feelings that are projected into him, the analyst needs to notice the manifestations accompanying these feelings, which he may experience in his own body. He will then be able to give them back to the patient by trying to give meaning to the patient's sensations and by helping him make the transition from sensation to affect, and then to representation and symbolism. Bodily phantasy can constitute a starting-point for mental representation. The analyst may also have the opportunity of drawing the patient's attention to a gesture he or she makes without being aware of its emotional significance. We have seen, in particular, how important it is for a patient to become aware of repeating a significant gesture and to move from the gesture itself to its meaning, as well as to the feelings which have given rise to it. It is by reconstituting the chain of sensations that the emotional significance of the gesture can be recovered by the patient; for it is often by getting in touch again with the bodily manifestations that accompany the affect that the patient will become aware that he or she has experienced the affect. For example, by rediscovering the emotional significance of 'turning her head away', Elise made contact again with a whole emotional context and the possibility of representing it mentally.

The absence of visual support in psychoanalysis can be invaluable

I have often found during analytic sessions that the absence of visual support can facilitate awareness of bodily experience, especially if the latter is barely differentiated; and, it can bring into play internal sensations that are difficult to locate as they are connected with the body as a whole, sometimes being linked to attitudes or to positions. My point of view relativises the opinion often expressed by psychoanalysts (Gibeault, for instance, quoted above) who recommend the face-to-face situation for patients of this type because of the importance for them of visual experience. I think that for these patients the phantasies linked to the earliest internal bodily experiences can be more important than those linked to visual experiences:

> the hallucinated breast is not to begin with a visual experience, but a bodily one. Early experiences, such as hunger or satisfaction, are experienced and interpreted by the infant in terms of object-relationship phantasies . . . Such primitive psychosomatic phantasies . . . can still play a dynamic part in later development.
>
> (Segal, 1993, p. 20).

For example, for Elise, the gesture of turning her head away was felt throughout her entire body; the fact of being deprived of visual support in the analysis had facilitated awareness of the bodily experience corresponding to this gesture and the related relational phantasies. On the couch, these patients, who need to get back in touch with early bodily experiences, often shut their eyes in order to be able to focus better on what they are feeling in their bodies and to find emotional meaning in it. The patient who recognises a 'lost' early bodily experience during the analysis can rediscover its emotional significance and reconstitute a bodily phantasy, which serves as a point of departure for mental representation. Sometimes, moreover, it is precisely because of the absence of visual support that psychoanalysis can on occasions be an invaluable asset for patients who have difficulty in symbolising; provided, however, as I have already pointed out, that they show an aptitude, even if it be minimal, for using the transference object, as well as a desire, albeit hidden, for inner unity.

The effect of surprise

As the development of the patients I have called heterogeneous is not linear, interpretations have to be found which, by creating an effect of surprise, cause the whole network of the patient's associations to vibrate. Interpretation thus creates a disequilibrium in the patient's psychic system, helping him to get out of the circle in which he is turning endlessly and to open himself to symbolisation.

Using a language with double meanings

These patients who are disconcerted by the paradoxes within them are touched by the use of a language that is capable of uniting different meanings within the same expression, thereby showing that the combination of opposites is possible. In his commentary on the 'Gradiva', Freud noted that Zoe-Gradiva, presented as Hanold's therapist, successfully used a double language to 'touch' Hanold: a language which had one meaning in the context of Hanold's sporadic bouts of delusion but also another meaning which took reality into account. For example, when she asked Hanold: 'I feel as though we had shared a meal like this once before, two thousand years ago; can you remember?' (1907, p. 26) she could have been referring to the period preceding the eruption of Vesuvius, but equally to their childhood. Now I think that Hanold can be taken as an example of a heterogeneous patient: a person who is adapted to social life but who, with his sporadic delusions, shows a psychotic part, while nonetheless wishing to reunify his ego and showing he is capable of using the object.

There are various ways in which language can operate on dual levels. It can be at the level of the words employed or at the level of discourse. Thus, 'pot' was a word with two meanings; it evoked several transference part-object representations: for instance, a 'saucepan' used for preparing food which can represent the full breast, but also the 'fluvial pot', a deadly hole that can represent the empty breast, hollowed out by the patient's cannibalistic aggressivity. A different aspect of the ego corresponds to each object-representation; for example, the dog corresponded to the deadly hole, but the panther corresponded to the hole created by erosion. Language can also have a double meaning at the level of discourse. When I said: 'Perhaps I am the pot . . .', I used a formulation corresponding to that of the symbolic equation since I did not say that I represented a pot, which would have been less mad. But it is only the formulation that evoked the symbolic equation; the general meaning of the sentence was open to symbolism. It was a way of taking both parts into account, the archaic and the more developed part of the patient. The double meaning of language obliges the patient to decentre himself, to differentiate himself from the object; for the patient thinks he has heard one thing and then realises that the analyst has been saying something different. This discrepancy creates a disequilibrium that mobilises thought and prepares the way for symbolism. This gap can make it possible to get out of the circle in which the dog goes round and round in the washtub of analysis.

Psychoanalysis is something living

I believe that future psychoanalysts will continue to do psychoanalyses if they are ready to take into psychoanalysis patients whom I have called 'heterogeneous'; that is, patients who use both neurotic psychic mechanisms and primitive mechanisms, even though these patients have at least a latent wish for integration and a capacity to use the transference object. This implies that the analyst should not confine himself to the domain of neurosis but needs to recognise the primitive psychic mechanisms used by the patient and know how to analyse them. It also implies that the psychoanalyst, who will be listening attentively to bodily phantasies, needs to speak a language that touches the patient. This language will be built up gradually, at the same time as the psychoanalyst discovers his own mad aspects and allows himself enough psychic liberty to accept them. Taking these heterogeneous patients into psychoanalysis corresponds neither to a stopgap measure, nor to a distortion or a concession with respect to the psychoanalysis discovered by Freud, which would be the case if Freud had passed on to us a rigid and dead object. Freud handed down to us a psychoanalysis that is living, and in order to remain faithful to him, what matters is not simply to respect its permanence but also its internal potential for development.

References

Bion, W. (1967). *Second Thoughts*. London: Heinemann.

Freud, S. (1907). Delusions and Dreams in Jensen's 'Gradiva'. *SE* 9.

Freud, S. (1924). The Loss of Reality in Neurosis and Psychosis. *SE* 19.

Freud, S. (1940). An Outline of Psycho-Analysis. *SE* 23.

Gibeault, A. (2000). In response to Otto F. Kernberg's: 'Psychoanalysis, psychoanalytic psychotherapy and supportive psychotherapy: contemporary controversies'. *International Journal of Psychoanalysis* 81: 379–383.

Green, A. (1986). *On Private Madness*. London: Hogarth.

Green, A. (1999). Genèse et situation des états limites. In: *Les états limites* (pp. 23–68). Paris: Presses Universitaires de France, Petite Bibliothèque de psychanalyse.

Kernberg, O. (1984). *Severe Personality Disorders: Psychotherapeutic Strategies*. New Haven, CT: Yale University Press. [*Les troubles graves de la personnalité*. Paris: Presses Universitaires de France, 1999.]

Mauger, J., Monette, L. (2000). 'Pure culture' 60th Congress of French-speaking psychoanalysts. *Bulletin Société Psychoanalyse Paris* 55: 9–78. Also *Revue Français Psychoanalyse* 5: 1391–1460.

Quinodoz, D. (1996). An adopted analysand's transference of a 'hole-object'. *International Journal of Psychoanalysis* 77: 323–336.

Quinodoz, D. (1998). A fe/male transsexual patient in psychoanalysis. *International Journal of Psychoanalysis* 79: 95–111.

Schmitt, E.-E. (1994). *Le visiteur*. Arles: Actes Sud-Papiers.

Segal, H. (1993). *Dream, Phantasy and Art*. London: Routledge. The New Library of Psychoanalysis. [French translation: *Rêve, Art et Phantasme*. Paris: Bayard Editions, 1993].

18 THE ANALYST'S RELUCTANCE TO BEGIN A NEW ANALYSIS
by Lena Ehrlich

Commentary

Mette Møller

Lena T. Ehrlich is a training and supervising analyst at the Michigan Psychoanalytic Institute. Her paper takes as the starting point the decline during the last decades in the number of full psychoanalyses in the average psychoanalytic practice today. Without denying the reality of a more negative socioeconomic climate towards psychoanalysis at present, the author does not believe this can be the main explanation for the decreasing number of psychoanalytic patients. Rather, she suspects that society's negative attitude is being used by analysts to obscure and rationalize individual reasons for a smaller intake of psychoanalytic cases. Given the fact that psychoanalytic training is long and demanding, the author wonders why analysts, when graduated, do not expect to get a psychoanalytic practice going, but instead have a generally negative expectation towards finding analytic patients. Out of many different, personal factors that could influence the analyst's ability to initiate analyses, the author isolates and examines what she names: 'the reluctance to begin'.

The author collects and summarizes important theoretical work by different American analysts, who, during the 1980s and 1990s, described aspects of the analyst's problems with functioning: for example Boesky's concept of the analyst's counter-resistance as a response to the patient's resistance to analysis (Boesky, 1990), Smith's idea of reluctance to engage in analysis because of reluctance to do the self-analysis needed (Smith, 1993), Ogden's description of how the fear connected with consultation actually is the fear that analysis will be undertaken (Ogden, 1992), Orgel's suggestion that resistance to analyse can relate to unresolved feelings towards the analyst's training analyst (Orgel, 1990), and several other contributions all focusing on internal obstacles to starting or practising analysis.

To these theoretical considerations the paper adds clinical demonstrations of how the reluctance operates. Through detailed clinical vignettes from the author's own work with consultations and decisions about recommending psychoanalysis, she shows how the reluctance manifests itself and how the awareness of it enables her to get productive analyses started. The change of focus from the patient's 'analysability' to the analyst's 'willingness to analyse', a focus most strongly brought forward by Rothstein more than ten years before (see this volume, p. 281), still needs to be consolidated. Lena Ehrlich demonstrates how we must understand the analyst's unwillingness to start analysis as just as natural a part of the profession as the ever-present resistance in the patient. In a paper published in 2010, she shifts the focus from the analyst's hesitation to take on new patients to the analyst's disinclination to 'continue and deepen an analysis' (Ehrlich, 2010, p. 516).

Psychoanalytic work is carried out in a kind of isolation, and it requires courage and conviction to keep going. It is not so strange that all sorts of reasons can be invoked not to do so. Maintaining the idea of the relevance of analysis in practice requires continual inner effort, and most especially in the actual, clinical situation, not just in challenging theoretical considerations. At the same time, each analyst most likely experiences a certain shame and insecurity in relation to his or her experience of how difficult the analytical effort is. It is reasonable to assume that one way to help analysts to overcome the reluctance is to acknowledge these difficulties and share them with colleagues, as Lena Ehrlich does in publishing this necessary paper.

References

Boesky, D. (1990). The psychoanalytic process and its components. *Psychoanalytic Quarterly* 59: 550–584.

Ehrlich, L. T. (2010). The analyst's ambivalence about continuing and deepening an analysis. *Journal of the American Psychoanalytic Association* 58: 515–532.

Ogden, T. (1992). Comments on transference and countertransference in the initial analytic meeting. *Psychoanalytic Inquiry* 12: 225–247.

Orgel, S. (1990). The future of psychoanalysis. *Psychoanalytic Quarterly* 59: 1–20.

Smith, H. (1993). Engagements in the analytic work. *Psychoanalytic Inquiry* 13: 425–454.

18 THE ANALYST'S RELUCTANCE TO BEGIN A NEW ANALYSIS[1]

Lena Ehrlich

At present in the United States we practice less analysis per analyst than ever before. The last full report (Brauer & Brauer, 1996) from a survey conducted by the Committee on Psychoanalytic Practice of the American Psychoanalytic Association presents the following findings: the number of patients in analysis per analyst has been steadily diminishing over the last twenty-five years, at a rate of roughly one percent a year. At the time of the last survey, certified or active members who had patients in analysis saw on average three analytic cases. The reported morale and level of satisfaction of those who practiced less analysis was low in comparison to that of those practicing more analysis. Troubled by these findings, we have been searching for an explanation of why psychoanalysis is practiced less. Widely accepted reasons include the public's negative attitude toward psychoanalysis, the current socioeconomic climate, and the public's expectation of a quick cure. While useful to consider at the organizational level, these realities cannot of themselves fully illuminate the factors affecting the individual analyst's practice. The analyst's interest, experience, confidence, energy level, skill, unconscious conflicts, personality style, social and professional affiliations, locale, attitude, and conviction are among the many variables that can affect an analyst's practice. My primary interest in what follows is to explore how one variable, the analyst's reluctance to begin an analysis, affects analytic practice. I do not intend to negate the role of external realities; instead I suggest that analysts can use adverse external realities to obscure this reluctance.

Psychoanalytic training, as demanding as it sometimes was, helpfully cushioned me from fully realizing the implications of being an analyst. During training, my anxiety about analytic work was mediated by the support that an analyst-in-training receives as a candidate (Kantrowitz *et al.*, 1989). My analysis and work in close supervision tempered some of my conflicts and insecurities about practicing independently, provided narcissistic support, afforded me the illusion of sharing the responsibility for the work,

[1] First published as: Ehrlich, L. T. (2004). The analyst's reluctance to begin a new analysis. *Journal of the American Psychoanalytic Association* 52: 1075–1093.

and offered me a fantasy of protection. I immersed myself in studying and practicing analysis and focused on becoming an analyst. The more I experienced the healing possibilities of the method, the more unwavering I became in my commitment to practicing analysis, or so I thought. While in training, I had been able to find analytic patients easily and speedily in order to fulfill the requirements of my institute. I had one low-fee, one moderate-fee, and one full-fee patient. Nonetheless, as I approached graduation I began to question whether it would be possible to develop an analytic practice. I listened anxiously to reports that the number of patients in analysis was decreasing. I worried about rumors that there were no patients willing to engage in a time-consuming, expensive, and out-of-favor endeavor – at least not with a beginning analyst. For a few months after my graduation, I thought my worry was justified by external reality. Gradually, however, I realized that I was failing to take into account my own experience: I had been able to find analytic patients in the recent past (I had begun my last control case within the last year). I then started to question whether the obstacle was indeed patient availability. Reassessing my practice, I realized that during the initial consultations with several patients who might benefit from more intensive work I had accepted too readily that they were unavailable for analysis. This puzzled me further. Reluctantly, I turned my attention to the possibility that, despite my conscious eagerness to practice as an analyst, I was hesitant to recommend and engage in analysis.

The analyst's reluctance

Starting with Freud (1912a, 1912b, 1913), analysts have portrayed analytic beginnings as predictable, grounded in reasonable considerations, and leading to objectively determined recommendations. Efforts to determine analyzability (Bachrach, 1990; Erle & Goldberg, 2003) and proper beginning technique (Lichtenberg & Auchincloss, 1989; Busch, 1995) dominated these discussions. This emphasis reflected the prevailing assumptions of the time that treatment outcome depends primarily on the patient's ability to participate in the analytic process (Kantrowitz, 1993) and the analyst's capacity to apply correct technique. Analysts' participation was portrayed as technically neutral, comparable, and uniform (Bachrach, 1983).

In recent years we have expanded our understanding of analytic process to include not only the patient's conflicts and resistances but also the analyst's inadvertent participation. Boesky (1990), in a seminal paper on psychoanalytic process, discusses the analyst's unconscious contribution to the patient's resistance: 'If there can be no analysis without resistance by the patient, then it is equally true that there can be no treatment conducted by any analyst without counter-resistance or countertransference, sooner or later' (p. 573). Smith (1993) writes about the analyst's reluctance to engage in analytic work as a manifestation of resistance to self-analysis. He proposes that all analysts in the course of their work face, and at the same time avoid facing, their own character difficulties. As the patient resists engagement, so too does the analyst.

Given my present task, the central questions are: How do the analyst's counter-resistances manifest themselves at the beginning of treatment? And, more specifically, how do they bear on the analyst's recommendations?

Jacobs (1988) is among the few analysts who have identified 'internal factors' in the analyst as a critical variable affecting the practice of analysis. As chair of the American Psychoanalytic Association's Committee on Psychoanalytic Practice he suggested, based on information collected from 71 analysts from several institutes, and including training analysts, senior non-training analysts, and recent graduates, that the number of referrals did not determine the size of an analyst's practice. According to Jacobs, the way the analyst conducted the consultation and the opening phase of treatment was more decisive. Jacobs concluded his report by stressing 'that internal factors operating in the analyst seem to be as important as such external conditions as the state of the economy, the intellectual climate, the kind of insurance coverage available and the prevailing attitude towards analysis in any given locale. Not surprisingly, ambivalence towards recommending analysis to patients is not uncommon in analysts. What feeds this ambivalence is not clear at this point and in any case is an issue beyond the scope of this report' (pp. 101–102).

Some writers have suggested that the analyst's ambivalence is a reaction to the intense affects generated in the analytic situation. Friedman (1988) speaks to powerful feelings engendered by the therapeutic situation and to the discomfort that is a constant companion to clinical work. He suggests that therapists do not acknowledge that they 'function in a sea of trouble' or that treatment is 'an uncivil, threatening, even brutal struggle, instigated by gently reflective intellectuals dedicated to delicate speculations' (p. 6). Elaborating on Friedman's ideas, Greenberg (2002) suggests that analysts at work are in a constant state of tension between their natural inclination to respond to the patient in a personal and unreflective manner and their professional inclination to analyze.

In an address to the Board on Professional Standards, Orgel (1989) also attended to the turmoil of analysis and the defensiveness that it evokes. He referred specifically to the emotional challenge of practicing as an analyst while simultaneously wishing not to analyze. Orgel described having witnessed analysts and candidates who, in parallel with their patients, defend against 'terrifying and/or forbidden drives' by resisting doing analysis. In another contribution, Orgel (1990) relates this resistance to doing analysis to analysts' unrecognized feelings toward their own analysts. He suggests that analysts must become well acquainted with their idealizations and aggression regarding their training analysts in order to function effectively as analysts. 'I have speculated that some candidates' difficulty in keeping patients, and their anxiety about losing them, are the results of unanalyzed fears of losing or destroying their training analysts, displaced into their patients' (2000, p. 735). Orgel further maintains that some analysts' lack of conviction about the therapeutic value of analysis reflects disappointment in aspects of their training analysis.

Observing the analyst's reluctance, Gabbard (2003) proposes that the analyst's love of analysis is continuously in jeopardy because of a countervailing unconscious hatred of it. As a result of that hatred, he suggests, analysts might be too quick to abandon the analytic method and impulsively resort to harmful actions; often the hatred is linked, in part, to envy of the patient for receiving the intensive and undivided analytic attention that the analyst unconsciously craves.

Many authors address specifically the analyst's anxiety and defensiveness at the beginning of treatment. Referring to the initial phase, Friedman (1988) proposes that the tension that characterizes treatment can be witnessed most dramatically at the beginning. Yet, he observes, therapists tend to consider beginnings as less tumultuous than the rest of the treatment. Orgel (1989) suggests that not recommending analysis, or not analyzing resistance in the months following a recommendation, can be a manifestation of the analyst's defense against aggression: 'An underside of our therapeutic ambitions' can be seen in 'contrary wishes – not to cure, not to help, not to understand, but to overthrow and defeat, sadistic wishes which are both satisfied and defended against by failing in the therapeutic task' (p. 534).

Poland (2001) speaks to the fear that attends analytic work and how it affects his every analytic beginning: 'So my career-long eagerness to have a new analytic patient is now accompanied by a hesitant fear, a small reluctance to start a new analysis. For as much as I want to do my work, as much as I enjoy doing my work, as much as I believe that the likelihood of success justifies the pains ahead, still there is something else I also know. And that is that whatever else happens this new analysis is going to go into areas I don't want to enter, into fears I would rather keep hidden away.' Ogden (1992) examines the sense of danger and fear associated with initial consultation sessions. Like Poland he attributes this feeling to the anticipation of becoming aware of his and his patient's inner life. Ogden suggests that beginning analysts misapprehend their own fear. While consciously they worry that patients will leave, unconsciously they are afraid that patients will stay. Chused (in Jordan, 2002) discusses how uncertainty influences analytic work. She focuses on how her doubts about whether she had been helpful to a small number of patients – who claimed they were not helped – make her fearful about the value of analysis. Bernstein (1990) is another who explores this uncertainty. He describes analysts who recommend analysis tentatively and in a manner that reveals their reservations about their motives for recommending analysis or about its usefulness. Bernstein suggests that analysts often manifest their reluctance by failing to interpret patients' resistances following a recommendation for analysis.

Bassen (1989) suggests that recommendations for analysis made during psychotherapy are not as simple or non-conflictual as they often appear. She regards such recommendations as possible enactments of transference–countertransference wishes or fears mobilized in the therapy. Similar considerations, she suggests, might apply to the recommendation process at the beginning of treatment. Of all analysts, Rothstein has written most extensively about the analyst's reluctance during the consultation phase. He proposes that the analyst's emphasis on analyzability (1994, 1998) and diagnosis (2002) can serve a defensive function. If taken at face value, this focus can obscure useful transference–countertransference manifestations. Rothstein (1998) proposes that 'there are many patients who are particularly disturbing to analysts both during the consultation and/or in the course of their analyses. It is not uncommon for analysts to respond to their own disturbances by deciding the patient is not suitable for standard analysis . . .' (p. 541). Rothstein considers the analyst's optimistic attitude (about a patient's capacity to work analytically and benefit from analysis) and conviction (about the usefulness of analysis) as critical variables affecting whether a patient will accept the analyst's recommendation for analysis (1994) and stresses how little able we are to predict at the outset who can benefit from analysis (1994, 1998). He recommends that most patients who consult an analyst should be considered analysands and be seen in a trial analysis. Rothstein maintains that analysts do not consider or recommend analysis as often as it is indicated, either because patients do not fit some strict criterion about analyzability or because they are disturbing to the analyst. He considers the analyst's inhibition, pessimism, and lack of conviction to be the result of a misguided educational focus (a focus on selection of patients who will respond primarily to interpretation of conflict and a focus on outcome) or the result of conflict evoked by a particular patient. Rothstein postulates that the analyst's attitude and sense of conviction about the therapeutic value of analysis is determined to a great extent by an 'unconscious bias' for or against analysis.

Whether referring to a 'hesitant fear' to begin a new analysis (Poland) or 'wishes not to cure, not to help, not to understand' (Orgel) or a fear that the patient will stay in treatment (Ogden), several analysts have explored the analyst's reluctance to analyze. Ogden implies that beginners are particularly unaware of their hesitancy to start an analysis. Orgel, however, suggests that students and graduate analysts can be identical in their lack of awareness and their hesitancy. Many analysts propose that analysts' reluctance is related to their fear of affects (Gabbard, Ogden, Orgel, Poland, Rothstein). Some authors view the analysts' reluctance as a momentary hesitation to begin (Ogden, Poland), while others suggest that it interferes with the actual beginning (Jacobs, Orgel, Rothstein). Several authors point to a lack of certainty about the efficacy of analysis as a critical variable affecting the manner in which analysts deal with recommendations for analysis (Bernstein, Chused, Jacobs, Rothstein).

To my knowledge, no detailed clinical contribution has demonstrated in detail the analyst's reluctance as it manifests itself during the consultation or the opening phases of a treatment. In what follows I offer detailed clinical material from my work with two patients who eventually settled into productive psychoanalyses. I focus specifically on the initial phase of treatment: the consultation with Mr. A and the early psychotherapy with Ms. B. I examine my developing awareness of my reluctance to engage these patients deeply, which bore directly on my recommendations for psychoanalysis. I describe the various manifestations of my reluctance, my understanding of its sources, and its effect on the work. In the discussion that follows, I examine how my own findings and understanding add to existing views on the analyst's reluctance to begin an analysis.

Clinical material

Mr. A

Mr. A, a senior at a local college, left a message on my answering machine saying that he was hoping to see me before he graduated and left town in nine weeks. When we spoke by phone, he repeated his wish to see me but asked if it made sense for us to meet since he was leaving so soon. Hesitantly, I replied that he must have had reasons to call me and therefore it might make sense for us to meet and talk things over in person. Although in his phone message he had sounded definite about when he was scheduled to leave, it turned out that he was less clear. He was to leave sometime after graduation, travel in Europe with a friend for the summer, and work as a waiter in New York in the fall. Because of Mr. A's plans to leave in the near future, we initially met on a weekly basis, with no clear goals or plans for treatment.

Mr. A, 21, had spent the last years in high school and his years in college using alcohol and drugs daily, had been in physically abusive relationships, and had been involved in two serious car accidents. Although adequate, his academic performance did not match his intellectual abilities or ambition. His career choice and plans for the future were unclear, with various and contradictory aspirations. During these first few weeks, Mr. A complained vaguely of not feeling good about himself and of being unable to find satisfying love relationships, although he had had a number of lasting friendships.

In what was to have been our last session, he announced that his upcoming summer plans had fallen through because his traveling companion was no longer available. Instead, he would now be looking for another companion. I asked if he had considered staying and continuing the inner travel that he had started. He responded that it had not occurred to him because this was the time of life to travel, experience other cultures, meet different people, and experiment.

Despite stating various objections, Mr. A postponed his departure yet again, this time until the end of the summer. At that time we increased to twice-a-week therapy. I saw it as my task to work with him in a short-term way to facilitate a referral to another analyst in another state once he settled down. As the end of the summer approached, symptoms that had vanished shortly after he started treatment now reappeared. I related these symptoms to his plans to end therapy and asked again if he had considered staying and working in an open-ended, intensive way on the unhappiness that had plagued him for years. Visibly relieved yet manifestly noncommittal, Mr. A in the next weeks made arrangements to stay. Within a few weeks, he increased to five-times a week and began using the couch.

My private response to Mr. A's first telephone message had been to question whether it made sense to meet with him, given that he was about to leave town. My second response was to think of my contact with him as 'just a consultation.' At the time, I considered these responses to be realistic reactions to his situation. A turning point came for Mr. A when his travel plans were cancelled. By that time, five weeks into an extended consultation, he had been responding to treatment with significant symptomatic relief. He showed dramatic improvement in his mood and energy level and stopped daily drug use for the first time in years. Despite this, I did not consider recommending more intensive treatment. One could argue that Mr. A was not ready to consider analysis and that I had responded empathically to him. However, regardless of his readiness, I was not ready because I did not, even privately, consider recommending analysis despite obvious indications. What is most striking about this is that I consciously was determined to practice as much analysis as possible.

Initially, I took at face value Mr. A's intention to leave soon and his lack of interest in committing to long-term treatment – at least in our locale. I experienced him as unavailable for analysis and questioned the wisdom of beginning with him when what he appeared to need most was a chance to experiment and exercise his independence. In retrospect, I privileged what I saw as his developmental needs, viewing his plans for out-of-town study and overseas exploration as consistent with those needs. I would add, being myself an immigrant, that this defensive inclination was particularly compelling to me. Inviting him to stay, but not in analysis, was my compromise of the moment.

It was not until Mr. A became symptomatic in anticipation of ending his 'short-term' treatment and leaving town that I was able to clearly recognize the potential value of analysis for him and was able to recommend it. I finally was able to give proper weight to his considerable, long-standing pain and his equally significant and chronic inability to use his ample resources to advantage in the present or to plan for his future.

Typical of several young adults that I treat in the college town where I practice, Mr. A was transient to the area. Yet he called on me with very real difficulties that had marked his life in important ways and were likely to derail or adversely affect his future. Although the decision was ultimately his, I was responsible for delineating his choices and providing a strong recommendation. Inadvertently, I had initially backed away from offering him the optimal treatment. That this young man engaged in five-times-a-week analysis was as much the result of my overcoming my own resistance as of him overcoming his. Had I not recognized my reluctance and recommended analysis, Mr. A, given his counterdependence and insecurity, would not have remained in treatment. One can view the reluctant beginning of this analysis in terms of transference and countertransference. From the outset, Mr. A and I enacted his difficulties. From the initial phone call, he conveyed that he was only temporarily available. Partly out of insecurity and fear of rejection, Mr. A had waited to call me until just a few weeks before moving out of town permanently. In a similar manner, I responded with the self-protective thought that it was just a consultation, proactively limiting my hopes for a longer involvement with him. During the first call, when he asked for my reassurance, I in turn felt reluctant to reassure him.

By declaring his provisional availability, Mr. A attempted to hide needs and yearnings that he considered shameful. Throughout his childhood and particularly during adolescence, Mr. A characteristically had dealt with rejection by making himself only fleetingly available and by being the first to leave. In his manifest independence, he concealed fierce counterdependence. In part because of my own fears of dependence and needfulness (especially at a time when I felt I needed another analytic patient), I identified with Mr. A's wish to leave. I thereby overlooked his needs and implicitly agreed with him that travel and education were more important than addressing his long-standing pain. Defending against my fears of dependency and yearning, which were mobilized by his looming departure, I denied that I wanted to work with him. Instead, I thought, I was 'generously' preparing him to see another analyst. We had joined together in denying needs and yearnings.

Anticipating that Mr. A was going to leave, I took at face value his plans and underestimated his motivation for intensive treatment. My anticipation of his leaving reflected in part my ambivalence about working with him in analysis: at some level I wanted him to leave. Only when I could recognize this could I function more effectively as his analyst. Specifically, I could facilitate the beginning of the analysis: give proper weight to his conflicts and distress; withstand his passive-into-active style of engaging; maintain confidence in the work and in my ability to be of help to him; and tolerate the inherent ambiguity in considering recommendations to a young adult. It was then that I found it within myself to assume responsibility for my judgment and to trust I was addressing the best interests of the patient.

When Mr. A became symptomatic on the eve of his departure, I finally was able to recognize my reluctance and to see through his denial. Only then was I able to extend to him an invitation for analysis. As he had been ready before I was, Mr. A promptly accepted. He is now in a productive analysis, which he is funding by working. In addition, he is taking classes at night in preparation for applying to graduate school.

Ms. B

An engineer in her thirties, Ms. B had ended several previous treatments prematurely and unhappily. The mother of two young children, whom she both adored and unconsciously wanted to destroy, Ms. B sought treatment because of her flickering recognition that she was at risk of hurting them and/or herself. She experienced her children as extremely demanding and attended to them in a masochistic way that increased her rage.

Although desperate for help, Ms. B was too afraid of criticism and too full of guilt and shame to hope that she could find it. She seemed in great distress, yet she also appeared indifferent and guarded. During the initial consultation, Ms. B made it clear that she had very low expectations for our work and referred frequently to her failed treatments. Given the nature and history of her difficulties and my experience of her during our meetings, I concluded that she could benefit from analysis and recommended to her that she attend as many sessions per week as she could. Although I had not specified the number of times she should attend and had not referred to 'analysis' while making my recommendation, she countered that she was not interested in a 'five-times-a-week analysis.' We began with a three-times-a-week psychotherapy. Hearing through her rejection of analysis her frightened interest in more engagement, I listened for the fears that prevented her from coming as often as she wanted. In the first few weeks of the therapy, Ms. B revealed her worries that she would fail as a patient; that she would be found to be defective and beyond repair; and that she would expose herself as inexplicably and indefensibly evil. Identifying these worries and particularly relating them to her reluctance to come more often, she resignedly accepted a fourth appointment. Still, she reiterated a refusal to consider a fifth session and lie on the couch, a stance she experienced as preserving her autonomy.

Ms. B reacted to the increased frequency with a reduction in her symptoms. Her rage toward her children and her sense of despair abated, and she began to speak about herself with some small measure of trust and a tentative sense of connection. Yet she continued to have intense, wearisome, even at times alarming (to both of us) reactions to interruptions of any kind in our work. Witnessing Ms. B's distress, I continued to believe that she wanted to come more often and that she was reacting with distress to not doing so. I also thought that her coming more often would allow us to address her conflicts more effectively. I felt frustrated by her reluctance. During this time, I consciously felt that I wanted to work with her, and I was pleased to have another analytic patient.

For about four months, I was convinced that the obstacles to more intensive engagement came from Ms. B. Then an interaction led me to reconsider this. One day, noticing that Ms. B had looked at the couch, I invited her to share her thoughts. She responded that she knew people who used the couch, but she could not imagine using it herself because she would fall asleep. She then asked me why people use the couch. I found myself responding with a clumsy explanation without any attempt to ask her for her thoughts, to address her fears, and without extending to her the obvious open-ended invitation to use the couch anytime she felt ready.

Reflecting on my response to her inquiry about the couch, I realized that despite my recommendation I had serious reservations about getting genuinely and deeply involved with Ms. B. Indeed, I recognized, I was unsure whether I wanted Ms. B to come more often after all. I knew that I had been feeling apprehensive about her narcissistic vulnerability and accompanying rage, her potential for regression, and her propensity for abrupt and unhappy leavings. I also knew that I feared she would hurt herself or her children. Yet until I reflected on the meaning of our exchange about the couch, I had not recognized how reluctant I felt about experiencing the intensity of those feelings in our relationship.

My fearfulness also reflected an identification with Ms. B's fear of attachment. Like her, I worried about precipitous endings to therapy and being hurt. In my unwelcoming response to her inquiry, I also was identifying with Ms. B's dismissiveness and aloofness, her characteristic ways of dealing with her deep fears of being left or feeling unwanted.

I recognized gradually that my focus on the fifth session had been a smoke screen for my reluctance to genuinely engage with Ms. B. My ostensible eagerness was a defense against my hidden reluctance. I was reluctant to bear her shattering sense of being inconsequential, insignificant, and powerless; to really know her profound shame and sense of inferiority; to experience my fears of being dismissed summarily, and my own wishes to dismiss her. Scared of her pain, I insisted on more contact, rather than truly encouraging her immersion.

This struggle was not just my response to fear of feelings or uncertainty about the work ahead and my capacity to do it. It was also a meaningful enactment between us. We have come to learn since that my initial conflictual engagement with Ms. B corresponds to a view of her mother as a self-centered, frightened, and controlling woman whose dread of attachment was manifested in a tyrannical, authoritarian, and depriving way of parenting. Reluctant to begin with Ms. B, I focused on the form rather than the essence of our analytic engagement and enacted a sadomasochistic struggle. In that struggle, control and distance substituted for engagement and understanding.

Becoming aware of my reluctance, I became freer to move toward her on her terms and to extend to her a more genuine, less conflicted invitation to begin analytic work.

Discussion

These two cases highlight several important issues regarding the analyst's reluctance. The case of Mr. A raises questions about the analyses of young adults. Because of their particular developmental tasks, young adults present particular challenges to analysts around recommendations for analysis. Young adults' competing, and at times compelling, choices test an analyst's belief in the value of psychoanalysis, as opposed to the value of education, travel, or other endeavors. Abend (1987) concludes that analysts have to live with uncertainty when recommending analysis to young adults: 'Hard and fast criteria do not exist, and it is possible that the degree to which the analyst believes in the special value of psychoanalytic treatment . . . may determine what he advises as much as any other single factor' (p. 34).

Although these considerations are most obvious with young adults, I have concluded from my work with Ms. B and other patients that they are relevant with analysands of any age. Most patients arrive with personal circumstances or reasons, with some basis in reality, why they should not or cannot be in analysis. The challenge of arriving at a recommendation is increased by the analyst's awareness that analysis is an expensive, time-consuming, and emotionally demanding treatment without a guaranteed outcome. Yet most analysts also know it to be true that psychoanalysis, even with all its limitations, remains a discontented person's best opportunity for a more fulfilled life. In agreement with Rothstein, I have come to think that if analysts do not privilege this point of view with a given patient, they should seriously consider that they are reluctant to analyze that patient.

In my view, one cannot consider analysts' doubts about the value of psychoanalysis or about their capacity to practice it without considering the influence of their training analysis. Although often alluded to, the ongoing influence of the analyst's personal analysis has not been fully acknowledged in our literature (Grusky, 1999). I speculate that analysts have not explored this topic more fully in part because of the expectation that a training analysis should leave no psychic residue – a remnant of the belief in the perfectly analyzed analyst whose conflicts and transferences would dissolve at the end of the analysis.

Addressing the clear need for more knowledge in this area, Smith (2001) gives evidence of analysts' ongoing internal relationship with their training analyst and how it manifests itself in their work. Smith suggests that 'the analyst's identifications and idealizations modify over time but, never fully given up, remain as compromised responses to both the analyst's and the patient's conflicts in a dynamic reciprocal relationship with the patient's inner life' (p. 809). As noted earlier, Orgel (2000) has explored the influence of the training analysis and suggested that analysts' lingering disappointment in their training analysis is one source of analysts' lack of conviction about analysis.

Based on my work with Mr. A and Ms. B, I would add that another source of some analysts' lack of conviction about the usefulness of analysis can be found in competitive feelings toward their own analyst. Analysts can express this competitiveness by denying the therapeutic value of their training analysis or the effectiveness of their analyst. Analysts can also express rivalry with the training analyst in their work. For me, functioning as an analyst stimulated competitive/aggressive strivings toward my own analyst. In turn, my conflicts over those wishes fuelled my reluctance to engage with these two patients. Specifically, by temporarily retreating from practicing as an analyst I defended against wanting to be the better analyst. For example, I was fearful that both Mr. A and Ms. B were going to leave. My worry that they would leave was also a wish: if they left, I would never be as successful as my analyst.

My uncertainty about the value of analysis not only reflected my aggression toward my analyst. It was also a defense against my love and gratitude. Thus, my fear/wish that my patients would leave was also a defense against my awareness of loving feelings. If my prospective analytic patients left, I would not have to practice as an analyst and be in touch with how much my analyst had helped me (and with the attendant sadness over the end of my analysis). Although questioning any strong inclination within me has become second nature in the course of my daily work as an analyst, I was particularly resistant to questioning my seeming eagerness to practice analysis. I suggest that one obstacle that blocks our considering our reluctance to begin an analysis is the idealization of our wish to analyze. Abend (1986) reminds us that, despite our intellectual understanding that analytic ability is a dynamic (rather than stable) function, we are still prone to 'unconscious narcissistic fantasies of perfection' and to 'unrealistic and unrealizable ideals' (p. 565). Analysts resist recognizing their conflictual contribution during the course of the analysis. It follows that they do not recognize or anticipate their 'resistance' at the beginning of an analysis. Despite what we know about the dynamic nature of psychic functioning, we often want to see the wish to begin an analysis as invariant. Although psychoanalysts have increasingly recognized and explored the tension and turmoil of analysis, Friedman (1988) has noted that many analysts still view the beginning of treatment as isolated from the irrational forces that govern the rest of the analysis. Similarly, the recommendation for analysis is often considered to be an 'objectively' motivated act (Bassen, 1989).

Based on my own experience recommending analysis, I concur with the view that the recommendation for analysis is from the outset infused with realistic and infantile wishes and fears from both therapeutic partners. This understanding has allowed me to consider how I might match or complement, with my own ambivalence, a patient's seeming unavailability or unwillingness to commit to analysis. To elaborate on Bassen's view of a recommendation for analysis during psychotherapy as an enactment, I believe it useful to consider that not making a recommendation for analysis during psychotherapy can also be an enactment, a manifestation of co-created resistance. This is seen in my work with Mr. A, where not making a timely recommendation was an enactment of conflicts about dependency fears and wishes.

As my clinical material demonstrates, the analyst's reluctance can influence analytic practice. At present the extent of its influence is not clear. However, from my own work, from reading clinical accounts in the literature, from listening to cases presented in various professional forums, and from anecdotal reports, I have concluded that reluctance to engage in analysis has an effect on analytic practice more frequently than is recognized. As is true during the course of an analysis, the analyst's reluctance at the beginning can significantly influence his or her attitude and performance. However, analysts' reluctance in the beginning, when the relationship with the patient is most tenuous, can more easily contribute to the premature end of a potentially useful, and often much-needed, treatment. My reluctance to consider or recommend analysis and my subsequent recognition of that reluctance each affected – though in opposite ways – the quality of my clinical work and the nature of my clinical practice.

Analysts' reluctance to begin an analysis is not new (one of its earlier manifestations has been a defensive focus on analyzability). However, because a less overt demand for psychoanalysis exists today than in past decades, psychoanalysts can more readily obscure their reluctance to analyze by citing patient scarcity. Given the reality of an atmosphere adverse to psychoanalysis, analysts can more readily rationalize their own reluctance to begin an analysis.

Conclusions

I have explored how the reluctance to begin a new analysis influences the individual analyst's thinking and practice and have considered the analyst's reluctance from different vantage points: as a response to intense affects mobilized by the consultation, as part of a co-created enactment, and as a manifestation of the analyst's conflicts. Analysts can use the compelling reality of an environment adverse to long-term treatments to rationalize their reluctance to engage patients in analysis. This reluctance to begin an analysis appears to be an underestimated factor in explaining why analysis is not practiced more.

One of the many paradoxes that characterize our 'impossible profession' is that we are reluctant to practice it. Although we might not wish it to be so, the reluctance to begin an analysis, like counter-resistance at any time during an analysis, appears ubiquitous. Whether it will become an interference or an aid to beginning depends in part on analysts' capacity to anticipate it in their consultations and to recognize how it manifests itself in relation to a particular patient. I have found it is clinically useful to anticipate that my reluctance to analyze will manifest itself with each new patient and to consider, also with each patient, how I play a part in their resistance to beginnings.

References

Abend, S. (1986). Countertransference, empathy, and the analytic ideal: The impact of life stresses on analytic capability. *Psychoanalytic Quarterly* 55: 563–575.

Abend, S. (1987). Evaluating young adults for analysis. *Psychoanalytic Inquiry* 7: 31–38.

Bachrach, H. (1983). On the concept of analyzability. *Psychoanalytic Quarterly* 52: 180–203.

Bachrach, H. (1990). The analyst's thinking and attitude at the beginning of analysis: The influence of research data at the beginning of an analysis. In: Jacobs, T., Rothstein, A. (Eds), *On Beginning an Analysis* (pp. 83–100). Madison, CT: International Universities Press.

Bassen, C. (1989). Transference–countertransference enactment in the recommendation to convert psychotherapy to psychoanalysis. *International Review of Psychoanalysis* 16: 79–92.

Bernstein, S. (1990). Motivation for psychoanalysis and the transition from psychotherapy. *Psychoanalytic Inquiry* 10: 21–42.

Boesky, D. (1990). The psychoanalytic process and its components. *Psychoanalytic Quarterly* 59: 550–584.

Brauer, L. D., Brauer, S. L. (1996). *Basic report about members who are graduates of institutes: Survey of psychoanalytic practice.* Committee on Psychoanalytic Practice, American Psychoanalytic Association.

Busch, F. (1995). Beginning a psychoanalytic treatment: Establishing an analytic frame. *Journal of the American Psychoanalytic Association* 43: 449–468.

Erle, J. B., Goldberg, D. A. (2003). The course of 253 analyses from selection to outcome. *Journal of the American Psychoanalytic Association* 51: 257–294.

Freud, S. (1912a). The Dynamics of Transference. *SE* 12: 97–108.

Freud, S. (1912b). Recommendations to Physicians Practising Psychoanalysis. *SE* 12: 109–120.

Freud, S. (1913). On Beginning the Treatment. *SE* 12: 123–144.

Friedman, L. (1988). *The Anatomy of Psychotherapy.* Hillsdale, NJ: Analytic Press.

Gabbard, G. O. (2003). Miscarriages of psychoanalytic treatment with suicidal patients. *International Journal of Psychoanalysis* 84: 249–263.

Greenberg, J. (2002). Psychoanalytic goals, therapeutic action, and the analyst's tension. *Psychoanalytic Quarterly* 71: 651–678.

Grusky, Z. (1999). Conviction and conversion: The role of shared fantasies about analysis. *Psychoanalytic Quarterly* 68: 401–430.

Jacobs, T. (1988). Unpublished report to the Executive Council by the Committee on Psychoanalytic Practice. Montreal.

Jordan, L. (2002). Panel report: The analyst's uncertainty and fear. *Journal of the American Psychoanalytic Association* 50: 989–993.

Kantrowitz, J. (1993). The uniqueness of the patient–analyst pair: Approaches for elucidating the analyst's role. *International Journal of Psychoanalysis* 74: 893–904.

Kantrowitz, J., Katz, A., Greenman, D., Morris, H., Paolitto, F., Sashin, J., Solomon, L. (1989). The patient–analyst match and the outcome of psychoanalysis: A pilot study. *Journal of the American Psychoanalytic Association* 37: 893–919.
Lichtenberg, J., Auchincloss, E. (1989). Panel report: The opening phase of psychoanalysis. *Journal of the American Psychoanalytic Association* 37: 199–214.
Ogden, T. (1992). Comments on transference and countertransference in the initial analytic meeting. *Psychoanalytic Inquiry* 12: 225–247.
Orgel, S. (1989). Address to the Board on Professional Standards. *Journal of the American Psychoanalytic Association* 37: 531–541.
Orgel, S. (1990). The future of psychoanalysis. *Psychoanalytic Quarterly* 59: 1–20.
Orgel, S. (2000). Thoughts on termination. *Journal of the American Psychoanalytic Association* 48: 719–738.
Poland, W. (2001). *The analyst's fear.* Paper presented at panel 'The Analyst's Fear and Uncertainty', American Psychoanalytic Association, New Orleans, May 5.
Rothstein, A. (1994). A perspective on doing a consultation and making the recommendation of analysis to a prospective analysand. *Psychoanalytic Quarterly* 63: 680–695.
Rothstein, A. (1998). *Psychoanalytic Technique and the Creation of Analytic Patients.* Madison, CT: International Universities Press.
Rothstein, A. (2002). Reflections on the creative aspects of psychoanalytic diagnosing. *Psychoanalytic Quarterly* 71: 301–326.
Smith, H. (1993). Engagements in the analytic work. *Psychoanalytic Inquiry* 13: 425–454.
Smith, H. (2001). Hearing voices: The fate of the analyst's identifications. *Journal of the American Psychoanalytic Association* 49: 781–812.

19 MAKING THE BEST OF A BAD JOB[1]

Rudi Vermote

Bion's last text, *Making the Best of a Bad Job* (1979/1987), is about what an analyst should do in the meeting with a patient. We may apply it to the first meeting.

> When two personalities meet, an emotional storm is created. If they make sufficient contact to be aware of each other, or even sufficient to be unaware of each other, an emotional state is produced by the conjunction of these two individuals, and the resulting disturbance is hardly likely to be regarded as necessarily an improvement on the state of affairs had they never met at all. But since they *have* met, and since this emotional storm has occurred, the two parties to this storm may decide to 'make the best of a bad job'.
>
> (Bion, 1979/1987, p. 247)

Maybe we are touching here at the heart of psychoanalysis. In the meeting of two people, a psychic change is created: neither of the two people will be the same after the meeting. This change happens inevitably. It happens to both participants of the meeting at an unknown, undifferentiated level. We hope that the special circumstances of an analytic frame will make it possible to be attentive to these unknown psychic powers and that analysand and psychoanalyst may use it for the best. In other words, that a psychoanalytic process, the growth of the patient's personality (Bion, 1979/1987), may ensue from it. In Bion's model, this psychoanalytic process is difficult to imagine without an accompanying growth of the analyst's Mind, but the central focus is the psychic change of the patient. The core question of this book is how to initiate this process from the storm in the first meeting.

Bion is clear in this respect, he advocates as a *conditio sine qua non* a mental attitude of maximal openness in the psychoanalyst (Bion, 1970). In terms of his Grid (Bion, 1963) this attitude of the analyst is reflected in the

[1] This paper was written for this book at the invitation of the editors.

C3-C4-D3-D4 categories. In the 1979 text, Bion further compares this maximal openness to Milton's verse. He does so because, from his point of view, the observation by the analyst is not only a sensorial observation; what the analyst should aim for is an observation of psychic elements, which are by definition of a non-sensuous realm. Sensorially perceptible phenomena such as anxiety and aggression, for instance, have a non-sensuous precursor in the Mind. The characteristics of the Living Mind are ineffable.

> Observation must play an extremely important part in it – which has always been recognized in a scientific inquiry – we should not be restricting our observation to too narrow a sphere. What then are we observing? The best answer that I know is provided by the formulation in Milton's introduction to the Third Book of *Paradise Lost*.
>
> So much the rather thou, celestial Light,
> Shine inward, and the mind through all her powers
> Irradiate: there plant eyes, all mist from thence
> Purge and disperse, that I may see and tell
> Of things invisible to mortal sight.
> (Milton, *Paradise Lost*, Book III)
>
> When the patient comes into the consulting room the analyst needs to be sensitive to the totality of that person; it should, for example, be possible to see a flush on the face as a physical manifestation of the blood system, as well as being able to hear the words which that person utters as a part of the operation of the vocal musculature – not particularly emphasizing the activity of the voluntary muscles, nor yet particularly the sounds which are created by the vocal cords and the vocal apparatus, but rather the total thing. Or, putting it differently, the analyst needs to be able to listen not only to the words but also to the music, so that he can hear a remark which is not easily translated into black marks on paper, which has a different meaning when it is made in tones of sarcasm, or in terms of affection or understanding, or by a person who has actual experience of authority – though his words might be the same in each instance.
>
> (Bion, 1979/1987, pp. 250–251, and Milton's verse in Bion, 1979/1987, p. 257)

Bion made a model of how elements become psychic. In his model, there is a stage where thoughts and feelings are not yet differentiated. Bion particularly stresses how important it is to be open to this unknown and undifferentiated zone from where thoughts emerge and where something psychic may already be present, but not yet appropriated by the mind (Bion, 1977/1989). He refers to the poet John Donne's verse to describe such psychic phenomena, which may be seen as beta elements.

> . . . her pure and eloquent blood
> Spoke in her cheeks, and so distinctly wrought,
> That one might almost say, her body thought;
> (Donne, *The Second Anniversary*, in Bion, 1979/1987, p. 257)

Bion compares the state of Mind of the analyst, in which he is radically open to what may happen in the meeting of analyst and analysand, to Faith. From this state of Mind in the session, something that has not happened yet is enabled to take place, which Bion calls an Act of Faith (Bion, 1970).

This kind of psychic change happens at the undifferentiated, infinite zone in the psyche (O), therefore Bion calls it a transformation in O or T(O). This level is non-represented and therefore unknowable, but it can be experienced. When it meets a form at a more differentiated level of the Mind, it becomes represented thought. There are several categories of representation (which are categorized in Bion's Grid: dreams, images, thoughts, pre-conceptions, conceptions, concepts, theories) with different degrees of vividness and sophistication. This process of representation and transitions between the different categories of representation Bion calls a transformation in knowledge (K) or T(K).

So, according to Bion (1965/1984), we may have transformations in O and in K in the analyst (TO and TK) and in the patient (TO and TK).

In this way of looking at the dynamics of the encounter, transformations in the patient and in the analyst can happen on at least four different vertices.

According to Bion, there are many possibilities of how the evolutions on these vertices may have an effect on each other or not. There may for instance be a T(O) in the patient – an experience, which did not meet a T(K) and therefore remains unthought, unrepresented in the analysand. It may have a great effect, but at this moment the analysand may not be aware of it and not be able to think it. The seed of transformation may be planted but resulting only much later in a perceptible and knowable change for the worst or the best. Or the analyst may have a T(K) for the T(O) of the patient, where the analyst can contain and name what happens in the patient at an experience level but may not be able to communicate it to the patient, because the patient is functioning in a closed way. Or the patient may pretend that he is affected by and understands the intervention of the analyst just to ward off change. In other words he used T(K) to close himself to T(O) (as represented in column 2 of Bion's Grid). At the outside something may look like a great progress or insight, but in this case the agreement is only at a knowing level and knowing is being used to ward off change. Bion describes this as a 'reversal of perspective': what one sees is in fact something else.

The fact that real changes happen at an unknown experiencing level, and that it is not clear how and when this will be represented, makes it very difficult or nearly impossible to foretell the effects. Bion compares this process to a game of snakes and ladders; what may look like a ladder may turn out to be a snake or vice-versa. It is only in retrospect that it may become clear if and how a change resulted from a meeting and an intervention.

A maximum openness in a radical not-knowing attitude may be the best guarantee that something may happen that eventually will lead to the initiating of a psychoanalytic process. This transformation is at an unknown, experiencing level and it is not clear when and how this will take the form of a discernible and knowable differentiated act or thought – in the patient and/or analyst. To try to grasp this powerful phenomenon, which may characterize first sessions in particular, and to put it in some concise thoughts that may ameliorate our work, is therefore extremely difficult. Moreover there are many pitfalls of pseudo-understanding that may block an eventual transformation. However, to try to be open and study these dynamics, which are at their strongest in a first meeting, seems rewarding as it is at the heart of our impossible job.

References

Bion, W. R. (1963). *Elements of Psychoanalysis*. London: Karnac.

Bion, W. R. (1965). *Transformations*. London: Karnac, 1984.

Bion, W. R. (1970). *Attention and Interpretation*, New York: Basic Books.

Bion, W. R. (1977). *Two Papers: The Grid and the Caesura*. London: Karnac, 1989.

Bion W. R. (1979). Making the Best of a Bad Job. In: Bion, W. R., Bion, F. (Eds) *Clinical Seminars and Four Papers* (pp. 247–257). Abingdon: Fleetwood Press, 1987.

INDEX